Submarine
DESIGN AND DEVELOPMENT

Frontispiece: The second most numerous Soviet submarine class ever built (76 plus since 1958 and continuing), the diesel-powered 300ft conventional 'Foxtrot' submarine of 1950/2400 tons (seen in 1973 or before) contrasted with USS *Michigan*, the second *Ohio* class nuclear-powered Trident ballistic missile submarine; at 560ft oa and 16,000/18,700 tons the largest built in the West. *Michigan* (SSBN 727) is seen under construction on the pier by her builders (Electric Boat of Groton, Connecticut) on 7 April 1979, two years after being laid down and a year before launch. The separate heel behind the crane belongs to her sister boat *Georgia* laid down that day (4th in the class). The lead boat *Ohio* (SSBN 726) is in the water newly launched that day. Compare with the jacket photograph which shows the launch of the *Los Angeles* class *Phoenix* on 8 December 1979. By late 1983 the US Navy had three Trident boats operational with seven more building or on order. Britain is to order her first of four Trident boats in the second half of 1985, so by the 1990s, and long into the twenty-first century, Trident submarines will be the principal bearers of the West's strategic nuclear deterrent.
US Navy

Submarine
DESIGN AND DEVELOPMENT

Norman Friedman

NAVAL INSTITUTE PRESS

For my wife, Rhea.

© Norman Friedman 1984

Published and distributed in the United
States of America and Canada by the Naval
Institute Press, Annapolis, Maryland 21402

Reprinted 1986

Library of Congress Catalog Card No.
83-43278

ISBN 0-87021-954-5

This edition is authorized for sale only in
the United States and its territories and
possessions, and Canada

Manufactured in the United Kingdom

Contents

Acknowledgements	7

Chapter 1	9

Stealth - the Nature of Submarine Warfare

Chapter 2	17

Design Constraints and Compromises

Diving depth and pressure hulls	18
Hull materials and forms	20
Conning towers and periscopes	23
Powerplants	24

Chapter 3	27

The Era of the Submersible 1900-1945

Before 1914	27
World War I	29
Submarine minelaying	32
Anti-submarine warfare	32
Between the wars: Britain	37
Between the wars: United States and Japan	39
Japanese midget submarines	41
Japanese submarines in World War II	42
World War II U-boats	42
France and Italy	43
World War II 'Wolfpack' tactics	43
The U-boat war 1939-45	48
US Pacific War tactics	51

Chapter 4	53

The Fast Submarine

Walter's hydrogen peroxide U-boat	53
Walter's later U-boats	54
The snorkel	56
Doenitz and the Type XXI U-boat	56
Type XXI armament and tactics	57
British Type XXI imitations	58
Postwar Allied evaluations	58
USS *Tang*	61
HMS *Porpoise*	61
The French *Narval*	63
US 'Guppy' conversion	64
Revision of ASW	66
'Bottom-Bounce' and 'Convergence zone' sonar phenomena	67
US ASW submarine fleet plans	67
New US submarine sonar	69
US 1950 'Hunter killer' tactics	69

Chapter 5	71

Postwar Development in the West

US radar pickets	71
Direct support of surface forces	72
US ASW submarines	74
US cruise missile submarines	75
Polaris	76

Silencing	76
Speed and ballistic missile submarines	79
Ballistic missile submarines and ASW	79
High underwater speed and the nuclear submarine	80
Noise and nuclear reactors	81
The hull revolution	82
Deep diving and new hull materials	82
US sonar and attack boat development	83
British developments	83
The British nuclear deterrent	88
French nuclear development	89
U-boats since 1955	90

Chapter 6 — 93
Some Soviet Views

Tactics and communications	94
Silencing	95
Operations today	96
Economic factors	97
Nuclear accidents	98
Strategy	98
Stalin's submarines	99
After 1945	100
Peak strength – 1957	101
Khrushchev's nuclear revolution	101
First missile submarines	103
Cruise missile tactics	104
Early ballistic missile tactics	104
Nuclear attack submarines	105
'Alfa'	105
'Yankee'	106
'Victor'	106
Current building programme	106

Chapter 7 — 107
Submarines in the Third World

Chapter 8 — 115
Diving and Underwater Manoeuvrability

Diving depth	116
Underwater control	117
Ballast tanks	118
Water densities	120
Diving	120
Surfacing	120
Diving planes	122
Modern control systems	126
Escape and rescue	127

Chapter 9 — 129
Propulsion-Conventional and Nuclear

Closed-cycle engines	130
Fuel cells	132
Batteries	133
Nuclear reactors	134
Submarine noise and silencing	136
Diesel or nuclear?	138
Hull forms	138
Reduced 'sails' and streamlining	140

Chapter 10 — 141
Sensors and Communications

Periscopes	141
Sound detectors	142
Sound behaviour under the sea	144
Sonar performance	145
Multi-target tracking	147
Towed arrays	147
Signal processing	149
World War II sonars	151
US and British sonars 1948 to date	151
Radio communications	152
Current communications systems	154

Chapter 11 — 155
Weapons and Tactics

Torpedoes	157
World War II torpedo tactics	159
Acoustic homing torpedoes	160
Torpedo fire control	161
Torpedo tubes	162
Torpedo stowage	164
Missile systems	165
Guns	169

Chapter 12

The Submarine's Enemy - Modern ASW

171

US ASW strategy after 1945	171
Active and passive detection	173
Non-acoustic detection	173
Countering sonar	175
'Dead time' and 'warning time'	176
ASW homing torpedoes	177
Nuclear ASW weapons	178
Evasion tactics	178
Submarine air defence	179
Countering mines and underwater detection	181

Chapter 13

Future Possibilities

181

Appendix: Third World submarine operations	188
Glossary	189
Index	190

ACKNOWLEDGEMENTS

No book of this type can be written without very considerable assistance. I would like particularly to thank Dr Edward Whitman; Charles Haberlein of the Naval Historical Center; Dr Bruce Johnson and Lt Cdr Michael Tracy of the US Naval Academy; David K Brown, David Andrews, and Bryan Pearson of the Royal Corps of Naval Constructors; Christopher C Wright; James T Westwood of E-Systems (Melpar Division); Arthur D Baker III; Norman Polmar; John Lewis; Paul Boyenga; David Isby; Jim Murphy; 'Ham' Caldwell; Karl Lautenschlager; and Dr Thomas Hone. Collectively, they caught many errors and suggested many improvements to the original manuscript. The errors which remain are, of course, my own responsibility. I am indebted to B Bruce-Briggs of the Hudson Institute, who pointed out the close analogy between modern 'stealth' concepts and submarine operations.

I am grateful to the staff of the US Navy Operational Archives for much assistance with General Board and early postwar material, and to the staff of the Navy Department Library and to Mildred Schneck, the librarian of the Hudson Institute, for assistance with open-source materials. Many of the photographs, particularly of modern submarines, were provided by the Photojournalism Branch of the office of the Chief of Naval Information and by the US Naval Sea Systems Command. My special thanks go to Ingenieurkontor Lübeck (IKL), the current German submarine design firm, and its founder Prof Ulrich Gabler for providing a copy of the latter's book *Submarine Design* (2nd edition, 1978) and allowing many of its excellent submarine drawings to be reproduced here. Other contemporary submarine builders who kindly provided illustrations are Vickers Shipbuilding and Engineering Ltd (W G Clouter, Public Relations Manager), Howaldtswerke Deutsche Werft AG of Kiel, and Kockums AB of Malmö (Sweden). F J IJsseling generously helped with Dutch material.

I would like to thank my wife, Rhea, for her patience and, more importantly, active support through a particularly complex and time-consuming research and writing project.

NOTE ON SOURCES

Although several official or semi-official accounts of World War II and earlier submarines have been published, complete accounts of postwar craft are relatively rare, and recourse has been made to technical journals such as *Defence*, *Maritime Defence*, the *Naval Engineers Journal*, *Marine Rundschau*, the *US Naval Institute Proceedings*, and the *International Defense Review*. The new US Submarine League has begun to publish a *Submarine Review* which discusses many current (and postwar) US submarine issues, and I have consulted both of its first two issues. I have also benefited from the proceedings of the Royal Institution of Naval Architects (RINA) Symposium on *Naval Submarines* (May 1983). They include detailed accounts of the technology of recent non-nuclear submarines. In addition, I have benefited from the lecture notes on submarine design distributed to students in naval construction at University College, London. The other major reference on modern submarine practice is a Soviet text (based on Western sources), V M Bukalov and A A Narusbayev *Atomic Submarine Design* (Moscow, Sudostroeniye, 1964, translated by the U S Government in December 1967 and available as AD 664961).

For US design practice, the standard sources are two technical papers, 'Recent Submarine Design Practices and Problems', by Rear Admiral Andrew I McKee, USN (Society of Naval Architects and Marine Engineers, 1959) and 'Naval Architectural Aspects of Submarine Design', by Captain E S Arentzen, USN (Society of Naval Architects and Marine Engineers, 1960); no comparable papers have been published in the more than two decades since 1960. Admiral McKee was responsible for a paper on the development of conventional American submarines, which appeared in the SNAME *Historical Transactions* published in 1945. It discussed the issue of surface v submerged performance in considerable detail, as the issue had been fought out before and during World War I in the US Navy. For modern German practice, I have relied on *U-Bootbau* by Dr Ulrich Gabler, the IKL designer (2nd ed, Wehr & Wissen Verlag, 1978). Special mention must be made of the series of tutorial articles on submarine design practice by K N Heggestad of the Royal Norwegian Navy published over the past several years by the journal *Maritime Defence* (London).

The standard histories of submarine design consulted were: A N Harrison *The Development of HM Submarines from Holland No 1 (1901) to Porpoise (1930)* (Ministry of Defence, 1979: BR 3043); Henri Le Masson *Les Sous-Marins Francais des Origines (1863) à Nos Jours* (Editions de la Cité, Paris 1980); Eberhard Rössler *The U-Boat* (Arms and Armour Press, as translated, 1981); John D Alden, *The Fleet Submarine in the US Navy* (US Naval Institute, 1979). For Japanese submarines I have relied primarily on material, derived from Japanese sources, published by Dr E Lacroix in *The Belgian Shiplover*. The account of Italian submarines is based on the Italian official history, by P M Pollina and A Cocchia *I Sommergibili Italiani 1895-1962* (Rome, 1963).

The account of British submarine development after 1930 is based on Ship Covers in the National Maritime Museum, which now (1983) include the experimental submarines *Explorer* and *Excalibur* and the 'T' class conversions. In addition, in 1984 the Royal Institution of Naval Architects published an account of British nuclear submarine development, 'UK Nuclear Submarines', by P G Wrobel, RCNC. The US account has been supplemented by materials from the Operational Archives at the Washington Navy Yard, including *FTP 224*, the formerly classified ASW magazine published 1946–49, the declassified proceedings of the OpNav ASW Symposia, and declassified issues of the formerly classified journal, *Combat Readiness*. Captain F A Andrews described the evolution of the SSK concept in 'Submarine v Submarine', in *Naval Review 1966* (US Naval Institute). The Trident story is taken from Chapter 6, 'Trident', of a US Government study, *Report of the Commission on the Organization of the Government for the Conduct of Foreign Policy* (June 1975): Appendix K, *Adequacy of Current Organization: Defense and Arms Control*. This appendix was based on a case study prepared by B E Carter and J D Steinbrunner. My account of early submarine tactics is based partly on Charles W Domville-Fife *Submarines of the World's Navies* (Francis Griffiths, London 1910).

The accounts of submarine tactics are based partly on such published sources as C Blair, Jr *Silent Victory: The US Submarine War Against Japan* (Lippincott, New York 1975); Rear-Admiral Ben Bryant RN *Submarine Commander* (Ballantine, 1958); Commander Richard Compton-Hall RN *The Underwater War 1939-45* (Blandford Press, Poole 1982); Grand Admiral Karl Doenitz *Memoirs: Ten Years and Twenty Days* (Weidenfeld & Nicholson, London 1959); Captain Matsaru Hashimoto, *Sunk! The Story of the Japanese Submarine Fleet 1942-45* (Cassell, London 1954); Commander F W Lipscomb *The British Submarine* (Conway Maritime Press, Greenwich 2nd edition 1975); Alistair Mars *British Submarines At War 1939-45* (US Naval Institute, 1971); Lieutenant-Commander C Mayers RN, *Submarines, Admirals, and Navies* (Associated Publications, Los Angeles, 1940); and Jürgen Rohwer *The Critical Convoy Battles of March 1943* (Ian Allan, Shepperton 1977).

Sources on the ASW campaigns of the two World Wars included R H Gibson and M Prendergast *The German Submarine War 1914-1918* (Constable, London 1931); R M Grant *U-Boats Destroyed: The Effect of Anti-Submarine Warfare, 1914-18* (Putnam, 1964); R M Grant *U-Boat Intelligence* (Putnam, 1969); Admiral of the Fleet Earl Jellicoe of Scapa *The Submarine Peril: The Admiralty Policy in 1917* (Cassell, London 1934); John Winton *Convoy: The Defence of Sea Trade 1890-1990* (Michael Joseph, London 1983); and OEG 51, a report of the US Navy Operations Evaluation Group; C M Sternhell and A M Thorndike *Antisubmarine Warfare In World War II* (Washington, 1946). The statistics on Axis and Allied operations at various phases of the battle have been taken from this report, which was originally classified.

For Allied exploitation of signals intelligence, I have benefited particularly from Patrick Beesly *Room 40: British Naval Intelligence 1914-18* (Hamish Hamilton, London 1982) and his *Very Special Intelligence:The Story of the Admiralty's Operational Intelligence Centre 1939-45* (Hamish Hamilton, London 1977); W J Holmes, *Double-Edged Secrets: US Naval Intelligence Operations in the Pacific during World War II* (US Naval Institute, 1979).

The discussion of nuclear power is based primarily on two papers: Rear Admiral Hyman G Rickover, Captain J M Dunford, T Roosevelt III, Lt Cdr W C Barnes, and M Shaw, 'Some Problems in the Application of Nuclear Propulsion to Naval Vessels' (SNAME, 1957); and Vice-Admiral Sir Ted Horlick (Director-General Ships and Chief Naval Engineer Officer) 'Submarine Propulsion in the Royal Navy', the 54th Thomas Lowe Gray Lecture before the Institution of Mechanical Engineers (London, 1982). The illustrations of British submarine powerplants were taken from the slides of Admiral Horlick's lecture. The notes on the noise characteristics of machinery plants were based partly on Kostas Tsipis, 'Underwater Acoustic Detection', in K Tsipis, A H Cahn, and B T Feld, eds, *The Future of the Sea-Based Deterrent* (MIT Press, 1973).

Norman Friedman

CHAPTER ONE

Stealth - the Nature of Submarine Warfare

The submarine was the first technologically 'stealthy' weapon system. Its great value, indeed its mystique, lies in its invisibility, and much of submarine technology is intended to preserve that invisibility in the face of increasingly sophisticated means of submarine detection. Submarine tactics and doctrine are often traceable to just that quality of stealthiness. Paradoxically, the submarine commander must shed his cloak in order to perform most of his missions. For example, a submarine reveals itself when it attacks its target. Thus, a successful commander must combine a talent for concealment with a willingness to abandon that protection at the moment of battle. This trade-off between preservation and combat effectiveness is central to submarine tactics and to submarine design.

In peacetime, stealth and invisibility seem all-important; the submarine is generally counted as a manageable threat as long as it can be detected by ASW forces. Training exercises, therefore, stress evasion and avoidance, which can be measured far more easily than effective damage to targets. Only in wartime does the destruction of enemy tonnage become the paramount value: risks are not only worthwhile, but required. The extent to which stealth was sacrificed on a routine basis during World War II would have shocked prewar experts. Perhaps that is a pointer to the future.

The largely psychological conflict between self-preservation (stealth) and combat effectiveness explains one of the most important operational lessons of submarine warfare, that a very few commanders are responsible for most of the sinkings. For example, the British found that the new effectiveness of the German U-boat arm in World War II declined considerably after a small number of aces were killed. However, the greatest number of sinkings was by commanders of medium aggressiveness. That is, the aces were relatively greedy; they kept attacking even as the odds shifted against them, and died relatively early in the war. Other submarine commanders tended to withdraw after a few successes; they balanced aggressiveness with some caution. As in air warfare, however, many commanders were not nearly aggressive enough.

In the US submarine force, the careful tactics drummed in, year after year, in peacetime were not nearly aggressive enough. About half of all serving US submarine commanders were relieved during the first 18 months of the Pacific War. For example, in prewar fleet exercises, submarines were counted as killed whenever they were detected by aircraft. In consequence, submarine doctrine called for very deliberate approaches which minimised periscope exposure, and which depended largely on passive sonar. In wartime, the most effective tactic was to attack on the surface at night, submerging only to escape counter-attack. For a prewar captain to operate that way was to deny all of his peacetime training. Indeed, a submarine commander who simulated a wartime-type night surface attack in a prewar exercise was severely reprimanded.

Until well after World War II exposure by attacking was the primary means by which submarines revealed themselves; that was a major justification for a convoy strategy, since only ASW craft near the targets could spot an attacking submarine. In World War I the cues were most often either periscope 'feathers' or torpedo tracks, and the main ASW problem was maintaining contact with a submarine after it had attacked. Sonar solved that problem, but not the problem of reliably detecting a submarine *before* it struck. Scanning sonar, which appeared after World War II, helped, but even now it is extremely difficult to resolve the locations of all submarines *before* they can attack. For example, through much of the postwar period, the 'flaming datum', a submarine location betrayed by a sinking, was considered a major clue for airborne ASW forces.

The stress of exposing a submarine by attacking was, for the first half of World War II in the Pacific, made considerably worse by the poor performance of US torpedoes. Numerous commanders suffered depth chargings after firing spreads of torpedoes (which failed to explode) into valuable targets, the wakes of their weapons giving away their locations. Late in the war, the submarine force received not only effective conventional torpedoes, but also wakeless electric ones, which further reduced the risk to the launching submarine.

Because submariners learn their trade partly by evading friendly ASW forces, their practice depends on the quality of those forces. For example, the US Navy has emphasised periscope-detection radar and electronic countermeasures, so that US submariners soon learn to avoid both exposure and electronic emissions. They therefore come to depend very largely on their passive sonars, and their tactics emphasise lengthy stalking of their targets. Soviet submariners seem much more willing to use their periscopes and radars, which may reflect the level of competence of Soviet ASW. These operational patterns filter back into the submarine design process, so that, for example, the US Navy has abandoned submarine air search radars.

Unfortunately such human factors rarely if ever figure in peacetime war games and in evaluations of the efficacy of the Soviet submarine force or of Western ASW. A related factor is the willingness of the average submarine commander to abandon an attack *after* he has scored a few kills, but before the ASW forces close in. That is, having made the decision to chance an attack, a submarine commander is unlikely to be deterred; but he is likely to be willing to take less than everything, to leave to fight another day.

It is also important to keep in mind the type of combat each navy envisages. At present the primary target of Western submarines is the Soviet submarine force, both anti-ship and strategic. Soviet emphases are mixed: in the 1950s they were concerned almost entirely with countering Western carrier and amphibious strike forces, but, particularly since the appearance of the 'Delta' class ballistic missile submarine, ASW (to protect

9

SUBMARINE DESIGN AND DEVELOPMENT

John P Holland's *Holland* was the direct ancestor of all American and British submarines. The stern view was taken in 1899, the bow view in 1900. *Holland* was single-hulled, and she was controlled in depth by her stern planes, which are barely visible outboard of her circular propeller guard. There was no periscope: the submarine commander navigated by bringing his boat just awash, so that he could see through the glassed-in ports let into the coaming around the circular hatch.
US Navy

submarine sanctuaries) has become very important. Since communication between submerged submarines is relatively inefficient, submarines in the ASW role tend to operate singly; the major tactical problem is the fear of accidental attack on or by a friendly ship. The Soviets prefer cooperative tactics, which are rational if they involve submarines attacking a non-submarine target when no Soviet surface ships are in the neighbourhood. It is not clear how the Soviets have dealt with the problem of interference when they employ tactics developed for anti-ship combat in an increasingly important ASW role.

In the past, wartime experience has rarely even approximated to peacetime forecasts (often made to plan the size of submarine fleets), to the great surprise of all parties. For example, the US Navy has been designed primarily to fight a general NATO-Warsaw Pact war, in which attack submarines would form an ASW barrier across the Greenland-Iceland-United Kingdom (GIUK) Gap and other narrow seas. Their targets would be transiting Soviet submarines. However, there are probably other more likely future scenarios such as limited wars in Third World waters in which most of the targets would be surface ships. Under such circumstances, submarines might well find themselves again trying to operate in 'wolf packs'.

Particularly since 1945, some submarine designs have been affected by rather special

STEALTH – THE NATURE OF SUBMARINE WARFARE

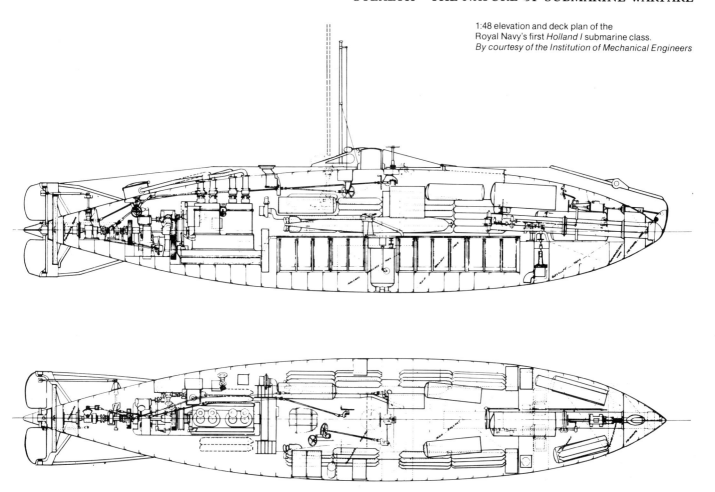

1:48 elevation and deck plan of the Royal Navy's first *Holland I* submarine class.
By courtesy of the Institution of Mechanical Engineers

requirements. For example, from the early 1960s onwards, US submarines were used extensively for electronic, photographic, and acoustic reconnaissance (intelligence collection) in Soviet fleet operating areas. When this story was revealed in 1975, particular reference was made to the *Sturgeon* (SSN 637) class. This had been developed from the earlier *Permit* (SSN 594) class, with additional masts, a larger sail, and some lengthening for additional electronics. All of which, in view of the 1975 report, suggests some considerable design attention to the requirements of covert reconnaissance. Submarine stealthiness makes reconnaissance a major wartime and peacetime mission, even though the conventional concept of the attack submarine emphasises attacks on enemy shipping and submarines. Special operations, such as landing small numbers of men behind enemy lines, also fall into this category, although generally they are met by specialised submarine conversions.

In the case of the Soviets, it is suggestive that the closed (diesel)-cycle 'Quebec' class coastal submarines were stationed in the Baltic and in the Black Sea, within submerged range of the Danish Straits and the Bosphorus. One can easily imagine a specialised seizure or minelaying or sabotage mission, to be executed at the outbreak of a general war, according to some standard Soviet scenario.

Many of the principal compromises of submarine design trade stealth for combat capability. For example, early submarines were effectively invisible simply because, at least in the immediate vicinity of enemy ships, they operated underwater, hidden from lookouts on board ship – although not always from lookouts in aircraft. Even on the surface, they were relatively difficult to spot because they were so low in the water. Fully submerged, however, a submarine was largely blind. Its commander had to give up some of his invisibility by piercing the water with a periscope, which a lookout in a surface ship might be able to spot. Later the same applied to a snorkel, and current submarine parlance includes an index of 'indiscretion', the fraction of the time the submarine subjects itself to detection by snorkelling. Similarly, in late World War II U-boats designed for high underwater speed, an important means of evading ASW ships, fast diving, had to be abandoned, so that when the submarine was on the surface it was easier to attack. That particular problem was solved at the time by the use of the snorkel, so that the submarine never had to surface. However, a submarine snorkelling was significantly slower than one cruising on the surface, so that some fraction of mobility had to be sacrificed.

As for the periscope, before 1941 the US Navy tried to maintain stealth by relying on passive acoustics for surface target detection and direction, with a 'single ping' active sonar to obtain a target range. Attacks were to be carried out from well below periscope depth. Such a doctrine proved largely ineffective, but it was some time before it could be forsaken.

The cautious attitude which goes with stealth survives in at least some modern submariners. One example is the frequent statement that a submarine is the naval unit most likely to survive a modern war. That is hardly a statement of military effectiveness. One veteran US submarine commander has said that a submarine captain could usually choose either to survive or to sink targets; he much preferred the latter. No account of submarine design and effectiveness, whether historical or current, can minimise this psychological dimension to the profoundly stealthy character of the submarine, the concentration on avoiding detection. That is most strongly emphasised in the modern ballistic missile submarine, whose peacetime mission is accomplished merely by avoiding detection. That mission was so at variance with the wartime emphasis on attack that, at least in the US Navy, wartime submariners promoted to command the new strategic submarines reportedly found the experience quite depressing.

It is striking that, in wartime, effectiveness was generally equated with audacity rather

SUBMARINE DESIGN AND DEVELOPMENT

Holland and her kin had very small silhouettes even when they ran on the surface, as here. However, demands for seagoing capability made for much larger and more elaborate bridges in later classes. Note, too, that when the submarine was trimmed down to the awash condition, to minimise its silhouette while retaining visibility, it had essentially no reserve buoyancy, and was easy to swamp; several were lost that way. Hence the development of conning towers, which began as unusually high hatch coamings.
US Navy

than with concealment. One might speculate that the Soviets have made a virtue of necessity (see Chapter 6) by developing tactics emphasising high speed and deep diving rather than silencing, although in fact their latest attack submarines ('Victor III' class) are reportedly very quiet. Moreover, it appears that the Soviets are much less concerned with avoiding detection than are their Western counterparts; they rely on aggressiveness, numbers and speed to attack and then to evade.

Such tactics can be extremely effective, particularly if the submarine has an alternative quiet-speed mode. If it varies operation between bursts of very high (noisy) speed and lower (but very quiet) speed, then it may be able to avoid attack by remaining one step ahead of the opposing ASW command and control system. That requires great coolness on the part of the submarine commander, and a rather sophisticated understanding of the opposing force, but it makes sense *if the submarine is fast enough in the relatively quiet mode.* The newest Soviet attack submarines may be well suited to just such concepts.

In effect, then, at least in the West, the submariner is taught in peacetime that to be detected is to be sunk, although in practice many submarines (at least during the two World Wars and in the Falklands War) successfully evaded the ASW forces which attacked them. This extends to submarine tactics which emphasise the stalking or ambush aspect of the battle. At least in the US and British submarine services, active sonar is generally eschewed because it gives away the existence of the submarine without gaining any commensurate advantage: the active 'ping' can often be detected at a greater range than that at which the active sonar can itself detect targets.

Invisibility is, to be sure, relative rather than absolute, and its extent depends in large part on the sensor from which the 'invisible' object is to be shielded. For example, to an eye on board ship, almost any underwater object is entirely shielded. To the same eye in an aircraft, however, a shallow object, particularly in clear water (as in the Mediterranean) is quite visible. The mere ability to dive to a moderate depth was sufficient to defeat visual detection under most circumstances, which is why submarines had only limited diving depths up through the early part of World War II. Since pre-snorkel submarines had to spend a large fraction of their time on the surface, the speed with which they could dive, ie with which they could gain a measure of stealth, was an important tactical factor.

The development first of passive and then

Low silhouettes made even surfaced submarines difficult to detect, but that made it difficult for them to operate in company with surface ships. The British 'K' class steam-powered fleet submarines suffered for just this reason in the 'Battle of May Island', when they collided with cruisers in the North Sea on the night of 31 January 1918, two (*K-4* and *K-17*) being sunk and two damaged. This unidentified K-boat is shown in her original, wet (low-bow) configuration, about 1917. The bows of these submarines were later raised considerably to increase buoyancy.
US Navy

STEALTH – THE NATURE OF SUBMARINE WARFARE

of active sonars considerably changed matters. The former (hydrophones) appeared during World War I, and could be defeated by effective silencing. That is, the hydrophone was (and is) useless unless the submarine co-operates by generating sufficient noise. Since World War I, and particularly since 1945, there has been a constant battle between passive sonar developers and submarine designers improving silencing. One reason the Germans developed surface submarine tactics in World War II was that they believed, incorrectly, that the primary British ASW sensor was still the hydrophone, and that it would be relatively ineffective against a surfaced submarine. Furthermore, only on the surface did a submarine have sufficient sustained tactical speed to carry out the type of attack required.

Active sonar was quite different, in that it did not require co-operation by the submarine. However, early World War II 'searchlight' sonars had a relatively low probability of detecting a submarine, due to their limited search rate. Thus most submarine contacts were still made as the result of observed submarine attacks, ie as a result of self-exposure by the submarine. In this sense very long-range homing and pattern-running torpedoes were a major contributor to maintaining submarine stealth in the face of sonars.

Once detected, the submarine would try to evade the sonar beam tracking it; its ability to survive depended on manoeuvrability (to break track) and the depth to which she could dive. That is, active sonar projected a narrow beam sloping downward at a shallow angle, with a blind area in a shallow cone directly under the ship. For example, one rule of

Stealth is psychological as well as physical; before World War I US doctrine emphasised the need to remain submerged in the face of the enemy. The General Board went so far as to keep down gun calibre so as to prevent submarine commanders from fighting on the surface. The fleet boat *Salmon* displays her 3in/50 calibre deck gun while running trials in 1938. As a result of wartime experience, submarines were fitted with 4in/50, then 5in/51 deck guns; ultimately a specialised 5in/25 'wet' gun was developed. The streamlining of *Salmon*'s fairwater is reminiscent of the pre-1917 emphasis on underwater performance. Such fairwaters were cut down in wartime to provide positions for light anti-aircraft guns.
US Navy

Stealth makes for unusual submarine missions. During World War I, the Germans built several U-boat merchantmen specifically to evade the British blockade. After the United States entered the war, they were converted into long-range cruisers. This is *U-151*, formerly the U-freighter *Oldenburg*, at Cherbourg in 1920. She was completed too late to see commercial service, but the first of the class, *Deutschland*, made two trips to America in 1916. The two boats in the background are French steam-driven submarines, from left to right *Fructidor* and *Thermidor*, completed, respectively, in 1909 and 1907. The frames attached to *Fructidor* are Drzewiecki 'collars', external torpedo launchers that were early and cheaper but more accident-prone rivals of torpedo tubes (especially in French and Russian boats).
US Navy

SUBMARINE DESIGN AND DEVELOPMENT

thumb for estimating the depth of a submarine was that contact would be lost at a range equal to one third of the depth. Thus a submarine could evade if it could dive rapidly enough *below* the sonar beam. That became more difficult after World War II, as sonar ranges increased. If surface ships worked in pairs, one could always keep contact on the submarine by appropriate manoeuvres. Deep diving could also bring the submarine below thermal layers in the sea capable of refracting sonar beams. As an adjunct to diving and manoeuvre, there were (and are) decoys and special noisemakers.

The latter are, however, very much a last resort. Underwater detection is ambiguous enough that there is always the possibility that a contact is a false target. The presence of a noisemaker resolves this ambiguity, and encourages ASW forces to try to regain contact.

Finally, great depth, if it could be attained rapidly enough, was a means of evading attack. Weapons such as depth charges dropped into the water take some considerable time to reach the depth of a submarine; the deeper the target, the more time it has to get out of the way. World War II ASW measures ultimately included tilting sonars, which could maintain contact even as a submarine dived, and faster-sinking weapons.

On the part of the submarines, there were also attempts to reclaim some measure of the invisibility lost with the advent of sonar. Modern anti-sonar measures include special shaping to diffuse the reflected sonar pulse, sheer small size (again to reduce sonar detection), and special anechoic (echo-deadening) coverings to absorb some portion of the sonar pulse as it strikes the submarine hull. Each of these approaches is analogous to recently discussed means of assuring 'stealth' in a new generation of bombers and fighters, the difference being that the chief sensor for the submarine is acoustic, whereas for the aircraft the active sensor is radar and the passive ones, infra-red and electronic support measures (ESM).

As this is written, acoustic sensors, either active or passive, remain the only consistently effective means of detecting a submerged submarine, which is why stealth is equated to sound absorption or deadening. From time to time alternative sensors are proposed, such as infra-red observation of the submarine wake, or radar detection of the disturbance of the surface created by a moving submarine underwater. The issue is always whether the submarine is to retain its ability to operate more or less invisibly. Although submerged operation has some inherent virtues (as demonstrated, say, by recurring proposals for commercial tanker submarines), from a naval point of view an easily detectable submarine is hardly worth the investment. Thus the claim of proponents of each radical new detection technology is that the ocean can be made 'transparent', ie that submarines can be reliably detected at extreme range, and therefore can be attacked easily and inexpensively.

The sort of invisibility enjoyed by a sub-

The inherent stealthiness of submarines makes them ideal for operations deep in enemy territory; several navies developed midget submarines for that purpose during World War II. The US *X-1* was inspired by British experience. She was also the only American submarine powered by hydrogen peroxide. With hull space and weight at a premium, she could not have a conventional bridge. Instead, when on the surface, she was steered from a deck position, protected by the folding spray shield shown, toward her bow. *X-1* is shown in April 1969, at the Naval Ship Research and Development Center, Annapolis, on Chesapeake Bay where she spent most of her career.
US Naval Institute/courtesy of Norman Polmar

STEALTH – THE NATURE OF SUBMARINE WARFARE

marine has its drawbacks. The key physical fact is that most electromagnetic waves, such as light and the radio waves of radar, cannot penetrate deeply into the water, which absorbs them very efficiently. That is why high-flying aircraft and satellites cannot easily detect submarines. Only sound waves combine long range in water and a wavelength sufficiently short to be useful, although they suffer from serious distortion over long distances. In each case, waves are a potential means of signalling as well as a means of detection; the two functions cannot be separated. The same physical laws which make detection difficult also interfere to a lesser extent with communication. That is, a communication signal must travel only one way, whereas active detection requires the signal to return as well, much weakened. Recently, for example, there have been claims in favour of blue-green lasers for air-to-submarine communication, but few seem to expect the lasers to provide a new means of detection.

Note, too, that at relatively short ranges submarines can be detected by their magnetic effects (magnetic anomaly detection, or MAD). However, MAD range is so short that this type of device is useful primarily for classification, ie for deciding that an acoustic contact is indeed submarine-like before actually expending valuable weapons.

The communication problem has been much publicised in connection with ballistic missile submarines. It is also very important in attack submarine operations. For example, lack of communication through the surface of the water makes it difficult (at best) for submarines to cooperate with friendly ASW aircraft. Similarly, World War II wolf pack tactics, in which several submarines attacked together, required all submarines to communicate via radio signals emitted on the surface. These signals, which could be detected at a great distance, were themselves a severe operational liability, at least to the German U-boat force. The Germans had to abandon important aspects of stealth in order to gain the tactical asset of co-ordination. Submarine IFF (Identification, Friend or Foe) is also a communication problem. Despite very great efforts, no reliable system has yet been developed, and thus co-operation between submarines, or between submarines, surface ships and aircraft is hazardous at best.

Similarly, a submarine attempting to sense its surroundings risks loss of stealth. If it shows a periscope, it risks abandoning invisibility; the same goes for a surface-search radar projected above water. Passive sonar does not give the submarine away, but a submarine using it must stalk its target for an extended time, risking detection by submarine-hunters in the vicinity. If, however, it uses an active sonar, to get information more rapidly, then it is vulnerable to detection, as passive sonars may pick up its own 'pings'. If the submarine depends on external sensors, such as those aboard friendly aircraft and satellites, then it needs some means of one-way communication.

One of the great surprises of both World Wars was that the stealth for which submarines were built was not always essential. In World War II, that realisation was reflected in increased gun batteries, as submarine commanders more frequently fought on the surface. In 1945 the US Navy was fitting out submarines as 'gunboats', partly because torpedoes were unsuited to attacking the small craft they encountered. Here *Blackfin* emerges from Mare Island Naval Shipyard (California) on 28 June 1946, armed with two 5in/25 and two 40mm machine canon. *US Navy*

SUBMARINE DESIGN AND DEVELOPMENT

This generally means deploying an antenna at or near the surface, itself detectable.

It is tempting to imagine that, because it is so difficult to detect and therefore to destroy, the submarine is the warship of the future. Clearly its role is increasing, but it is important also to keep in mind its very real inherent limitations, in terms of classic warship roles. The two primary naval roles are sea control and power projection. Sea control requires a navy to be able to guarantee free use of the sea in the face of a spectrum of threats including not only submarines and surface ships but also aircraft. Power projection generally requires an ability to transport and land considerable numbers of troops, in the face of opposing enemy land and air forces.

In the sea control mission, probably the greatest drawback of the submarine is that the same physics which makes it nearly invisible also denies it detection of aircraft and missiles at long range. Moreover, a submarine has only very limited internal volume, so that it has little capacity for anti-aircraft weapons. It is an effective anti-ship and anti-submarine weapon, but even in these roles it is somewhat affected by its limited ability to communicate. Tactical combination is difficult; although submarines can be (and have been) used as escorts for surface forces, they cannot entirely replace the surface ships.

Limited internal volume becomes a particularly acute problem in power projection. As a rule of thumb, a submarine of a given displacement has about half the internal volume of a surface ship of the same displacement, since the surface ship has much more structure above water. In 1956 the US Navy's Bureau of Ships, seeking radical new concepts of ship design, proposed a submersible aircraft carrier. Even on a submerged displacement of 40,000 tons, it could carry no more than six aircraft, and to provide that large a hangar the designers had to limit power to a cruiser plant, for a maximum underwater speed of only 5 knots (20 knots on the surface, at a displacement of 24,000 tons). Dimensions were set by landing requirements (500 × 120ft), and there was no question of providing catapults, as their slots could not have been made watertight. Aircraft would have been launched by a combination of jet assisted take-off and a 5-degree ski-jump. The BuShips designers concluded that such a ship was useless except for nuclear strikes, and that missile submarines would be more effective in that role. In particular, there was no hope of carrying enough aircraft or non-nuclear weapons to carry out traditional carrier roles. A parallel study of a submersible landing ship was even more disappointing.

There is no question that a submarine, by submerging, can avoid many of the worst threats that conventional surface ships face. That does not make it a viable replacement for such ships; stealth and associated advantages carry major costs. Moreover, mere ability to survive is not the test of a successful warship. That is particularly true of submarine virtues in war as opposed to peace.

Two US 521-ton O-class submarines at Boston on 28 September 1922 illustrate the unusual American disappearing gun mount. *O-10* (SS 71), in the foreground, has it stowed, visible only in the form of a protrusion from her deck forward of her fairwater. *O-4* (SS 65), in the background, has the gun fully erected, her deck fairing plate forming a shield. Both have their tall radio masts fully erect.
US Navy

CHAPTER TWO

Design Constraints and Compromises

All warships are the result of compromise, but submarine design is particularly difficult because of the range of conflicting conditions the designer must meet. In the broadest terms, he must balance surface performance against submerged performance, the latter both near the surface and, in many cases, deeply submerged. Another broad compromise is between unit capability and unit size, many submariners markedly preferring minimum size for a wide variety of reasons. Beyond their preferences is the issue of numbers versus quality which always enters warship design. This dilemma becomes acute in an era of extremely expensive nuclear attack submarines.

The most fundamental condition levied on the designer is that the same submarine floats neutrally buoyant submerged, and remains buoyant enough on the surface to keep the seas. That is, submerged, the displacement of the watertight part of the submarine, the weight of water which would fill that volume, must just equal the total weight of the submarine, structure and all. According to Archimedes' Law, which governs submarine and surface ship alike, that is the condition for the submerged submarine neither to sink nor to rise towards the surface; clearly small deviations can be controlled by diving planes and forward propulsion, but the basic condition must be met.

This is a far more severe constraint than the one the surface ship designer faces. For him, too, displacement must equal the total of all the weights in the ship, but it is only the underwater volume of a larger hull. For example, if he must accommodate added weight, he can add to the submerged volume (displacement) by allowing his ship to sink a bit deeper in the water. Similarly, extra volume can be provided by adding deckhouses, perhaps at a small cost in added draught (ie in added displacement) to balance any addition in weight. The construction of the current missile cruiser USS *Ticonderoga* on a hull originally designed as a destroyer (*Spruance*) is a case in point.

The submarine designer has no such luxury. He can add displacement only by enlarging the pressure (watertight) hull, which is a major modification. Alternatively, he can allow for later modification by providing lead ballast in his original design, at a price in performance. To some limited extent, equipment can be added outside the pressure hull, as in the current US project to fit vertical missile tubes to later *Los Angeles* class boats, but the price is an imbalance between underwater displacement and weight, which must somehow be corrected.

Submarines are difficult to design because of this direct relation between weight and buoyancy. Weight and space are truly interconnected, so that any change, even a minor one, affects virtually the entire design. As a result, submarine designs cannot be divided up nearly as neatly as surface warship design; each element has too much effect on each other. A British designer has commented that submarine design is far more tedious than surface ship design because of the need to take details into account, but that 'it is much more satisfying to achieve a balanced design, because there are comparatively few loose ends'.

The fundamental design quantity is volume rather than weight. Submarine designs begin with estimates of required internal space, often in the form of compartment length or deck area; the pressure hull is, in effect, wrapped around this volume. This is now a typical situation in warships, but it has always been the case with submarines, because generally the components of the submarine are considerably lighter than water. In consequence, submarines are 'volume critical', tightly packed with components. Because these components are generally not very dense, weight-saving does not reduce total displacement, since it does

Running on the surface in Manila Bay about 1912, the early US submarine *A-2* (SS 3), formerly named *Adder* when completed in 1902 as the lead boat of the US Navy's first (6 boat) submarine class, illustrates the fundamental compromise of submarine design: submerged v surfaced performance. She was carefully streamlined for maximum underwater speed, but that entailed minimising her above-water structure. However, extended surface operation was impossible without some kind of bridge, and the rudimentary framework shown was built up. Surface performance was the key to extended overseas submarine operations, and the United States was relatively slow to emphasise it.
US Navy

SUBMARINE DESIGN AND DEVELOPMENT

In drydock at Mare Island (California) in 1933, the US fleet submarine *Bass* (SS 164) of the 1924 *Barracuda* class illustrates a surface-orientated hull design, with a bulbous bow surrounding her torpedo tubes, and a flared bow typical of surface ship practice. In effect, her hull is a surface ship type containing the necessary tankage. This type of design was rejected in favour of German-type knife bows, that could cut through seas instead of bouncing over them, and there was little point in keeping unmanned decks dry.
US Navy

not reduce the space they require inside the pressure hull. But the weight thus freed can go into a thicker pressure hull, and thus into deeper diving. As submarines dive deeper, a point is reached where the weight of the pressure hull is so great that they become 'weight critical'. Massive increases in powerplant (eg reactor and turbine) weight almost certainly have the same effect. Some current nuclear submarines, for example, cross this boundary, as do the extremely deep-diving 'submersibles'.

Aside from the pressure hull, the powerplant is the major very dense component of a submarine. In diesel-electric submarines, batteries are often relatively heavy; they also consume a great volume. The reactor, heat exchangers, and turbines of a nuclear submarine are also quite heavy. Thus one can imagine trade-offs between propulsion weight and pressure hull thickness (ie between speed and diving depth). If the hull or the powerplant is dense enough, the submarine becomes weight-critical, and special provision must be made for it to be buoyant enough not to sink. That is the case, for example, with very deep-diving research submersibles. Thus, the strong pressure hull of the famous bathyscape *Trieste* was so thick that it was much heavier than water; it was actually suspended from a tank filled with light gasoline, which supplied the necessary positive buoyancy for the combination to achieve the neutral buoyancy required. Note that the current Soviet 'Alfa' class of nuclear attack submarine combines a lightweight hull material, titanium, with a very compact reactor plant (reportedly unmanned) to achieve its combination of high speed and very deep diving.

DIVING DEPTH AND PRESSURE HULLS

Diving performance places other limits on the designer. The fundamental tactical issue is the optimum operating depth. To a submariner, depth has many virtues. If he is being attacked, the more he can use the third dimension (depth) in evasion, the better his chances. The deeper he can dive, too, the better his chances of being able to use the acoustic structure of the sea, hiding under layers or, if he can dive really deep, exploiting the deep sound channel. A hull built to withstand great pressure can also withstand a more violent explosion, although some would suggest that the shock effect of the explosion can penetrate even a very strong pressure hull.

Particularly before World War II, submarines were often longer than their operating depth, which meant that a steep dive could bring one end or the other below operating, or even crush, depth. For example, the US 'T' class, designed during World War I, was 268ft 9in long, and had a rated operating depth of only 150ft. American 'fleet boats' of the interwar and early war programmes were about 300ft long, but had rated operating depths of only 250ft. The modern equivalent of this problem is the effect of a sudden stern plane jam (in the down position) at high speed; the submarine may pass beneath its design depth before its crew can recover. As a result, submarines typically operate in a restricted depth band. Above a depth fixed by speed (and roughly proportional to the square of the speed), their propellers cavitate, losing power and radiating noise. Below a depth set by speed, they risk crushing due to a stern plane casualty. If the designer accepts too great an operating depth, he must pay heavily in hull weight and thus in total submarine size. In particular, submarines built to operate in relatively shallow water, as in the Baltic, benefit from their limited diving depth.

In principle the ideal pressure hull is a sphere, the strongest shape, and the one frequently used in very deep-diving sub-

DESIGN CONSTRAINTS AND COMPROMISES

mersibles such as bathyspheres and *Trieste*. However, usable volume is very limited, since the strength of the sphere decreases as it is made larger. Submarine designers tend instead to use stiffened cylinders, which are the most practical compromise between weight, strength, and arrangement. They may be externally framed (to limit losses of precious internal volume), with hemispherical caps at the ends. Despite its cost in volume, internal framing has important advantages. Water pressure tends to press the skin of the pressure hull *into* the frames. By contrast, it tends to tear the skin *away* from external frames. Their welds, moreover, are more vulnerable to stress-enhanced corrosion. Truncated cones are sometimes used as a concession to overall hull shape, to improve hydrodynamics. Several World War II submarine designs had non-cylindrical end sections. These were accepted to gain space for more torpedo tubes, at a considerable cost in structural complexity or, perhaps, weakness. Some British submarines had non-reloadable bow tubes external to the pressure hull, a compromise which made for a powerful initial torpedo salvo without requiring a weakening of the pressure hull.

For any cylindrical pressure hull, strength declines as diameter increases; deeper diving requires either a narrower or thicker (hence heavier) pressure hull or a new hull material. On the other hand, sometimes hull diameter must be increased to fit essential equipment. There are several American examples. The nuclear attack boat *Narwhal* (built 1966–69) apparently required considerably increased diameter to take a carefully silenced power plant. The subsequent *Los Angeles* and *Ohio* classes required more space to fit more powerful reactors. It is not clear to what extent diving depth limitations had to be accepted in any of these cases; the alternative would have been increased hull strength bought with thicker plating or frames brought closer together, both of which add weight. The other major limitation on diving depth is the strength of the many connections at which the pressure hull is penetrated; examples include the propeller shafts, the periscopes, and the seawater inlets of a nuclear submarine. As submarines dive deeper, it becomes harder to maintain absolute watertightness in these hull penetrations.

A circular cross-section is an awkward space, relatively difficult to use fully. One early twentieth century designer, the Italian Laurenti, tried to use elliptical pressure hulls, but he was defeated because he could not achieve sufficient strength on the available weight. His successors tried multiple cylinders instead, to gain internal volume without excessive length. The first such submarines to be built came in 1944, the German Type XXI and the Japanese *I-400*; the former with a figure-8 and the latter with side-by-side cylinders. In the Type XXI, the extra volume was used to gain volume for extra batteries; in more conventional submarines,

The US submarine *O-1* was typical of single-hull craft of her period. She is shown in drydock at Portsmouth Navy Yard, New Hampshire, 5 September 1918, newly completed. The entire circular-section hull shown is the pressure hull, with a free-flooding casing on top. Her starboard forward diving plane can be seen folded back against the casing, and a bow torpedo tube is visible. There were no stern tubes.
US Navy

the batteries were stowed below the deck in the space remaining within the usual cylinder. At about the same time the Dutch naval constructor M F Gunning in Britain suggested a triple-hulled cargo submarine, the hulls forming the apexes of a triangle; postwar his ideas were applied to several Dutch attack submarines. The new Soviet *Typhoon* class missile submarine appears to employ a pair of side-by-side pressure hulls, with missile tubes between them.

Presumably the Soviets were unable or unwilling to build a single circular-section hull of sufficient diameter to accommodate these missiles more conventionally. Alternatively, they may have wanted to continue to use the industrial plant built up to construct pressure hulls for the 'Yankee' and 'Delta' classes. In the *Typhoon*, the elliptical cross-section is formed by fairing the gaps between the two cylinders. A truly elliptical hull would be far too weak to be worthwhile.

19

SUBMARINE DESIGN AND DEVELOPMENT

A prefabricated section of a US World War II fleet submarine illustrates double-hull construction. The circular-section interior is the pressure hull proper. The big external tanks, which are closed at the end, are for ballast. Two circular frames are visible inside the pressure hull itself; the braces will be removed as the submarine is fitted out. This photograph was taken at Manitowoc Shipyards on Lake Michigan, Wisconsin.
US Navy

HULL MATERIALS AND FORMS

New hull materials introduce their own problems of modern welding technology. For example, the USS *Thresher*, which was lost on diving trials in 1963, introduced the new HY80 steel in place of the earlier STS, and suffered from defective welds. As a result, the US Navy decided to build a small submarine for experimental purposes prior to introducing the new HY130 steel in full-size submarines. However, this Nuclear Hull Test Vehicle (NHTV) was ultimately cancelled together with the HY130 project.

A simple change in hull material can have a dramatic effect on diving performance. The United States entered World War II with submarines built of mild steel, rated to dive routinely to about 250ft, ie with a collapse depth of about 375ft. Late in 1941 the two leading US designers found that they could save enough weight to increase hull plating from $9/16$in to $7/8$in; that alone would increase collapse depth to 650ft. They also expected to introduce a new high tensile steel (HTS) that would bring collapse depth to 925ft. Operating depth was therefore set at 450ft in the new submarines. But none of the essential machinery, such as the trim pump, had been tested at the greater depth, and the new submarines were rated only at 400ft. In practice, this sufficed, as the new HTS was downgraded due to wartime shortages, and the 1941 calculations were therefore over-optimistic.

Given a fixed demand for internal deck space, the submarine designer can choose from a variety of external hull forms. A submarine intended for high surface speed has to be relatively long, for a favourable speed-length ratio. This requirement was, if anything, exaggerated by the scarcity of internal volume for diesel engines for surface propulsion. Until after 1945, then, submarines were build on a single principal deck level, with batteries (relatively heavy) below it; and the principal compartments distributed along the boat's length, namely torpedo rooms (fore and aft in some boats), limited berthing, a control room, and engine spaces.

Underwater, by contrast, for a given hull form, drag is proportional to the surface area of the submarine. A long hull has a relatively high ratio of surface area to volume, and in any case reductions in volume (displacement) reduce surface area as well. However, note that in the case of the current *Los Angeles* class, increased power was equated to much longer machinery spaces, hence to greater overall length. Note that outside the engine and reactor rooms the key requirement for internal space is for deck space (with adequate headroom), not for volume per se.

Thus modern submarines, intended for high underwater speed, are generally built with multiple decks. Smaller hulls could be wrapped around the same deck area, if it was arranged differently. For example, *Skipjack*, launched in 1958, was the first US submarine with four deck levels. She had about the same total deck area as the three-level *Nautilus*, but much reduced total pressure hull volume, for a noticeable saving in displacement, and also in hull surface area, hence drag.

Given a fixed hull volume, appendages such as the fixed sail and the diving planes contribute heavily to hull drag, and advocates of high underwater speed have proposed that the sail be eliminated altogether. For example, the *Thresher* class hull was much larger than that of the earlier *Skipjack* largely to fit a new bow sonar and a much quieter (hence more voluminous) powerplant. Their cost in speed was to be held to a minimum. The designers could not increase power, as it would have taken far too long to design an entirely new reactor. The only choice was to minimise the increase in drag, and that was achieved in part by cutting down the sail structure and the masts it contained. An example will illustrate the lengths to which the designers were prepared to go, although it should be noted that a proposal to eliminate the sail altogether was rejected.

In the *Skipjack* class the superstructure other than the sail had been reduced to a spine which covered the intake and exhaust piping of the emergency diesel engine, housed in the engine room and connected to a snorkel in the sail. That spine had to be dispensed with, but there was no space within the hull to pass the piping through. The solution was drastic. The emergency diesel was moved out of the engine room, and placed in a separate space almost directly under the snorkel in the sail, which itself was drastically reduced in size. Some speed had nevertheless to be sacrificed, but not nearly as much as would have been the case had earlier design practices been continued. Ironically, within a few years the *Thresher* design had to be modified to increase the number of masts and the height of the sail, apparently for near-surface performance, and speed had to be sacrificed anyway. It seems likely that the sacrifice was limited by the careful hydrodynamic design of the original *Thresher*.

Submarine evolution can be read in part as a balance between surfaced, submerged, and diving characteristics. That is, until 1945, surfaced performance equated to strategic mobility, while submerged performance counted primarily at the point of attack. The higher the surfaced speed, the better the chance a submarine had of closing with high-speed surface targets, and also the faster its transit to the war patrol areas. World War I experience, particularly in the German Navy, showed how much more important surfaced speed was, and the US Navy actually re-designed its submarines for better surface performance at the expense of underwater speed. For example, the 1918 American 'S' class was designed with carefully streamlined bridges and fairwaters, and with deck guns able to retract for minimum underwater resistance. However, in response to war experience they were redesigned with larger, drier bridges, and with more powerful deck guns. At the same time surface safety features such as permanent life rails and wood decks were added. The total cost of the change in emphasis was about 3 knots in underwater speed.

The other great issue in surface performance is reserve buoyancy, essentially the volume of the tanks the submarine floods to submerge. In the US Navy, for instance, the evolution from coastal defence to seagoing submarines was measured in part in the increase in reserve buoyancy from 12 per cent in the original *Holland* of 1900 to 13, 16, and 19 per cent in the later 'D' (1909), 'E' (1912), and 'F' (1912) classes, the latter capable of going about 1000 miles out to sea. Even then there were problems. Most of the reserve buoyancy was amidships, so that boats tended to nose under in head seas rather than rising to them. Aft, propellers and diving planes were too near the surface, coming out of the water too easily in rough weather.

This issue is somewhat clouded by the practice of providing submarines with free-flooding superstructures for better sea-keeping. Some early designers, such as the American Simon Lake, made their casings watertight, controlling their flooding. Such designs were relatively complex, and made for slow diving. However, a fully free-flooding casing could flood in a heavy sea, and make a submarine bow-heavy. The typical solution was to provide buoyancy tanks forward, watertight except for flooding holes; they improved surface performance, and could be flooded on diving.

The three basic submarine hull forms, single-hull, double-hull, and the intermediate or saddle tank, are alternative approaches to the surface v submerged problem. A classic single-hull submarine carries all of its tankage inside the pressure hull. In consequence it is the simplest to build, at least in small sizes, and it has the least hull surface area, for minimum underwater resistance. However, that internal tankage detracts from the limited internal volume of the submarine. The greater the reserve buoyancy required for surface cruising, the worse the problem. In modern single-hull submarines, moreover, considerable internal space is lost to reinforcing frames, which can be external (hence inexpensive in space terms) in double-hulled craft. John P Holland's early submarines were intended primarily to operate submerged, for coastal defence, and so emphasised underwater performance; they had single hulls. The US Navy, for example, abandoned the single hull during World War I in order to achieve greater surface reserve buoyancy, and did not return to it until the era of the 'true submersible' nuclear submarines.

Most Western submarine designs are described as single-hulled, but they differ from their classic ancestors in that all of their main ballast tanks are outside the pressure hull. Instead, they occupy portions of the streamlined hull fore and aft of the pressure hull. Many of the earlier single-hull submarines had some of their ballast fore and aft, but they also had internal ballast tanks. Probably the earliest all-external single hull class was the German Type XXIII coastal submarine of 1945; internal space was at a premium due to its unusually large battery capacity.

Double hulls were introduced in 1896 by a French designer, Maxime Laubeuf, who advocated 'submersibles', ships which would spend most of their time on the surface, diving only in the presence of their targets. His approach was to superimpose a floodable ship hull, adapted from contemporary torpedo boat practice, atop a submarine-type pressure hull. To keep this casing well out of the water, he had to provide substantial reserve buoyancy in the form of floodable saddle tanks between pressure hull and casing.

By contrast, the French in particular commonly referred to single-hull boats as submarines, ie as craft suitable only for submerged operation. For example, the earliest French undersea craft were propelled only by batteries, and they were intended to operate underwater almost all of the time. Single hulls had the least underwater resistance and

The incomplete US submarine *Walrus* (SS 437), being launched at Electric Boat on 20 September 1946, illustrates the tanking of a standard US fleet boat (*Tench* class). She was complete except for her casing and her conning tower. The framing visible amidships belonged to the pressure hull, which was almost completely surrounded by tankage. The bow was complete because it contained the buoyancy tank. The Electric Boat house flag flies from the stub that would have led into the conning tower, which in American practice was (in effect) a secondary pressure hull. *Walrus* was delivered incomplete, and broken up in 1959.
US Navy

SUBMARINE DESIGN AND DEVELOPMENT

The most efficient pressure hull shape is a sphere; the next best is a cylinder. The highly automated 800-ton research submarine USS *Dolphin* (AGSS 555) shown being launched at Portsmouth, New Hampshire, on 8 June 1969, was intended to operate at very great depths; hence the form of her single hull.
US Navy

so economised on battery power. The double hull, then, was associated with surface performance and with fuel capacity. Submarines typically had only a 6 to 10 per cent reserve buoyancy, compared to as much as 30 to 40 per cent in a submersible, in which a ship-like outer hull surrounded the pressure hull.

The submersible was much more seaworthy, with its substantial freeboard, and could attain higher speeds on the surface, due to its finer hull form. It was also much safer on the surface, due to its greater transverse and longitudinal stability (from its greater waterplane area). The space between the two hulls was generally used for ballast, but it could also stow fuel oil, for greater range. External ballast tankage could even be used for stowage of weapons in pressure-proof containers. Finally, framing between the two hulls could increase pressure hull strength without any cost in valuable internal space. On the other hand, all of that superstructure had to be flooded as the submarine dived. The recent British official history notes that the relatively long diving times of double-hull submarines were of little import before 1914, although war experience soon changed that.

The Royal Navy came to the double hull via an intermediate step, the saddle tank, in which external tanks were built around the pressure hull. In the 'D' class (approved in 1906) reserve buoyancy was gained by carrying most of the ballast water externally, although some internal tanks were retained. The extra internal space made for much better habitability rather than for extra fuel (for greater range), since the earlier single-hull 'C' class already had a theoretical radius of action beyond the endurance of the crew. The saddle tanks also greatly increased waterplane area, hence longitudinal (and transverse) stability on the surface.

At this time the French and Italian navies were already using more or less completely double-hulled submarines. British constructors rejected them for the time as too complex, with unduly bulky ballast piping. However, by 1910 many British officers felt that the double hull might be worth testing, and in February 1912 a Submarine Committee called for both overseas and coastal submarines of double-hull design. Only later would it become clear that small double-hull submarines were inefficient. The following year there were reports that nearly all of the German programme was for medium double-hull overseas submarines, and the Admiralty chose to follow suit with a 'G' class.

The Royal Navy continued to develop large double-hull submarines during 1914-18, but abandoned the type altogether postwar. The recent official history notes that its single great disadvantage was excessive diving time; all of the stability and reserve buoyancy problems of the single-hulled boats could be solved by appropriate saddle-hull design.

The Germans chose double-hull construction from the first, apparently in part because they demanded good seakeeping. They initially went to single-hull designs only for small coastal types intended to operate from the Belgian bases (Types UB and UC), although a much larger minelayer (UE) was also designed with a single hull, for simplicity of construction. In both UE and later versions of UB, small saddle fuel (not ballast) tanks were added for range, but, from the point of view of ballasting, all of these submarines were pure single-hull types. With the later version of the UC minelayer, the designers returned to the double hull for improved surface seakeeping.

In 1917 the Germans returned to the single hull for a new 364-ton UF class intended specifically to operate in the English Channel and the North Sea. They believed that by confining oil tanks to the interior of the hull they could eliminate leakage under depth charging, and thus improve the chances for escape. A single hull also made for much quicker diving, and for simpler (hence faster) construction. Later an enlarged UF, UG, was designed to replace the relatively complex double-hulled UBIII; the single-hull concept was relaxed to the point of allowing water ballast (but not oil fuel) externally. Compared with UBIII, this design was considered simpler and stronger, having greater stability (if reduced surface performance). Neither UF nor UG was completed, due to the end of the war.

Postwar, German designers at first continued to develop their wartime double-hull or nearly double-hull designs, culminating in Type IA. But the standard 1939-45 U-boat was Type VII, begun as a single-hull type. It had small saddle diving tanks while the main diving tank was in the pressure hull under the control room. Fuel oil was carried inside the pressure hull, to avoid leakage, as in the UF class. But, as the design was developed, the easiest way to increase range was to store fuel oil in enlarged saddle tanks (Type VIIB/C as compared to Type VIIA).

Modern American and British designers favour single-hull submarines because they have a minumum of wetted surface, hence minimum drag, for a given internal volume. The new *Los Angeles* is a particularly extreme example, with all ballast tanks concentrated at the ends, outside the pressure hull. They have relatively little reserve buoyancy, and virtually the entire length of the pressure hull is also the outer skin of the submarine. By contrast, Soviet designers appear to favour double hulls for a variety of reasons. Their submarines often operate in ice fields, in which a single hull might be punctured. Great reserve buoyancy is thus an important safety factor. In addition, a double hull provides a measure of protection against contact attack, eg by ASW torpedoes. Many writers have suggested that Western lightweight torpedoes, such as the ubiquitous Mark 46, cannot penetrate both hulls of most Soviet craft. Others would argue that the shock effect of even such small warheads would suffice, and that the resulting outer hull rupture would dramatically increase the submarine's noise signature, hence its detectability.

Full double hulls are relatively difficult to build and to maintain, because the compartments near the ends are necessarily very narrow and therefore difficult to inspect or to paint. Indeed, it appears that Soviet submarines have to be partially dismantled for hull maintenance. And, below a substantial displacement, the external tanks consume so much volume that the submarine proper is badly crowded. Thus, although the Royal Navy favoured saddle hull designs, essentially partial double hulls, its two smallest 1914-18 submarines ('H' and 'R' classes, about 400 to 430 tons surfaced, 500 tons submerged) were single-hull types.

Professor Ulrich Gabler, the designer of the current German IKL submarines, has claimed that, for a given diving depth and cruising speed, the single-hull submarine will generally be smaller and less expensive than its double-hull counterpart. It will also present a smaller sonar cross-section, but, on the other hand, the larger the expected radius of action, the more valuable the external tankage inherent in a double-hull design. Thus, although a single hull was the natural solution for German coastal submarines, double hulls were far better for the first generation of postwar ocean submarines. Nuclear power is the exception, since external tankage does not contribute to the range of a nuclear submarine, only to the resistance of its hull.

Submarines designed to spend most of their time on the surface had to be able to dive very quickly in an emergency, so that the reserve buoyancy so valuable on the surface had to be shed very quickly. Moreover, although much of the freeboard of a submarine was a free-flooding structure, there was some question as to how rapidly it could be flooded. Hence the standard World War II modification to US fleet submarines, in which numerous additional free-flooding holes were cut in their casings. These same holes added considerably to underwater drag, as well as to flow noise at high underwater speeds. The same submarines had already suffered when their streamlined superstructures were cut down to provide additional platforms for light anti-aircraft guns – a nice illustration of choosing surface over underwater qualities.

The British 'R' class of 1914-18 illustrates the elements of compromise as they were understood at the time. British submarine commanders in forward patrol areas had often sighted U-boats transiting on the surface, but had been unable to close them to attack. Between 1 January 1917 and 1 October 1918 there were 364 sightings but only 13 successful attacks. The earliest proposal for a fast ASW submarine was made in March 1917, but work began only later in the year. Anti-submarine attack required not only high speed, to get into position, but also a very powerful torpedo salvo, as the targets were small and agile, and as there would be little hope of a second shot. Thus the original design called for a submerged speed of 13.5 to 14 knots and four 18in tubes, but the final design was for 15 knots and six bow tubes.

The price paid was in surface speed and in surface seagoing qualities. In both, British requirements conflicted with those of the Germans, the latter determining much postwar American and Japanese policy. The Germans saw surface performance as a means of reaching their often farflung operational areas. Days lost in transit could not be made up, and underwater speed would matter little to a submarine spending most of its patrol time on the surface. By contrast, a British submarine in German waters would have to operate largely submerged after a short transit time so the cost of a day could be discounted. Hence the 'R' class designers were able to concentrate on underwater speed and manoeuvrability, at the expense of surface qualities.

They chose a single-hull design for minimum underwater drag, and further reduced drag by cutting away the free-flooding superstructure abaft the conning tower. Hull lines aft were very fine, for a combination of propulsive efficiency and agility (reduced deadwood). Inside the hull, an unusually high fraction of the length, 35 per cent, had to be devoted to machinery, consisting of a 240bhp diesel and two electric motors, for a total of 1200bhp (15 knots for 30 minutes, or 12.5 knots for an hour and 48 minutes). By way of comparison, the contemporary conventional 'H' class, of similar size, had a 480bhp diesel for surface power and 620bhp submerged (13 knots and 11 knots, respectively), and the battery consisted of 120 cells (220 for the 'R'). Postwar, the 'R' suffered in comparison with more conventional submarines due to very low surface speed (8 knots), and poor seakeeping; they were easily 'pooped' by following seas, due to very limited buoyancy aft.

CONNING TOWERS AND PERISCOPES

The bridge structure or fairwater, now usually termed the 'sail', (called the fin by the Royal Navy) is a special case in surface seakeeping. If it is dry enough, even a submarine with relatively low freeboard can operate on the surface; hence the significance of the changes in the American 'S' class in 1917-18. The earliest submarines were provided only with small armoured watertight conning towers, in which their commanders could stand when they were submerged. Before the development of periscopes, the only view was from ports in this tower, and it was standard practice for the submarine to rise intermittently to just awash during its approach to the target. Surface performance was another matter. At first, there were no permanent bridges, and orders had to be shouted down an open conning tower hatch. The conning towers of early British submarines were so short that high waves could wash over them, swamping the boat.

SUBMARINE DESIGN AND DEVELOPMENT

It was natural for the early periscopes to pass through the conning towers into the control rooms below. But the British view was that the conning tower per se was no more than a passageway between the control room and what became a permanent bridge. There was little point in passing the periscopes through this relatively narrow tube. The first British submarine with this type of conning tower was *C-19* in 1909, and this system persisted in all later boats. A recent British official historian observed that there was a conflict between a desire to increase the length of periscopes (to increase periscope depth for safety) and the need to be able to dive in shallow water, which in turn made a low silhouette attractive. Typically British conning towers had upper and lower watertight hatches, to provide extra security against flooding by waves breaking over the bridge.

The US Navy followed a rather different path. From the large *V-4* on (1927), it placed periscope eyepieces in large conning towers rather than in the control room located in the pressure hull proper. Total periscope length was fixed by the height of the structure above the bridge, which determined in part the size of the silhouette the submarine presented on the surface; when housed, the lower end of the periscope was nearly at the keel. However, periscope depth was determined by the height of the eyepiece above the keel; by placing its eyepieces in the conning tower, the US Navy (and other navies employing similar configurations) gained about 10ft. They also gained in periscope height above water, hence range, when the periscope was used for look-out on the surface. In most US fleet type submarines, the conning tower contained an attack centre from which the captain operated, although most of the ship controls were in the compartment below. This separation led to later demands for amalgamation of the attack centre and the control room.

The separate conning tower's great disadvantage was its bulk adding resistance underwater. That was no great problem as long as high underwater speed was not demanded, but in 1946 the US Navy began to develop a fast (underwater) submarine, which became the *Tang*. One of the first measures taken was to forego the conventional conning tower, to reduce the bulk of the fairwater enclosing the periscopes, snorkel, and surface bridge. Perhaps surprisingly, the loss of periscope depth was not universally accepted, and both *Darter* (diesel) and *Seawolf* (nuclear) of the mid-1950s had small conning towers justified entirely in terms of increased periscope depth. Later designs lacked conning towers; underwater speed was far too important.

Conning tower design is only one factor affecting another important aspect of submarine design, performance near (but by no means at) the surface. The classic problem of a submarine at very shallow depth is that sudden changes in trim (as when a torpedo is fired) or even violent waves can so change its buoyancy as to cause it to surface inadvertently, to broach, and so to expose itself. The entire issue might be thought obsolete in an era of nuclear submarines, but that is so far not the case that attempts to eliminate the sail (as a major source of underwater drag) in US submarines have generally died in the face of requirements for periscope-depth performance.

Historically, depth keeping was essential if an attacking submarine was to be able to make periodic periscope observations of its target; the periscope was the only effective attack sensor. Then near-surface depth keeping became important for snorkelling; the snorkel had to be kept out of the water, but not too far out (ie too detectable). For example, at least in early installations, each time a wave shut down the snorkel air intake the diesels would begin to suck air out of the boat so violently that air pressure would drop rapidly. Nuclear propulsion solved that problem, and it might be argued that the periscope is of little value in submarine v submarine duels. But this is not the only important current submarine role. For instance, the covertness of the submarine makes it an ideal platform for collecting electronic and even photographic intelligence, for both of which it must project sensors out of the water. The public discussion of US submarine intelligence missions into Soviet fleet operating areas (using *Sturgeon* class boats) can be read alongside statements that this design shows a much taller sail than its predecessors, a feature which would keep the submarine deeper under water when at periscope depth, and thus would make it less responsive to surface wave motion.

POWERPLANTS

Then there is the powerplant. One of the two central problems of submarine development, until late in the nineteenth century, was to provide reliable underwater power. The first solution was the electric motor, supplied by a storage battery. The major drawback was very limited endurance, just as in an electric car. Even so, a fully electric boat capable of submerging and of travelling a limited distance submerged was clearly useful for harbour defence, and a number of such submarines were built at the end of the nineteenth century, especially by the French Navy. Limited high speed underwater endurance is still a problem for conventional submarines. Submarine underwater speeds are usually quoted at a maximum battery discharge rate, which cannot last for more than an hour or two. Hence the need for surface operation, in which the submarine could be powered by a long endurance fossil-fuelled engine also able to recharge its batteries. That was provided by John Holland, who combined a gasoline engine with batteries at the end of the nineteenth century to create the modern submarine. He still thought in terms of coastal operations, primarily submerged, as demonstrated by his choice of hull form, ill-suited to extended surface running in anything but calm weather.

The other nineteenth century problem was trim control. Early submarine inventors tended to fill their ballast tanks only partly, to compensate for water density and details of weight aboard their craft. As a result, they suffered badly from the effects of free water surface. They also tended to try to hover; without any waterplane area, their boats had little longitudinal stability. John Holland solved both problems by relying on dynamic as well as static forces, by using the lift generated by hull and hydroplanes as his submarine moved through the water. That controlled lift could balance off weight and trim imbalance, so that, for example, ballast tanks could always be entirely filled.

The combination of separate surface and underwater powerplants was the key to strategic mobility, and even to the ability to deal with high-speed targets in the open ocean. In the latter case, a typical 1939–45 submarine tactic was to run on the surface, just out of visual range of a target ship or convoy, either submerging to attack or waiting for night to deliver a surface attack. The surfaced submarine would dive to frustrate pursuit. In either case, high surface speed was vital, and that in turn required relatively large surface engines, which made claims on limited internal space. They competed with battery space and with electric motors and generators. The size of the latter determined, at least to a large degree, underwater endurance, since they recharged the batteries when the submarine ran on the surface (or, later, snorkelled).

Here there was much room for complicated compromises. For example, the US Navy ultimately chose to connect its diesels to generators, always running the propellers on electric motors. When a fleet submarine ran on the surface, it would always be charging its batteries, since power would always be fed through them. This was a relatively cumbersome system, and represented a sacrifice of space and weight. The benefit was a higher surface speed when charging batteries; in some other navies diesels had to be de-clutched in order to connect them to the generators.

Diesels were by no means the only surface powerplants tested. Compared to steam turbines, they produced relatively little power for their weight. Steam engines seemed attractive for high surface speed. Their major drawback was twofold; they required many more openings in the pressure hull, a potential diving hazard, and they took much longer to start up and to secure. The first problem was particularly evident in the fast British 'K' class submarines of 1914–18, which needed steam turbine power to reach battle fleet speed. The second was exemplified by the early French steam submarines sometimes taking as long as 15 minutes to submerge. Even so, when the US Navy sought very high surface speeds after 1945 for submarine radar pickets, it returned to steam

DESIGN CONSTRAINTS AND COMPROMISES

plants. One result was the pressure-fired boiler for a steam turbine, a machinery plant ultimately employed only in surface ships.

The entire concept of using two separate powerplants was extremely expensive for anything as volume-critical as a submarine, but it was inescapable; only fossil fuels could store sufficient energy for sustained high power in a limited volume. They in turn required oxygen, and no submarine could carry a sufficient volume for extended underwater operation. There were attempts to use high power underwater, the most notable being the German Walter turbine, but they were all very limited in endurance by the volume of oxidiser the submarine could carry. Thus, until the advent of the snorkel, high sustained power meant surface operation. A submarine exercising its long-range mobility became, temporarily, a surface ship, giving up its stealth entirely. Even while snorkelling, the snorkel head itself is detectable (and it is larger than an attack periscope) so there is still a sacrifice of invisibility. One former ASW pilot referred to a snorkelling submarine as 'a small surface vessel' which had abandoned its essential submarine quality. Typically submarines snorkel intermittently in hopes of avoiding excessive exposure, and, therefore, detection.

Moreover, when it is snorkelling, a submarine is limited in speed, partly to avoid damage to the snorkel itself. Partly, too, the snorkel is generally used to charge batteries, so that only a fraction of the power being developed goes directly into propulsion. For example, a modern German IKL submarine may make only 5 knots on its snorkel, but as much as 22 knots at maximum battery rate submerged.

The nuclear submarine is at present unique in combining underwater and long-range propulsion, because it alone packs very high energy densities into a fuel requiring no oxygen for its combustion. Nuclear plants are also unique in that they are so powerful that excess energy becomes available for many auxiliary functions. For example, it is typical for nuclear submarines to renew their atmospheres by hydrolysis, extracting oxygen from the water through which they steam. A conventional submarine attempting to remain underwater for an extended period usually uses chemical devices such as 'candles', which are less effective. Almost certainly, too, only a nuclear submarine has sufficient excess electrical capacity to power a very large active sonar; certainly commanders of nuclear aircraft carriers have remarked on the degree to which their powerplants assured them of sufficient energy for their electronic systems. The principal drawback of nuclear power is that it imposes a very considerable minimum size and cost on the submarine. It is not clear whether this factor accounts for the continuing popularity of diesel-electric submarines in the world's smaller navies; one would have to add that the five nuclear submarine operators have shown no willingness whatever to export such craft.

This section of the second British nuclear submarine HMS *Valiant* (seen at Barrow-in-Furness when Vickers laid her down in January 1962) typifies externally-framed pressure hull structure. *Central Press Photos*

The case for advanced non-nuclear plants is still open. For example, there are very energetic reactions which could, in theory, power a non-nuclear submarine for weeks on end (albeit only at low speed), given the volume available for fuel in such a craft. Many of these reactions are quite violent, and no such submarine has yet been built, but the non-nuclear fully submerged submarine is probably a real prospect for the 1990s or the early years of the next century. Fuel cells are often mentioned in this connection. This issue will be explored more fully in Chapter 9. For now, the world's submarines are divided into two classes: non-nuclear submarines, with limited underwater mobility by battery, requiring contact with the atmosphere (via their snorkels) for sustained mobility; and nuclear submarines capable of essentially unlimited underwater endurance. A third category, the submersible, designed for surface operation with intermittent underwater mobility, is essentially extinct. Design criteria, tactics, and ASW countermeasures suited to these three classes are very different, as the reader should keep this distinction in mind in what follows.

Beyond all of these detailed questions is the great strategic issue of sheer submarine size. As in every other warship class, most of the issues of compromise are most easily solved by increasing unit size. Many (though by no means all) submariners traditionally prefer the smallest possible size, for a combination of manoeuvrability (in three dimensions) and relative invisibility, the theory being that the larger the submarine, the better the sonar target it presents. Larger size should also make for easier detection by a variety of current and potential non-acoustic sensors. As for manoeuvrability the longer the submarine, the easier it is for it to exceed test depth in an acute dive. Planners often prefer smaller submarines on the usual ground that cost is roughly proportional to size, so that numbers and unit size are (at least apparently) opposed.

But experience suggests that small size per se does not make the target undetectable. For example, much of the size difference between the US *Permit* class and the earlier *Skipjack* can be traced to elaborate arrangements for engine silencing. Since passive acoustic detection generally can be done at much greater range than can active, it seems likely that silencing is more important than a reduction in sonar cross-section in enabling the submarine to survive.

CHAPTER THREE

The Era of the Submersible 1900-1945

The history of the modern submarine, a warship capable of protracted underwater operations, began only in 1945. The great submarine campaigns of the two World Wars were fought with submersibles which spent much of their time on the surface, submerging only for concealment. One pre-1914 writer described submarines as good-weather torpedo boats, substituting submergence for the cloak of darkness or foul weather which surface torpedo craft required for their approach. Underwater mobility was so limited that in his memoirs Admiral Doenitz described German U-boats as little better than intelligent mines.

A typical World War I U-boat, *U-111* of 1917 (which the United States acquired after the war) could make 16.4 knots on the surface and 8.4 knots submerged, the latter at the one-hour battery rate. Her *sustained* underwater speed was far less, 5 knots for 10 hours. No submarine commander would willingly exhaust his batteries by running at sustained speed for the full ten hours. He would always keep a sufficient reserve of electrical power to deal with any emergency, such as an ASW attack. Thus a constant theme in accounts of submersible warfare is the need to conserve battery power, and to 'top up' batteries whenever possible by running on diesels, on the surface. This problem was complicated by the need to maintain some degree of forward motion to balance out any positive or negative buoyancy. The greater the excess buoyancy, the greater the minimum required speed, and thus the greater the drain on the batteries, and, tactically, the more frequent the need to re-charge.

These limitations endured until 1945. The German Type VIIC fought most of the Battle of the Atlantic and was credited with only 4 knots at its 20-hour battery discharge rate, 2 knots at the slowest discharge rate, at which it could remain submerged for 65 hours. Conversely, the maximum underwater speed of about 7.6 knots could be sustained for only about an hour.

Despite its limitations, the submersible was a new type of warship, the only type able to defy command of the *surface* of the sea on a regular basis. Its ability to operate more or less freely in enemy areas was the basis of the German submarine blockade of Britain, as well as of many more conventional operations. Almost seven decades later, the *inability* to enforce sea control both on and under water remains one of the most significant realities of naval warfare.

BEFORE 1914

Before 1914 the primary submarine design goal was to transform it from a coastal craft to a long range or 'overseas' submarine with sufficient strategic mobility to reach distant, enemy-controlled waters. 'Overseas' performance resulted from a combination of greater size (for seakeeping) and the diesel engine (for endurance). The precise meaning of 'overseas' depended on the distance between home and enemy waters. For the Royal Navy, a typical figure was Portsmouth to Wilhelmshaven, 620 nautical miles. At 10 knots a submarine would cover 240 miles per day. Thus an endurance of 3800 miles would suffice for over ten days on patrol in German waters. The German point of view was very different. To intercept shipping en route to the British Isles, a U-boat would have to be able to pass around Scotland into either the Atlantic or the Irish Sea. Hence the Germans tended to require a range of 5000 or 6000 miles for effective 'overseas' operation. But 2000 or 3000 miles would suffice for offensive operations in the English Channel, off the Allied Channel ports.

The first effect of submarines on naval warfare was to make close blockade of enemy ports obsolete. The sheer strain of awaiting surprise attack would surely exhaust the crews of blockading warships. Admiral George Dewey, the victor of Manila Bay in 1898 and, from 1900, Chairman of the US

The first role of the submarine was as an 'equaliser', a relatively inexpensive means of countering expensive foreign capital ships. Even the major powers, which did operate large battlefleets, considered them a useful means of defending their overseas possessions. Here three small US 'A' class submarines (from left to right *A-6*/SS 7, *A-4*/SS 5, *A-2*/SS 3) sit in the floating Dewey Drydock at Olongapo in the Philippines, about 1910-12. *US Navy*

27

SUBMARINE DESIGN AND DEVELOPMENT

The 495-ton D-boats, completed from 1908, were the first British 'overseas' submarines (range 2500 miles at 10 knots); *D-1* is shown at Portsmouth before 1914, with two smaller C-class submarines in the background. Her saddle tanks are clearly visible as protrusions from her pressure hull, and her radio mast (the first for a British submarine) is rigged, with cross- and star-shaped spreaders marking the cage antennas slung from it. Note the absence of any protection for her bridge, and the prominent ventilators surrounding her fairwater.
US Navy

operations, even though relatively few warships were actually sunk by submarines when steaming at speed. But the great surprise of the war was the submarine campaign against shipping.

Pre-1914 British strategy called for a blockade of enemy bases and harbours, both to deny an enemy the means to fight and to protect British commerce. Submarines had two major effects. First, as early as 1904, Sir John Fisher, the new First Lord of the Admiralty, argued that seagoing submarines and surface torpedo craft would be able to dominate the North Sea, to the virtual exclusion of large warships. He had begun his career as a torpedo expert, and was uncomfortably aware of the vulnerability of large warships. Second, *if* Britain could build 'overseas' submarines capable of operating off the enemy coast, they could form the first line of the blockade, effectively immune to enemy countermeasures. In 1906, at his urging, the Admiralty Board approved the first British 'overseas' submarine design, the 'D' class, with an endurance of about 3000 miles at 8 knots. That year Captain Reginald Bacon, commanding the British submarine force, claimed that all existing British submarines could fight as much as 200 miles from their bases. Four years later *D-1* steamed unaccompanied from Portsmouth to the western coast of Scotland (a distance of about 500 miles) for fleet exercises, notionally torpedoing two cruisers as they sortied.

By the end of 1912 the Admiralty War Staff had concluded that the main means of detecting a German fleet sortie would have to be long-range ('overseas') submarines on sustained patrol in enemy waters. The same submarines might well also be the only units able to engage German warships, as the British fleet might be unable to make contact. In fact the British were able to use radio intelligence to improve their chances of intercepting the German fleet at sea, but before 1914 (with its remarkable early recoveries of German merchant and naval codebooks) no one could envisage that.

The Royal Navy also saw its submarines as a means of defending distant colonies without detaching major units from the battlefleet in home waters, a practice both Britain and the United States would follow after 1918. As in the case of preventing blockade, it could be assumed that submarines would have a disproportionate effect on any hostile commander intending to mount an assault. Six of the early 'B' class were assigned to Gibraltar and Malta as the British battlefleet withdrew from the Mediterranean from 1906 onwards; in 1910 six of the larger 'C' class were towed to Hong Kong, three remaining on that station in August 1914. *B-11*, one of the Malta boats, made the first wartime penetration into the Dardanelles.

In 1914, due largely to Fisher's enthusiasm, the Royal Navy operated the largest submarine fleet in the world, 74 boats built, 31 under construction, and 14 more either on order or projected. But the bulk of

Navy's General Board, argued that with two submarines in Galveston, 'all the navies in the world could not blockade that place'. Nor did he feel that his fleet would have been able to seize Manila in the face of submarines, had the Spanish possessed any in 1898. Faced with the prospect of some Japanese attempt to seize the Phillipines, the United States very early deployed its own submarines to the Far East, on just this theory.

The Royal Navy in 1914–18 had virtually to abandon areas of the North Sea near German naval (ie U-boat) bases, shifting to a strategy of blocking the North Sea exits. Hence the choice of Scapa Flow, rather than traditional bases such as Portsmouth, as the war base of the Grand Fleet. The threat of submarine attack strongly affected fleet the existing units were coastal or short-range single-hull types of the 'A' (8 left of 13 built), 'B' (10 left of 11 built), and 'C' (37 left of 38 built) classes; only 8 'D' and 6 of an improved 'E' (typical endurance 3800 miles at 10 knots) overseas classes had been completed. The latter class eventually contributed the bulk of British operational submarines during the war. However, as early as 1912 the British Submarine Committee recommended the next step, an 'overseas' submarine capable of operating directly with the main fleet, ie with a surface speed of about 20 knots. This concept continued to attract the major navies through the early postwar period, the most extreme example being the unfortunate British steam-powered 'K' class.

WORLD WAR I

In August 1914 the Royal Navy assigned its overseas submarines to patrols in the Heligoland Bight. Most of the intermediate 'B' and 'C' classes in home waters joined Surface Patrol Flotillas operating from major ports, such as Dover. The less capable submarines were assigned to harbour defence. All suffered from insufficient endurance: the overseas boats were towed part way to their patrol areas, and the Dover boats tied up at buoys laid across the Straits, on alert for enemy reports. Although local patrols continued at least until 1917, they were never particularly effective, war experience entirely vindicating the decision to abandon coastal submarines for the overseas type.

Even so, defensive submarines at Yarmouth and at Lowestoft sortied when the German battlecruisers bombarded those ports in 1914 and 1916. In the latter case the Germans may actually have cut short their attack after sighting a surfaced British submarine coming into firing position. Later the Admiralty would describe submarines in port as the principal British defence against coastal bombardment. The German raids themselves were possible because the Royal Navy could not maintain anything approaching a close blockade of German naval bases, due largely to its own perception of the underwater threat from both U-boats and mines.

On the offensive, submarines proved most valuable to the Royal Navy for their ability to operate in enemy waters, such as the Baltic, the eastern North Sea, and the Sea of Marmora. In each case, although relatively few submarines operated, and although net tonnage sunk appears not to have been very large, the moral and disruptive effect was enormous. For example, the Turkish army in the Dardanelles was almost deprived of ammunition for a time. Submarine minelaying in German home waters was a major British ASW weapon. Finally, British submarines were a useful means of attacking U-boats when the latter were surfaced.

German prewar naval doctrine emphasised coastal defence, and U-boat strategy reflected it. On 3 January 1912 the Torpedo Inspectorate, responsible for U-boat construction, drafted a programme for future development. U-boats were to be organised in flotillas of 12, each of which could cover a 60-mile front (5 miles between boats). One flotilla at sea would cover Heligoland. Each boat at sea would have to be backed by another in port, relieving it daily, and a third flotilla would be held at Kiel in reserve. A fourth flotilla would patrol the approaches to Kiel, and a fifth, of longer range, would be based at Emden for North Sea operations. Since current experience showed that about one out of six U-boats would be under repair at any one time, the Inspectorate proposed an additional 10, for a total of 70 U-boats, of which only 14 would have to be ocean-going.

But the Germans did not really distinguish between coastal and overseas craft. From *U-1* onwards they were double-hulled. *U-1* herself sailed 587 miles round Denmark from Wilhelmshaven to Kiel in bad weather as early as September 1907; three years later the British would consider this 'overseas' performance. At the same time the Germans were designing 500-ton boats with an endurance of 2000 miles at 15 knots. Endurance was much increased, to 6700 miles at 8 knots, in *U-17*, which was the first true long range boat capable of operating to the west of the British Isles, athwart the shipping routes.

Before 1914, submarines were not perceived as potential commerce raiders because they were clearly incapable of obeying the international laws of such warfare, as they had been formulated at the Hague between 1899 and 1907. They could not really be expected to stop and search merchant ships before seizing or destroying contraband; they were far too vulnerable when surfaced, and it could even be argued that fast merchantmen could sight them far enough way to evade them altogether. Most naval officers concluded that submarines were effective only attacking without warning, while submerged, and therefore were for almost exclusive use against warships. This was not to dismiss them; their threat to surface warships was frightening enough, particularly since there were no effective means of counterattack. A few, including Admiral Sir John Fisher, concluded rather that the classic rules of commerce warfare would be discarded, and that submarines would be a terrible threat to the seaborne commerce upon which Britain depended. Perhaps remarkably, the German Imperial Navy showed little prewar interest in such a strategy; one British naval historian has remarked that the Germans found the great British vulnerability almost by accident.

Certainly the submarine was an ideal blockader, *if* the prize rules could be discarded. No individual merchant ship could expect to detect a submerged submarine. Nor was there any countermeasure in sight, since the submarine could so easily escape detection by warships as well. In 1914 submarines revealed themselves only either by attacking (ie by showing periscopes or torpedo tracks) or by showing periscopes or by surfacing. Even so, a submarine commander could generally count on detecting surface ships before they became aware of him. Most submarine fleet manoeuvres

The K-boats were the first US submarines (launched 1913–14) capable of keeping the sea for any protracted period, and thus were considerably behind European practice. The 392-ton *K-8* (SS 39) is shown in drydock at Honolulu shortly after World War I; note the absence of any permanent bridge to shield personnel while she ran on the surface.
US Navy

SUBMARINE DESIGN AND DEVELOPMENT

The 212ft *U-35* was the highest-scoring submarine (224 ships worth 535,900 grt in 25 patrols) of either World War. She is shown at Cartagena (Spain) in 1916, alongside the German freighter *Roma*. Built under the 1912 programme, she was delivered in November 1914, and was representative of U-boat development at the outbreak of war. She displaced 685/844 tons, was double-hulled, armed with two bow and two 20in stern torpedo tubes (with two reloads) and two 88mm guns, and manned by a crew of 35. The very tall masts were necessary to achieve sufficient radio range.
US Navy

The seizure of Belgium led to German interest in small, easily transported U-boats for North Sea operations. They were also well-suited to the Adriatic. Transported by rail, they were assembled at Antwerp and Pola. Here the 92ft *UB-1* of 127/142 tons, the first of the series, transferred to Austria as *U-10*, is lowered by crane, 1915. She had been completed in only 75 days. Unlike sea-going U-boats, the UBs were only single-hulled. They had no reloads for their two 17.7in torpedo tubes.
US Navy

demonstrated these points, yet the surface navies did not really appreciate their implications until German and British commanders achieved a series of spectacular successes against cruisers during the first months of the war.

At the same time, German submariners on patrol around the British Isles began to appreciate the density of the merchant shipping in such areas of concentration as the Downs. By the end of 1914 they were beginning to agitate for shipping warfare. The German naval staff began to estimate the sinking rate which would force Britain out of the war; late in 1915, for example, the stated figure was 600,000 tons per month for six months. In 1917, on the eve of the great unrestricted submarine campaign, the duration of the required sinkings was extended to nine months. The U-boats sank 540,000 tons in February 1917, 593,000 tons in March, and a terrifying 881,000 tons in April, when British food stocks were only equal to ten days' consumption. Convoy tactics brought the figures back down, to 596,000 tons in May and 687,500 in June, but the shipping war was not really under control until the end of 1917.

Perhaps the most important quality of the German submarine blockade was its ruthlessness. The prize rules were a vestige of an earlier hope that the savagery of warfare could be limited. Sinking merchant ships, including liners, without warning seemed to be part of the new and terrifying practice of 'total war', in which non-combatants were as much at risk as were the uniformed services. The Germans argued that the reality was far more complex, that the British practice of considering foodstuffs contraband made their blockade of Germany as much an assault on German civilians as the submarine war was on British civil society.

The horror associated with unrestricted submarine warfare persisted after 1918, but Allied ASW *did* succeed in containing the submarine threat, albeit at a high price. Thus it was not difficult for the major sea powers to agree to revive the prize rules, and to prohibit unrestricted submarine warfare, as part of the interwar naval arms limitation treaties. Doctrine in most navies concentrated on submarine operations against purely naval targets. After 1939, however, such limitation was difficult to maintain. Unlike Germany

THE ERA OF THE SUBMERSIBLE 1900-1945

before 1917, none of the combatants was inhibited. It may be noteworthy that Admiral Doenitz took pains in his post-World War II memoirs to claim that he had returned to such tactics only under Allied provocation.

Until the spring of 1917, Germany faced three linked strategic problems. First, after the Western Front stalemate on the Marne, she had to seek some other means of achieving a decision. Second, she had to keep the United States, with vast industrial and manpower, from entering the war on the Allied side. Third, as the war progressed, the British blockade on raw materials and also on food gradually weakened the German economy. It is not clear to what extent the German government perceived the blockade as a driving force, although its weakening effect was certainly evident in many ways by 1918. From late in 1914 on, the German Navy pressed for a submarine blockade in the face of a civilian government which feared incidents that would drive the United States into the war. The key tactical problem was that a submerged submarine could not be expected to distinguish one type or even one nationality of merchant ship from another, with the result that no satisfactory rules of engagement could be framed.

The German government sought security without any real appreciation of the operational consequences of its restrictions. The submariners and the naval staffs rebelled against the concept of the rules, and even so there were enough incidents to cause the suspension of all submarine warfare on several occasions. Postwar, the German submariners could quite correctly point out that the US decision to go to war had been taken without reference to the resumption of submarine warfare. But one might also argue that the American 'Preparedness' campaign of 1916, which helped provide the mobilisation base of 1917-18, was inspired partly by submarine operations. Certainly the series of incidents, from the *Lusitania* onwards, helped prepare US official and public opinion, so that the final provocation of the Zimmerman telegram was effective.

The U-boat arm's frustrations are familiar to students of more modern limited wars; political considerations took precedence over practical (purely military) ones. But, given the consequences of US intervention, one might argue that the political questions were in fact extremely practical in a military sense. Current discussions of rules of engagement often engender similar contempt for impractical foreign policy, yet most realistic scenarios for future naval conflict involve limited rather than general war. It is not clear that a better grasp of military realities by civilian authorities will solve the problem; certainly the German Imperial government was never able to resolve its own dilemma. Postwar, Vice Admiral Andreas Michelsen, the U-boats' wartime commander, complained that as early as May 1915 there were no fewer than 146 special restrictive orders, and 'soon the submarine commanders were not able to get about on account of the mass of papers'. The naval staff consistently argued that operations would be impossible if conventional prize rules were enforced; for example, the British employed disguised armed merchant ships ('Q-ships') against submarines surfaced to stop and board them.

Even stiff rules did not prevent dangerous incidents. Despite orders prohibiting attacks on liners (but permitting attacks on armed merchantmen and military transports), the Channel steamer *Sussex* was torpedoed, the U-boat commander arguing that she appeared to be a troopship, with many uniformed men on her decks. In fact she was an unarmed liner and one of the 80 victims was an American. The German government then restricted the U-boats to the prewar prize rules, and in protest the U-boat commanders suspended operations against merchant ships altogther. The political nature of the problem shows in German willingness to continue virtually unrestricted submarine warfare in the Mediterranean, where there was little danger of sinking American ships or killing Americans aboard British liners.

It is difficult to evaluate German claims for the efficacy of unrestricted submarine warfare. Certainly Britain was in great danger during the spring and summer of 1917, before convoys were formed, and while shipping was essentially uncontrolled. Yet the tonnage war eventually failed, and the U-boat leaders had to explain why. Admiral Michelsen claimed that, although 600,000 tons per month might well have been decisive in 1916, when the offensive was planned, by 1917 the British blockade's impact on Germany had upset the calculation. In any case, with the failure of late 1916 peace initiatives the German General Staff appears to have decided that a submarine campaign offered the only hope for a decision during 1917, and the six-month estimate was actually published. Unrestricted submarine warfare actually began on 1 February 1917, albeit with some restrictions.

The Germans had to choose between the dense shipping zone around the British Isles and more spectacular operations farther afield. They never tried to operate in the open ocean, where merely finding targets would have been a problem. Rather, they placed medium U-boats on 12 patrol stations around the Western Approaches to the British Isles. Shorter-range U-boats operated in the English Channel and in the southern North Sea. By 1917 there were also U-cruisers capable of cruising all the way to the US East Coast and to Dakar in West Africa. In Michelsen's view, the long cruises were perhaps valuable for propaganda and for diverting Allied ASW efforts, but they were uneconomical. In tonnage warfare what counted was merchant tonnage sunk per ton of U-boat. The closer the patrol area to the German base, the more time a U-boat could spend on station. The smaller the U-boat, the more efficient.

It took 36 U-boats merely to occupy the Western Approaches blockade stations. As a

The submarine was an important 1914-18 ASW measure: here four US 450-ton L-class submarines (launched 1915-16) lie alongside their tender at Berehaven, S Ireland. The 'A' prefix distinguished them from the very different British L-class. The short vertical objects on their foredecks are 3in/23 deck guns, which could retract part way into the casing, for streamlining while submerged. The US Navy of this period tended to emphasise submerged more than surface performance, so its boats were designed either without bridges or with very cramped ones. Note the rudimentary canvas screens of AL-10 (SS 50) and AL-4 (SS 43), which contrast with the 'chariot-type' bridge of AL-11 (SS 51).
US Navy

rule of thumb, a U-boat spent one-third of its time on station, one-third en route to or from its patrol station, and one-third in refit. En route time was much reduced for the boats based in Flanders, operating in the Channel. As for the U-cruisers, Michelsen complained that they took much too much time en route, that they were too large (and too expensive in foregone opportunities to build smaller boats), and that their refits were too lengthy. He noted, too, that the Germans had been unable to attack the transatlantic troop transports at least partly because they never had the U-boats to spare from the essential shipping war around Britain. Throughout the campaign, there were only about 90 boats available on average in the theatre; others operated in the main distant theatre, the Mediterranean.

SUBMARINE MINELAYING

The other major theme of shipping warfare was submarine minelaying. Neither Britain nor Germany appears to have designed submarine minelayers before 1914, although the Russian Imperial Navy ordered the specialised *Krab* in 1912, and Krupp patented a scheme for mine tracks atop a U-boat hull early in 1913. The first German minelayers were small UC-class submarines designed to operate from newly-seized bases in Flanders; by 1915 they were designing longer-range minelayers, and were planting small fields around the British Isles. They ultimately accounted for about a quarter of all shipping lost to U-boats during World War I. Their victims included many warships, notably the cruiser HMS *Hampshire*, carrying Lord Kitchener to Russia in 1916. Overall, U-boat minelayers were credited with sinking about 2.9 million tons of shipping, compared with about 11 million sunk by gun and torpedo.

The first British minelayer was *E-24*, completed in January 1916 but lost that March. There were no specialised designs; instead six each of the medium 'E' and 'L' classes were fitted with mine tubes protruding through their ballast tanks. Both they and the UCs carried their mines externally, without any access from the pressure hull. War experience suggested that this had two major disadvantages. First, mines had to be preset (eg with a particular tidal height) before loading. Second, they tended to deteriorate in the tubes, so that they could not be considered reliable (at least in the British case) if they remained there for more than three days. That limited them to short-range operations, and precluded tactical mining or waiting on station for enemy ships to come out of port. The Germans therefore built submarines (UE class) with dry storage for 34 mines (compared with wet stowage for 12 in a UC, or 20 in each of six 'E' class minelayers); they considered it an ocean, rather then a coastal, minelayer. There was no British equivalent, but in 1920 the Admiralty authorised studies of a specialised minelayer.

One conclusion was that full internal stowage cost precious limited space within the pressure hull. The British compromise was to carry mines externally, on tracks atop the hull but beneath the floodable casing. They were both dry and accessible when the boat ran on the surface, at no cost in pressure hull volume. This system was tested in 1927, when the submarine monitor *M-3* was converted with tracks atop her hull, to carry 100 mines externally. A similar arrangement was adopted for the *Porpoise* class, the only British submarine minelayers built as such from the keel up, in 1930. Except for France, which duplicated the external vertical tube system, other navies copied the German internal system.

From a strategic point of view, the mine tended to be an area denial weapon rather than a means of accounting for British tonnage or of sealing British ports. Historically, minefields have been most effective when they have been kept under surveillance and periodically renewed. Submarine-laid fields are difficult to renew because precise underwater navigation is relatively difficult, so that a boat risks destruction on the remaining mines of the original field. On the other hand, a submarine force can do considerable damage by mining areas just ahead of enemy operations. For example, the October 1939 *U-47* attack on Scapa Flow, which sank the battleship *Royal Oak*, was co-ordinated with submarine minelaying in several areas Admiral Doenitz thought might be alternative fleet anchorages, to which the Home Fleet would have to transfer after discovering that Scapa was unsafe. One of the mines laid at this time damaged the Fleet flagship, the battleship *Nelson*; another broke the back of the new light cruiser *Belfast*.

Relatively few specialist minelayers were built in the decade before World War II, largely because the London Naval Treaty of 1930 limited total submarine tonnage for each major navy. The United States, Britain, Germany, and Japan all developed mines to be laid through torpedo tubes, although the Germans had to build several specialist boats (Types VIID and XB) partly because their torpedo tube weapons were not ready in time. The Royal Navy actually designed several minelayers in 1938-39, and ordered three in January 1941. But British submarine-building capacity was limited, and patrol submarines seemed more valuable, and certainly more flexible. The three standard wartime classes ('S', 'T', and 'U') were therefore fitted to carry torpedo-mines.

ANTI-SUBMARINE WARFARE

Geography was a vital factor both in submarine and in anti-submarine warfare. It changed radically in 1914 when the German Army seized the Belgian (Flanders) coast. The U-boat base at Zeebrugge was only 65 miles from Dover, a saving of about 300 miles ($2\frac{1}{2}$ days at sea) compared with Wilhelmshaven. There was also a subtler saving. Given the very short range required for Channel operations, the Germans could radically reduce the size, hence the cost, of their submarines, and thus could greatly increase their numbers.

Similar geographical shifts shaped the 1939-45 Battle of the Atlantic, and may be decisive in any future ASW war. At first, the German Navy had to pass its submarines around Scotland to reach the Atlantic trade routes, given the position of the British Isles athwart the path from Germany to the open sea. The long transit time was one reason for the relative inefficiency of the U-boat force. That changed radically from June 1940, after the seizure first of Norway and then of the French coast. Now U-boats could proceed directly into the North Atlantic, saving several days (and exposure to a combination of weather and a British blockade).

As this is written, much of the NATO ASW strategy depends upon the geography of the 'choke points' between the major Soviet bases and the open sea. Modern technology makes it possible to erect reasonably effective barriers across these straits and gaps in wartime provided NATO retains control of their shores. NATO planners appear not to have taken one possible outcome of a land campaign entirely into account here. For example, some analysts envisage a rapid Soviet advance through Western Europe. It is entirely conceivable that nuclear weapons would *not* be used on either side, and that the United States and, perhaps, Britain, would find themselves in a strategic situation not entirely unlike that of 1940. Once again, the enemy might be in possession of an open coastline, and once again the war might prove much more protracted than expected.

Just as the World War I U-boat campaign was a prototype for World War II, the Allied counter campaign displayed, sometimes in embryo form, the full spectrum of later ideas. On one plane, British ASW displayed a very basic conflict in naval tactics, the desire to pursue offensive tactics despite the greater efficiency of apparently defensive ones. This deeply felt preference is often blamed for the failure to adopt a convoy strategy until 1917. Yet it may have been a fortunate coincidence that convoy tactics were adopted just as effective ASW weapons, such as depth charges, became available. Certainly the early history of World War II ASW suggests that ineffective convoy escorts could not prevent severe losses. Note, too, that the rival mining strategy was hampered by ineffective weapons until late 1917.

The basic strategies were to restrict submarine mobility, to route shipping away from known submarine positions, and to deny the submarines access to shipping, through a combination of blockade and convoy. There was also a secondary strategy intended to bring submarines into proximity with ASW forces. Both convoy and the earlier Q-ship tactic shared aspects of it as ways of overcoming the lack of any reliable submarine detection system.

Submarines were mobile only on the surface, where they were exposed to

THE ERA OF THE SUBMERSIBLE 1900-1945

World War I experience convinced the US Navy of the inferiority of its submarine designs, and made the acquisition of U-boats particularly valuable. *U-111* is shown under American colours, immediately after the war. The US Navy adopted German-type raked bows like hers about a decade later. The United States also built German-designed MAN diesels under license. Completed in 1917, *U-111* was sunk in 1920 bombing experiments.
US Navy

observation and attack. Early in World War I a submarine had so small a silhouette (and so high a vantage point, in its periscope) that it could generally hope to spot a surface ship before being seen. Aircraft and ASW submarines changed matters radically. Because of their vantage, observers aloft could cover enormous areas, so that, at least near the British coast, unobserved areas might become the exception rather then the rule. This idea was extended to observation balloons towed by surface ships. Submerged British submarines were themselves effectively invisible. A U-boat commander had to accept that they might be anywhere in his patrol area. He had, therefore, either to remain underwater (invisible) during daylight, or to zigzag at high speed like a surface ship. From 1915 onwards ASW was the primary British submarine mission, culminating in the design of the specialised 'R' class. The British were frustrated by the number of U-boat sightings not converted into attacks, but the threat of an invisible enemy appears to have had a strong psychological effect on the U-boat force itself. The only effective countermeasures were mining, which sank several British boats, and diving upon spotting a periscope. Submarine ASW was considered so important that a flotilla of US craft joined the British force after 1917. Altogether the British patrol submarines sank 17 U-boats, another two being torpedoed by submarines operating with Q-ships. Michelsen argued that '...in view of the relatively small number of submarines employed on this service one must admit that this offensive measure was relatively the more important...the submarine is also an offensive weapon for the stronger power, contrary to the formerly acknowledged doctrine'. This strategy was not continuously adopted during 1939-45 (although British submarines sank 35 Axis U-boats on an ad hoc basis), but it was revived after the war, in the US SSK programme. The current NATO submarine ASW concept is a modern version (see Chapter 4).

Surface mobility was essential to reach a favourable attack position on a relatively fast-moving target. Typical World War I tactics called for a boat to submerge just out of sight, then attack. Even then it might find the approach difficult, and before World War II

A 417/473-ton UC II class minelayer (64 built 1916-17), probably *UC 31*, surrendered to the Royal Navy and flying the White Ensign in 1918. The built-up portion of her 213ft hull, forward, contains her six vertical 39in mine tubes (18 UC 200 mines). They are flanked by two 20in external torpedo tubes (one stern, 7 torpedoes in all); a torpedo is visible stowed on deck at the aft end of the mine casing. The deck gun was an 88mm/30 calibre and the crew numbered 26.
CPL

Another captured UC II class minelayer, *UC-58*, is shown at Cherbourg in 1920. Note the separate helm forward of her navigating bridge, and the prominent 'jumping wires' intended to carry anti-submarine nets over her.
US Navy

33

SUBMARINE DESIGN AND DEVELOPMENT

The Royal Navy built several specialised minelayers during the 1930s. The 1810/2157-ton *Rorqual* displays the high casing that housed her 50 mines, and the stern door through which they were laid. Minelaying was hazardous because it brought the submarine close to enemy shores: she was the only one of the six ships in her 293ft class to survive the 1939–45 war although their mining did sink 36 Axis merchant ships and 6 Axis warships. *US Navy*

Captain Karl Doenitz developed night surface attack tactics to make up for the U-boat's lack of sustained underwater speed. Aircraft could so extend the detection range of a surface force that, at least in theory, they could preclude attack altogether. This was the rationale for the visual ASW patrols which figure in so many accounts of US task force operations during 1941–45, and also for early escort carrier tactics.

Aircraft were so impressive that at the outbreak of World War II US submarine attack doctrine was designed specifically to avoid exposure to them. Submarine commanders were trained to approach their targets while relatively deeply submerged, obtaining bearings by passive sonar, and a range by a single sonar 'ping'. In fleet exercises, submarines detected from the air were accounted sunk, but there were no realistic tests of the underwater sound attack. War experience proved the opposite; submarines often escaped air attacks, but sound systems were not nearly accurate enough.

The key World War II development was airborne radar. It extended air search to night and bad weather, and finally drove the U-boats from the surface. The air problem motivated the modern revolution in submarine operations described in the next chapter. On the other hand, assurance of timely air warning would increase the amount of time a submarine could spend on the surface, since it could be sure of diving in time to avoid attack. Hence early US and British interest in submarine air warning radars. Still later in the war, ASW aircraft were able to home on submarine radar emissions, and submarine air warning turned to passive ECM.

Evasive ship routing was a very important ASW measure. As early as the end of 1914 the British were able to ascertain U-boat patrol areas by radio intelligence. They could route particularly important ships and, later, convoys clear of known U-boat positions. This appears to have been a relatively successful measure until the Germans had enough U-boats to cover the entire Western Approaches. Patrick Beesly argues in his recent account of 1914–18 British naval intelligence that the *Lusitania* sinking was a relatively unusual event, in that by May 1915, special routing was common for such important ships. He concludes that the disaster can best be traced to unusually poor staffwork, which in itself shows how important signals intelligence was at the time.

Once convoys had been formed, they, too, could be routed away from known U-boat positions. This improved naval control of shipping was entirely separate from the defensive or offensive value of concentrating ASW ships around the U-boat targets.

Although hunting groups were sometimes dispatched to patrol areas revealed by radio interception, there was no effective means of pinpointing these U-boats for attack. That had to wait until World War II. However, the basic idea of tracking the entire U-boat force through German signals was important in both World Wars. In the second it was the basis for routing convoys clear of wolf packs.

The third type of ASW measure took two forms in 1914–18. The first and most obvious was to mine choke points through which U-boats had to pass; its most extreme expression was the US Northern Mine Barrage, across the Northern exit of the North Sea, between the Orkneys and Norway, a distance of 250 miles, covered by 100,000 mines. The Royal Navy attempted to close the Straits of Dover as early as 1914, using indicator nets, but did not succeed until December 1917 when 4000 mines were in place. Extensive fields were also laid off the German coast, in the path of exiting U-boats, and around Britain, in areas U-boats might be expected to frequent. In the end, mines accounted for more U-boats than any other ASW measure: a total of 44, plus another 12 for mine-nets and indicator nets. By way of comparison, depth charges sank 38; submarine torpedoes 19 (including two to Q-ship/submarine combinations); gunfire 16; ramming 14; Q-ships 12; aircraft 6; and high-explosive sweeps 5. But the expenditure of mines was gigantic, and mining could be both expensive and dangerous. At one time British submarine minelayer losses were averaging one in three. Further minefields were of limited value if they could not be kept under surveillance. Although the Germans could not sweep the big barrages, they could discover paths through them, and without constant patrol they could keep their losses to a minimum. Michelsen was particularly critical of the Allied performances in the Northern Barrage and in the fields and nets closing off the Mediterranean Strait of Otranto.

Convoy is usually described as the single decisive ASW measure of World War I; the opposition to it is often taken as the greatest example of official prejudice and stupidity. Yet convoy tactics were used from the beginning of the war to protect particularly valuable ships, such as troopships. There is also abundant evidence that the Admiralty and the US Navy were unwilling to exchange offensive ASW tactics for what they perceived as a defensive and rather desperate measure. Proponents of convoy spent much of their time postwar explaining that in fact it *was* an offensive technique. But Admiral Sir John Jellicoe, who as First Sea Lord was accused of having delayed the introduction of convoy, argued after World War I that it could not really have been instituted much before mid-1917 anyway.

First, until 1917 the British did not have effective ASW weapons. The depth charge was invented only in 1916, and few were available for some time. Arguably, a convoy *without* escorts was no more than a concentration of targets. It might escape detection by U-boats, but the potential for disaster was enormous. Second, until the United States entered the war there was no really satisfactory port for forming a convoy in the Western Hemisphere. There was no reason to imagine that merchant ships could navigate well enough to assemble at some offshore point, and the neutral United States would not have allowed British warships into her waters to fuel and provision before forming up convoys. Third, without the US Navy, there were not nearly enough escorts: the Royal Navy was very much at full stretch by this time. Finally, many, including those with considerable sea experience, doubted that merchant ships could steam in close proximity without collisions. In practice much of the voyage, outside U-boat waters, was used merely to train the merchant masters in station-keeping. Finally, even after the United States entered the war, Jellicoe always felt that he could not provide strong enough escorts, and he feared that the Germans would one day simply overwhelm them, as in fact they did with wolf pack tactics just over two decades later. The same might be said of American attacks on poorly-escorted Japanese convoys in 1943-45. Even the strongest ASW escort was incapable of protecting against a determined surface ship attack, such as the British Scandinavian convoys encountered twice during 1917. In both cases, by concentrating the targets, convoying would actually increase the effectiveness of the attack.

The convoy strategy operated on two planes. First, by concentrating shipping it swept the oceans almost clear of submarine targets. Shrewd commanders could still wait near likely areas of assembly and dispersal or near probable convoy destinations, but even then they would be unable to maintain a steady rate of attacks. Faced suddenly with a large convoy, a submarine could sink only a fraction of the ships. Second, by bringing the submarines into contact with ASW ships, convoying solved the primary problem of submarine detection. A U-boat commander contemplating attack on a convoy had also to contemplate a severe counter-attack; the convoy acted as a kind of U-boat trap, deterring attack. In this sense convoy tactics were an (unconscious) continuation of the clearly offensive Q-ship idea. By the end of World War I, more than nine out of every ten Allied merchant ships were being convoyed, and losses in the Atlantic had been reduced from a quarter to a tenth of total shipping per year, or down to 1.5 per cent per month. Nonetheless, Michelsen did claim that the convoy system in itself reduced Allied carrying capacity by one third.

Analysis of World War II convoy operations showed that very large convoys were far more effective than smaller ones, in that the number of ships lost in a convoy battle was virtually independent of the total number in the convoy, as there were always many more potential targets than submarine torpedoes. Before that battle the probability that U-boats would detect a large convoy was little greater than the chance of their detecting a smaller one. Finally, the number of escorts required was proportional to the perimeter of the convoy, whereas the number of ships convoyed was proportional to the *area* ie to the square of the perimeter. Thus, the larger each convoy, the better it could be protected. On this basis, P M S Blackett, a British physicist and operations analyst, predicted early in 1943 that convoy losses could be reduced by 98.5 per cent by increasing the average number of ships per convoy from 32 to 54.

That is, the sheer number of convoys, hence the number of times U-boats could attack, would be cut by 56 per cent. The number of escorts per convoy would be increased from 6 to 9, reducing losses per convoy by a quarter. Escorts would also be released for more intensive training, and that in itself would increase their average effectiveness by 61 per cent. The limited number of long-range ASW aircraft could better be distributed among the smaller number of convoys, and Blackett estimated that the assurance of an average of eight hours of air coverage per day would reduce losses in a convoy by 64 per cent. Finally, since there were more escorts per convoy, spacing within a convoy could be doubled, to halve the chance of loss to a long-range ('browning') torpedo shot. In fact Blackett's figures proved pessimistic; the enlarged convoys did even better than he had guessed.

Most of these considerations remain valid 40 years later. There are three important exceptions. First, convoys, even in the open ocean, are subject to air as well as submarine attack. Because of their extremely high speed, aircraft can attack again and again. If the convoy escorts cannot destroy them (or their stand-off missiles), the aircraft can destroy *all* of the ships in a convoy. If aircraft are most vulnerable when they are searching for targets, then it can be argued that the most effective counter to enemy air attack is some form of dispersal. That becomes even more attractive if it is feared that an enemy may use nuclear weapons, which might be capable of

Several navies experimented with large cruiser submarines after 1918. This is the USS *Narwhal* (ex-V-5), originally designated Submarine Cruiser One (launched 17 December 1927), on trials off Provincetown (Massachusetts), July 1930 two months after commissioning. She and her sister boat *Nautilus* (SS 168, ex-V-6), were the largest pre-nuclear American submarines (2987 tons surfaced and 371ft oa), and were armed with 'wet' versions of the standard cruiser gun, the 6in/53 being on raised platforms. The similar *Argonaut* was a specialist minelayer.
US Navy

SUBMARINE DESIGN AND DEVELOPMENT

destroying an entire convoy at a single blow. Finally, a classic dense convoy is ill-adapted to countering modern nuclear attack submarines, which may be able to use the sheer bulk of the merchantmen as a hiding place. It may, therefore, be necessary to disperse the merchant ships and to mix them with ASW escorts, so that noise within the convoy is reduced, and escorts are much closer to their potential targets. In such a convoy the number of escorts is proportional to the area of the convoy, and some of the value of very large convoys is lost.

The Q-ship was a pure decoy, designed to look like a merchant ship but armed to destroy a surfaced U-boat. As long as the U-boats obeyed prize rules, they had to board and search their targets, automatically bringing themselves within range of their hidden armament. Michelsen cites these 'submarine traps' as a major motivation for abandoning the prize rules, and their value did decline steeply as the U-boats adopted submerged attack. However the basic concept, that a submarine could be forced into danger by placing its target and the ASW forces together, carries over into convoy operations. The difference is that in the case of a convoy the targets were real, and the hope was to deter the submarine from attacking in the first place.

World War I ASW differed sharply from World War II practice in that it was almost entirely coastal, a reflection of U-boat performance and, above all, their lack of reconnaissance support; the open sea was far too empty to be worth searching for targets. Thus ocean convoys were typically escorted by cruisers on anti-raider duty; a surface ship did have a sufficient visual range to be useful in the open ocean, particularly if she could launch an aircraft or even a balloon. The U-boat danger zone was considered to extend 300 to 400 miles from the British coast, and in it the ships were escorted by ASW craft, usually destroyers or sloops.

As for their role ordained before 1914, submarines achieved relatively little against first-class warships during World War I. There were spectacular successes, but submarines were just too slow to catch fast ships, even when they were surfaced. The Royal Navy tried to develop submarines fast enough to accompany the battlefleet, but propulsion technology was not equal to the problem. The diesel-powered 'J' was not fast enough, and the fast steam-powered 'K' class suffered from crippling operational problems. With their small silhouettes they found close cooperation with fast surface ships hazardous at best. Current 'direct support' tactics encounter much the same problems of IFF and communication. It is just too easy for the surface force to conclude that any nearby submarine is unfriendly.

On the other hand, submarines could provide a surface fleet with invaluable services, particularly distant scouting, where any surface ship encountered could be presumed hostile. And a submarine scout would have a better chance of survival than a cruiser.

The radar picket submarine was a later equivalent of this idea; it would normally operate on the surface or awash, but it could submerge to avoid air attack. Like the 'K' class, such submarines sometimes subordinated underwater performance to high surface speed, for operation in conjunction with a fast task force. The largest of the early US nuclear submarines, the *Triton*, was designed before 1956 specifically to achieve a high surface speed. The most recent application of this idea was the use of British nuclear submarines during the recent war in the Falklands, operating in waters at least nominally controlled by the Argentinians. Although they had not been designed as pickets, they were able to warn the Task Force of outgoing Argentine air strikes. Presumably they spent most of their time nearly awash, with their radar antennae projecting above the surface, ready to submerge at the approach of enemy forces.

At the end of World War I, then, most naval experts considered the submarine a failure in the anti-shipping role. It was not that individual submarines were easy to locate and sink, but rather that successful shipping warfare required each submarine to attack defended convoys so frequently that the odds would soon become overwhelming. These odds were further tipped by the interwar development of sonar (Asdic in British parlance at the time), which, unlike the 1914–18 hydrophones, was finally able to

Like Britain and the United States, the Netherlands employed submarines to protect distant colonial possessions from the large Japanese fleet. The small 670-ton submarine *K XIII* (one of the 3 *KXI* class launched in 1924), in drydock at the Mare Island US Navy yard shows her two after 17.7in torpedo tubes. She was unusual in having a two-calibre battery, with two 21in and two 17.7in tubes in her bow (12 torpedoes in all). Note the placement of the stern planes directly behind her propeller: planes were not placed forward of the screws until the development of the modern *Albacore* type hull.
US Navy

THE ERA OF THE SUBMERSIBLE 1900-1945

France built up a large submarine force between the wars. This is the *Minerve* class 662-ton coastal submarine *Junon* (launched 15 September 1935). The outline visible on the side of her 223ft casing aft covered a trainable triple 15.7in torpedo tube, a typical feature of French submarine design. The ONI caption reads 'HMS' because *Junon* operated with Free French forces based in Britain; hence the British-style pennant number.
US Navy

locate a submarine precisely in range as well as in bearing. The proliferation of maritime patrol aircraft also promised to eject submarines from the coastal areas they had infested during World War I. In the open ocean, they were unlikely to be able to locate convoys, let alone attack them. But there remained the threat of surface attack on convoys screened primarily against submarines.

BETWEEN THE WARS: BRITAIN

Submarines were one possible solution. Late in 1922 the Royal Navy sent the battlecruiser *Hood* against a mock convoy screened by 3 light cruisers and 5 submarines (including submarine monitors armed with 12in guns). The cruisers and the convoy had to flee, but the submarines merely dived and interposed themselves between the raider and her target. *Hood* was judged hit by four torpedoes as well as by a dummy 12in shell (at a range of about 1000 yards) and was declared disabled. Her captain was apparently particularly impressed by the submarine monitors. Later the British experimented with an entire squadron of 5 battleships against a 7-submarine screen. The submarines were again judged successful. Similar tactics were tried on the 1941–45 Murmansk run, where convoys faced a combination of U-boats and capital ships. In each case, the submarines had to remain surfaced long enough to be seen, hence to present their threat, and to move into a blocking position. They were difficult enough gun targets for such tactics to be reasonable, although their practical effect is not clear.

For the US, British, and Dutch navies, war against Japan was the central scenario through most of the interwar period. Submarines were the only warships that could be expected to operate in Japanese home waters. Given the need to concentrate battlefleets, they were also the most effective means of defending Far East colonies. Hence, for example, the US Asiatic Fleet's large submarine force stationed in the Philippines in December 1941. The analogous British force had already long been withdrawn to fight in European waters.

For the Royal Navy, the end of World War I drastically changed the meaning of 'overseas'. From about 1919 onwards Japan became the most probable future naval opponent. Existing overseas submarines could barely reach Japanese waters from the nearest British base, Hong Kong. For example, in 1924 the Naval Staff asked commanders afloat to suggest qualities for new submarines. The choice was between a relatively expensive long-range type (see below), and the existing, well-liked 'L' (overseas under pre-1919 definitions) class (essentially an updated 'E'), which had a radius of action of about 1700 miles. Commanders afloat argued that about 1500 miles would suffice since 'reconnaissance reports which cannot be acted upon at once are of little value' and 'reconnaissance at so great a distance as Japan from Singapore [is] impracticable'. In fact it was 1500 miles from Hong Kong to the Inland Sea. An 'L' could operate off the entrance to the Inland Sea for a week, but it would have only a very thin margin of fuel (15 per cent) for shadowing and attacking ships. As in many other warship categories, this was an indication of how much more expensive it would be to exert British sea power in the Far East.

A new kind of submarine was needed. In 1922 the C-in-C Atlantic Fleet suggested that a new Overseas Patrol Submarine be developed specifically for the Far East; at this time there were enough shorter-range craft to meet any (at that time unlikely) European requirements. In her original form *Oberon* had an endurance of 10,000 miles and was adapted for operation in the tropics. She displaced 1480 tons, compared to 890 for an early 'L' and only 670 for an 'E', and was chosen as the standard for new construction.

Meanwhile the Admiralty debated requirements for a fleet submarine, in effect a successor to the wartime 'K' class. The primary issue was speed; the Overseas Patrol Submarine could make only about 15 knots, but 23 to 24 knots were desirable for a submarine intended to operate with the fleet; 21 knots was a bare minimum. Flag Officer (Submarines) called for a general increase in submarine speed, from 18 to 19 knots; commanders afloat agreed. At this time, too, the British government hoped to achieve a general limitation on submarine size. The abortive 1927 Geneva Conference had chosen 1800 tons; 2000 would be approved at London in 1930. Any new submarine had to fit within these limits, and that in turn made it impossible to achieve as much as 23 knots. The outcome was a fast overseas patrol submarine, the *Thames* class, which was expected to replace the earlier overseas type. Twenty were planned, but submarine policy changed in 1933 and only three were completed. Instead, the Royal Navy turned back towards the earlier overseas patrol type; the new 'T' class displaced about 1300 tons on the surface, and had a surface speed of about 15 knots. Endurance was reduced to 4500 miles at 11 knots, presumably because it was expected that any submarine in the Far East would be able to operate from a local base such as Singapore.

After 1918 the British Fleet also included single-hull coastal submarines of the 'H' class, displacing only about 420 tons surfaced, but with roughly the same endurance as the larger 'L'. They were well-liked, and were employed largely for submarine and anti-submarine training. The latter function was extremely important for a navy, like the Royal Navy, which had to maintain sea control in the face of enemy submarine fleets. The 'H' boats aged through the 1920s, and about 1928 work began on a replacement. The new class would be based on a patrol area 500 miles from base, partly because that suited several areas of interest, and partly because it was a practical range limit for the radio outfit in a small submarine. Patrol endurance was initially set at ten days. This alone drove size above that of the 'H',

37

SUBMARINE DESIGN AND DEVELOPMENT

since war experience showed that the latter were too uncomfortable to patrol for more than 5 or 6 days. Later these figures were modified; the new short-range submarine would have to be able to patrol at a distance of 1200 miles in order to fulfill part of the British war plan of the time. The resulting *Swordfish* of 1931 displaced 640 tons (standard), and endurance grew to 5750 miles at 8 knots. Twelve were built prewar, and they were successful enough that another 50 were ordered in wartime.

The 'S' was still too large to replace the 'H' altogether. In 1936, then, a new coastal or local defence/training boat, which became the wartime 'U', was ordered. At 600 tons it was much slower than the other classes (11 knots, compared to about 15 for the others), and endurance was only 3600 miles at 10 knots. In fact the 'U' was considered ideal for Mediterranean operations, and 74 in all were built. That made the earlier small submarine, the 'S', intermediate in size between the Far East types and the coastal boat. This spread in size reflected, not any indecision, but rather Britain's central strategic dilemma: the Fleet had to deal with two very different theatres, Europe and the Far East, yet she could not really afford two disparate navies.

There were two opposing forces at work. The variety of requirements made for a range of different classes. At the same time, economics and the treaties limited the total size of the submarine fleet, and thus made some degree of standardisation attractive, so that most submarines could perform the entire range of missions. Wartime production problems made standardisation even more

HMS *Shakespeare* (seen entering Algiers in early 1943) was typical of the standard British wartime 842/990-ton medium submarine, her class of 50 boats (built 1940–45) among the most numerous ever built for the Royal Navy. Note the external stern 21in torpedo tube, to fit which the free-flooding casing was extended right aft. There were also six internal bow tubes, and the 20mm AA gun and Type 291 air search radar on her superstructure. Unlike the larger T-boats, these submarines were not fitted with extra external bow torpedo tubes.
US Navy

The British 'H' class of 364/434-ton coastal submarines (44 boats built 1915-20) survived World War I and between the wars were employed largely for ASW training; the U/V class of World War II eventually replaced them. Ten were ordered from Vickers (Montreal, Canada) and 10 from Fore River (Electric Boat) in the USA; the US Neutrality Act prevented their release until 1917. *H-272* was one of a longer (171ft instead of 150ft) subsequent repeat series, 6 of the earlier boats being given to Chile in part payment for warships seized by Britain in 1914 and 8 others going to Italy.
CPL

THE ERA OF THE SUBMERSIBLE 1900-1945

HMS *United* (seen in Home Waters 1944) was typical of a large group of British 630/732-ton coastal submarines (68 boats built), designed initially as ASW targets. The object abaft her bridge fairwater is a D/F loop, and a Type 291 air search radar antenna is visible atop her mast. This group (crew 31-33) of 191-196ft boats served primarily in the Mediterranean.
US Navy

attractive, and in 1941 work began on a single type to replace both the 'S' and the 'T'. Within a few months Singapore had fallen, and minimum range requirements for Far Eastern operations had risen accordingly. Ultimately this new 'A' class had an endurance of 15,200 miles at 10 knots with fuel in one main ballast tank; surface speed was 18.5 knots, roughly what had been requested 15 years earlier. War experience showed in an increase in diving depth to 500ft from the former standard 300ft.

BETWEEN THE WARS: UNITED STATES AND JAPAN

American submarine development was much simpler, because the US strategic situation was simpler; the primary war plan, Orange, envisaged a fleet movement across the Pacific, supported by submarines operating near Japan. For most of the Orange war plan's life, there was little expectation that the Philippines could hold out long enough for relief; the submarines had to be able to operate over very great ranges. High surface speed was attractive partly because such craft had to cover immense distances merely to reach their patrol areas. And unless they were fast, they would use up all their stores en route to or from those areas. At 10 knots, for example, it would take a submarine 33 days to cover the 8000 miles from the US West Coast to the Far East. A typical patrol might last 60-75 days.

Thus the US prewar submarine developers concentrated on propulsion; on making engines more reliable, more compact, and more economical. The first post-1918 types were large 'cruisers', which failed largely because their diesels were unreliable. Later, the Navy went so far as to help sponsor the diesel conversion of the US railroad industry, to assure it of a source of reliable high-speed engines. The tactical and strategic emphasis was consistent throughout, resulting by 1941 in the *Gato*, the prototype of the mass-produced 'fleet boat'. Displacing about 1525 tons, she could exceed 20 knots on the surface; endurance was 11,000 miles at 10 knots, for a 75 day patrol. There was some very limited interest in a smaller alternative, which might be useful for the defence of the Panama Canal Zone or the Philippines, but only two, *Marlin* and *Mackerel*, were built. As in Britain, it was far more efficient to choose a single standard type.

Japan had the inverse strategic problem. She expected to fight the United States in or near her home waters. Particularly after 1921, the US Fleet was assured by treaty of a numerical superiority, at least at the beginning of the war. Japan had the advantage of position: a US fleet steaming across the Pacific would have to survive lengthy exposure to submarine attack. Hence, from 1918 onwards, an intense Japanese interest in very long-range cruiser submarines, modelled on the wartime German U-cruisers.

Japanese reading of wartime experience focused on two other types: the fast fleet submarine, roughly analogous to the British 'K' class (but always diesel-powered), and the very long range minelayer (initially copied from the German UE). Existing Japanese shorter-range submarines, many of which had been based on contemporary British practice, were effectively relegated to coast defence. Relatively few short or medium-range submarines were built between the wars, presumably because it was imagined that they could be manufactured rapidly in an emergency. Indeed, the two ordered under

Japanese experience in high-speed submarine design led ultimately to the construction of the *I-201* class; *I-202* is shown running her 1944 Inland Sea trials. This 1070-ton design was quite different from the contemporary German Type XXI. The horn-like object atop the periscope shears is a search radar. These boats had high-speed, lightweight MAN diesels, and had much higher underwater (5000shp) than surface (2750bhp) power (19 to 15.8kts). Endurance was just under an hour at full submerged power. Unlike Type XXI, they were not deep divers.
US Navy

SUBMARINE DESIGN AND DEVELOPMENT

Japan followed a very distinctive course of submarine development, typified by the three *I-401* class submarine aircraft carriers shown after their surrender in 1945. The catapult track of the nearest submarine is obscured by sailors unloading stores. Note the large hangars passing through the superstructures of all three, and the snorkels abaft their bridges. At 3530 tons and 400ft oa they were the largest submarines built until the advent of ballistic missile craft.
US Navy

the 1931 programme were explicitly mobilisation prototypes. The minelayers were included in several programme, but were never built in numbers.

Two new operational requirements were recognised in the late prewar period: the defence of the island chains through which an attacking US Pacific Fleet would have to come, and support of long-range seaplane bomber operations through refuelling at remote atolls. The Japanese carried out only one such operation during World War II, a March 1942 raid on Hawaii, but they planned others, including an attack timed to coincide with the Battle of Midway. It was abandoned when the refuelling site, the French Frigate Shoals, was occupied by US warships. The island chain mission was partly responsible for Japanese interest in very fast submarines. There were also midget submarines which some of the larger craft were designed to launch.

The two primary types, the cruiser ('J', later Type 'A') and the fast fleet submarine ('KD', later Type B), were designed for relatively high speeds and for great ranges. Design work on the latter began in 1918, even though as yet Japan possessed no suitable diesel engine. They were designed to make about 20–22 knots, with an endurance of 10,000 to 12,000 miles at 10 knots. The cruisers, essentially copies of the German *U-142*, were designed for about twice the endurance (24,000 miles) at a somewhat lower speed, 17.5 knots. Since they would have to operate independently, they were armed with cruiser guns (two 5.5in, rather than one 4.7in in the fleet type), as in such foreign submarine cruisers as the British *X-1*, the US *Nautilus*, and later the French *Surcouf*.

From the fifth unit (1933) onwards they were provided with a scouting aircraft and a catapult. Several navies experimented with submarine-borne aircraft, but only the Japanese made them a standard design feature. They were an attempt to expand the inherently limited area of vision of the submarine, both for strategic scouting and for commerce raiding. During World War II, the Germans tried a particularly ingenious variation on this theme, a helicopter-like kite, which was far more compact than a powered aircraft. Both aircraft and kite required the submarine to remain on the surface, vulnerable both to discovery and to attack. That was no problem as long as the submarine was far from enemy observers, particularly aircraft, in the open ocean. The U-boats flew their observation kites in distant, sparsely travelled waters such as the South Atlantic and the Indian Ocean. It became unacceptable only with the proliferation of ASW aircraft. Given their experience with scout aircraft, the Japanese naturally developed submarine-borne attack aircraft for special missions. A scout float plane was actually used to bomb the US West Coast during 1942, and later in the war several cruiser submarines were completed to carry two bombers each. A much larger *I-400* type (over 5000 tons) was designed (and built) to carry three, and attacks on the Panama Canal were planned.

Fleet submarines needed no aircraft because they were organised in flotillas led by aircraft-bearing light cruisers. The cruisers could also serve as information relays, since submarine radio was relatively ineffective. Cruiser submarines, by way of contrast, had to be able to operate independently, in the open ocean, with their own sources of intelligence. However, two of them (*I-7* and *I-8*) were designed as submarine flagships, with special command and control spaces. Their precise role is not clear; the prewar Japanese fleet was divided into squadrons of 10 submarines, each consisting of a flagship and three divisions of three boats each.

The early distinctions survived through much of the interwar period. Thus in 1928 the Japanese Navy classified its proposed submarines as Type A, for 'oceanic operations', with an endurance of more than three months; Type B, for 'fleet operations', with a two-month endurance; Type C, for 'restricted area operations', with an endurance of about $1\frac{1}{2}$ months; and Type D, a proposed oceanic minelayer. As time passed, apart from the scout plane, the two series came to have very similar maximum speeds and rated endurances. Thus the 1931 fleet submarine (which became the KD6a class of 6 boats) was designed for 23 knots and an endurance of 14,000 miles at 10 knots (on 1400 tons), while the corresponding cruiser (*I-6*) made 21.3 knots on trials (1900 tons, 20,000 miles at 10 knots).

40

THE ERA OF THE SUBMERSIBLE 1900-1945

In 1936 both long-range types effectively merged. Three variations were envisaged: 'A', the 2200-ton cruiser, with a float plane and a 5.5in gun; 'B', an intermediate type (1950 tons), similarly armed, but with somewhat reduced range (14,000 versus 16,000 miles at 16 knots); and 'C', a fleet submarine (1500 tons) with cruiser endurance (14,000 miles at 16 knots, compared to 8000nm for the last of the KDs), armed with a gun but without any aircraft although it could carry a midget submarine in a cradle forward of the bridge. All three types were expected to make 23 knots on the surface.

Great endurance and high surface speed necessarily translated into large submarines of limited manoeuvrability, and relatively slow to dive. Nonetheless, Japan was able, despite (presumably) inferior diesel engine and battery technology, to achieve higher performance (speed and range) within a given displacement (or hull envelope) than was the United States; Japanese fleet submarines were superior to the US 'fleet boats' in this respect. Postwar accounts emphasised how tightly packed such craft were, which is only another example of the extent to which submarines are volume-critical. Thus performance had its cost, in this case in free internal volume. One might add that Westerners found Japanese warships generally extremely cramped, although it appears that the Japanese themselves were able to tolerate these conditions quite well. Several of the large submarines were re-engined in 1942 with much less powerful diesels of Japanese (as opposed to German) design, originally designed for medium (*Ro-35* class) submarines. The postwar American report on the Japanese submarine force suggested that this standardisation increased diesel production; in the large submarines, the substitution of smaller engines considerably increased fuel capacity and, therefore, endurance.

It certainly cannot be claimed that excessive size destroyed the Japanese submarine fleet; the almost equally large US craft were extremely successful. Japanese concepts of naval warfare were much more important. As soon as America was deemed the primary enemy, the destruction of an advancing US Pacific Fleet became the absolute priority. Shipping warfare was unimportant compared with sinking enough American warships to help the outnumbered Japanese battle line. Thus prewar planning apparently envisaged a cruiser submarine fleet (the Sixth) harrying the US fleet as far east as Hawaii; most of the submarines would be assigned to the principal battlefleet, which is why they needed their speed.

JAPANESE MIDGET SUBMARINES

The Japanese were well aware that submarines attempting to attack fast warships suffer from their own limited speed, particularly underwater. In the mid-1930s they hit upon a solution: the fast, short-range midget submarine, carrying only one or two torpedoes. Although the initial proposal (1932) was for a piloted suicide torpedo, by the spring of 1933 work began on a craft which the crew might be able to escape. The small, short-range submarine was potentially effective because, at least in theory, it could be much faster than a conventional craft. That is, although a small submarine experiences more resistance per ton than does a larger streamlined one, the midget could devote a much greater percentage of its volume to batteries and motors, since it required neither reload torpedoes nor surface endurance. And since the midget would not have to operate on the surface, it could be streamlined to a degree inconceivable in a larger craft.

The first calculations showed a speed of 30 knots and an operational range of about 30,000 yards, but in fact the first midgets, codenamed Target A, were designed for only 25 knots (1 hour rate). A modified Target B, built at Kure in 1938, was capable of 24 knots. Both types were intended to operate at 100m (328ft), with a crush depth of 200m. Some reports suggest maximum speeds as high as 27.5 knots. Experiments were completed in December 1934, and four special midget-submarine carrier ships (*Chitose*, *Chiyoda*, *Mizuho*, and *Nisshin*) were built in 1936-39, each capable of carrying 12 midgets, and of launching all of them over a stern ramp in about 20 minutes. The first two ships were converted in 1940-41; the last two were never fitted. Midget submarine exercises were actually carried out from *Chiyoda* in late 1941.

At about that time their commander, a Captain Furuiwa, suggested that, carried by submarines, they would be an ideal means of attacking ships inside harbours, such as Pearl Harbor. As a result, five 'C' class submarines (*I-16*, *I-18*, *I-20*, *I-22*, and *I-24*) were modified to carry midgets between October and mid-November 1941. The midgets themselves were modified for greater endurance, with a quarter of their batteries replaced by compressed air tanks, and fitted to penetrate nets; so cutting speed from 19 to 14 knots. In this form, the midgets made their only operational attacks in the Pacific, beginning with Pearl Harbor and including Sydney, Australia. The basic midget design was also modified for local defence, a diesel engine being added and the crew increased to two or three. Craft of this type were, for example, carried to the Aleutians in June 1942. From 1944 onwards there was a resurgence or interest in both midgets and manned torpedoes, this time to defend Japan herself. These craft roughly parallel the late-war German midgets, and are outside the scope of the present work. The earlier Japanese midgets are worth mentioning because they led directly to full-scale attempts to build a very fast submarine.

In practice, they were relatively unsuccessful. A similar scheme was apparently proposed by several British submarine officers in the 1930s but received no official backing. There is no evidence that either side was ever aware of what the other was developing, and no account of the British proposal was published until 1941. But it supports the view that, given existing technology, *only* a very

Although the British, German, and Italian navies all developed midget submarines during World War II, none developed anything resembling the Japanese midgets, which were intended originally as piloted high-speed torpedoes for use in fleet engagements. Their development stimulated Japanese interest in high underwater speeds, and led directly to the construction of a full-size high-speed submarine, *No 71*, in 1937. The Japanese Navy was compelled to employ most of its midgets for coast defence; this craft was sunk in 1945 at Okinawa. Her torpedo-like lines were duplicated in the wartime fast submarines of the *I-201* and *Ha-201* classes.
US Navy

SUBMARINE DESIGN AND DEVELOPMENT

short-range midget could achieve the sort of underwater speed needed in a battle-line engagement.

The special Japanese requirement for local defence of outlying island bases appears to have been formulated in the late 1930s. The earliest concept was a very fast short-range submarine; the prototype was built under the 1937 Fleet Programme, as *No 71*, based on midget submarine practice. It was designed beginning early in 1936, and begun in December 1937. Built under conditions of extreme secrecy, *No 71* was, in her day, the fastest submarine in the world. Displacing only 280 metric tons (including free-flooding spaces), she was designed to achieve 25 knots underwater, although on trials she made only 21.34. Designed surface speed was 18 knots, but the planned Daimler diesel was not available, and in practice surface speed was only 13.2 knots. As an indication of battery capacity, submerged endurance at 7 knots was 231 miles, or about 33 hours; 25 knots was to have been sustained for just under an hour. Armament was three 17.7in torpedo tubes, without reloads; a short-range submarine would be able to reload at her base. Although *No 71* was conceived as the operational prototype, her design was abandoned for a variety of technical and operational reasons, and she was broken up in the summer of 1941. Lessons learned in her design were later applied to two classes of fast submarine, *I-201* and *Ha-201*.

Meanwhile, a much more conventional design, the *Ro-100* class, was adopted for mass production for short-range work around island bases. The Japanese Navy considered them effective both in their designed mission and in the open ocean; for example, they attacked to the east of Saipan during the American landing there.

As for the seaplane mission, a large *I-351* class submarine was designed before the war to carry gasoline, bombs, ammunition, and provisions. Such submarines had a relatively low priority, and the first was not laid down until 1943. These submersible seaplane tenders carried an impressive gasoline load, 365 tons, in tanks outside the pressure hull, separated from it by ballast tanks, with a gasoline pump in the after portion of the conning tower. Their gasoline tankage actually exceeded that in contemporary US light fleet carriers. As Japan seized a vast island empire in 1941–42, interest shifted to special assault transport submarines. A new *I-361* class was hurriedly designed in the summer of 1942, to carry 120 armed officers and enlisted men. Large numbers were to have been built, so the design incorporated existing, relatively low-powered machinery. By the time the first had been laid down, in 1943, their role had changed to supplying isolated garrisons, and the design was changed to cargo carrying. In 1944 it was changed again to include gasoline tanks, but the programme was cancelled after ten submarines, so that production could shift to smaller transports and to coast defence craft.

JAPANESE SUBMARINES IN WORLD WAR II

Although the prewar planning scenario never unfolded, Japanese naval policy in wartime was to concentrate submarines against naval, rather than shipping targets. As in World War I, even extremely fast submarines could not perform well, particularly in the face of sonar and aircraft. In 1942 the order of priority was carriers first, battleships second, with other warships following. Merchant ships were considered legitimate targets only in the absence of warships. Even the number of torpedoes to be used was fixed: all available ones against carriers and battleships; three against cruisers; and only one per merchant ship or destroyer. In the latter case a hit was considered extremely unlikely beyond about 800 yards. Only once was a large-scale anti-shipping campaign even contemplated. In June 1942 the Imperial Navy decided to wipe out the Midway defeat by attacking Allied shipping in the Indian Ocean and Australasian areas. The operation had to be cancelled when Allied forces began their attack in the Solomons. Once Japan had lost sea control, she was compelled to use much of her submarine force for subsidiary duties such as covert resupply of island garrisons.

One might speculate further that the failure of Japanese defensive ASW reflected the Imperial Navy's neglect of anti-shipping submarine warfare. Others have speculated that both failures stemmed from the character of *Bushido*, the Japanese military tradition; it was, on the one hand, relatively dishonourable to attack non-combatants (ie merchant shipping) and, on the other, much better to attack than (as in ASW) to defend.

Throughout the war, the Japanese Navy learned from the Germans, although clearly it did not copy German designs. It appears that the German shift towards high (underwater) speed submarines, such as the Type XXI, inspired Japanese interest in similar performance (as in the *I-201*), although the Japanese approach to the problem was quite original. Unlike the German craft with their increased number of batteries, the Japanese chose to use new high-capacity, short-life batteries, to obtain more electrical energy storage in a limited volume. Similar batteries were used in late-war types of midget submarine. For instance, the *I-201* initially had a battery designed for only 100 charging cycles, and good for only about 80; later units of the class, not completed by the end of the war, had a 300-cycle battery. As in analogous German submarines (see Chapter 4), they had a snorkel to permit battery charging submerged. It sufficed to run one out of the two main diesel engines. This class was designed to achieve 19 knots underwater, but on trials made 16.3–17 knots; had it appeared in numbers in the Pacific, it might have had an impact comparable to the German Type XXI's had it become operational in the Atlantic. They did differ considerably from U-boats, being designed for much shallower operation, with a design depth of only 110m, about 360ft. Only the first three boats of the *I-201* class had been completed by the end of the war, together with nine of the smaller (but analogous) *Ha-201* class.

As in the case of U-boats, dynamic stability was a major issue. However, perhaps accidentally, the Japanese found that their hull form was stable even when without fixed fins or planes. They tried to eliminate bow planes altogether, but found that their submariners demanded them for low-speed control and to avoid broaching while firing torpedoes.

Design work on *I-201* began early in 1943, reportedly as a reaction to *German* experience of high submarine losses. Answering postwar US interrogators, the Japanese submarine designers equated high submerged speed with relative immunity from airborne radar detection, although they had been interested in very high underwater speeds for some time. Construction began in March 1944, with the goal (unrealised) of completing one boat per month. Design of the smaller *Ha-201*, particularly well adapted to mass production, began in mid-1944.

Japan did copy the German snorkel (which they used only for auxiliary engines aboard conventional submarines), from a U-boat which called at Singapore in mid-1944. Snorkelling speed was limited to 4 to 5 knots; virtually all Japanese submarines had been fitted by the end of the war. There was also a 'creep', or silent low-speed, motor as in the later U-boats.

WORLD WAR II U-BOATS

The U-boat fleet contrasts sharply with these examples. From the beginning, there was a sharp conflict between advocates of a conventional battlefleet and those pressing for a World War I style anti-shipping campaign. The other factor was the treaty limit on total submarine tonnage. The anti-shipping faction won and plans for fleet submarines were rejected. Instead, the minimum acceptable attack submarine, which became the Type VII, was designed and placed in production. In theory Type VII was suited only to the North Sea and to Britain's Western Approaches although in fact it operated across the Atlantic. In all 628 of these single-hull boats were built, far more than any other submarine class ever built.

The design was extremely austere, to the point where Allied submariners found it difficult to imagine how the Germans had been able to continue to operate effectively in terrible Atlantic conditions. The US fleet type seemed particularly luxurious by comparison. Certainly Admiral Doenitz was well aware of the limitations of a type able to carry only 14 torpedoes in its most widely-produced version (Type VIIC). That was one reason for his short-range attack tactics (see below). One might argue that the Type VII was at or even below the lower limit of submarine size for effective ocean operation, and that the austerity exercised in its design made

THE ERA OF THE SUBMERSIBLE 1900-1945

The giant French 3205-ton *Surcouf* (launched 18 October 1929) was the wonder submarine of the interwar period, a specially designed 360ft cruiser and commerce raider. She is shown after a September 1941 refit at the Portsmouth (US) Navy Yard. Note the section of deck under the twin 8in gun mount (the guns were heavy cruiser weapons with an effective range of 13,000yds), which turned with it.
US Navy

later modification, for example for deeper diving, virtually impossible.

The other major design of the prewar period was the 'ocean-going' double-hulled Type IX (210 built) intended to fight in distant theatres, and so to dissipate Allied ASW resources. However, much of the war in the Atlantic had to be entrusted to the relatively short-range Type VII. One solution was resupply at sea, for which ten Type XIV 'Milch Cows' were built. They introduced a new vulnerability; in order to refuel or rearm a U-boat at sea, a rendezvous had to be set up by radio. Once the Allies could break the relevant codes, by 1943, such arrangements guaranteed attack, both on the supply boat and on the U-boats nearby. All ten boats were sunk during the war, most of them during the crisis of 1943.

FRANCE AND ITALY

The other major submersible fleets were those of France, Italy, and the Soviet Union; the latter is discussed in Chapter 6. French naval policy always differed substantially from that of sea-control powers such as Britain, Japan, and the United States. First, from the later nineteenth century onwards, there was always a strong school of thought (originally the *jeune école* or 'young school' of naval theorists) maintaining that the torpedo made conventional capital ships obsolete, and that command of the seas was an effective impossibility. Initially such thinking led to large numbers of torpedo boats; submarines were their natural successors. The fortunes of the *jeune école* varied with French financial ability to maintain the alternative naval strategy, that of a substantial battlefleet. Unlike the three sea-control powers, France had to pay first for a very large peacetime army.

Thus the French reaction to the financial disaster of World War I was to abandon capital ship construction (even before the Washington Treaty) and to emphasise light surface and subsurface craft. At Washington, French delegates strongly opposed any attempt to limit submarine forces, describing them as purely defensive. Through the interwar era, France built large numbers of 600 to 800-ton submarines well-suited to operations in the North Sea and in the Mediterranean, ie against her most probable enemies. Like Britain, she had overseas imperial interests, which presumably explain her construction of a considerable number of 1500-ton submarines, all capable of about 17 knots on the surface, with endurances of about 10,000 miles. However, the correllate of the *jeune école* sea-denial strategy was commerce raiding. France therefore built a large submarine cruiser, the *Surcouf*, armed with two 8in guns. She had a hangar for a scout plane.

In effect, *Surcouf* was the physical expression of the classic prize rules, applied to a submarine. Her guns gaver her an ability to stop merchant ships, and they were powerful enough to fight off any light warships present. Her scout plane suited her for operations in the open ocean, far from 'focal points' and hostile aircraft. She could even take prisoners; the rules demanded that merchant seamen be brought to 'a place of safety', emphatically not a lifeboat. That these consequences were somewhat absurd in operational terms was evident even in World War I, and *Surcouf* was only another demonstration. She was not unique; in 1920, long before the French submarine was designed, the British developed the long range *X-1*, armed well enough to take on destroyers, with two twin 5.2in gun mounts. She proved a failure, partly because the diesel engine technology of the time was not up to providing sufficient power, and partly because she dived extremely slowly, reportedly requiring 3 to 4 minutes to submerge.

Italian interwar naval strategy appears to have been designed largely to deal with France, the historic rival. Her submarine force included ocean-going craft suitable for operations outside the Mediterranean (ie against French shipping in the Atlantic) as well as medium and coastal craft for the Mediterranean. Italy also built several specialised minelayers. Perhaps the most remarkable of her craft was the four-boat *Ammiraglio Cagni* class of 1939, conceivably the only design ever to address the critical issue of weapon limitation in commerce-raiding. That is, time spent sailing to and from bases or tenders is time lost; in addition, each transit exposes the submarine to attack. The larger the weapon load, the fewer transits per attack. A small-diameter (17.7in) torpedo was chosen deliberately so that a large number of tubes (14) and reloads (36 torpedoes in all) could be carried. The small torpedo was unsuited to attacks on warships, but sufficed to destroy merchantmen.

WORLD WAR II 'WOLFPACK' TACTICS

During the interwar period, the efficacy and practicality of submarine warfare against commerce was controversial even in Germany. Too much had been promised, and it was too obvious that the U-boat had not been the miraculous weapon the German public had been led to expect. Many in the interwar Navy believed that the unrestricted campaign's abject failure proved that U-boats could never be other than a secondary arm in the future. Even prospective U-boat officers were demoralised by the threat of the new British secret weapon, Asdic. Karl Doenitz was an exception. He believed that a new anti-shipping campaign could be decisive, and he was skeptical of Asdic's attributed performance. On both points he had to overcome considerable opposition with the German naval staff. Within the U-boat arm, he had to overcome a fear of Asdic analogous to the fear of ASW ships inculcated in other navies' submariners. His group (wolfpack) tactics were designed specifically to overcome convoy, the previous war's single most effective pro-shipping tactic and contrasted dramatically with the modified

43

SUBMARINE DESIGN AND DEVELOPMENT

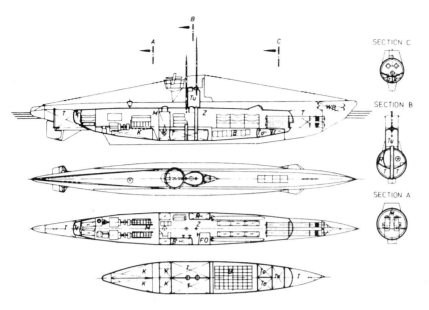

Type IIB U-boat deck plans, elevation and sections.
courtesy of IKL and Prof Gabler

LEGEND

T	BALLAST TANK
K	FUEL TANK
TB	BALLAST/FUEL TANK
R	COMPENSATING TANK
RB	COMPENSATING FUEL OIL TANK
U	NEGATIVE BUOYANCY TANK
Tr	TRIM TANK
To	TORPEDO TANK
WB	WATERTIGHT BOW
WH	WATERTIGHT STERN
Z	CONTROL ROOM
B	BATTERY COMPARTMENT WITH BATTERY
M	ENGINEROOM
F	COMMUNICATION ROOM
O	SONAR ROOM
Tu	CONNING TOWER
Ot	UPPER DECK CONTAINER FOR RESERVE TORPEDOES
Sch	SNORKEL

The World War II U-boat arm hoped that the snorkel would solve the problem of Allied ASW aircraft. This unit is stowed aboard a Type IX U-boat. The mesh coating was intended to reduce radar reflectivity. Note the exhaust below the intake head in the view of the snorkel folded away.

World War I (single ship) submerged attacks of other navies.

The greatest problem was simply locating targets. It had to be assumed that air patrols would prevent U-boats operating in coastal waters, near natural concentrations of shipping. Farther out to sea, the ocean would be almost empty, since convoys would concentrate ships otherwise spread over many thousands of square miles. First, the U-boat arm therefore needed to locate the convoys themselves in the open ocean, despite the individual boat's very limited visibility. Second, the U-boats needed some means of overcoming escorts around the convoys themselves. Finally, no individual U-boat could sink the sheer number of targets represented by a large convoy. Each convoy, when sighted, had to suffer as many attacks as possible.

There were only two possible solutions to finding the targets in the first place. In relatively narrow seas, submarines acting together, on the surface, could form a scouting line (line roughly abreast). If they were fast enough, they could concentrate against a target spotted by any one of them, this information being relayed by radio. Doenitz developed such tactics in the Baltic and the North Sea during 1938–39, a few years after virtually the same concepts had been developed by the British China Fleet. The only difference was that Doenitz planned to engage on the surface, whereas the China Fleet submarines expected to dive upon sighting the Japanese Fleet.

THE ERA OF THE SUBMERSIBLE 1900-1945

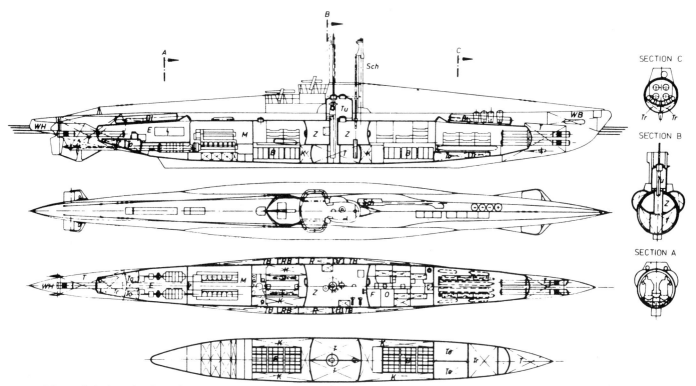

Type VIIC U-boat deck plans, elevation and sections (see legend opposite).
courtesy of IKL and Prof Gabler

The 220ft Type VIIC (749/851 tons) was the most common U-boat in the Battle of the Atlantic. *U-251* has just returned to Narvik after attacking convoy PQ-17, July 1942. She is flying a flag from her attack periscope. A sky search periscope was normally housed forward, where the officers are standing. There was no search periscope of the type employed by US and British submarines. Note the wind deflector surrounding the bridge, with a spray deflector lower down, at the level of the anti-aircraft gun platform. The bulge at the fore end of the fairwater housed the magnetic compass. This boat illustrates the original Type VIIC superstructure, before radar (housed in a bulge on the port side) and extra anti-aircraft weapons were added. The deck gun was an 88mm/45 calibre (ready use ammunition came from watertight containers in the casing) and the anti-aircraft weapon a 20mm cannon. The small saddle tank can just be seen at the waterline. Note also the double row of limber holes in her casing, to make diving faster by speeding flooding. Most of the crew (44 was the normal total) are on deck.
US Navy

In wider waters no scouting line could be really efficient. There had to be some longer-range means of detecting targets; the submarine or submarines could then be cued into detection range. Most prewar tacticians expected long-range maritime patrol aircraft to perform this scouting function. During World War II, however, various forms of signals intelligence (codebreaking and radio direction-finding) were far more effective, at

45

SUBMARINE DESIGN AND DEVELOPMENT

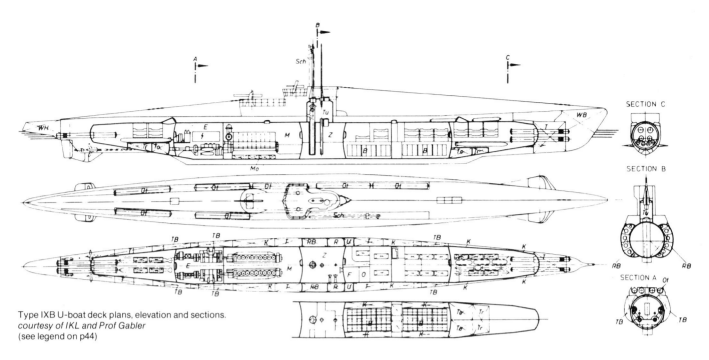

Type IXB U-boat deck plans, elevation and sections.
courtesy of IKL and Prof Gabler
(see legend on p44)

U-873, another Type IXD2, displays some of her underwater details in drydock at Portsmouth Navy Yard, New Hampshire, 30 June 1945, after her surrender. The streamlined shutters of her stern tubes are visible abaft her paired rudders, with ballast tank vent slots abaft them.
US Navy

least in the British, German, and US navies. In both cases, information was rarely exact enough to guide a submarine directly to its target. Even when codebreakers could divine the planned course of a convoy, the convoy navigators themselves might well make errors taking the convoy outside a submarine's detection range at its expected position.

Reliance on information generated outside the individual submarines automatically implies some degree of centralised control of the submarine campaign; there must be someone who can form an accurate picture of enemy targets as a group, and allocate submarines efficiently. That in turn implies a need for a command link, at least from the submarine commander ashore to the boats at sea.

The scouting line could make up for the degree of imprecision implicit in long-range reconnaissance and signals intelligence; it also concentrated enough submarines both to overwhelm the escorts and to sink many of the merchant ship targets. That was really necessary only in the Atlantic, where the Allies ran large convoys. Both in the Mediterranean and in the Pacific, single submarines (British and American, respectively), successfully attacked and virtually destroyed convoys, because the merchant ship targets were far less numerous. Ironically, although Doenitz invented wolfpack tactics, he was unable to use them for the first year of World War II because he had far too few operational U-boats to concentrate. Thus it is sometimes claimed that the wolfpacks were direct counters to early wartime British ASW tactics.

American submarines in the Pacific were able, at first, to operate in areas of natural concentrations of Japanese shipping. Later US codebreakers were able to direct them to convoys and also against specific naval units; codebreaking was so precise that submarines sometimes missed their targets due to Japanese navigational errors. From September 1943 onwards the US Navy employed its own wolfpacks against Japanese convoys.

Both centralised control and submarine group co-operation only were possible thanks to improved radio communications after 1918. Admiral Doenitz remarked in his memoirs that he had taken part in the only attempted (and, as it happened, failed) multiple submarine (two) attack of World War I. At that time, any submarine attempting to transmit or receive radio signals had to surface and erect special masts; even then ranges were very short. By way of contrast, 1939-45 submarines could often receive long-range broadcasts while submerged to periscope depth. They still had to surface to transmit, but none had to accept the delay of rigging special masts.

Doenitz initially believed that wolfpacks should be commanded from special flagship U-boats. Gradually, he realised that the flagships would be ineffective unless they were kept out of the immediate battle. Once

The forward and after torpedo rooms of a Type IX U-boat. Note the overhead rails for moving torpedoes by hand and the bunks rigged above the stowed torpedo in the after room. *U-505* of this class is on display at the Chicago Museum of Science and Industry.

that was done, there was little real difference between the information available aboard the special U-boat and that available by radio to a shore-based HQ; indeed, the latter was much better adapted to receiving and using the great variety of information available. Rigid control to the point of engagement was followed by uncontrolled individual attacks. Even this degree of control required unrestricted use of U-boat radios, as the commander ashore needed to know conditions at the scene of battle. If radio communications were inadequate, the U-boat high command radioed the most experienced captain present.

These tactics were initially rejected by a German naval staff probably all too conscious of British World War I radio intelligence successes. Doenitz argued, first, that coordination was inescapable, as long as the U-boat offensive had to be conducted against convoys, far from 'focal areas'. He also expected to rely on the relatively new technology of high-frequency radio, doubting

SUBMARINE DESIGN AND DEVELOPMENT

that an effective shipborne direction-finder could be devised. Without one, shore stations could not locate communicating U-boats precisely enough to call in attacks. Here he erred; high-frequency direction-finders (HF/DF) were the *only* long-range shipborne submarine detectors available to the Allies during the war. Yet until mid-1943 Doenitz was certainly borne out by operational results even though the Allies were able to exploit U-boat radio traffic heavily from mid-1941.

Typically the first U-boat to spot the convoy would shadow it on the surface, reporting its position to home in the other members of the pack, and also to allow Doenitz himself to concentrate other U-boats. Shipborne HF/DF was a valuable Allied ASW sensor because it could detect these shadowers, allowing fast escorts or aircraft to neutralise them. Similarly, aircraft escorting a convoy could prevent both shadowing and the assembly of the pack on the surface.

Since he could not control the attacks themselves, Doenitz tried to spread the available U-boats around convoys, to ensure maximum damage, and also to prevent individual ships from escaping. In practice even this degree of co-ordination was difficult to achieve, given limitations on U-boat speed and convoy manoeuvres. But the sheer weight of multiple U-boat attacks often broke up convoy formation, drawing escorts out of position and creating opportunities for further attacks. Doenitz insisted that U-boats attack at short range, generally at night on the surface, so that single-torpedo salvoes would hit.

THE U-BOAT WAR 1939-45

In practice, until about June 1940, U-boats tended to make conventional submerged attacks on independently-routed ships. On average, Doenitz could maintain about six U-boats in the Atlantic, each sinking an average of four ships (about 18,000 tons) per month. That required considerable aggressiveness, the average cost of which was the loss of two U-boats per month, so that a U-boat's operational life was only about three months; a rate of loss far worse than any during World War I. It also actually reduced the net size of the U-boat force. At the same time orders were placed for large numbers of new boats which became operational during the next two phases of the war. From the Allied point of view, too, although the U-boats were being contained, other forms of enemy action were destroying merchant ships much faster than they could be built. Total average monthly shipping losses were about 280,000 tons (106,000 to U-boats, 58,000 to mines, 27,000 to aircraft, and 14,000 to surface raiders), compared to a new construction rate of about 88,000 tons. Thus almost 2 million tons of merchant ships, out of a total Allied fleet of 40 million tons, were lost in the first ten months of the war, with every prospect that losses would accelerate after the fall of France.

In July 1940 the U-boats gained access to the French and Norwegian ports. Operations could, therefore, be extended much farther into the Atlantic. At the same time many British escorts had to be concentrated in home waters against the threat of German invasion. By late 1940, too, the Royal Navy was routing its convoys evasively, a postwar US summary noting that 'this thorough diversion of convoy routes seems to have been the main factor in the reduction of shipping losses, just as it had been in World War I'. With an average of 10 U-boats at sea, Doenitz still had too few to employ wolfpack tactics, but his captains did begin to attack convoys at night, on the surface. U-boat losses fell (average life increased from three to four months), and efficiency increased, so that on average each sank 16 ships of 88,000 tons before being sunk. Commissionings finally overtook losses, so that the total U-boat force approximately doubled between July 1940 and March 1941. For the Allies, this was a bleak time. Total Allied and neutral shipping losses averaged 456,000 tons per month, an increase of about 60 per cent, but new construction grew only to 114,000 tons leaving a net loss of about 342,000 gross tons per month. Of this figure, U-boats accounted for about twice as much as in the previous period, 224,000 tons, surface ships increased to 87,000 tons, and aircraft to 61,000. But mining was much less effective, partly because the British succeeded largely in neutralising the new German magnetic mine.

Through 1941 Doenitz was able to increase the number of U-boats at sea, and to form effective wolfpacks. He also moved his operations west, away from British air cover. As a result, the British were forced to escort convoys through their entire voyages rather than only through the Eastern Atlantic, and that made for some weakening of each convoy escort. From the U-boats' point of view, this period, roughly April-December 1941, was somewhat disappointing. Even though on average three times as many (about 30) were at sea as during the preceding period, and the average operational life per boat was about doubled (to nine months), the U-boat arm's rapid expansion greatly reduced crew experience, and many more crews were being lost on their first cruise. The average U-boat was sinking only about ten ships before itself being sunk, and the average U-boat was sinking only a little over one ship of about 5500 tons per month at sea, on average, about a quarter less than in the previous period. On the other hand, about 174 new U-boats were commissioned while only 28 were lost. Clearly the war was not being won. On the Allied side, average monthly total shipping losses fell to 363,000 tons, against new monthly deliveries of 175,000; the net monthly loss was almost halved and U-boats accounted for only about 175,000 tons of this total loss.

In January 1942 as the United States entered World War II, Doenitz shifted much of his offensive to the unprotected shipping of the Western hemisphere, with spectacular results. He now had many more U-boats, so

The engine and motor rooms of a Type IX U-boat, looking aft. Note that the big diesels almost fill the available space. On the surface, submarines are very fast in terms of their speed/length ratio so they require high power in proportion to their displacement. Diesel development was therefore a major issue between the two World Wars.

that the average number in the Atlantic increased from 22 in January to 93 in September, even though about 20 apiece were employed in the Mediterranean and on the convoy route to the Soviet Union. U-boats in the Atlantic were at their safest, with an average life of 13 months, and they were also at their most productive, sinking, on average, 19 ships of about 100,000 tons before being sunk. Such figures were achieved by concentrating on the weakly protected American area; out of 57 U-boats at sea in the Atlantic at any one time, 37 were off the US East Coast. Similarly, against a new average loss of $4\frac{1}{2}$ U-boats per month, the rate in the US area was only about $2\frac{1}{3}$. For the Allies, total shipping losses reached 700,000 tons per month, but the accelerating building rate reached 515,000 tons, so that the net monthly loss actually declined slightly. U-boats now accounted for about 78 per cent of losses, so that their defeat would clearly be decisive. These net figures do not reflect the severity of tanker losses: during this period, 190,000 tons were lost each month, compared with about 70,000 tons built, for a 10 per cent net decline in tanker tonnage each month at a time of sharply increasing demand for oil.

As US coastal escorts were strengthened, the U-boats were forced back into the North Atlantic for their decisive battle. The wolfpacks came close to cutting the convoy routes between late 1942 and mid-1943, but after May 1943 their losses grew so sharply that Doenitz had to withdraw them pending the availability of new weapons and tactics. As the escorts became more numerous, Doenitz tried larger and larger wolfpacks, as many as 20 U-boats sometimes attacking together. They proved relatively inefficient, each boat sinking far fewer ships. In addition, Allied air coverage of the central North Atlantic much improved, making it much more difficult for U-boats to operate on the surface. Allied losses reached their wartime peak, 862,000 tons, in November; fast, independently-routed merchant ships were the major sufferers. After November, monthly losses began to decline, even though they remained high. Between October 1942 and June 1943 the average loss rate was 491,000 tons (of which 394,000 were lost to U-boats); Atlantic losses fell but U-boat activity in the Mediterranean increased, partly to counter increased Allied activity there. The average number of U-boats at sea increased to 104, but each was far less effective than in previous periods; the average life fell to $8\frac{1}{2}$ months and during it an Atlantic U-boat sank only $4\frac{1}{2}$ ships of 28,000 tons before being sunk. At the same time, new construction (1,026,000 tons) finally exceeded losses.

Doenitz still had about 400 U-boats in service at the end of June, and he tried to recover the initiative. In July 1943 with 85 U-boats at sea, he attacked largely outside the North Atlantic, in areas previously largely untouched, but even so, only 244,000 tons were sunk. Allied aircraft and escorts became more and more effective. Moreover, as the summer of 1944 approached, Doenitz began to husband U-boats to defeat the expected Allied assault on France. Thus only 50 U-boats were at sea in the Atlantic in April, and only 40 in May. A postwar US assessment was that most of these were intended for reconnaissance, weather reporting, and also to force the Allies to convoy their shipping; there was little attempt to achieve any great result against Allied merchant ships. By November 1943 wolfpack tactics had been abandoned altogether, in favour of individual attacks. This much looser technique permitted U-boats to remain submerged during daylight.

Admiral Doenitz had considered the existing type of U-boat obsolete as early as late 1942 (see Chapter 4); from mid-1943 onwards, his goal was to keep the U-boat fleet in being while awaiting production of new types of boats. The U-boats' strategic defeat meant average monthly sinkings fell to 101,000 tons (17 ships) out of 184,000 tons lost to all causes; only about 45 per cent of the former being in the Atlantic where the average U-boat now survived only four months. Losses, about 200 U-boats, were balanced by the completion of about 250 new boats. They would presumably have been much higher had Doenitz not drastically reduced offensive operations.

In the final phase of the war from June 1944 snorkel-equipped U-boats began to concentrate in British home waters, using their snorkels to remain continuously submerged. A postwar US report noted that U-boat captains tended, at first, to avoid snorkelling due to the many discomforts involved, but soon discovered that, given the sheer number of aircraft they faced, they had no choice: 'After six U-boats were sunk by aircraft attacks in the Biscay Area between 7 and 10 June, the U-boats began to appreciate the value of snorkel and quickly learned how to use it efficiently.' As the campaign in British coastal waters intensified, some U-boats moved back into the Atlantic, partly to capitalise on the movement of escorts from the mid-Atlantic into those coastal waters. By the war's end the Germans were beginning to introduce the new fast submarines discussed in the next chapter: six Type XXIII operated with some success off the East Coast of Great Britain, and several new Type XXI reached Norwegian bases in preparation for war patrols, although in fact none carried out attacks. Had large numbers come into service before Germany was overrun, presumably the sea war would have shifted very considerably. As it was, the downward trend in U-boat effectiveness continued.

For although monthly sinkings of U-boats in the Atlantic declined from 16 to 13, that was out of 39 at sea rather than 61, so that a U-boat's average life declined to three months, as low as the unacceptable figure of the war's start. That is, despite the introduction of the snorkel, inshore waters were statistically quite as dangerous as they had been in 1939. Worse, the Atlantic exchange rate was only 0.6 ship sunk per U-boat sunk. Inshore, matters were only slightly better.

The postwar US evaluation was that wolfpack tactics succeeded only because there were too few convoy escorts. By 1943 more surface ships were available, and convoys could enjoy air cover throughout the North Atlantic; pack tactics were revised. The U-boats were instructed to fight both the air and the surface escorts, rather than to attempt to

This may convey some impression of how crowded U-boats were. Even the Type IX was small by US standards. These are officers' quarters next to No 2 battery room. Most of the enlisted men had to 'hot bunk' (use the same bunks in rotation).

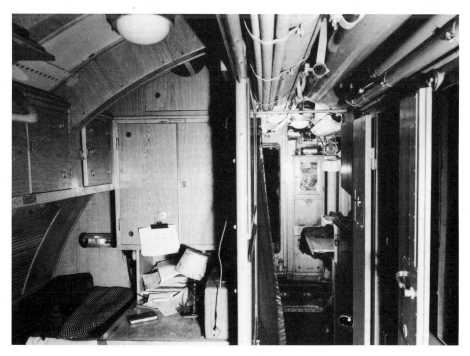

SUBMARINE DESIGN AND DEVELOPMENT

The conning tower of *U-889* shows the pipe connection to her snorkel; the snorkel itself is folded down into the deck (left side of the picture). The port side of the tower has a bulge mount for the radar mast and the DF loop is on the opposite side of the bridge.

U-boats could be ordered to attack. Long-range communication was so central to this type of warfare that the Germans could not avoid it, even though they suspected that it was their most serious vulnerability.

The Allies ultimately exploited U-boat tactics – themselves a consequence of the basic character of the submarine force – in two quite distinct ways. One was to locate transmitting U-boats using HF/DF, both ashore and afloat; aircraft running down HF/DF 'cuts' accounted for many U-boats. The other end of the German net was the command circuit emanating from the U-boat HQ (mainly near Lorient and at Berlin). Once that code had been broken, the Allied naval command could anticipate planned U-boat dispositions, re-routing convoys and ordering hunter-killer groups to attack.

Surface attack tactics were an integral part of the wolfpack technique. Mindful of the failure to sink enough Allied tonnage in World War I, Doenitz ordered his captains to attack from ranges so short that every torpedo would be effective. He reasoned that at night a surfaced U-boat would have so small a silhouette as to be effectively invisible, so that she could operate within a convoy as a surface torpedo boat, diving only after attacking so as to evade counter-attack. A surfaced U-boat could expect to fire at 600 yards; hits would be nearly certain and salvoes would be unnecessary.

Similar ideas were proposed in other navies, but they were generally rejected as suicidal. For example, a US S-boat commander who penetrated the Fleet Train during a fleet manoeuvre, attacking on the surface, was severely reprimanded. British submarine commanders were indoctrinated in the supposed effectiveness of sonar. Similar ideas prevailed in the German Navy of the mid-1930s; submarine doctrine required that torpedoes be fired outside the presumed 3000 yard sonar range. But Doenitz doubted that sonar would perform very effectively, possibly because German experiments with active sonar had been unsuccessful.

Perhaps because of the corresponding German success with passive directional sonars, Doenitz based his tactics on presumed British dependence on such sensors. He argued that, unlike a submerged

evade them; they were provided with additional anti-aircraft guns and acoustic (anti-escort) torpedoes. In theory the first measure would prevent aircraft from breaking up packs, and the second would allow the U-boats to break up the surface screen before attacking the merchant ships. In fact, neither measure was effective. The aircraft drove the U-boats from the surface, and that in turn destroyed the radio net and the mobility required to concentrate the pack.

Recent accounts of World War II convoy battles show a complex series of moves and countermoves. German cryptanalysts would determine the planned convoy route, and the U-boat command would throw a patrol line of U-boats across it. The Allied ASW command, decoding the German signal setting up that line, would order the convoy re-routed, and the Germans might break that signal in turn to redeploy the U-boats. Individual U-boats on the patrol line would, in turn, report to the centralised command when they sighted the convoy, so that other

U-889, a Type IXC, running on the surface at 17 knots, her best speed, under the White Ensign (Royal Canadian Navy) after the war. Note that her superstructure has been enlarged to take additional AA weapons, not mounted.

50

submarine running at speed, a surfaced U-boat would not be detectable by either hydrophones or by active sonar. U-boats were instructed to evade counter-attack at very low speed, to minimise noise. However, surface attacks became more and more dangerous as the British introduced effective surface search radars, and from 1941 onwards the Germans tended more and more to fire from underwater, as they had in 1914-18. Wakeless (electric) torpedoes and special devices to eliminate splash on firing made detection of the firing submarine more difficult. As before, detection of a submerged submarine *before* firing was extremely difficult, and did not have to be taken into account.

To some extent Doenitz's ideas played to Allied strengths. World War II sonars were essentially contact-holding rather then search sensors. A submarine revealing its approximate position by attacking could often be caught in a sonar beam, and then tracked for attack after attack. Low-speed evasion tactics made it easier to keep the submarine in the sonar beam. Contact-holding in general was effective, according to a postwar British study, not because it led to destruction by depth charge, but because a U-boat could be held underwater until it had to surface to replenish either its battery or its air supply, at which time it might be sunk by gunfire.

Airborne radar forced the Germans to abandon wolfpack concentration on the surface, ie to surrender their initial mobility. In 1944-45 they tried to restore invisibility to the submarine via the snorkel, which permitted continuous underwater operation, albeit at a loss in maximum speed. A postwar British account described this as a real change from the 'submersible' to the 'snorkel-fitted submersible'. Pack tactics had to be abandoned because communication (both with the U-boat command and with other U-boats) became much more difficult, and the submarines had to return to the inshore 'focal points' of World War I tactics. This they could do only because they were no longer detectable visually or by radar. Only sonar could still detect them, and it was hampered by interference from wrecks, tide rips, and an uneven bottom.

German late-war inshore tactics indicate just how effective Allied ASW had become. The U-boats operated almost entirely submerged, navigating by dead-reckoning, by using electronic aids (a chain of 'Electrasonne' transmitters and beacons), by echo-sounding, and by taking periscope bearings of lights and landmarks. Since aircraft could sometimes detect the snorkel itself or its characteristic exhaust, U-boats attempted to snorkel only at night, for about four hours out of 24. While snorkelling and therefore at its most vulnerable, the U-boat kept both periscope and radar detection watch. It stopped its diesels every 15 or 30 minutes to conduct an all-around hydrophone sweep, in the expectation that any approaching surface

Radar detectors carried by *U-889* at the time of her capture. The curved reflector was part of *Tunis* (FuMB 26), operating at S- and X-band to counter Allied airborne sea-search radars. The cone is presumably an active microwave surface search radar.

ASW craft could be detected in time. Once in the patrol area, it would attempt to lie on the bottom, under a convoy route, listening. Only when a convoy was detected by hydrophone would the U-boat rise to attack, firing salvoes of pattern-running torpedoes at the merchant ships, or else single acoustic torpedoes at the convoy or at its escort. In either case, the attack could be conducted from relatively long range. Once an attack had been completed, the U-boat would try to evade counter-attack either by lying on the bottom, or by creeping off at about 3 knots or less, using special low-speed motors.

By mid-war a surfaced submarine could expect to be detected on escort radars at ranges of three or four miles at night. Escort sonar screens in the van of convoys increased minimum torpedo firing range to 5000 yards or more, which in itself greatly reduced torpedo effectiveness. A postwar US submarine tactical manual claimed that any submarine trying to come closer would have about an even chance of being detected and attacked immediately, as well as a reduced chance of escaping unscathed after launching its torpedoes. By the later stages of the war, U-boats rarely attacked convoys. When they did, they generally had to fire from ranges as great as 2000-4000 yards. In effect this experience vindicated the pre-Doenitz German doctrine, with the very important addition of radar to deny submarines the surface at night.

US PACIFIC WAR TACTICS

Doenitz was not unique in his need for two-way communication. The US Navy also used centralised intelligence to direct an anti-shipping campaign. Well aware of the operational success of shipboard direction-finding, it tried hard to avoid the return circuit from the submarines. One American advantage was the breaking of the Japanese convoy code; the US codebreakers could estimate the positions of particular submarines, and even the number of torpedoes left aboard, by listening for Japanese attack reports in the submarines' patrol areas. As a corollary, American wolfpack practice was to delegate command to the pack's senior officer so as to minimise radio traffic.

American wartime submarine experience was summarised in the 1946 edition of the standard fleet manual on submarine warfare. Perhaps the greatest limitation of the fleet boat was its inability to detect targets at a great range. A surface ship radar 100ft above the waterline could detect shipping at ranges beyond 30,000 yards (almost 15 miles). By way of contrast, according to the manual, the fleet boat could expect to achieve:

	QB/JK	JP	Enemy Sonar	Periscope	SJ-1
Single Merchant Ship	7	10	17	12.5	17
Convoy	10	15	17	17	19
Warship	7	10	17	10	10.5
Escorted Warship	15	20	17	17	25

SUBMARINE DESIGN AND DEVELOPMENT

The figures are ranges, for various sensors, in thousands of yards. Half the time the range would be shorter; *reliable* ranges, for planning purposes, were counted as 75 per cent of the averages. In this table, QB/JK was an active sonar, JP was a passive receiver of propeller noises, and the 'enemy sonar' column indicates counter-detections of enemy pinging. In each case the target is treated as a point target, so that the distance a scout can spot a formation increases with formation size.

US doctrine kept the submarine surfaced as long as possible so as to move into the most favourable position, a few miles ahead of the targets. That required effective warning of the approach of enemy aircraft, so that the submarine need not dive *except* when in danger. Thus a submarine warning radar, SD, was among the first products of the American naval radar industry. Unlike conventional surface ship sets, it had no fire control function; it merely indicated that an aircraft was nearby. That was not enough. First, it proved relatively easy for the Japanese to home on the omni-directional SD emissions. Second, the SD was triggered even by aircraft not flying towards the submarine. Later models were made directional; they were also more difficult to intercept. By 1944 the Japanese were using their own primitive airborne radars, and US submarines were being equipped with countermeasures receivers. They could, then, dive long before being detected, and they gave off no tell-tale signals of their own.

Heading toward the target from ahead, even submerged, the submarine would make the maximum possible speed *relative* to the target. It could, therefore, expect to be able to counter target manoeuvres (such as zigzags) and yet close to effective torpedo range. The faster the targets, the more difficult this manoeuvre, so that some attacks had to be made from beam or quarter positions. In those cases torpedo runs would be longer, with a greater chance that target evasive action *after* firing (such as zigzags) would cause misses. More generally, given fixed torpedo, submarine, and target speeds, there is a relative bearing beyond which a submarine cannot approach to within effective torpedo range.

Standard practice was to avoid coming within visual range of the target. At night that minimum range was sometimes more than 6000 yards, and sometimes so short that torpedoes could be fired on the surface. Submerged, the submarine would try to sidestep the escorts, run as silently as possible, and avoid sonar detection by not presenting its beam aspect (the greatest sonar cross-section). Statistical analysis showed that night attacks and submerged daylight attacks were about equally common.

Only loaded torpedo tubes were fired since reloading required withdrawal and a fresh approach to the target. A US fleet submarine had 10 torpedo tubes, 6 forward and 4 aft. Statistics covering the entire war showed an average of 3 torpedoes per salvo, and about one in three hit. Acoustic torpedoes were generally fired singly with the same success rate. Thus the bow tubes were good for two targets, the second to be attacked as soon as a fire control solution could be obtained. To shift from bow tubes to stern tubes, or vice versa, required a course change of about 140 degrees and, according to the manual, 'therefore entailed a somewhat longer delay, but was usually attempted unless activities of enemy escorts made it inadvisable'.

Once it had attacked, the submarine would generally have to evade the escorts, going as deep as possible and steering to minimise the sonar cross-section presented to the enemy. Tactics depended on whether the escorts had passive or active sonars. The Germans and Italians, for example, depended largely on passive equipment, and that in turn shaped British tactics. Thus, an evading submarine had to increase speed gradually to avoid cavitation noise as speed through the water built up to the equivalent of the propeller rpm. War experience showed that often the best place to evade was the noisiest, right under the formation just attacked, where propellers and exploding depth charges would mask the noise of radical high-speed manoeuvring. A submarine might turn into a noisy surface ship wake or run beneath a moving ship. If the target had stopped, the submarine might still wish to hide beneath her, but it would have to balance on a heavy water layer, or back down to do so.

Active sonar carried its own vulnerabilities. Its downward-angled fan-shaped beam could not hold contact with a submarine at very short range. Allied ASW forces used as a rule of thumb that submarine depth was one-third of the range at which contact was lost. Density and thermal layers reflected sonar signals and so could shield a submarine able to dive deep enough. There were also many false targets: wrecks, eddies, currents, even the submarine wake itself. A violently-turning submarine would leave a 'knuckle' in the water simulating the submarine's own echo. A submarine under attack might dodge by accelerating to full speed when the ASW vessel was committed to attack, and therefore about to lose contact. A full-speed dash would create a wake, an artificial target of about the right size; the submarine would then glide with its machinery stopped, making a slow withdrawal. Sonar decoys gave the same effect without the dash. Manoeuvre could also reduce the sonar echo strength itself; the sonar cross-section of an end-on target is far smaller than a broadside target's.

Attack by a hunting ASW ship could be expected 'when (i) the true bearing remains steady; (ii) the ASW ship shifts to short scale on her echo-ranging gear; (iii) the ASW ship speeds up and an up-doppler of target noise is detected. When the attack is believed coming in, the submarine should make a radical turn towards the target at high speed... [and] maneuver to put the ASW ship on her quarter. When depth charges explode, depth charge direction indicator should be watched very closely and submarine should be maneuvered to keep the ASW vessel astern.'

Once the attacker had been shaken off, the submarine could withdraw at periscope depth to observe enemy moves. The British claimed, however, that the best anti-sonar measure was a torpedo in return followed up on the surface with gunfire. By 1944 the Germans were using homing torpedoes as an anti-escort measure, and the late-war US submarine designs showed special tubes for small diameter anti-escort homing torpedoes.

From January 1943 to April 1945 US submarines on average attacked 32 per cent of all merchant ships sighted, hitting 75 per cent of those attacked, and sinking 66 per cent of those hit. Against large warships, the corresponding figures were 17 per cent of those sighted, reflecting the protective effect of high speed; 66 per cent hits on ships attacked, but only 35 per cent of those sunk, reflecting large warships greater ability to survive. Against smaller warships, primarily escorts, only 49 per cent of ships attacked were hit (presumably due to their agility), but 72 per cent of ships hit were sunk.

The 1946 manual claimed that many ships sighted but not attacked were either not considered worth attacking, or could not be engaged because the submarine was not fast enough (submerged or surfaced) to reach a firing position. Thus greater underwater speed or a longer-range torpedo might have increased the ratio of ships attacked to ships sighted. Speed, particularly surfaced speed, limitations were even more severe in other navies, and many World War II submarine memoirs describe the frustration of sighting a target too distant to attack.

The other possibility was to reduce the number of torpedoes expended per target, so that a submarine could fire at more ships in a convoy before retiring to reload or being forced to defend itself against escorts. According to the 1946 manual, however, 'A study of cases in which a group of ships was contacted but not attacked indicates, however, that... probably about two-thirds of all ships which presented an opportunity for attack were actually attacked.'

CHAPTER FOUR

The Fast Submarine

All modern submarines are descended from the German Type XXI of 1944. It had two radically new features. First, it could manoeuvre and attack entirely submerged, thanks to its high sustained underwater speed. In normal sea states, submerged, it could often outrun surface ASW ships. Second, its snorkel permitted it to operate entirely submerged. Type XXI could also dive much deeper than its predecessors, manoeuvring more violently as it did so. It was clearly capable of defeating the successful Allied ASW tactics of 1939-45; the threat from large numbers of Soviet equivalents was the primary motivation for Western ASW development during the decade after 1945. Moreover, most postwar attack submarines can be characterised as adaptations of the Type XXI concepts, although none was really a direct copy. Examples include the US *Tang*, the British *Porpoise*, and the Soviet 'Whiskey'.

Tactically, the Type XXI reversed classic submarine design priorities, substituting high submerged speed for surface seakeeping and sustained speed. It was introduced as a specific counter to the Allied radar-equipped aircraft and surface ships that had driven Admiral Doenitz's wolfpacks from the surface. Denied its surface speed, the Type VIIC U-boat could not expect to achieve submerged attack positions against even moderately fast convoys. Type XXI restored mobility; submerged, it was nearly as fast as a surfaced Type VIIC.

Ironically, the Germans were able to build Type XXI not because they had foreseen this development, but because a young engineer, Helmuth Walter, had spent the previous decade working on a revolutionary fast U-boat. Doenitz supported his project before the war, but apparently only as a long-term possibility. Given the problems of the few actually built, he may have been fortunate that he had to settle for an intermediate solution. Thus, although the Walter closed-cycle submarine was widely regarded in the early postwar period as the design of the future, all postwar non-nuclear submarines are, in effect, modern versions of the Type XXI concept. The nuclear submarine simply substitutes a reactor for the disintegrator and combustion chamber of the Walter plant.

WALTER'S HYDROGEN PEROXIDE U-BOAT

Walter first proposed his fast submarine in October 1933. He does not appear to have been inspired by any particular reading of 1914-18 U-boat experience. Rather, he claimed that a submarine capable of 25-30 knots underwater would have revolutionary effects, comparable to those of the aeroplane. It would be able to operate with surface fleet and also to engage fast ships, the reasoning that had produced the British 'K' class. But Walter sought high *underwater* speed. That meant a fuel-burning engine, ie a source of oxygen for underwater operation. Walter proposed a closed-cycle diesel, in which exhaust gas would be cleansed of carbon dioxide, enriched with new oxygen, and then reused. Surfaced, the submarine would draw in air. Submerged, it would draw oxygen from the breakdown of hydrogen peroxide, which Walter considered superior to pure oxygen or air as a method of oxygen storage. He had as yet no idea of how treacherous a substance bulk hydrogen peroxide can be, and considered it safer than oxygen.

Walter soon discovered that the catalytic reaction which broke down peroxide into water and oxygen itself generated considerable heat, that could be used for propulsion. That in turn made external combustion, ie a steam engine, much more attractive than the diesel system which made no use of the heat produced by catalysis. Thus in the mature Walter system, the products of

The 30-ton *V80* was Walter's test boat, inspiring Admiral Doenitz to approve construction of full-scale hydrogen peroxide U-boats. She was also the first U-boat to sacrifice surface performance to underwater speed and to rely almost entirely on dynamic control.
Aldo Fraccaroli

SUBMARINE DESIGN AND DEVELOPMENT

disintegration were led into a combustion chamber and burned, to make use of the oxygen generated. In the 'direct process', the combustion chamber itself was used as a boiler, more water being injected with the fuel. Temperature (hence thermal efficiency) fell, but it was simpler than the 'indirect process' in which the hot exhaust gas of the combustion chamber was used to heat a separate boiler. In fact in the Walter prototype submarine, the experimental *V80*, all combustion was foregone, the steam created by catalysis being used directly in a turbine. The oxygen bubbling away formed a visible trail, so that *V80* could not function as an operational boat.

Walter sought to minimise drag by eliminating the traditional above-water floodable superstructure. As a result, even when surfaced, his submarine ran nearly awash; it needed a projecting pipe to assure a supply of air to the diesels. It was only a short step to the later concept of the snorkel, to supply air to a submarine just under the surface. High underwater speed also changed the basis of submarine depth control, from buoyancy to dynamic forces like those governing aircraft and airship motion. Thus the drag inherent in substantial ballast tanks (and the complexity of valves) could be avoided.

The German Navy was sufficiently interested to commission a study contract at the end of 1933 for a 300–400-ton, 24-knot steam turbine U-boat which it designated Type V. As early as 1936 the Germania engine works could report successful operation of a 4000hp Walter direct-process turbine installation. An order for the 80-ton *V80* followed early in 1939. It had Walter's fish-shaped hull, designed on the basis of wind-tunnel tests, and provided with only a minimal superstructure. As predicted, at high speed, surfacing and submerging were achieved by the motion of control surfaces rather than by emptying and flooding ballast tanks, so that the boat could be operated by aircraft-type controls.

V80 achieved 28.1 knots underwater during her April 1940 trials, by which time the design for a larger operational prototype had already been ordered. It was to have had three separate powerplants: two low-power diesels for surface operation (600hp total), two turbines for high underwater speed (total 4000shp), and two small electric motors for underwater endurance. All three would work through two sets of gearing, powering a single propeller. As in the prototype, Walter relied on dynamic control as far as possible, using one control-stick for both lateral and vertical motion.

Like all subsequent closed-cycle submarines, this one was limited in underwater endurance not by fuel capacity, but by the volume of oxidiser (hydrogen peroxide) it could carry. Unlike fuel oil, which could be carried externally, peroxide could not be allowed to come into contact with sea water; it would react much too violently. The pressure hull, however, was limited in diameter to maintain strength. Walter's solution was to provide a second cylindrical pressure hull below the primary hull, specifically for peroxide tankage. The resulting hull form, much deeper than its beam, was often described at the time as 'fish-shaped', and was later justified on hydrodynamic grounds, but it appears at the time to have been adopted primarily to gain internal volume. The postwar Allied view was that the figure-8 hull was too difficult to build, and that it was easier to accept the problems of greater hull diameter.

WALTER'S LATER U-BOATS

At this time the German submarine industry was being pressed for maximum production of the standardised Type VIIC U-boat, for the ongoing tonnage war in the Atlantic. Moreover, during 1941, there was no reason for Doenitz to believe that his existing designs were in any sense obsolescent. It says much for the Admiral's belief in the Walter boat that he ordered three prototypes, and demanded a high priority for their completion: he met with Walter in Paris in January 1942 to press for a peroxide boat suitable for the Atlantic campaign. Walter was then fighting a losing battle to hold down the operational prototype's size, and the German Navy was about to order a 600-ton type capable of only 19 knots. Walter argued that a submarine should be at least as fast as a destroyer running against a medium sea. In addition, it was expected that within a few years Allied convoys would be much faster. A speed of 25 knots seemed necessary to deal with a 16-knot convoy. Walter therefore turned to a 300-ton, 25-knot boat powered by two 2500shp turbines. It became the Type XVIIB, the first three of which were delivered only in January 1945. They were essentially coastal and North Sea submarines. Walter also designed a much larger Type XVIII, an Atlantic U-boat displacing 1750 tons (submerged), powered by two 6000shp turbines, and expected to achieve 25 knots submerged and 17.5 on the surface, with two diesels. It was not built, but its hull became

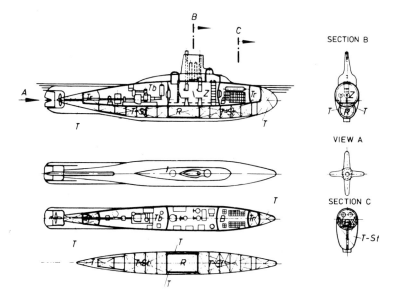

LEGEND

T	BALLAST TANK
K	FUEL TANK
R	COMPENSATING TANK
Tr	TRIM TANK
To	TORPEDO TANK
Tu	TORPEDO OR NEGATIVE BUOYANCY TANK
T-St	OXIDANT (H_2O_2) TANK
WB	WATERTIGHT BOW
WH	WATERTIGHT STERN
Z	CONTROL ROOM
B	BATTERY COMPARTMENT WITH BATTERY
M	ENGINEROOM
Tb	TURBINE ROOM
F	COMMUNICATION ROOM
O	SONAR ROOM
Sch	SNORKEL
W	BULBOUS BOW FOR LISTENING GEAR

V80 U-boat elevation, deck plans and sections.
courtesy of IKL and Prof Gabler

THE FAST SUBMARINE

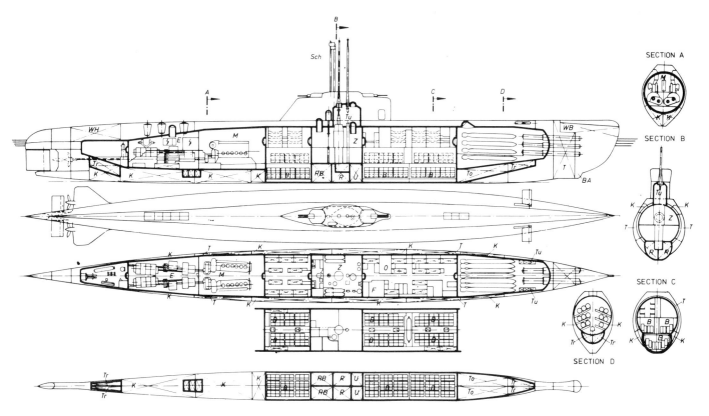

Type XXI U-boat elevation, deck plans and sections. *courtesy of IKL and Prof Gabler* (see legend opposite)

The German Type XXI U-boat was the direct ancestor of all modern submarines. *U-3008* is shown in US service, 25 July 1947, with her sail somewhat modified. A US submariner who served aboard her was impressed by her extremely rugged construction, developed after the experience of four years of depth-charging in the North Atlantic, and also by her relatively simple and austere design. Type XXI U-boats served operationally in the French and possibly the Soviet navies after 1945, and experimentally in the US, Soviet, and Royal Navies. One boat, which had been scuttled in 1945, was raised to become the West German experimental submarine *Wilhelm Bauer*.
US Navy

the basis of the very successful Type XXI. Work stopped in 1944; effort shifted to a compromise design, the 800-ton Type XXVI. The first was scheduled for delivery in the summer of 1945, and the turbine was found, partially dismantled, at the Walter factory. It was so promising that orders for the earlier XVIIB were cut from 24 to 6 in its favour.

No Walter boat ever became operational, but six were captured by the Western Allies in 1945. Four had been sunk; one (plus a complete test installation for a 2000shp engine) was retained by the US Navy, and a sixth, *U-1407*, became the British experimental submarine *Meteorite*. She had been scuttled, but was raised in June 1945, sealed up, and towed to Vickers, at Barrow-in-Furness, and refitted with virtually a completely new set of machinery also captured in Germany. It appears that, upon obtaining all this material, the Royal Navy decided that the Walter cycle was the submarine power plant of the future; it ordered two experimental Walter boats, *Explorer* and *Excalibur*, in August 1947.

In January 1942 the fast U-boat was a

55

SUBMARINE DESIGN AND DEVELOPMENT

future possibility, essentially of academic interest. However, during the spring of 1942 German submariners began to encounter Allied microwave radars, particularly aboard aircraft. Doenitz foresaw the defeat of his entire campaign, even though Allied analysts would place the moment of crisis almost a year later. Radar, either airborne or seaborne, attacked 'our whole method of conducting submarine warfare, which was based on mobility and operations on the surface, and which reached its culmination in the wolfpack tactics we had evolved'. As soon as destroyers or aircraft could reliably detect surfaced submarines far enough out to force them to dive before reaching attack positions around a convoy, the submarines would be neutralised. Moreover, if mobility could be denied in mid-ocean even in bad visibility, that 'would mean the end of the employment of the U-boat as a mobile instrument of war and its relegation to a purely stationary role – and that, with no prospect of success, except in sea areas which are less strongly defended'.

Doenitz argued that the ideal solution was a U-boat with 'an underwater speed so high that it would no longer be compelled to proceed on the surface in order to reach a position ahead of target, but could instead close with any enemy and reach a position from which to attack while still submerged'. In 1942 the Walter boat held exactly this promise. Doenitz soon discovered that its priority had not been nearly high enough. Not only were the prototypes as yet incomplete, but supplies of essentials such as peroxide would not be available for some time. At an otherwise depressing Paris conference in November 1942, Dr Friedrich Scheurer and Fritz Broeking, who had conceived the Type VII, suggested an alternative, the 'electro-boat', in which increased battery capacity went some way to substitute for peroxide.

The Walter hull already had unprecedented internal volume, intended for peroxide tanks. Devoted to batteries, it could double existing capacity. Walter had already realised excellent streamlining for minimum underwater resistance. Electric motors more powerful than those of earlier submarines could exploit its possibilities. Perhaps most importantly, because it incorporated existing technology (albeit in a new form), such a submarine might be built in time to meet the crisis Doenitz expected. Although it would not match Walter performance, this intermediate type of submarine would certainly be much faster than existing types – fast enough to attack convoys entirely submerged.

THE SNORKEL

The only major objection was that the extra battery capacity would require longer time on the surface for re-charging: Walter revived his old breathing-pipe idea, which became the snorkel. Given an external source of air, a submerged submarine could run its diesels to charge its batteries or, indeed, could travel for long distances on diesel power alone. Doenitz saw the snorkel not merely as an element of the new 'electric' U-boat, but also as a solution to the vulnerability of his existing fleet.

The idea was not altogether new; the pre-war Dutch Navy had already adopted an air tube of this type. But both the British and German navies had rejected it upon obtaining submarines so equipped in 1940. They had argued that it could not function in rough water. When the tube was closed due to wave action, the diesel, still running, had to have an alternative source of air. The Dutch, expecting to operate in the calm seas of the Dutch East Indies, used a small compartment and some air bottles to 'cushion' against intermittent closure. Walter's contribution was to use the entire internal volume of the submarine as an air chamber; he estimated that the diesels could run for as long as a minute at 7 knots on this internal air supply only. From the crew's point of view, having the air temporarily sucked out of their lungs would be extremely unpleasant, but now the submarine could operate entirely submerged. Tests began in August 1943.

The snorkel did not quite restore the U-boats' previous mobility, speed being limited to 5 or 6 knots. Thus a snorkelling Type VII still could not close a convoy. It could, however, avoid destruction by aircraft, even when operating relatively close inshore. It could therefore revert to the pre-wolfpack tactic of waiting at a 'focal point' of shipping, hoping that targets would pass within range. The Germans were well aware of this limitation, and by the war's end they were experimenting with a new reinforced streamlined tube, good they hoped for 10–11 knots. Type XXI could snorkel at 10 knots from the start.

DOENITZ AND THE TYPE XXI U-BOAT

Denied the Walter boat, Doenitz considered Type XXI the best possible solution. He could not afford the usual development cycle, which as of June 1943 envisaged building two experimental boats within 18 months. Mass production could not begin until trials had

Type XXIII U-boat elevation, deck plans and sections.
courtesy of IKL and Prof Gabler

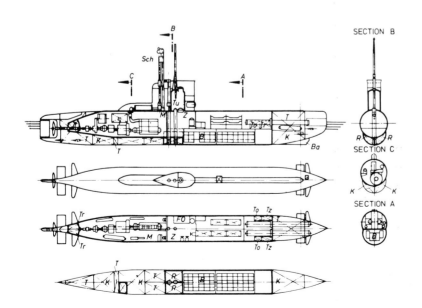

LEGEND

T	BALLAST TANK
K	FUEL TANK
R	COMPENSATING TANK
B	COMPENSATING FUEL OIL TANK
U	NEGATIVE BUOYANCY TANK
Tr	TRIM TANK
To	TORPEDO TANK
Tu	TORPEDO OR NEGATIVE BUOYANCY TANK
WB	WATERTIGHT BOW
WH	WATERTIGHT STERN
Z	CONTROL ROOM
B	BATTERY COMPARTMENT WITH BATTERY
M	ENGINEROOM
F	COMMUNICATION ROOM
O	SONAR ROOM
Tu	CONNING TOWER
Sch	SNORKEL
Ba	BALCONY FOR LISTENING GEAR

56

been completed in 1945, which meant no operational craft until the end of 1946. Even these dates could not be met without continuous production (no bombing damage) and with top priority.

Doenitz took the radical step of ordering production without trials, and prefabrication was adopted to minimise time on the slip, when boats would be vulnerable to bombing. The results were impressive; production actually accelerated in 1944-45 despite intensified bombing. This improvement was due in part to the improved U-boat production process, but also to the elimination of numerous inefficiencies remaining in the German economy even after six years of warfare. Careful design reduced labour per boat, from 460,000 man-hours for an earlier U-boat of similar size, to 260,000-300,000. Although the yards never met the production goal of 40 per month, they did complete 98 (Type XXI and the smaller Type XXIII) in the second half of 1944, and 83 in the first quarter of 1945. The price of this rapid production was teething trouble, and the first few boats became operational only at the end of the war, demonstrating a new order of capability but not affecting the outcome.

Compared to Type VIIC, Type XXI had better habitability, longer underwater range (360:108 miles) higher speed, (5:2 knots 'silent'; 12:5 knots 'high' and 16:7 knots maximum); and had no need to surface except for morale. Postwar tests showed a 72-minute endurance at full speed, 5 hours at 12 knots, 15 hours at 9, and 48 hours at 6 knots. At the 'creeping' speed of 5 knots, endurance was 72 hours, far in excess of Type VIIC performance, which by 1943 was only 5-6 knots for 45 minutes.

Wartime active sonar was effective only down to 400ft, but Type XXI was rated at a safe depth of 435ft. Since the safety factor was 2.5, it could actually operate, at least at low speed, at 600-800ft, making full use of the thermal layer for concealment. Due to streamlining, Type XXI presented a smaller sonar target than the physically smaller Type VIIC. The bulk of the echo came from the conning tower and other irregular surfaces of the submarine. It could be argued, however, that streamlining would not much reduce effective sonar range, since a 15 per cent loss in sonar cross-section equated only to a 4 per cent loss of range. Designed when the German Navy placed much more stress on passive than on active sonar, it was extremely quiet. Postwar US tests at Key West in Florida showed that, submerged at 15 knots, Type XXI was equal to the quietest US fleet submarine at 8 knots. At 10 knots, it was equivalent to the fleet submarine at 6; on its special motor at 5.5, it was equivalent to the US boat at its slowest creep speed, and in fact merged with background noise as it could then be measured. In another test, a Type XXI at 5 knots was so quiet that it could detect and get a bearing on a 16-knot destroyer from several times the destroyer's detection range.

The World War II Type XXIII coastal U-boat formed the basis of German postwar designs. Two of them, which became *Hai* and *Hecht*, were reconditioned for service in 1956-57. Their figure-8 hull form, which they shared with Type XXI, is particularly visible here; since they were single-hull boats there was no fairing to cover it. CPL

Nor would aircraft be able to maintain anything like their former detection ranges. Even relatively simple airborne radars were effective against surfaced submarines at tens of miles. By way of contrast, even the best existing airborne radar, the APS-20 could not detect a snorkel at more than 13 miles in smooth Sea State 2; it was useless in slight Sea State 3 or more. Even if it was surprised on the surface, Type XXI could dive extremely fast; to periscope depth in 10 seconds, to 100ft in 40 seconds after the diving alarm was sounded. In one blow, then, Type XXI neutralised all the major wartime tactical ASW systems.

Submerged Type XXI could patrol a station as efficiently as the surfaced Type VIIC, independent of weather. At 1600 tons it was much larger than earlier Atlantic U-boats, but longer ranger allowed it to operate without support submarines – which were being picked off on the basis of signals intelligence. It could also fire torpedoes even when moving at high speed. Perhaps most important, the new U-boat had a passive sonar to detect convoys at long range, completely submerged. Doenitz argued that the new submarine was fast enough to engage convoys entirely underwater 'for it was unlikely the enemy would be able in the foreseeable future, to increase the average speed of his convoys beyond about 10 knots'.

TYPE XXI ARMAMENT AND TACTICS

There was, to be sure, still a handicap. No matter how mobile, Type XXI still could not easily communicate while underwater. Wolfpack tactics were no longer practicable, and Doenitz had to seek some alternative means of achieving maximum kills each time he attacked a convoy. The Type XXI design therefore emphasised heavy torpedo armament, including rapid reloading of tubes. The initial design provided six rapidly-reloaded bow tubes (compared with a total of five in VIIC), but this seemed insufficient, and wartime designs showed one (XXIB) or two (XXIC) triple banks of rearward-facing tubes on each side.

New capabilities demanded new tactics. Doenitz recommended that, upon hearing a convoy, the submarine go to maximum speed to get ahead of it, then approach at maximum underwater speed. When detected, it was to crash the escort screen, 'paying no attention to pursuit or depth charge attack during the approach run'. If possible, the U-boat was to fire during its approach. Otherwise it would go *under* the convoy, on a parallel course, attacking from below, protected by the merchant ships. Homing or pattern-running torpedoes could be fired without precise fire control information, so that the U-boat would never have to come to periscope depth; it could fire from a depth of 100-150ft. High underwater speed would keep the U-boat with the convoy for a long time, for multiple attacks. Afterwards, it would go deep and crawl, then turn about and move off laterally astern of the rest of the convoy.

The Type XXI and the smaller coastal Type XXIII had immense influence on postwar development both in the West and in the Soviet Union. Another wartime fast submarine series did not: the Japanese Navy

SUBMARINE DESIGN AND DEVELOPMENT

The 842/990-ton HMS *Seraph* was the first of 7 British S-boats to be specially streamlined in 1944 to provide a high-speed underwater target for Allied ASW forces. She is shown in the same role passing the new destroyer HMS *Battleaxe* during the first postwar Anglo-US joint naval exercises, May 1948.
CPL

built two classes of fast attack submarines as described in Chapter 3. Although some of their capabilities matched those of the German craft, they sank into almost total obscurity postwar. Postwar US classified ASW publications contain no discussions of their designs. This may reflect the relatively high prestige of the German, and the very low prestige of the Japanese, wartime submarine arms.

BRITISH TYPE XXI IMITATIONS

The Royal Navy became aware of Type XXI early in 1944; it was reported capable of 20 knots surfaced and 16 submerged. A British equivalent was needed if ASW tactics were to be developed. The Director of Naval Construction, Sir Stanley Goodall, considered converting an existing submarine, fairing fittings, blanking off the torpedo tube ports, removing the gun, replacing the bridge with a smaller streamlined structure and removing one periscope and the radar masts. Higher capacity batteries would be fitted and the motors upgraded. Both the large 'S' and the small 'U' class were considered, HMS *Seraph* being chosen. She was completed in August 1944, after a two-month conversion at Devonport. Underwater resistance was reduced by 45 per cent, *Seraph* achieving 12.52 knots (1647bhp) compared to 8.82 knots (1460bhp) for a conventional 'S' class submarine. High speed target duty (to train ASW forces against the new U-boats) was so urgent that *Sceptre, Satyr, Statesman, Selene, Solent,* and *Sleuth* were later converted. HMS *Scotsman* was later used for high-speed tests. She had high-power ('A' class) motors, which took up so much space that her original diesels had to be replaced by the small units of the 'U' class. As a result, she took about a day to recharge after a high-speed run, but she demonstrated that a high-speed conversion was practicable, and inspired the 'T' class reconstruction programme.

The conversion showed that Type XXI was not so radical as might have been imagined; suitably modified conventional submarines could approach its performance. Postwar, both Britain and the United States were able to modify many war-built submarines to match Type XXI's underwater speed, although not its diving depth. As with the wartime conversions, the initial rationale for this work was ASW training.

POSTWAR ALLIED EVALUATIONS

Thus the Germans produced three revolutions in submarine performance virtually simultaneously: the snorkel, the 15-17-knot 'electric' submarine (Types XXI and XXIII), and the 25-knot Walter boat. In 1948 the US evaluation was that World War II ASW developments had essentially solved the non-snorkel submarine problem; for example, the 'fleet type' could expect to exchange 2 boats for every merchant ship sunk. Even a snorkel submarine with limited underwater speed and endurance would be almost completely ineffective; it was estimated that the Type VIIC (snorkel) would exchange 1 submarine for every 6 merchant ships sunk.

Existing escorts would find attacks on a 17-knot submarine relatively difficult. For example, *Odax*, the first US 'Guppy' (effectively a Type XXI equivalent) was able to outrun a destroyer escort in any substantial sea by heading into it. The fast submarine could cover the range of wartime sonars so quickly that it could escape detection by speed alone. This tactic was defeated only with the advent of reliable long-range sonars such as the US SQS-4 and its successors; as late as 1973 the Soviets, who generally lag behind in sonar design, were credited with reliance on speed, rather than on deep diving and silence, for evasion.

A 25-knot submarine like Type XXVI would be able to counter-attack; it could

58

THE FAST SUBMARINE

expect to outrun attackers in the North Atlantic. Even so, it would be limited by the need to refuel: the submarine could not, in effect, recharge underwater power plant by creating new peroxide while snorkelling. On the horizon was the nuclear submarine able to sustain 25 knots for 60 days rather than 10 hours. It would be able to attack a convoy with very long-range torpedoes, never coming within sonar range.

The British view at this time (about 1948) was that the greatest advance was in intermediate speeds and in underwater endurance at low speed. Increased torpedo performance was equally important, because it permitted a fast submarine to attack from beyond sonar range. Range was tripled, and speed increased, with lethality maintained by the use of homing and pattern-running torpedoes. The new torpedoes could be adjusted to take any target angle. The Allied navies already had periscope ranging radars to achieve better torpedo fire control. In effect, there were no longer submerged limiting lines of attack for target speeds below about 25 knots. They had been replaced by limiting *areas* of approach.

The Royal Navy discounted the 15-knot underwater speed as an improvement in survivability; wartime experience showed that the best hope for a detected submarine was counter-attack, possibly with homing torpedoes. Shortly after the war it expected the next step to be the underwater wolfpack, co-ordinated by underwater telephone. The fear of detection was considered over-rated; only one wartime case had been found of a submarine being heard, and in that case it was transmitting directly at an escort, at short range and at full power.

During 1944 and 1945 the extent of the revolution became apparent to the US and Royal Navies. They had to react on two levels; submarine development proper, ie the exploitation of the new technology, and new countermeasures, which latter required a wholly new concept of ASW.

At the simplest level, the snorkel (snort in British parlance) could be fitted to many submarines. With the 'A' class under construction late in 1944, a snort was hurriedly designed. Tested in HMS *Truant* the following year, it was placed in production for the entire 'A' class and for most other British submarines. Actual installation was slowed by the end of the war, but the programme showed what could be done rapidly. Meanwhile, a design was prepared for an improved 'A' class submarine. It began with relatively minor changes (including snort), but by July 1945 Flag Officer (Submarines), Rear Admiral George Creasy, wanted a wholly new design comparable to Type XXI, with large battery capacity, a snort, and much streamlining; there would be no deck gun. There was some hope that the conventional powerplant would ultimately be replaced by a Walter turbine, but, within a few months this design, too, had been rejected in favour of a purely experimental Walter boat, which became HMS *Explorer*. Ironically, the first British submarines actually completed after the war

The Royal Navy fitted snorkels to many of its submarines immediately after World War II, without making any other major modifications. The 1300/1575-ton HMS *Thorough* (one of 53 T-boats launched 1937–45) is shown returning to Portsmouth in December 1957, on her return from Australia. The snorkel was folded down on deck abaft the sail, and its head can be seen just abreast the sonar dome (which housed an underwater telephone). Note the external (one-shot, non-reloadable) bow tube, which was fitted to many wartime British submarines to strengthen their torpedo salvoes, and the saddle tank visible as a bulge on the pressure hull, amidships. *CPL*

SUBMARINE DESIGN AND DEVELOPMENT

The *Tang* class attack boat *Trigger* (SS 564, seen in May 1967) typified the US equivalent of Type XXI. Note the slot for her retractable bow plane, and the absence of deck fittings; her safety lines retracted into the slots visible on deck. The small sonar dome probably housed an underwater telephone.
US Navy

THE FAST SUBMARINE

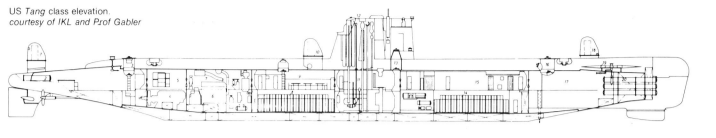

US *Tang* class elevation.
courtesy of IKL and Prof Gabler

1 SONAR DOME
2 AFT TORPEDO TUBE
3 AFT ESCAPE TRUNK
4 ELECTRIC PROPULSION MOTORS
5 CONTROL ROOM
6 DIESEL GENERATOR SETS
7 MACHINERY SPACE
8 AFT BATTERY ROOM
9 CREW MESS AND GALLEY
10 SONAR DOME
11 C.I.C.
12 HOISTING EQUIPMENT
13 ACCESS TRUNK
14 FORWARD BATTERY ROOM
15 OFFICERS CABINS AND RADIO ROOM
16 FORWARD ESCAPE TRUNK WITH TORPEDO HATCH
17 TORPEDO SPACE
18 SONAR DOME
19 BOW PLANES, TO BE RIGGED OUT
20 TORPEDO TUBES

were closer in concept to the original 1945 design: the *Porpoise* class.

USS TANG

Meanwhile an American Type XXI version took shape as the *Tang*. She was conceived early in 1946 as an experimental submarine, but became the prototype of the US postwar submarine fleet. Although a German-type figure-8 hull was considered, the Bureau of Ships designers adopted a conventional cylindrical pressure hull surrounded, except at the ends, by ballast tanks. They increased battery volume by compressing the diesel engine spaces, using a new compact high-speed 'pancake' diesel. The latter showed less than half the volume and weight of the conventional 1000bhp opposed-piston diesel, so that 4000bhp could be fitted in a 22ft length, compared with 6400bhp in a fleet boat or a 'Guppy' conversion. However, the 'pancake' was notoriously difficult to maintain, and ultimately had to be withdrawn from service. Some *Tang*s experienced breakdowns so severe that they had to be towed home, across the Atlantic. A Submarine Service jingle ran '*Harder, Darter, Trigger, Trout*/Always in, never out'.

Streamlining for high underwater speed required that deck guns as well as the former conning tower be eliminated altogether, the attack centre being relocated in an enlarged control room, as in contemporary British practice. At first, following German wartime practice, the stern was made very fine, so that there was no space for stern tubes. Instead, there were two 12in countermeasures tubes aft. Later, however, the design was modified to show two swim-out tubes aft, firing acoustic (ie, anti-escort) torpedoes. A contemporary account suggests that underwater manoeuvrability would make up for the reduced torpedo battery.

The hull form itself was a compromise; US designers were still unwilling to abandon surface performance. They already suspected that a short, fat hull would be most efficient underwater, but argued that it would be very slow on the surface. Given a conventional single-deck layout, great length was necessary in any case to fit the usual equipment. The *Tang*s were substantially shorter than their 'fleet submarine' predecessors, and above 15 knots they experienced less resistance submerged than surfaced.

High underwater speed, ie high battery power, had a price: low surfaced speed while recharging. The *Tang*s were the first US submarines designed specifically to snorkel, and appear to have been successful; the standard problems of snorkel conversions, described in 1953 as excessive battery gassing and high engine blower temperatures, were overcome.

The new design also increased operating depth to 700ft rather than 400ft (with a collapse depth of 1100ft). In 1948 the standard submarine steel had a yield stress strength of 42,000lb/sq in, and a new 75,000lb steel was under development; it would increase test depth to 1000ft without any change in hull weights. In fact the new steel did not become available until the late 1950s when, as HY80 (80,000lb yield) it was introduced in the *Skipjack* and *Thresher* nuclear classes. Note that it could be argued that a faster submarine *had* to be able to dive deeper, if only to avoid collapse during violent manoeuvring.

The US Navy appears to have considered the *Tang* a transitional design; like the Royal Navy, it expected to build a closed-cycle submarine based on the same hull in the near future. By 1948, projections showed a boat capable of sustaining 25 knots for 10 hours, in service by 1952. The design requirements of the *Tang* herself included suitability for 25 knots speed, and space for installation of a closed-cycle engine to match.

HMS PORPOISE

Britain and France built their own *Tang* equivalents, the *Porpoise* and *Narval* classes. Like the American design, neither used Walter's figure-8 hull. The British had actually considered a figure-8 hull design before the war, to store fuel oil *within* the pressure hull so that tell-tale leakage would not occur under depth charge attack. They concluded then, and later, that the lines of intersection of the two sub-hulls were too likely to be concentrations of stress. Instead, like US designers, they chose conventional circular-section designs. Like *Tang*, *Porpoise* minimised diesel engine room length to maximise battery volume. The Royal Navy did not employ an exotic short diesel; instead, it used relatively conventional in-line types, in a single engine compartment. The major design issue, then, was how to maintain the strength of this unusually long unbroken space. Like *Tang*, *Porpoise* had six torpedo tubes forward and two, for anti-escort homing torpedoes, aft. There was no provision for a deck gun, and the bridge fairwater was a streamlined 'sail'. Unlike the *Tang*s, the British submarines carried their sonars in big domes above their bows. The American boats employed the passive fixed BQR-2 array in a chin sonar dome as their primary sensor, whereas the British relied on a trainable searchlight sonar, Type 187.

Work on *Porpoise* began early in 1949, after the British concluded that they would not have an operational High Test Peroxide or HTP (Walter) submarine soon enough. They initially considered building a slightly modified *Tang*, but instead developed their own design. But US-type ('Guppy') batteries were adopted to simplify wartime supply. The basic design requirement was for a maximum underwater speed (at the half hour rate) double that of the existing 'A' class, ie about 16 knots. Draft staff requirements called for a speed of 17 knots to be sustained for 20 minutes. ASW was to have been the primary mission, and the six bow torpedo tubes (12 reload torpedoes) were designed to be fired at great depths. Ultimately, however, like the *Tang*s, the *Porpoise*s were fitted with a pair of stern tubes (primarily for short ASW torpedoes) in addition to their bow armament.

Like *Tang*, the new British submarine was intended to dive considerably deeper than her predecessors. In mid-1949 it was expected that she would operate at 650ft, with a safety factor of 1.75 (collapse depth 1140ft); the designers hoped for 750ft. This compared with 550ft for the experimental HTP submarines, *Explorer* and *Excalibur*. In fact materials development lagged, and by 1953 the new *Porpoise* class was rated only at 500ft. Yet, at least from 1949 onwards, the British submarine designers aimed at a 1000ft operating depth, corresponding to a collapse

SUBMARINE DESIGN AND DEVELOPMENT

The Royal Navy pursued hydrogen peroxide propulsion largely because it needed an ASW target that could simulate the most effective Soviet submarine. The 225ft experimental boat HMS *Explorer* (780/1000 tons) is shown in London's West India Docks, 19 March 1957, just over 3 months after her completion She was known as 'Exploder' because of numerous minor mishaps. Note her unusually short sail and the Type 187 sonar dome. *CPL*

depth of 1750ft. This compares with a US policy which appears to have kept to the 700ft of the *Tangs* until the design of *Thresher* in 1957–58. Thus, like the US Navy, the Royal Navy made considerable efforts to develop new high-yield submarine steels. By mid-1949, for example, it had a UKE steel with a yield strength of 54,000lb/sq in, and expected soon to have 70,000 or even 90,000lb steels. Reportedly the modified

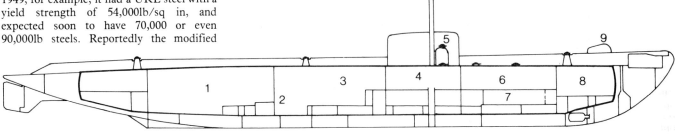

General arrangement of HMS *Explorer*. 1 Turbine space; 2 Turbine control platform; 3 Motor room; 4 Control room; 5 Bridge; 6 Living space; 7 Battery; 8 Diesel room; 9 Sonar dome.

British *Oberon* class elevation.
courtesy of IKL and Prof Gabler

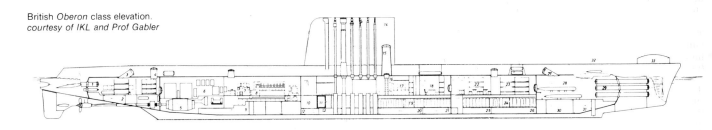

1 AFT TORPEDO TUBES	9 FRESH WATER TANK	17 WEAPON CONTROL EQUIPMENT	25 FRESH WATER TANK
2 AFT TRIM TANKS	10 PROVISIONS SPACE	18 OFFICERS' QUARTERS	26 FRESH WATER TANK
3 TORPEDO LOADING HATCH	11 DEEP FREEZE SPACE	19 BATTERY ROOM	27 TORPEDO LOADING HATCH
4 AFT ESCAPE TRUNK	12 SLUDGE TANK	20 COMPENSATING TANKS	28 TORPEDO STOWAGE SPACE
5 ELECTRIC PROPULSION MOTOR	13 COMPENSATING TANKS	21 FRESH WATER TANKS	29 TORPEDO TUBES
6 CONTROL ROOM	14 BRIDGE FIN WITH HOISTING EQUIPMENT	22 CREW MESS	30 FORWARD TRIM TANKS
7 GENERATORS	15 ACCESS TRUNK	23 CREW QUARTERS	31 TORPEDO TANKS
8 DIESEL ENGINES	16 STEERING CONTROL CONSOLE	24 BATTERY ROOM	32 BOW PLANES
			33 SONAR

THE FAST SUBMARINE

Porpoise (Oberon) class could operate below 1000ft, which suggests that the 1949 goal was soon met.

THE FRENCH NARVAL

Both the US and British navies envisaged only a single type of general purpose submarine. France was different. Before the war, she had required two very different classes, and this practice continued postwar. Her first effort towards submarine modernisation was to complete two prewar 1500-ton units with streamlining and a snorkel, for better underwater performance. It does not appear that battery capacity or motor power was increased. The next step was the design of a successor 1500 tonner, which became *Narval*. Like Britain and the

The 2030/2410-ton HMS *Porpoise* (launched 16 April 1958) was the first postwar British attack submarine, at 290ft oa broadly analogous to the US *Tang*. She leaves Malta's Grand Harbour on 13 October 1966, having had her name and pennant number painted out at a time when the Soviet Navy was reported to have up to a dozen submarines circling the island from their bases in Algiers and Egypt. It is standard US Navy practice to paint out submarine hull numbers.
CPL

United States, France sought very long range. In her case, submarine size was dictated by the need to patrol Indo-Chinese waters for 8-12 days after the long passage out, without refuelling. Unlike the US and British designs, this French one incorporated the German-style 'knife' stern. It was, therefore, impossible to fit a pair of conventional after tubes. The French were unwilling to dispense with them so they mounted two, firing to starboard, in the after part of the casing.

The *Narval* design was begun in 1947. Five years later work began on a modern counterpart to the prewar second class submarine, which became the *Daphne*. The parallel extended to the sort of extremely heavy torpedo battery common before the war: four tubes forward and four more aft (two right aft, and two angled aft, all external to the pressure hull). Finally, there was a specialised ASW submarine to be described later in this chapter.

The Dutch Navy was unique in employing

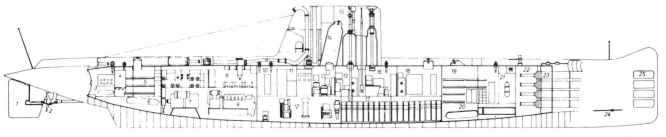

French *Daphne* class elevation.
courtesy of IKL and Prof Gabler

1 RUDDER	9 DIESEL GENERATOR SET	17 BATTERY ROOM
2 PROPELLER	10 GALLEY	18 OFFICERS' QUARTERS
3 AUX. MACHINERY SPACE	11 COOLING SPACE	19 CREW QUARTERS
4 WASH ROOM	12 AUX. MACHINERY SPACE	20 H.P. BOTTLE STOWAGE
5 CREW QUARTERS	13 C.I.C.	21 WASH ROOM
6 H.P. BOTTLE STOWAGE	14 ACCESS TRUNK	22 TORPEDO ROOM
7 ELECTRIC PROPULSION MOTOR	15 BRIDGE FIN	23 TORPEDO
8 CONTROL ROOM	16 RADIO ROOM	24 BOW PLANE
		25 TORPEDO TUBE DOORS

SUBMARINE DESIGN AND DEVELOPMENT

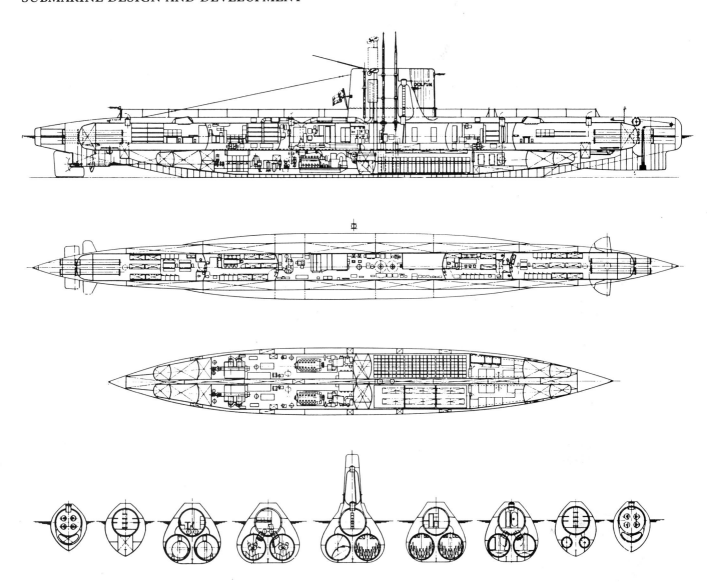

The Dutch *Dolfijn* class was a unique solution to the internal volume problem. Each of the two lower cylinders housed a complete powerplant, comprising a diesel engine, motor and batteries (one 1500hhp MAN diesel, one 2200bhp motor and 168 battery cells). The designer, M F Gunning, thought that this design might solve the heat-dissipation problems that had plagued earlier steam-propelled submarines since the boilers would be physically separate from the crew. Similarly, he regarded the triple hull as ideal for nuclear power. Her upper hull was arranged like those of earlier submarines and her relatively great length (260ft oa) made for greater underwater resistance than from an *Albacore*-form hull, so that, on about the same power as *Zwaardvis* she could make only 17 knots under water at a smaller displacement, 1830 tons.
Courtesy of Mr P Jalhay (Kon Marine-bureau Maritieme Historie)/De Boer Maritiem

a multi-hull design, in its case the triple-hull scheme evolved by M F Gunning, who had been chief naval constructor in the wartime Dutch government-in-exile. He had sought extra internal volume for cargo-carrying, but postwar he argued that the same basic scheme was extremely well suited to the new type of submarine since it minimised total length while providing additional volume for batteries, motors, or Walter-type boilers. Gunning also argued that, because the power cylinders were isolated from the pressure hull, his design was particularly well adapted to steam propulsion, the major drawback to which had been the need to absorb the heat involved. Later the same argument was made with respect to nuclear powerplants, although in practice the sub-hull diameters were hardly adequate. In the *Dolfijn* class (launched from 1959), each of the two lower cylinders accommodated an independent power unit, consisting of a diesel, a battery unit, and a motor and shaft; the longer upper cylinder contained four torpedo tubes at each end, as well as a control room and crew spaces. Gunning also argued that his cylinders could be of smaller diameter, and thus that his type of submarine could dive deeper than a conventional one.

US 'GUPPY' CONVERSION

Neither in Britain nor in the United States was there any willingness to buy large numbers of new submarines, given the vast and recently-built fleets left over from World War II. The only alternative was a conversion programme. In retrospect it is remarkable that in both navies vessels originally of quite conventional design could be modified to a fair approximation of the exotic Type XXI. The US version cost about $2.5 million each. These 'Guppies' (for 'Greater Underwater Propulsive Power') were deficient only in diving capability; like the wartime boats, they were capable of operating only at 400ft. They could match or exceed the U-boat in underwater speed and endurance. 'Guppy' conversion was initially justified by fleet requirements for ASW training. However, particularly after the outbreak of the Korean War (1950-53), it became evident that a large modern US submarine fleet was well worthwhile, and the 'Guppies' helped reduce the fiscal strain that a major new construction programme would have represented. Even they were relatively expensive, and the US Navy resorted to a more austere 'fleet snorkel' conversion programme, the products of which were suitable for later 'Guppy' modernisation.

The full 'Guppy' conversion replaced the original pair of 126-cell batteries by four new 126-cell units, each two-thirds the weight, but with about 75 per cent more capacity. That almost doubled available underwater

THE FAST SUBMARINE

power at the high-discharge rate (4250 vs 2638shp for one hour). At the medium (6 hour) rate, the 'Guppy' battery had 50 per cent more energy, and at low speed, 40 per cent more. But the new battery used twice as much lead as a conventional one, and wore out twice as fast, with an estimated life of only 18 months. There was some fear, in the late 1940s, that there would not be enough lead for the conversion programme; the existing foreign sources were either in hostile hands (Balkans) or in an unstable area (Burma). Later conversions ('Guppy II') employed a more conventional 'Sargo II' battery, and were limited to 15 knots underwater, compared to the 17 of a 'Guppy'-battery submarine.

Moreover, the thin plate construction of the 'Guppy' batteries made them more susceptible to abuse, and they tended to reach higher temperatures on charge. Air conditioning capacity had to be increased to dissipate the additional heat, and the submarines had to be rearranged internally which included removing an auxiliary engine and four reload torpedoes.

Externally, the 'Guppies' were carefully streamlined, and the mass of fittings aboard the typical fleet boat removed or made retractable. The effects could be dramatic. At periscope depth on batteries, over the 8-10 knot range, an unstreamlined fleet submarine required 2.25 times as much power as a 'Guppy'.

The 'Guppies' came quiet close to *Tang* performance. A 1953 comparison shows the latter no faster submerged, and actually slower on the surface, but its specialised design (and shorter hull) showed in much better manoeuvrability and better longitudinal stability. These qualities made for improved depth control and easier rapid depth changes.

The US fleet submarine was so large that battery capacity could be more than doubled, and motor power greatly increased, without any change to the outer hull. British submarines were smaller, and their equivalent

So urgent was the need to build high-speed underwater targets that the US Navy completed the reconstruction of its first two 'Guppies' even before it could develop a snorkel for them. This is the newly converted *Tench*-class boat *Pomodon* (SS 486) off Mare Island, 2 July 1947. Her sail is bulged to fit her air-search radar, which was turned athwartships to reduce the overall length of the sail. Streamlining also entailed rebuilding the bow, and making all deck fittings retractable.
US Navy

USS *Caiman* (SS 323), *Balao* class, off Mare Island on 25 September 1951, was a standard 'Guppy', with a streamlined fairwater and bow. The small dome enclosed an active high-frequency BQS-2 sonar; note the unpainted 'window' covering most of its surface. Abaft it, and unenclosed, was a passive BQR-3, a modernised version of the wartime JT. Such a submarine would also have a chin sonar dome enclosing a longer-range passive sonar (BQR-2) and a bottom dome for a second active sonar (BQS-2). Although the 'Guppies' were attack (ie anti-ship) submarines, they were designed for later conversion to the SSK (ASW) role.
US Navy

conversion was more drastic. Eight welded 'T' class boats were streamlined, fitted with snorts, and lengthened by 14ft 6in (16ft 6in in two), so that additional motors could be added on each shaft without any sacrifice in diesel (ie battery-charging) power. A fourth

SUBMARINE DESIGN AND DEVELOPMENT

'Guppy' conversion was relatively expensive, and 19 fleet submarines were subject to a simpler modernisation as 'fleet snorkels': their deck guns were removed and their bridges streamlined at the same time. The conversion was arranged so as to facilitate later reconstruction as 'Guppies', but no boats were so converted. This is USS *Charr* (SS 328, *Balao* class) off Mare Island in November 1951, following her conversion.
US Navy

battery section was also added; underwater speed was approximately doubled, to 15 knots. They were, then, rough equivalents (albeit much smaller) of the US 'Guppies'. At the same time, the Royal Navy streamlined the riveted 'T', replacing the original batteries with new higher-capacity ones, but without adding underwater power. Here the primary motive was to reduce cavitation noise by reducing underwater resistance, ie propeller loading. Trials in October 1952 showed an increase of 1.4 knots underwater. In both cases, streamlining entailed removal of the usual British external torpedo tubes, so that four forward and two after tubes remained. Twelve 'S' class submarines received an even more austere conversion, with snorkels (snorts), and improved radar and sonar (asdic). Most had their 4in guns removed as a rudimentary form of streamlining. The other major surviving wartime class, the large 'A', was also rebuilt. It was long enough to fit enlarged batteries, and reportedly the original electric motors were not replaced. Like the fast 'T', the rebuilt 'A' had an underwater speed of 15 knots, and a much-reduced torpedo battery of six tubes.

REVISION OF ASW

The new generation of submarines called forth a new kind of ASW. Wartime evaluations were optimistic, on the theory that high speed equalled radiated noise and thus long passive detection ranges. In fact, as noted, Type XXI was extremely quiet even at

Many existing 'Guppies' were refitted in the early 1960s; USS *Pickerel* (SS 524) is shown off Hawaii on 17 January 1963. Under the FRAM Program, she was converted to 'Guppy III' configuration, which included the capability to fire the wire-guided Mk 45 nuclear torpedo. That in turn entailed lengthening her by 10ft, so that a plotting room could be added. The three large sonar domes atop her casing were parts of the PUFFS (BQG-4) passive ranging system, and her new plastic sail raised her bridge (for better seakeeping) and also reduced underwater resistance. Although only 9 'Guppies' underwent the full conversion, many US and allied submarines were fitted with new sails and, in many American boats, PUFFS gear.
US Navy

THE FAST SUBMARINE

high speed. The combination of fast submarine and long-range torpedo seemed to restore to the submarine much of its World War I advantage: once more, it could not really be detected by surface ships, let alone attacked. Radical new strategies seemed to be in order. In fact they bore a strong resemblance to the pre-convoy ideas of 1914–18: direct attacks on enemy submarine bases, barriers (largely of mines and submarines in forward areas). For example, the US Navy characterised the proposed aircraft carrier *United States* as an anti-submarine weapon, her heavy bombers necessary to deal with submarine pens.

Submarine v submarine ASW development was practicable because it was discovered that snorkelling submarines could be detected, and therefore engaged, at very long ranges. From a strategic point of view, it could be expected that submarines would snorkel to make good their passage to operational areas, where they might trade that mobility for silence and safety. Only submarines could come close enough to enemy bases to catch such transitting boats; farther out, they would have too much ocean to cover.

'BOTTOM-BOUNCE' AND 'CONVERGENCE ZONE' SONAR PHENOMENA

It appears that scientists at Woods Hole Oceanographic Institution Laboratory on the US East Coast were responsible for the initial concept of very long listening ranges. They were the first to predict the bottom-bounce and convergence-zone phenomena, although the later would not be named as such for some years. In August 1947 the submarine USS *Quillback*, balanced dead in the water in a density layer about 400 miles west of Bermuda, with a hydrophone suspended on a cable to a depth of about 300ft. She was able to detect the destroyer *Witek*, dropping sound bombs at the convergence zone ('sound peak') ranges of 35, 70, 105, and 140 miles. In further trials in September, the fleet submarine *Sennet* employed two remote hydrophones, one 100ft above, and one 200ft below her. She was able to identify *Witek*, making 30 knots, out to 70 miles and then 105 miles. Even in Sea State 5 (rather rough) she was able to detect the destroyer at first convergence zone.

Woods Hole concluded that the existing maximum listening range of 30,000–40,000 yards (14–20 miles) might be doubled in practice. It found that sound absorption at low frequencies was far less than had previously been believed, that sound would bounce off the bottom out to about 60,000 yards (30 miles), and that it would focus near the surface at 70,000 yards (35 miles), so that a target should be continuously tracked out as far as the first convergence zone, given sufficient ocean depth (about 2200 fathoms or 13,200ft) for sound rays to descend and then be refracted back up. The only limits on performance against a loud target, then, would be background noise (in both the sea and the submarine) and the sensitivity of the listening gear.

Later experiments were directed specifically towards developing a submarine ASW capability; in 1949 the Chief of Naval Operations ordered that one submarine division in each Fleet have the sole task of solving the submarine versus submarine ASW problem, as Project KAYO. The first and most significant unit of this type, Submarine Development Group Two, was commissioned into the Atlantic Fleet in May 1949, with two 'Guppies' and two World War II-type fleet submarines. It carried out its first submarine v submarine exercises in the Norwegian and Barents Seas in July 1949.

By this time Submarine Squadron 6 at Guantanamo (Cuba) and Panama had detected snorkelling targets at up to 24,000 yards, holding them to 37,000; and echo ranging (active sonar) was limited to 8700 yards. Subrons 3 and 7 at San Diego were able to detect a 10-knot snorkeller at 21,600 yards. These were what would later be called direct-path ranges. Much more could be achieved under bottom-bounce/convergence zone conditions. For example, the *Sea Dog* was able to detect the submarine *Diodon* at the first convergence zone (70,000 yards), even without a very powerful passive sonar.

These results were all achieved under unusually good conditions. The wartime JT line-array hydrophone aboard fleet submarines could be expected to detect the standard threat, a cavitating, snorkelling, 8-knot submarine transitting with occasional zigzags, at 4000–7000 yards. Such short ranges were partly the result of the noisiness of a fleet submarine, which was covered in external wires and other protuberances. Thus, rigged for ultra-quiet operation, with all motors and other equipment such as ventilation blowers and air-conditioning compressors shut down, a fleet submarine could expect to detect a snorkeller at 12,000 yards. The new BQR-2 sonar, which appeared aboard the new fleet submarines and the new ASW boats, could extend this to a reliable 20,000 yards, almost 10 miles.

US ASW SUBMARINE FLEET PLANS

The Fiscal Year 1948 Program included a specialised anti-submarine submarine (SSK), to lie in wait on enemy transit routes, listening for snorkellers and for surface transits. In each case the target's diesels were expected to give it away. The 1947 tests showed that the key to long-range performance was careful silencing. *Quillback*, for example, was able to shut down her motors, relying on the density layer to keep her at the desired depth. Without it, she would have needed some ahead speed to maintain depth. Given effective passive sonar, a specialised American ASW submarine would be able to detect, and thus to ambush, Soviet submarines leaving their ports, when they would be at their noisiest, snorkelling at high speed to make good the long distance. The new technology of acoustic torpedoes would provide the weapon. At this time it was assumed that a submarine would have to snorkel virtually continuously to make good any considerable distance as it sailed towards its patrol area.

This was a modern equivalent of the British 1914–18 submarine strategy, with visual detection of surfaced submarines replaced by passive detection of snorkellers, at a much greater range. Even so, it was clear from the first that very large numbers of such ASW submarines would be needed. In 1948 American ASW planners expected a short-term Soviet fleet of 356 modern submarines, and a long-term threat of 2000. On these figures they were able to calculate production requirements for the ASW submarine; three boats were needed to keep one on station in the forward areas. They would operate near Soviet bases, and also in barrier formations in the open sea. Others, whose numbers were not calculated, might form barriers around convoy routes, or work with hunter-killer teams. Two different strategies are evident. Against the immediate 356-submarine threat, the ASW submarines would operate well inshore, near the Soviet bases:

	On Station	Total
North Cape-Cherry Island -Spitzbergen (Norway)	56	168
Petropavlovsk (Kamchatka, Far East)	6	18
North End Sakhalin (Sea of Okhotsk)	6	18
La Perouse Strait (Japan/Sakhalin)	7	21
Tsugaru Strait (Hokkaido/Honshu)	2	6
Training		19
Total	77	250

Against the longer-term threat, however, they would form barriers much farther out to sea. The reasoning is not clear; it may have been assumed that Soviet ASW would be much more effective by the time the 2000-boat fleet materialised, perhaps about 1960. Presumably the numbers were all predicated on an assumed 20,000-yard range against a snorkeller:

Greenland-Iceland-Scotland	124	372
NE Coast Kamchatka	10	30
Wales-Spain	86	258
Petropavlovsk	6	18
Kurile Islands	30	90
Tsugaru	2	6
Kyushu-China	42	126
Training		70
Total	210	970

Note the need to seal the southern exit of the English Channel in the 2000-submarine case. Presumably it was expected that minefields in the Baltic would seal in the entire Baltic Fleet in either case. By this time a snorkelling submarine had been detected out to first convergence zone, 35 miles, and there were claims that 'any submarine which exceeds cavitation speed becomes noisy and would be

SUBMARINE DESIGN AND DEVELOPMENT

detected. They give up quiet operations when they exceed 6 knots...'

Modern sonars are much more effective, as is indicated by the shrinkage in barrier requirements. Although the present numerical breakdown of US submarine deployment is classified, clearly the number required to fill the Greenland-Iceland-United Kingdom Gap barrier cannot much exceed 10. There are only about 90 attack submarines altogether, some of which are rated as 'second line' and thus probably excluded from so demanding an assignment. Each carrier battle group is to have one or two, which suggests a total of about 10 submarines so occupied in peacetime at any one time (or 30 so dedicated, given the usual ratio); others would surely be assigned to convoys, to the Pacific, even to SSBN escort duty. In that case the ratio of early ASW submarines to current-type attack submarines is probably about 10:1, for the same barrier. That is probably not far from the ratio of sonar ranges, which suggests that current boats expect to detect targets at about two to three convergence zones (say up to 210,000 yards or 103 miles), although attacks will occur at much shorter ranges. Another way to look at these figures is to suggest that any very severe reduction in US passive sonar range would effectively destroy the barrier strategy, since impossible numbers would be required.

In 1948 the proposed solution was a boat so simple that it could be mass produced, even by builders not familiar with submarine practice in wartime. It was not a fast submarine, but it is included here because it was directly inspired by the advent of the Type XXI. The major simplification was to trade submarine performance (hence size) for *torpedo* performance. Much slower than attack submarines, at 8.5 knots submerged (one-hour rate; 6 knots when snorkelling), the very quiet SSK would not have to close its targets. Instead, it would detect them passively at 20,000 yards or more, and attack with fast homing torpedoes.

The design was adapted to mass production and operation in several ways. First, it was limited to a diving depth of 400ft, whereas the new attack submarines were intended for 700ft. Given its low submerged speed, there was no need to be able to rig in the bow planes. The carefully silenced diesel engine was 'packaged' for unit replacement at a forward base, and the engine room was to be unmanned, to reduce crew size. A con-

The threat posed by Type XXI-type submarines was so severe that it prompted the US Navy to seek radical solutions: the ASW submarine, or SSK, was one of them. SSKs would have been required in enormous numbers, and two alternatives were tried: a very small submarine well suited to mass production, and an SSK conversion of an existing fleet submarine. This is the mass production type, *K-3*, off Mare Island on her completion day (11 February 1952). Her most important feature was the big BQR-4 passive sonar in her bows; the small object atop it was BQS-3, a powerful 'single-ping' active sonar. The three K-boats proved too small for operations in their prospective wartime patrol areas. Even so, in 1955-57 the US Navy tried to design a small nuclear SSK, which became the *Tullibee*.
US Navy

THE FAST SUBMARINE

temporary Navy account suggests that silencing was expected to be easier for a small, low-powered diesel; the original design showed a single screw.

The SSK did follow attack submarine design standards in having no conning tower in its sail; instead a command and intelligence centre was combined with the control room. It also resembled the larger submarines in having a passive sonar in a chin position. Mission requirements included provision for underwater anchoring on a picket station and paired fathometers, one on the keel and one atop the hull, tiltable for under-ice operation.

As in many other warship designs, size kept creeping upward. In the case of the SSK, the original 480-ton hull could take enough batteries to allow for sufficient loiter time. It turned out that even passive electronic equipment was a sufficient drain on battery charge to require much more capacity, and by the time the SSK was ordered it had grown to 750 tons, with two propellers in place of the original one, and four rather than two torpedo tubes. It was also limited to production by specialised yards.

NEW US SUBMARINE SONAR

On the other hand, the Woods Hole theories made it clear that a large low-frequency passive sonar would greatly extend listening range. This was BQR-4, an Americanised German World War II GHG, 20ft×10ft× 10ft, with sufficient bearing discrimination to permit the submarine to close a target. Design sketches show it wrapped around the SSK sail, but it was actually installed in the bow, presumably to isolate it better from engine and propeller noise. This installation was typical of later American ASW submarine practice. The higher-frequency BQR-2 (the sole sonar of the original design, adapted from the German 'Balkon') was a 3ft high circular array of vertical line hydrophones, 5ft in diameter, in a keel dome. With a claimed bearing accuracy of $\frac{1}{10}$ of a degree, it would be used for fire control (attack). A hydrophone could be suspended clear of the hull for very long range (but non-directional) listening, and there was also a modified World War II JT passive sonar (BQR-3) intended as a back-up for the newer sets. Although space and weight were reserved for the possible installation of an active sonar, none was ever fitted.

Performance was spectacular: off Bermuda in 1952, the prototype, *K-1*, detected a snorkeller at 30 miles, and tracked it for 5 hours. Even so, no mass production was ordered. Instead, interest focussed on the large number of existing fleet submarines. An SSK conversion was developed and carried out in small numbers, but the 'Guppy' and fleet snorkel conversions were designed so that they could later be modified to SSK configuration. The BQR-4 array in the bow generally displaced two of the six forward torpedo tubes. Although ultra-quiet operation had originally been needed, the Bureau of Ships was able to modify these submarines to the point where they could listen while running equipment such as air conditioners, which, according an official account of the period, 'improved habitability and also reduced electronic maintenance problems'.

US 1950s 'HUNTER KILLER' TACTICS

A Submarine Development Group Two officer described typical ASW operations at the 1952 Undersea Warfare Symposium. Each submarine on war patrol would occupy a single patrol area, which would be closed to air and surface forces: IFF was very much an unsolved problem. If the submarine were to remain continuously submerged, conventional navigation would be impossible, and some novel ideas were being investigated such as RAPOS (2 position sound navigation) and gravimetric navigation. RAPOS used small charges detonated in the deep sound channel on a carefully timed schedule; accuracy per reception was expected to be at least 5 miles. A receiving hydrophone would be dangled 4000ft down, and hydrophones on the hull itself would also be used. As of 1952 signals could be received at a range of 950 miles in the Atlantic, and this was expected to double. Gravimetric navigation did not require any external assistance, but it was credited with a 12-mile error, given a two-day survey carried out by the submarine itself when it entered the patrol area.

Several passive sonars were available. The wartime JT, mounted above the hull, was still good only for an average of 8000 yards, but a similar sensor *below* the hull was good for at least 12,000 yards, and for 40,000 yards (almost 20 miles) under ideal conditions. The massive BQR-4 was expected to detect

Grouper (SSK 214) was representative of 7 US fleet submarines converted to the SSK role. Her BQR-4 sonar was wrapped around the front of her bridge fairwater: although at first glance she appears to be a conventional 'Guppy', the men on her bridge are some distance away from its front edge and that, unlike a 'Guppy', it carries no windows on its upper level.
US Navy

SUBMARINE DESIGN AND DEVELOPMENT

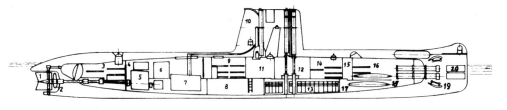

1 RUDDER
2 PROPELLER
3 CREW QUARTERS
4 MACHINERY SPACE
5 ELECTRIC PROPULSION MOTOR
6 SWITCHBOARD
7 DIESEL GENERATOR SET
8 AUX. MACHINERY SPACE
9 CREW QUARTERS
10 BRIDGE FIN
11 CONTROL ROOM
12 C.I.C.
13 BATTERY ROOM
14 OFFICERS' QUARTERS
15 TOILET
16 CREW QUARTERS
17 SPACE TORPEDO STOWAGE SPACE
18 TORPEDO ROOM
19 BOW PLANES
20 TORPEDO TUBE DOORS

French *Aréthuse* class elevation.
courtesy of IKL and Prof Gabler

surfaced submarines at 10-50 miles, and snorkellers at 20-50 miles. It could hold contact at a submarine speed of 4 knots, and often at speeds as great as 9 knots. The smaller (higher frequency) JT could be used at shorter range for fire control; typical practice at this time was to use JX, an improved JT mounted fore and aft, to triangulate, using the ship's length as a base line. Good ranges could be obtained at 2500 yards, 30 degrees on the beam, and at 5000 yards when abeam.

Straight-running steam torpedoes were to be used against surfaced or snorkelling submarines. Hits would probably be limited to 35 per cent of torpedoes fired, since they could be heard and evaded at 2000 yards. Homing torpedoes were expected to be better. It was predicted that the war-developed US Mk 28 would make 60 per cent hits on a target making 8-15 knots. Submarine v submarine exercises had already taught US submariners to snorkel only intermittently. Typically they charged batteries for less than an hour at a time; they expected to be able to hear another submarine far enough away before beginning to snorkel to be able to react in time. But many of these assumptions broke down if the approaching submarine was quiet and deep.

A February 1954 exercise SW of Iceland illustrates SSK tactics and performance. The new *K-1* operated against the converted fleet submarine *Cavalla*, for a total of 36 runs. *K-1* achieved an average detection range of 28 miles (11 runs); *Cavalla* was limited to an average of 13 miles (25 runs). In 26 cases one submarine or the other was able to get into attack position, and 21 attacks were judged successful. By this time the big BQR-4 was being used for attack as well as search and track; it was credited with half-degree accuracy at firing range. *K-1* used the new technique of estimating range by plotting target motion as she manoeuvred, but she was limited by errors due to an insufficiently stable gyro: she could not adequately measure her own motion.

One run began at a range of 60 miles, the target submarine running for two hours on batteries at noncavitating speed (4.5 knots), alternating with one hour snorkelling at 6 knots, while zigzagging (short legs superimposed on longer ones to make target motion analysis difficult). She was essentially undetectable while on batteries. Even so, contact was made at 38 miles, and 6 hours 35 minutes later the ambushing submarine was in attack position, 1200 yards off the target's beam. This remarkable performance was attributed to the effectiveness of the self-noise reduction programme and to the range of the BQR-4 array sonar, about ten times that of the wartime JT.

The SSK's great defect was its limited speed: it could detect a target much farther away than it could attack. Several solutions were tried. The SSK could relay data to a destroyer by underwater telephone, which had a range of 8-11 miles but also disclosed the submarine's position. Alternatively it could vector in a carrier- or land-based attack airplane. Patrol plane-SSK operations were quite common in the 1950s. Reportedly the Atlantic Fleet war plan included an SSK-air barrier off Argentia (Newfoundland), barring Soviet submarines from the US East Coast, as late as 1962. This concept survives in some forms of 'direct support' of battle groups. Finally, the submarine itself could be provided with a much longer-range weapon, which became Subroc, the underwater-launched ballistic ASW missile, with a nuclear depth bomb warhead. Subroc was generally employed in combination with a more effective sonar, the spherical BQQ-2, in nuclear submarines, but it was conceived in the SSK era.

Although all of the other NATO navies emphasised ASW, only one of them, the French, built specialised submarines for the purpose. The four *Arethuse* class were intended for basing at Mers-el-Kebir in Algeria, to intercept submarines which might have attacked Mediterranean traffic. NATO exercised a considerable degree of integration at the time of their design (1951), and they were presumably expected to cooperate with an ASW barrier across the Straits of Gibraltar. They were hunters, not pickets like the American SSK, with a high underwater speed (15 knots). As hunters, too, they needed (and had) no stern tubes; the stern tubes of postwar attack submarines were *aids to post-attack escape*, not ASW weapons.

The Royal Navy also planned an SSK, the '1953 Submarine', a small single-screw streamlined boat with a relatively small crew. It was not built, largely because a financially strapped Royal Navy could not afford to develop both a general purpose (*Porpoise/Oberon*) *and* a specialised mass-production submarine. Details have not yet been released.

CHAPTER FIVE

Postwar Development in the West

For the Western navies, World War II changed both the technology and the rationale of submarine operations. Just as the new German designs changed the entire concept of the submarine, so the need for classic submarine forces appeared to decline. Unlike the Axis powers against whom prewar Western submarine fleets had been planned and built, the Soviets had no substantial merchant fleet. They did have a surface fleet, but it was largely limited to operations in home waters. It appeared to many in the US Navy that future naval operations would be limited to attacks on land targets (eg by carrier task forces) and protecting shipping against a possible Soviet naval offensive. Moreover, funds for new construction and even to maintain the Fleet were scarce, so the Navy's different elements found themselves in hot competition.

This image of future sea power was by no means a universal one. Wartime experience of convoy operations in the face of powerful surface warships appears to have convinced the Royal Navy that modern Soviet cruisers were a very real threat, sufficient to justify a wide range of postwar naval projects, such as the rapid-fire destroyer and the tactical nuclear (anti-ship) carrier bomber, The British did not follow American attempts to develop specialised ASW submarines during the first postwar decade though by 1950 they did consider ASW the primary role of all their general-purpose boats.

As the wealthiest of the Western Navies, the US Navy was able to develop a wide variety of submarine technologies and types after 1945. Most other navies had to limit themselves to general-purpose attack submarines, and only Britain and France were able to afford nuclear power. The Netherlands sought American nuclear assistance, and was refused; which is why the second pair of diesel-electric *Dolfijn*s lagged behind the first by eight years (1954–62). Thus the account which follows emphasises US developments. Note that, soon after it succeeded in developing nuclear submarines the US Navy made a conscious decision to abandon all construction of non-nuclear types. That left the field for advances in such craft open to the smaller navies, particularly, in the 1960s and 1970s, Sweden and West Germany. France, Italy, Japan, and the Netherlands also developed domestic diesel submarine designs, but on the whole they have been less innovative.

The US Submarine Force followed two parallel paths. It developed the new technology in a series of conversions and new classes, such as the 'Guppies' and *Tang*s described in the previous chapter. To some extent they could be justified as a means of anticipating probable Soviet developments, and thus as a vital development tool for ASW, but they were also a hedge against some change in the naval environment which would again demand new submarine construction.

At the same time the submariners explored a range of new missions: direct (radar picket) support of fast carrier task forces; transport (for covert amphibious operations); ASW (including both pickets and tankers for their support); and shore bombardment with the new long-range missiles.

US RADAR PICKETS

The picket idea originated in 1945, as US surface radar pickets suffered heavily off Okinawa from Japanese suicide and conventional air raids: a submarine might be able to detect attackers at long range, yet submerge as they approached to avoid destruction. The original picket (SSR) programme, Project Migraine, called for the conversion of 24 fleet submarines to operate their SV air search radars at periscope depth. At the war's end four had been completed,

The world's first nuclear-powered warship, USS *Nautilus* (SSN 571), heralded the second postwar submarine revolution – atomic power. Her 3533/4092-ton, 323ft hull undergoes initial sea trials in May 1955. She became a museum boat in 1982.
US Navy

71

SUBMARINE DESIGN AND DEVELOPMENT

In 1945 the US Navy began to experiment with radar picket submarines. Unlike destroyer pickets, they could submerge so as to avoid destruction by Kamikaze. This is *Spinax* (SSR 489), second of 10 conversions (1946–53), with a big SR-2 air search radar mounted on her fairwater. The two antennae aft are a YE beacon for fighter control, and a height-finder, SV-2. The submarine picket programme ended in 1959, as reliance shifted to carrier-based pickets. Note the snorkel forward of the radar mast.
US Navy

and two more were in various stages of conversion. They would have been limited by the absence of any means of altitude estimation, required for fighter control.

Early warning was clearly so important that Project Migraine continued postwar, first with much more elaborate fleet boat conversions (including lengthening to fit fighter direction centres), and then with specialised designs. By 1950, the notional future carrier task force included at least one radar picket submarine capable of steaming with it. But then the entire submarine picket concept was dropped about a decade later as all-weather carrier early warning aircraft, such as the current E-2C Hawkeye, took over.

The picket (SSR) was in effect a throwback to submersible concepts, in that the boat was expected to spend most of its time surfaced at high speed, submerging only intermittently. Thus the early 1950s *Sailfish* design was based on the earlier fleet submarine, modified to provide enough space for a command intelligence centre and for the radars themselves. She was expected to operate awash, with her radars high enough above the surface to be effective. However, even postwar diesels could not suffice to achieve anything resembling task force speeds, and there were several projects for alternative SSR powerplants. One of them became the pressure-fired steam engine, which was actually used in two classes of ocean escort (surface) ships. The radar picket *Triton* was the only American nuclear submarine designed to achieve higher speeds on the surface than submerged, again in order to operate with the carriers.

DIRECT SUPPORT OF SURFACE FORCES

Task force support remained an important issue even after the pickets' demise; it merely shifted from anti-air to anti-submarine sensing, using the acoustic advantage inherent in a submerged submarine sonar. Such employment was inconceivable before the advent of nuclear submarines. Yet, as early as 1952, a US study of the relative merits of nuclear and closed-cycle powerplants pointed out that a fast nuclear submarine could supplement or supplant task force ASW escorts. It would, for example, be much faster in rough weather, and it already appeared that its sonar would outperform those in surface ships. By the late 1960s the Royal Navy saw the submarine as a manned equivalent of the variable depth sonar then in vogue. HMS *Dreadnought* was so employed, in what was probably the first example of the current 'direct (ASW) support' mission. Her great defect was her limited ability to communicate with the surface craft which would have to act on her information. The solution at the time was to station a surface ship near her, within underwater telephone range.

By the 1960s the Soviets had numbers of nuclear attack submarines fast enough to engage carrier task forces, and, as in the years immediately after 1945, new ideas were being developed to deal with them. Direct support, discussed on and off for years, finally became an operational technique. Modern direct support operations apparently began in the US Sixth Fleet, cursed with particularly poor acoustic conditions in the Mediterranean, during the late 1960s. At about the same time a new very fast nuclear submarine, which became the *Los Angeles*, was designed specifically for the carrier battle group escort role. A fast submarine in the van of a carrier battle group can, at least in theory, detect waiting submarines over a long range. It can either engage them directly or, perhaps more efficiently, it can vector in ship-based aircraft or long-range patrol aircraft also operating in direct support. The major design require-

POSTWAR DEVELOPMENT IN THE WEST

ment is high speed coupled with very long-range sonar. Although the United States achieved the former in the *Skipjack* design of 1956, the latter required a high degree of silencing as well as a massive bow sonar. The *Thresher* and her immediate successors introduced the latter, but as a result they were much larger than *Skipjack* – and therefore somewhat slower, since they used essentially the same powerplant. It therefore took a considerable leap in horsepower, achieved in the current *Los Angeles*, to redress the balance, ie to achieve *Skipjack* (or better) speed coupled with true long-range sonar performance.

All direct support missions require a high degree of co-ordination between submarine and surface fleet. The lack of reliable and continuous two-way communication makes this difficult. Totally pre-planned operations get round the problem. That is, a submarine with an effective inertial navigational system can follow a pre-arranged fleet course accurately enough not to be mistaken for an interloper. It can come to periscope depth at fixed intervals to receive messages of formation course changes and other information. A recent unclassified article mentions SOSUS-aided carrier battle group screening, which implies regular reception of submarine intelligence information from shore stations. Such communication intervals are likely to be relatively infrequent, since, even it does not transmit, the submarine exposes itself to a greater risk of detection each time it comes to periscope depth. At high speed its propeller cavitates there; it is much quieter at great depths.

Surface and air forces may wish to communicate with the submarine at unplanned intervals, eg to transmit emergency course changes. A variety of more or less unsatisfactory solutions have been proposed. Loud underwater signals or ELF radio messages can act as 'bell-ringers' to bring the submarine to periscope depth for radio reception. Proponents of the blue-green laser claim that aircraft will soon be able to transmit messages to submarines at depths as great as 400ft.

The submarine is effective in direct support only so long as it can communicate back to the surface force. That is much more

The SSK idea survived into the nuclear era, and Admiral Rickover's reactor group tried to design an atomic powerplant small enough for a mass-produced SSKN. They were only partially successful, and the 1960 prototype, USS *Tullibee* (SSN 597) grew too large (2316/2607 tons, 272ft). She was never copied. The US Navy's 14th operational nuclear submarine is shown on 3 October 1960 during initial builder's trials in Long Island Sound before formal completion. She had PUFFS sonar domes fore and aft. She introduced bow spherical sonar and amidships torpedo tubes (4 × 21in) into US service and was the last American attack submarine with a deck casing.
US Navy

SUBMARINE DESIGN AND DEVELOPMENT

difficult. To transmit radio messages it has to pierce the surface with an antenna, and the resulting signals are subject to direction-finding. The alternative is a buoy floated to the surface with a pre-taped message inside. Again, there is a risk of detection, and again there is an uncomfortable rigidity to the procedure: the absence of two-way communication within a single tactical force (a battle group) is difficult to accept.

One result of communication limitation is that the 'direct support' submarine typically steams so far ahead of the force that it can afford to wait to be apprised of tactical shifts. This distance depends on force speed and on communication frequency. However, it must be considerable. If the submarine communicates every two hours, then an interval of 60-70 miles (two convergence zones) might be necessary, and then the submarine might be unable to keep up with really radical course changes. In any case, there will be a substantial gap in sonar coverage through which an approaching enemy submarine may slip. In consequence, the ideal form of direct support is a multi-submarine formation, presenting so wide a front that nothing would be able to slip through. That in turn would seem to require efficient submarine-to-submarine communication.

The natural solution, an acoustic link with surface ships (which would also make inter-submarine co-ordination much easier), is generally rejected because its operation gives away the position of an otherwise very quiet boat. Nor are ranges very great. Declassified accounts of the American UQC underwater telephone (not considered secure in any sense) generally quote ranges of 5-15 nautical miles. A long history of failures to develop anything better, either in range or in security, testifies to the difficulty of the problem.

Submarine transport had a varied wartime history. For the United States, it was a means of landing small raiding parties for reconnaissance, often just prior to a major attack, as in Makin and the Aleutians. The Japanese went so far as design their own submarine transports (see Chapter 3). Some in the US Marine Corps suggested that larger submarine transports might have averted a number of wartime amphibious disasters, by increasing the element of tactical surprise. Indeed, the Dutch triple-hull submarine design concept was very well received on this basis in Washington in 1947. But there was never enough money for specially-built submarine transports so all of those used by the US Navy were conversions of existing hulls. The cruise missile submarines, designed with large hangars, were particularly well suited to this task.

US ASW SUBMARINES

The last two new missions took over the US submarine force. ASW was the major theme of American naval development during the first postwar decade. The three specialist 'K' class were built and several war-built fleet submarines converted, all entering service in the early to mid-1950s. A few years later the first nuclear submarines entered service. Experience in the 'K' design showed clearly that dependence on batteries for extended picket service was a design problem. Moreover, the small hull (adopted to make mass production practical) could not cope with rough Northern seas, where the 'K' would have to operate in wartime. A small nuclear SSKN, which became *Tullibee*, was designed and built. Like the SSKs, she was designed around a long-range passive sonar; she was the first really quiet nuclear submarine.

By the late 1950s, it was clear that the United States could not afford to build expensive nuclear attack and ASW submarines, so the *Thresher* design, in effect the direct ancestor of all modern US attack submarines, was biased heavily towards the classic ASW requirements of very long range sonar and very quiet operation. Later Admiral Hyman G Rickover tried to revive the distinction between the fast attack submarine and the slower, but much quieter, barrier submarine, proposing that the United States build two parallel classes: the *Los Angeles* for attack and some development of the *Glenard P Lipscomb* or *Narwhal* for the barrier mission. Economics made this impossible. This time the decision went against the specialist barrier submarine, because the present numerous and faster *Los Angeles* could carry out a new ASW mission, the direct support of fast carrier groups. At the same time she was quiet enough for barrier work. It is sometimes suggested that *Los Angeles* was the result of substantial

The post-1945 search for submarine roles led the US Navy to develop submarine-launched strategic weapons, in direct competition with carrier strike bombers. Here USS *Halibut* (SSGN 587) launches a Regulus I in the Pacific on 28 February 1961, with the then-attack carrier *Lexington* in the background. Major operational defects of the Regulus system were that it could be fired only on the surface, after the missile had been assembled, and that the submarine could not survive the flooding of the large missile hangar, eg in heavy seas.
US Navy

POSTWAR DEVELOPMENT IN THE WEST

At her commissioning on 7 March 1958, the Regulus submarine USS *Grayback* (SSG 574) illustrates elements of the Regulus weapon system: the missile on its launcher, the massive hangars forward (for 4 missiles), and the shrouded missile guidance radar, which was used to issue steering commands to the weapon. The shrouded object at the rear of her sail is her snorkel. *Grayback* and the four other Regulus boats carried out Pacific Fleet deterrent patrols until replaced by Polaris in 1964.
US Navy

pressure to match the assessed maximum speed of Soviet nuclear submarines, independent of any submarine role. But American efforts to develop a carrier escort submarine, to restore the speed advantage of the earlier *Skipjack*, considerably predate the 1968 appearance of the first really fast Soviet submarine, the 'Victor'. It seems more likely that the comparative speed issue made *Los Angeles* much more attractive than the quieter *Glenard P Lipscomb*, when production funds were sought from the late 1960s onward.

From time to time the submarine, with its superior sonar performance, was proposed as the primary anti-submarine vehicle. In February 1962 Rear Admiral Ralph K James, then Chief of the Bureau of Ships, suggested that in future surface ASW ships should be confined to shallow waters and protecting convoys threatened by air attack.

It was argued at the time that Admiral James was overemphasising detection, and ignoring limitations on effective submarine attack ranges. Nor was there much hope of an early solution to the communications problem. At this time about two surface escorts could be bought for the price of a single submarine.

US CRUISE MISSILE SUBMARINES

The other major current mission is strategic attack. The Germans experimented with submarine-launched missiles during World War II, and postwar US naval shipbuilding programmes included projects for a German-inspired 'submersible missile barge' by means of which a fleet submarine could tow and then fire a V-2 missile. At the same time, as part of the general search for novel submarine missions, the fleet submarine *Cusk* was modified to carry and fire a Loon (US-built V-1) cruise missile. In principle, the missile-firing submarine was attractive because it could approach an enemy coast by surprise. Although it could not deliver anything like the firepower of a carrier air group, nuclear warheads made total deliverable weight much less important. As conceived before about 1955, then, submarines and nuclear-capable carrier bombers were considered complementary, to move towards enemy coasts just before or during a conflict. Of course they could also be used during escalation, as a deterrent threat. The United States then intended to use nuclear weapons to balance a perceived Soviet superiority in non-nuclear forces.

But, as the Soviets developed their own nuclear weapons, the feeling grew that American nuclear forces were primarily a means of deterrence, ready in peace and capable of rapidly retaliating against any Soviet strike. The later cruise and ballistic missile sytems were designed in this light; submarines would be maintained

75

SUBMARINE DESIGN AND DEVELOPMENT

continuously on patrol in missile-launch areas, ready to attack upon command. They are valued for their survivability: even were the Soviets to destroy the carriers and the weapons based in the United States, they would be unable to avoid retaliation from under the sea. Many would say, in fact, that the deterrence mission is the single most important naval role, either in the surface or in the submarine fleet. It certainly represents a considerable shift in tactical and technical emphasis.

Missile submarine design characteristics are determined, first, by missile characteristics, and second by the paramount need to avoid detection and destruction while on patrol. For example, the Regulus cruise missile, the first US submarine strategic weapon, was quite large in proportion to the submarines carrying it. It required servicing before firing, either on the surface or in a hangar within the pressure hull. In either case the submarine had to surface to fire. The longer it spent on the surface, the more vulnerable it became, so that specially-designed Regulus submarines all had large pressure-proof hangars. They introduced another danger; their volume was so great that, if the hangars flooded while the submarine was surfaced, it would turn turtle or sink. The final Regulus design, (never built) had four separate tubular hangars instead of a single large one for just this reason.

POLARIS

Polaris and its successors were much more attractive. Each missile was enclosed in its own tube (ie in its own hangar) and could be serviced, adjusted, and fired while the submarine was submerged. As originally designed, the Polaris missile had to have its gyro lined up before flight. In the original *George Washington* design, that was accomplished by reference to a master gyro, the position of which was transmitted optically down the row of missiles. Hence there was a fixed requirement for access to windows in each tube, with a clear optical path back to the control room. Adjustment and servicing have become less and less important as missile reliability has increased, to the point where separate encapsulated weapons, linked to the firing submarine only by an umbilical, are suggested from time to time.

Although it could be argued that the submarine itself could be located by its missile trajectories, it was clearly more secure than its surface-launched cruise-missile predecessor. Note that the current US Tomahawk cruise missile, like the ballistic weapons, is fired from a low-volume one-weapon tube, and, at least as importantly, from underwater.

SILENCING

In recent years, then, design emphasis has gone into silencing and other security features. Quieting in particular has gone from relatively simple to extremely elaborate measures, escalating rapidly in cost as the former are exhausted. In the years

The three *Barbel*-class boats (built 1956-59) are the last US diesel submarines. They employ the *Albacore* hull form and although completed with conventional bow planes, were converted SSN-type sail planes, as in this 7 November 1973 photograph of the name boat (SS 580) off Hawaii. Note that, despite her underwater hull form emphasis, she retains a substantial flat-decked casing. Her two periscope and surface-search masts are raised. *US Navy*

POSTWAR DEVELOPMENT IN THE WEST

The diesel-powered experimental 210ft USS *Albacore* (AGSS 569) transformed postwar submarine design when built in 1953. Once the possibility of very high underwater speed (a reported 33 knots in final form) had been demonstrated, the submarine community demanded it in operational craft; the *Skipjack*s were the result. This wind tunnel model clearly shows the relatively fat *Albacore* hull form developed on the basis of airship practice. Note the numerous vents and limber holes and the total absence of bow planes.
US Navy

SUBMARINE DESIGN AND DEVELOPMENT

Although a continuously curved hull form is best, it is almost as efficient to use a cylindrical middle body, which is much easier to build. This is the *Los Angeles* class nuclear attack submarine *Omaha* (SSN 672) launched on 21 February 1976 at Groton, Connecticut. Note her relatively small sail, its size minimised to reduce resistance in a submarine built for very high speed. As a result, the planes cannot be rotated to the vertical position, and thus the *Los Angeles* class cannot break through ice. From units built under the FY83 Program onwards, *Los Angeles* class submarines will have their forward diving planes relocated to their hulls, primarily for under-ice operation. *US Navy*

immediately after 1945 the emphasis was on reducing propeller noises such as cavitation. One might describe three stages, each reducing noise by roughly the same amount: special propellers, then bubble screens (in surface ships) costing perhaps three or four times as much; then pump-jets, which cost about 50 times as much as the bubble screens and add to the vessel's size and complexity. The next noise source was the machinery proper, and modern practice is to isolate it from the hull by mounting it on a suspended raft. That adds considerably to vessel cost, although less so to its size. Such noise isolation requires an extraordinary level of quality control, both in construction and in maintenance, to avoid acoustic 'short circuits' which can transmit internal noises to the hull proper. Since a larger submarine requires less power per ton of displacement, it is easier to maintain a given speed in a larger silenced boat. If acoustic sensors continue to be the primary threat, then, efficiencies of scale favour larger rather than smaller missile submarines. The current *Ohio* class is an application of this idea: it has 24 missile tubes rather than the 16 of earlier types. The latter were already the largest submarines of their day.

Submarine silencing is usually designed to allow the submarine commander to choose between relatively noisy and relatively quiet speed ranges. It has two aspects, propeller noise and machinery noise. Since the former is largely due to cavitation, and since cavitation does not occur below perhaps 150-200ft, a submarine can often move at high speed without regard to it. Machinery noise is a different issue, since some silencing measures may be much more difficult at high power levels. In effect, then, the extent to which a submarine commander is silencing-limited depends upon the sophistication of the passive sonars he faces. This point will be developed further in Chapter 9.

SPEED AND BALLISTIC MISSILE SUBMARINES

Speed is a somewhat controversial virtue in the context of an SSBN. It has three quite separate aspects. First, there is transit speed to the patrol area. The typical submarine patrol lasts 60-70 days, and transit time must be subtracted from effective deterrent coverage. The shorter the range of the weapon, the longer the transit. Depending upon the target coverage desired, a submarine with a 1500-mile missile might well have to occupy stations almost in Soviet territorial waters, and perhaps 3000 miles from US bases. At a quiet speed of (say) 10 knots, that would be 300 hours, or more than 12 days; the submarine would lose almost a third of its patrol time in transit, counting the trips forward and back. American dependence on the bases at Guam (Central Pacific), Holy Loch (Britain) and until recently Rota in Spain is understandable on this basis. The longer the missile range, and the higher the quiet transit speed, the greater the percentage of each patrol that contributes directly to deterrence. Thus forward basing in Europe will no longer be necessary as Poseidon is increasingly replaced by the longer-range Trident missile.

An alternative formulation is that deterrence requires X missiles on station at any one time. Submarine refit schedules as well as submarine speed determine what percentage of the force can be maintained on station, and thus the relation between X and the total number of submarines which must be built.

The second aspect is quiet speed on patrol. A patrol area is probably defined by the requirement that a boat on patrol be able to reach a firing position within some fixed (and relatively short) time. The faster the boat (or the longer the missile range), the larger the potential patrol area for some particular target set. In theory, any enemy seeking to destroy the deterrent force would have to search the entire patrol area, and that force's survivability is often calculated in terms of the sheer area the submarines can occupy.

Then there is maximum quiet speed. If the deterrent submarine is somehow detected, it must be able to escape. The quieter it is on patrol, the better the chance of detecting a searcher or attacker before the latter can detect it (let alone set up a fire control solution) thanks to the enhanced effectiveness of its own passive sonars as much as to its enhanced relative undetectability. Once the missile submarine senses a potentially hostile boat approaching, it has to try to evade. If it can run without increasing the probability of detection, then evasion is likely to be successful. Although it is unlikely that any very large missile submarine will be able to outrun a fast attack type, relatively silent high speed evasion will probably make a considerable difference.

BALLISTIC MISSILE SUBMARINES AND ASW

The political concept of SSBN operation is very important here. Until the mid-1970s, there was an implicit expectation among many Western strategists that any war would escalate extremely rapidly to a general nuclear exchange. SSBNs would have to evade attempts to trail them in peacetime and during periods of prewar tension, but they could expect to fire relatively soon after the outbreak of war. However, at least since about 1975 there has been a growing realisation that a war might well go on for some considerable time before (if ever) it escalated to a general nuclear exchange. SSBN commanders, then, might be permitted to shoot at approaching enemy attack submarines. Although the destruction of anti-SSBN craft could never be a primary consideration, certainly torpedoes *coupled* with high-speed (sprint) evasion would be useful.

In addition, the 1970s limited-war theorists had to contemplate the use of very small numbers of undersea ballistic missiles. It had to be assumed that an enemy would be able to detect such weapons soon after they emerged from the water, and that (at least within a short time) he could attempt to fire long-range nuclear missiles into the submarine operating area so revealed. Such counter-battery fire would be well worthwhile because the submarine would still have most of its offensive weapons on board, after executing its limited strike. The higher the speed with which it might escape the firing zone, the better its chance of survival under such a delayed attack. Alternative solutions included encapsulated floating missiles (not to be fired until well after the submarine had cleared the area) but they were generally rejected because of the paramount need to keep tight control over nuclear weapons.

The *Ohio* design illustrates these points. She has a new reactor, more powerful than those of earlier missile boats, and also much quieter, thanks to its natural circulation design. Clearly there was a trade-off, since, ton for ton, the quieter reactor is considerably less powerful than a pumped one. When the Trident system was first proposed, its submarine carrier was envisaged as an enlargement of the existing Poseidon type, with the same 15,000shp pressurised water reactor, and with speed reduced from about 20-23 knots to 19-20 knots. But by this time a much quieter natural circulation reactor had been developed for the 1966 attack submarine *Narwhal*. It could have been upgraded slightly to make up for increased submarine size with minimum loss of power. However, ultimately the choice was for maximum speed, about 25 knots on 35,000shp. One implicit argument was that, once expensive quieting measures had been adopted, it was much more economical to carry more missiles per submarine. The submarine therefore grew, and that in turn made higher power necessary.

There is, however, a very natural feeling that, somehow, the larger the submarine, the more detectable it is. Obviously the larger hull is a target for active sonar. The central issue, then, is whether passive sonar is so clearly the premier submarine detector that silencing is to take precedence over virtually all other defensive measures. At present the American view seems to be that passive acoustics will dominate for the foreseeable future, and therefore that large size is a reasonable price to pay for much-diminished noise levels.

As with the task force support submarine, communication is a major issue for any strategic submarine. The retaliatory threat is effective only so long as it is credible. Any enemy would seek to attack the system's weak point – the communication link to the submarine. The great problem is that radio waves, except for those of very low frequency, penetrate water so poorly. And the lower the frequency, the shorter the message passable in a given time. Higher frequency links, which are more desirable, require the submarine to trail an antenna at a limited

SUBMARINE DESIGN AND DEVELOPMENT

depth and, perhaps as importantly, at a limited speed. One solution is to use the lowest-frequency signals as 'bell-ringers', then transmit more detailed orders at much higher frequency, accepting the implicit brief exposure.

The current submarine missions have evolved from a series of distinct major post-war hull/machinery developments. First came high underwater speed with conventional propulsion, as in Type XXI; this class of submarines is described in Chapter 4. High burst speed and deep diving enormously complicated the standard ASW problem. For example, a submarine capable of operating at 700ft, as were all the early US postwar attack boats, could often operate under the thermal layer that reflected sonar signals. Even though a snorkeller could generally be reliably detected at about 12,000 yards (due to the noise of collapsing exhaust bubbles; diesel noise itself was often detectable at much longer ranges), that hardly assured a successful attack.

In the early 1950s most surface-launched ASW weapons were still unguided devices with only a small lethal radius (4-40ft) sinking at 8.5-42.5ft/sec. That gave a fast submarine below 600ft a long time to evade. A 1952 study showed kill probabilities for the best existing operational weapons (such as the US Alfa and the British Squid) as 5-40 per cent against a 'Guppy' at 300ft and 15 knots, but only 0-8 per cent against a *Tang* at 600ft and 18 knots, and only 0-1 per cent against an even faster closed-cycle or nuclear submarine, operating at a similar depth and at 23 knots. The much larger Limbo mortar, not yet in service, was credited with about twice the kill probability of Squid in such circumstances.

Torpedoes were also limited, in that a target submarine could detect their propeller noises and evade. The US World War II ASW Mark 24 provided a 70-second warning sufficient to protect an 8-knot submarine. Even postwar torpedoes, such as the Mark 35, were considered so noisy that the new fast submarines could be sure of evading them.

HIGH UNDERWATER SPEED AND THE NUCLEAR SUBMARINE

The next stage was a new powerplant for higher sustained underwater speed. The choice was between a closed-cycle system (SSX) with limited endurance and the much more effective nuclear plant (SSN). In the US case, they were developed together until 1953, when the non-nuclear plants were abandoned because nuclear development was proceeding so well that no inferior hedge was needed.

Both advanced submarines offered enormous advantages over existing craft. In 1952 the comparison in underwater high-speed endurance appeared to be between a 'Guppy' or *Tang* capable of about 15-17 knots for one hour; SSX, capable of 24 knots for 10 hours on its oxidant (either pure oxygen or hydrogen peroxide), and then operating as a snorkel-battery submarine with a somewhat lower endurance than a 'Guppy'; and the full SSN, capable of 23 knots for 25 *days*. It also appeared that the advanced submarines would be no easier to detect than the diesel-electric types except for cavitation at high speed; no one yet suspected that nuclear submarines had major inherent sources of noise. As for cost, exclusive of

HMS *Dreadnought*, Britain's first nuclear submarine, steams to sea for trials, 12 December 1962 off Barrow-in-Furness. Note the distinct break in her casing aft, which is associated with the combination of a US-designed machinery space and a British forward end.
CPL

research and development expenses and nuclear fuel, the SSN was expected to be no more than 20-25 per cent dearer than an equivalent diesel submarine of much lesser capability.

In the important barrier ASW role, higher sustained underwater speed would permit the SSX or SSN to attack a higher proportion of enemy submarines trying to transit. A 1952 analysis showed that each SSN or SSX could kill two to four times as many as a conventional submarine, if the enemy boats had no effective sonar of their own. If they had effective sonars, ie could take evasive action, then the nuclear submarine was clearly superior as it would never have to give away its position by snorkelling. Perhaps more telling was an estimate that no barrier could be effective against a nuclear submarine attempting to penetrate it. That of course assumed that the SSN was inherently quiet, which turned out not to be the case.

The nuclear submarine's very high sustained speed had numerous other consequences. For the first time a submerged submarine could keep up with a task force or convoy, as already noted. In any type of distant operation, such as forward-area ASW, minelaying, or attacks on enemy shipping, this sheer sustained high speed would greatly reduce transit time, particularly important for a US Navy typically operating far from home. That in itself might help make up for the SSN's higher cost. For minelaying, it was estimated that higher transit speed would give an SSN force the effectiveness of a diesel-electric force twice its size. It was already well understood that a very fast submarine would be able to close with a higher percentage of detected surface targets, and would probable be able to evade enemy ASW forces far more effectively.

When it materialised in 1955, the nuclear submarine largely fulfilled these expectations, to the point where it could properly be considered an altogether new type of warship. Anti-submarine warfare would never be the same: a nuclear submarine could sustain 20 knots indefinitely, and avoid making cavitation noise merely by going deep. Snorkel submarines could be controlled, because from time to time they had to show themselves for an extended period. The SSN, however, would never show more than a few feet of periscope or ECM mast, and that for only a few seconds. The elaborate existing mechanism of hunter-killer groups and aircraft dependent on visual or radar contact would fail altogether. Low frequency passive sonars could no longer expect to pick up diesel noises, although perhaps some substitute could be found.

The surface ships would need a new generation of very long range active sonars. Otherwise the submarine would always be able to attack at will and shoot first. It would not even have to avoid attacking the escorts, because it would be able to fight them on even

HMS *Conqueror* (shown in 1978 at Portsmouth) became the first nuclear submarine to torpedo and sink a ship in war when she sank the Argentine cruiser *General Belgrano* off the Falklands on 2 May 1982 after shadowing her for over 30 hours. *Conqueror* is typical of the first generation of British nuclear attack submarines with her high bow planes and a relatively sharply-tapered stern.
L & L van Ginderen

or better terms. The standard search plan for use against a retiring submarine would merely bring the surface escorts back within torpedo range. That appeared to imply that future ASW escorts would have to be faster than nuclear submarines in all sea conditions, or else replaced with ASW submarines. The SSK barrier concept had already been accepted; it appeared to be time to consider submarine escort of convoys and task forces.

The future was so bleak that radical solutions seemed in order. They included very long range sonars such as SQS-23 and SQS-26, and stand-off weapons (DASH and Asroc) to match, with alternative nuclear and conventional warheads. Nuclear depth bombs were particularly attractive because fast submarines could evade even homing torpedoes easily. The 1952 analysis called for attack within seconds of contact, at maximum range. Many years later an ASW officer would comment that real nuclear submarine contacts could always be recognised because they vanished so quickly. They must be attacked at once.

NOISE AND NUCLEAR REACTORS

There was one surprise: nuclear machinery was quite noisy, so that early nuclear submarines could be detected passively at considerable distances, much like snorkellers. Yet the situation was not quiet analogous. A diesel-electric submarine could operate in two very different modes; a quiet mode, on batteries, and a relatively noisy one, snorkelling. Mobility depended on how its commander mixed the two. Nuclear machinery was inherently noisy; even at very low speed reactor coolant circulation pumps and turbo-generators could not be turned off. Turbine reduction gearing added its own noise.

The drawback was a serious one, but once it had been solved nuclear submarines no longer had to trade much of their mobility for silence. They could then more than fulfill the expectations of the 1952 paper.

The advent of nuclear power had one other important consequence. It proved relatively difficult to change a nuclear powerplant's output once parameters had been set. That is, it is conventional in warship design to begin with performance requirements and deduce engine power; engines are considered 'rubber' until the design reaches an advanced stage. Reactors were very different. They were much more difficult than a submarine to design, so they were specified at the outset. Admiral Rickover was well aware of this problem, and initially proposed a range of reactors, suitable for small, medium, and large submarines, and for several different types of surface ships. As reactor design became more complex, he appears to have been unable to carry as many projects simultaneously, preferring to improve a few standard plants.

There were design consequences. For some years the S5W, reportedly of about 15,000shp, was the submarine standard. It was first employed in the *Skipjack* class, which had geared turbines. Much improved silencing without loss of speed was demanded for the follow-on *Thresher*. The designers had several alternatives. They could adapt the inherently quieter turbo-electric drive then being built into the nuclear ASW submarine *Tullibee* (launched 1960), at an enormous cost in weight, complexity and redesign. Instead,

SUBMARINE DESIGN AND DEVELOPMENT

Dutch *Walrus* class elevation, section and plans.
courtesy of Mr P Jalhay (Kon Marine-bureau Maritieme Historie) De Boer Maritiem

they chose to silence the much noisier standard geared plant by careful sound-mounting. That in turn added greatly to powerplant bulk, and hence to hull volume and resistance. In a non-nuclear vessel, the natural counter would have been a compensating increase in engine power. That was impossible with a reactor, at least at the time, and instead the *Thresher* hull was re-designed.

THE HULL REVOLUTION

Just as the first American SSN, *Nautilus*, was nearing completion (1955), a parallel revolution in hull form was proceeding. The fast U-boats had all tended to pitch at high underwater speeds. The 'Guppies' and *Tang*s showed similar defects. Above 8 knots, small changes in pitch angle would grow to the point where control would be lost if the boat were allowed to 'fly'. Yet very high underwater speeds could not be exploited fully unless submarines steered freely, in the vertical as well as in the horizontal planes. The US David Taylor Model Basin (outside Washington) tried to solve the problem in 1948 by testing a series of 'bodies-of-revolution', based in part on airship practice. It appears that the Royal Navy independently developed its own new generation of roughly similar submarine forms at the same time. When the two British hydrogen peroxide propelled submarines were completed, their designer was asked why they did not have *Albacore* hulls. He could only reply that *Albacore* had not existed when they were being planned, but that their hull form was based on the shape of the airship *R101*. Ironically, that in turn was based partly on towing-tank tests of the earliest British (Holland-designed) submarines.

The results were startling. The new hull was dynamically stable at all speeds, yet easy to dive. For a given displacement, it was much shorter than a conventional submarine, hence much more manoeuvrable. Its greater ratio of diameter and length made multi-deck layouts more attractive than before. Submarine length requirements could be translated into deck-area requirements, and in turn could be met within a smaller total volume, ie a lesser displacement for a given set of requirements. That in turn reduced underwater resistance. The new single propeller was far more efficient than conventional twin screws, and the hull form as a whole could be driven faster for a given powerplant, since it had much less surface area for a fixed displacement.

An experimental diesel-electric submarine, the USS *Albacore*, was built specifically to test the new hull form. As first completed in 1953, she could make 26 knots submerged for half an hour, compared with a sustained speed of 23.3 knots for the nuclear prototype *Nautilus*. Equipped with new silver-zinc batteries and propelled by contra-props, she later made 33 knots submerged, which shows the speed potential of her hull form. Perhaps as importantly, she could turn at 3.2 degrees per second, compared to 2.5 degrees per second for the much larger (and much longer) *Nautilus*. Nuclear power and the *Albacore* hull were combined in the *Skipjack* design in 1956; for the first time a submarine could *sustain* task force speeds underwater.

DEEP DIVING AND NEW HULL MATERIALS

A third parallel force was the drive for much deeper diving, pursued for several reasons.

First, a fast submarine could not manoeuvre freely unless it had a 'cushion' of effective diving depth beneath, sufficient to recover from a jammed diving plane. It had to cruise relatively deep (typically at 300-500ft) in the first place to avoid making noise by cavitation. Second, diving depth in itself improved the submarine's chances under ASW attack. All sinking weapons would take longer to reach the boat, as it was steered to evade them. The stronger hull, moreover, would improve resistance to underwater explosions, above collapse depth. A submarine capable of diving deep enough could even exploit the 'deep sound channel', which trapped low-frequency sound over immense distances.

The success of *Nautilus* during the late 1950s led to speculation, much of it in the un-classified US press, that within a decade America would have submarines capable of diving to 4000ft and also of achieving 45 knots submerged. In some cases only slightly less impressive performance was attributed to *Nautilus* herself. It may be that this publicity was partly responsible for the Soviet design project leading to the 'Alfa' class during the late 1960s and 1970s. These boats actually do approach the 1955-56 claims.

The reality was less impressive, but still had a major impact on submarine design. After 1945 the United States developed a series of high-yield steels, HY80, HY100, HY130, and so on, the number always indicating the yield stress in lb/sq in. For the *Tang* design, the mere substitution of what would have been HY75 for conventional high tensile steel would have increased operating depth to 1000ft. *Thresher*, the first US submarine designed to be built of HY80, was reportedly designed to operate at 1300ft.

POSTWAR DEVELOPMENT IN THE WEST

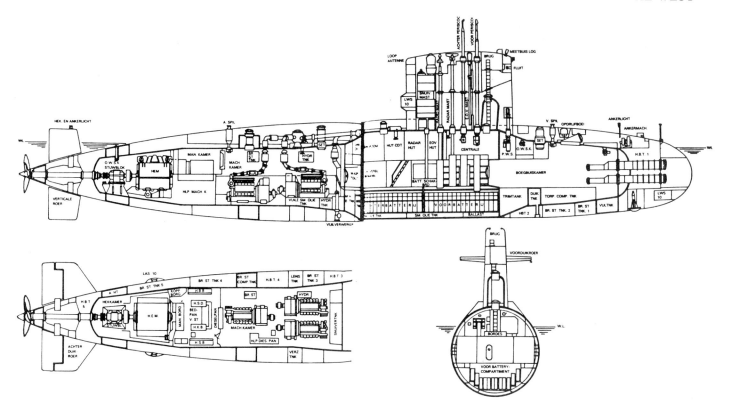

The Dutch *Zwaardvis* (launched 1970) was loosely based on the US *Barbel* except that the American boat had her three diesel generators staggered over two deck heights, to save length. The 219ft *Zwaardvis* displaces 2350 tons surfaced (including 330 tons of fuel oil) and 2640 tons submerged. She carries 18 torpedoes (6 bow tubes) and a crew of 71. The 4200shp electric motor (420 battery cells) drives her at 20 knots submerged, but only at 13 on the surface.
Courtesy of Nevesbu

That required a new generation of designs for auxiliary machinery and hull-penetrating fittings able to resist almost twice the pressure encountered at 700ft. It appears that HY80 fabrication met snags, some suggesting that *Thresher* was lost in 1963 primarily because of the failure of welds. In any case, the US Navy later announced that it intended to build a steel fabrication prototype before taking the next great step, to HY130 steel.

There is another side to the drive for new hull materials. The pressure hull and the powerplant proper are the only major potential sources of weight-saving in a modern nuclear submarine. Displacement and hull surface area are so closely connected for a given hull form that, for a given speed and a given powerplant output, displacement is very nearly fixed. It follows that a very fast submarine may have to sacrifice pressure hull weight for speed, since engine output may not increase fast enough to make up for increased powerplant weight. That is probably one reason the Soviet 'Alfa' requires a lightweight titanium hull. American interest in HY130 steel or titanium may reflect a similar desire to improve either speed or diving depth, or, more likely, both, in new submarines.

US SONAR AND ATTACK BOAT DEVELOPMENT

The other major design force was sonar development. The early passive sonars, composed of vertical line hydrophones, had beams which were steerable only in the plane. They were, therefore, relatively poorly adapted to make full use of bottom-bounce and convergence zone sound propagation, in turn required for reliable very long-range sonar operation. In the mid-1950s the US Naval Underwater Sound Laboratory began to experiment with arrays steerable vertically as well as horizontally, and also with 'spot' hydrophones arranged conformally along a curved submarine hull.

The vertically and horizontally steerable array technology led immediately to proposals for spherical sonars. They in turn would have to be mounted directly in a submarine bow. Their projected performance was so impressive that the submarine community was willing to pay a very high design cost. In order to reduce turbulence noise, and to keep the bow clear, torpedo tubes had to be relocated amidships, angled outwards at ten degrees. Enhanced sonar performance also made silencing much more profitable. Hence the combination of features in *Thresher* and subsequent US attack submarines: very quiet machinery, torpedo tubes amidships, and a big bow sonar for active and passive search and attack (ie fire control). The latter was generally coupled with conformal arrays, for passive search and classification, built into the hull proper. After *Thresher*'s loss this first generation of truly modern US attack submarines is generally referred to as the *Permit* class, after the next boat, SSN 594.

Thresher/Permit thus defined the major lines of subsequent US attack submarine development. For instance, *Los Angeles* is essentially an attempt, within the same overall configuration, to retrieve the speed lost in the transition from *Skipjack* to *Thresher*. In the early 1970s came a much larger fast attack submarine design, called the Advanced High Performance Nuclear Attack Submarine (AHPNAS). It differed from *Los Angeles* mainly in having a much more powerful reactor and vertical launch tubes (for anti-ship cruise missiles) in addition to the usual torpedo tubes. Admiral Elmo R Zumwalt, the then Chief Naval of Operations, killed it off on grounds of excessive cost, but it probably represents the ultimate expression of the design theme begun in the late 1950s with *Thresher* and *Permit*. We still await another radical design stage. Candidates will be explored in the final chapter.

BRITISH DEVELOPMENTS

As for the other Western navies, their priorities and their courses of action differed considerably. The postwar Royal Navy, for example, was not chosen as the bearer of the national nuclear deterrent; that role was reserved to the Royal Air Force. It therefore developed no missile submarines, but it did embrace nuclear power enthusiastically. Early proposals for a gas-cooled reactor system, (analogous to early British nuclear power generating stations ashore) were dropped because a submarine so powered would have been far too large. By 1953 studies were underway on alternative thermal (steam-generating) reactors cooled either by pressurised water or liquid metal, and there was even interest in a larger aircraft carrier plant. As British work proceeded, it became clear that the US Navy was considerably

SUBMARINE DESIGN AND DEVELOPMENT

US *Los Angeles* class (SSN 688) elevation.
Author's drawing

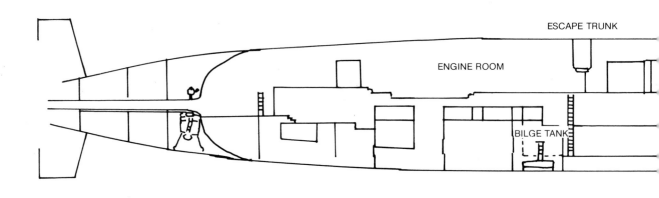

US *Sturgeon* class (SSN 637) elevation.
Author's drawing

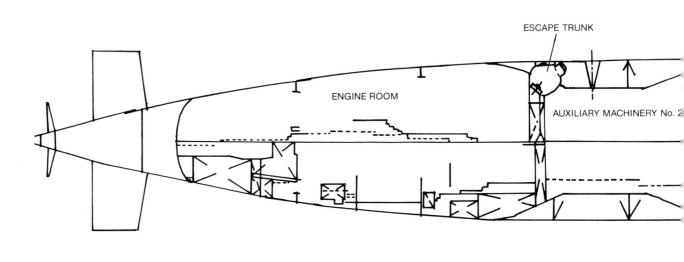

US *Los Angeles* class weapon layout (deck plan).
Author's drawing

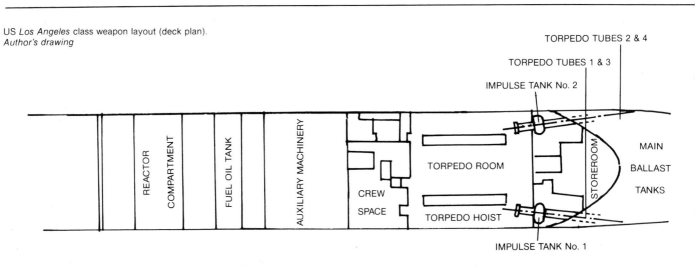

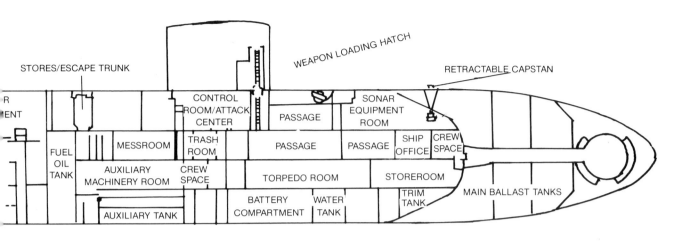

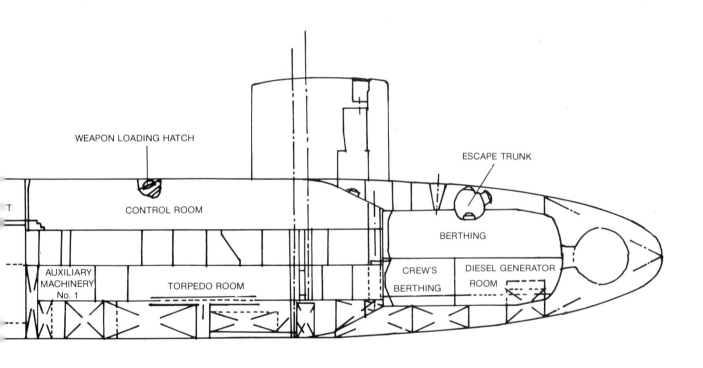

further advanced, and by early 1957 the United States had offered to share critical design information. Later that year the American and British governments reached an agreement under which the United States would supply a complete S5W plant for the prototype British nuclear submarine (HMS *Dreadnought*), while a national industrial team continued to develop an independent powerplant.

In consequence, the first Royal Navy nuclear attack submarine (launched in 1960) was a hybrid, combining British sensor and weapon concepts with an existing US powerplant. At this time the all-British design much resembled that being drawn in America for *Thresher*, with a large bow sonar array (except that the British one was conformal, on the outside of the hull, rather than spherical, on the inside) and sound-isolated (raft-mounted) machinery. As drawings of *Dreadnought* show, her turbine plant was mounted as in *Skipjack*, with little or no sound isolation. The design differed from the US Navy's in placing the forward planes in the bow, for better control at low speed, particularly at periscope depth. Their positioning also allowed the use of a smaller sail, which reduced both hydrodynamic resistance and snap-roll. The great disadvantage was greater self-noise, reduced by careful detailed design. The *Dreadnought* design also introduced a new water-ram torpedo tube, usable at greater depths than in previous classes. Given the forced adoption of the after end of the US *Skipjack* class, the designers had to make special efforts to effect a smooth structural transition between it and the British-designed front end of the hull.

The next step was to revert essentially to the original all-British submarine design, including raft-mounted machinery, in the *Valiant* class from 1963. There were actually three separate propulsion modes. For moderate speeds, as when the submarine was operating in direct support of a convoy or a task force, the raft isolated the machinery from the hull. However, at very high speeds, as when the submarine was intercepting targets, evading, or transiting, it had to be locked in place, and noise isolation was lost.

SUBMARINE DESIGN AND DEVELOPMENT

At the other end of the spectrum, there was a very low-speed electric motor independent of the reduction gearing, and reminiscent of wartime German 'creep' motors. There is also a retractable 'get home' motor to provide insurance against a main propulsion failure. Self-noise was reduced by moving the bow planes away from the bow sonar.

This basic design was slightly modified, in the late 1960s *Churchill* class, to fire the new British Tigerfish wire-guided torpedo (Mark 24 Mod 0). HMS *Conqueror* of this class sank the Argentine cruiser *General Belgrano* on 2 May 1982. Because she was fitted only to fire the anti-submarine version of the Tigerfish, she had to rely on conventional straight-running torpedoes (Mark 8) for that attack. The *Churchill* class also formed the basis of the British Polaris submarines (*Resolution* class). The latter differed technically from earlier attack submarine practice only in requiring better control at low speeds, an ability to hover (while firing), and more electric power. This basic design was somewhat older than the American *Thresher/Permit* one, itself the basis of the series-production *Sturgeon* class (launched 1963–74). It was, therefore, larger and slower than the US submarine, and could not dive as deep. By the mid-1960s a basic redesign, which led to the 1970s *Swiftsure* class, was in progress.

This new design was intended to be able to dive significantly deeper, and to have a higher speed, yet with less radiated and self-noise than in the previous design. It was developed about two years before *Los Angeles*, the US successor to *Sturgeon*. Although it was intended for increased speed, it did not display the US design's emphasis on speed. The cylindrical portion of the pressure hull was extended as far aft as possible, to eliminate structural transitions that had caused stress problems in previous British designs. For increased speed, a new reactor core (B) provided some increase in power, while the hull's overall size was restricted to reduce drag. Sail height was also reduced, which in turn reduced periscope depth where control was maintained by moving the bow planes down in the hull. They were made fully retractable for the first time in British practice, ie could be housed to avoid damage when coming alongside. Ironically, although

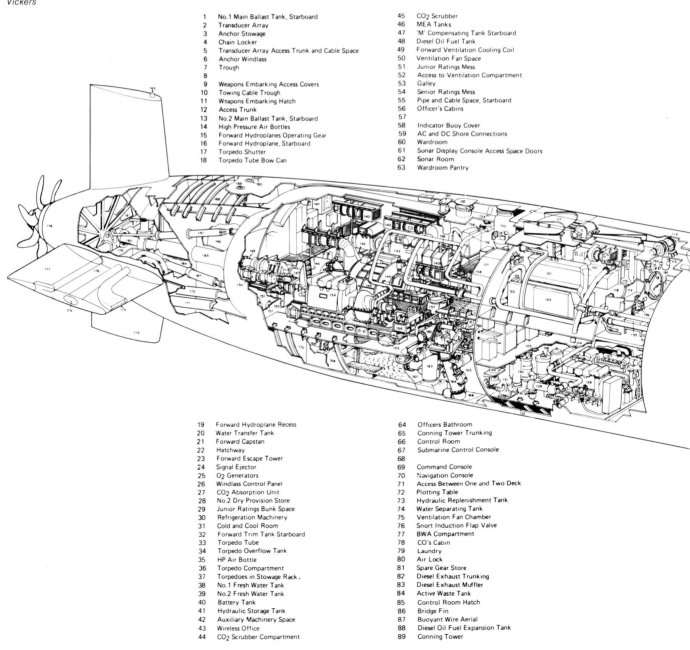

Cutaway of the Vickers British *Swiftsure* nuclear attack submarine class.
(unnamed figure numbers relate to security classified areas)
Vickers

1	No.1 Main Ballast Tank, Starboard	45	CO$_2$ Scrubber
2	Transducer Array	46	MEA Tanks
3	Anchor Stowage	47	'M' Compensating Tank Starboard
4	Chain Locker	48	Diesel Oil Fuel Tank
5	Transducer Array Access Trunk and Cable Space	49	Forward Ventilation Cooling Coil
6	Anchor Windlass	50	Ventilation Fan Space
7	Trough	51	Junior Ratings Mess
8		52	Access to Ventilation Compartment
9	Weapons Embarking Access Covers	53	Galley
10	Towing Cable Trough	54	Senior Ratings Mess
11	Weapons Embarking Hatch	55	Pipe and Cable Space, Starboard
12	Access Trunk	56	Officer's Cabins
13	No.2 Main Ballast Tank, Starboard	57	
14	High Pressure Air Bottles	58	Indicator Buoy Cover
15	Forward Hydroplanes Operating Gear	59	AC and DC Shore Connections
16	Forward Hydroplane, Starboard	60	Wardroom
17	Torpedo Shutter	61	Sonar Display Console Access Space Doors
18	Torpedo Tube Bow Cap	62	Sonar Room
		63	Wardroom Pantry
19	Forward Hydroplane Recess	64	Officers Bathroom
20	Water Transfer Tank	65	Conning Tower Trunking
21	Forward Capstan	66	Control Room
22	Hatchway	67	Submarine Control Console
23	Forward Escape Tower	68	
24	Signal Ejector	69	Command Console
25	O$_2$ Generators	70	Navigation Console
26	Windlass Control Panel	71	Access Between One and Two Deck
27	CO$_2$ Absorption Unit	72	Plotting Table
28	No.2 Dry Provision Store	73	Hydraulic Replenishment Tank
29	Junior Ratings Bunk Space	74	Water Separating Tank
30	Refrigeration Machinery	75	Ventilation Fan Chamber
31	Cold and Cool Room	76	Snort Induction Flap Valve
32	Forward Trim Tank Starboard	77	BWA Compartment
33	Torpedo Tube	78	CO's Cabin
34	Torpedo Overflow Tank	79	Laundry
35	HP Air Bottle	80	Air Lock
36	Torpedo Compartment	81	Spare Gear Store
37	Torpedoes in Stowage Rack	82	Diesel Exhaust Trunking
38	No.1 Fresh Water Tank	83	Diesel Exhaust Muffler
39	No.2 Fresh Water Tank	84	Active Waste Tank
40	Battery Tank	85	Control Room Hatch
41	Hydraulic Storage Tank	86	Bridge Fin
42	Auxiliary Machinery Space	87	Buoyant Wire Aerial
43	Wireless Office	88	Diesel Oil Fuel Expansion Tank
44	CO$_2$ Scrubber Compartment	89	Conning Tower

POSTWAR DEVELOPMENT IN THE WEST

they can be retracted at medium speed, they must be deployed at high speed for safety, to improve recovery in the event of a stern plane jam. In this sense US-style sail planes would probably have been better; the US Navy is turning to British-style hull planes just as the Royal Navy is beginning to appreciate the virtues of the American solution.

From an American point of view, perhaps the new *Swiftsure* design's most exotic feature was the replacement of a conventional propeller by pump-jet propulsion. New machinery features included circulating water scoops in the leading edges of the tail fins; through a large part of the power range, natural flow suffices, and main (sea water) circulation pumps (a source of radiated noise) need not be run. The raft was enlarged to carry not only the turbines and generators, but also the condensers. That in turn reduced the need for flexible couplings, a source of complexity and weakness in earlier designs. And the raft no longer had to be locked in at maximum power.

The new hull form was much fuller aft than earlier ones. It was initially thought that a fuller tail-cone would make for greater propulsive efficiency, but the effect is probably marginal though it did provide increased buoyancy to support the machinery, including the pump-jet.

The usual bow sonar array was relocated to the 'chin', reducing the effect of surface reflections. To fit it, the torpedo tubes had to be moved well abaft the bow, angled out, much as in American designs, and the total reduced from six to five. Hull sonar arrays were added to improve coverage to the boat's sides (flank arrays in British parlance).

The new *Trafalgar* class for the 1980s is essentially a modified *Swiftsure*, capable of firing the anti-ship variant of the Tigerfish torpedo (Mod 1) and also the sub-Harpoon missile. HMS *Trafalgar* incorporates anechoic hull coatings, and has evolutionary noise-reduction features. However, several much more radical proposals were rejected as too risky or too expensive. They included a natural-circulation reactor and a new type of machinery raft, mounted, not on the hull, but suspended instead from the transverse bulkheads.

Upon developing a successful nuclear attack submarine, Britain effectively

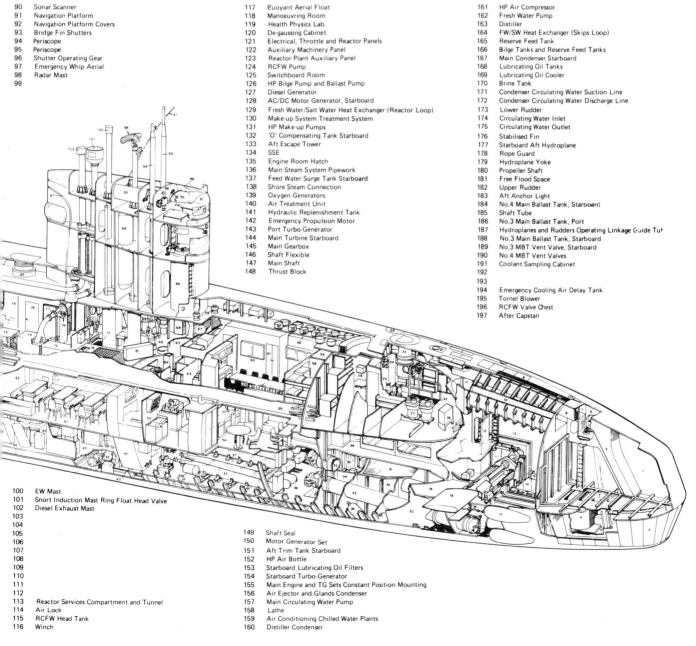

90	Sonar Scanner	117	Buoyant Aerial Float	161	HP Air Compressor
91	Navigation Platform	118	Manoeuvring Room	162	Fresh Water Pump
92	Navigation Platform Covers	119	Health Physics Lab.	163	Distiller
93	Bridge Fin Shutters	120	De-gaussing Cabinet	164	FW/SW Heat Exchanger (Skips Loop)
94	Periscope	121	Electrical, Throttle and Reactor Panels	165	Reserve Feed Tank
95	Periscope	122	Auxiliary Machinery Panel	166	Bilge Tanks and Reserve Feed Tanks
96	Shutter Operating Gear	123	Reactor Plant Auxiliary Panel	167	Main Condenser Starboard
97	Emergency Whip Aerial	124	RCFW Pump	168	Lubricating Oil Tanks
98	Radar Mast	125	Switchboard Room	169	Lubricating Oil Cooler
99		126	HP Bilge Pump and Ballast Pump	170	Brine Tank
		127	Diesel Generator	171	Condenser Circulating Water Suction Line
		128	AC/DC Motor Generator, Starboard	172	Condenser Circulating Water Discharge Line
		129	Fresh Water/Salt Water Heat Exchanger (Reactor Loop)	173	Lower Rudder
		130	Make-up System Treatment System	174	Circulating Water Inlet
		131	HP Make-up Pumps	175	Circulating Water Outlet
		132	'O' Compensating Tank Starboard	176	Stabilised Fin
		133	Aft Escape Tower	177	Starboard Aft Hydroplane
		134	SSE	178	Rope Guard
		135	Engine Room Hatch	179	Hydroplane Yoke
		136	Main Steam System Pipework	180	Propeller Shaft
		137	Feed Water Surge Tank Starboard	181	Free Flood Space
		138	Shore Steam Connection	182	Upper Rudder
		139	Oxygen Generators	183	Aft Anchor Light
		140	Air Treatment Unit	184	No.4 Main Ballast Tank, Starboard
		141	Hydraulic Replenishment Tank	185	Shaft Tube
		142	Emergency Propulsion Motor	186	No.3 Main Ballast Tank, Port
		143	Port Turbo-Generator	187	Hydroplanes and Rudders Operating Linkage Guide Tub
		144	Main Turbine Starboard	188	No.3 Main Ballast Tank, Starboard
		145	Main Gearbox	189	No.3 MBT Vent Valve, Starboard
		146	Shaft Flexible	190	No.4 MBT Vent Valves
		147	Main Shaft	191	Coolant Sampling Cabinet
		148	Thrust Block	192	
				193	
				194	Emergency Cooling Air Delay Tank
				195	Tornel Blower
				196	RCFW Valve Chest
				197	After Capstan
100	EW Mast	149	Shaft Seal		
101	Snort Induction Mast Ring Float Head Valve	150	Motor Generator Set		
102	Diesel Exhaust Mast	151	Aft Trim Tank Starboard		
103		152	HP Air Bottle		
104		153	Starboard Lubricating Oil Filters		
105		154	Starboard Turbo-Generator		
106		155	Main Engine and TG Sets Constant Position Mounting		
107		156	Air Ejector and Glands Condenser		
108		157	Main Circulating Water Pump		
109		158	Lathe		
110		159	Air Conditioning Chilled Water Plants		
111		160	Distiller Condenser		
112					
113	Reactor Services Compartment and Tunnel				
114	Air Lock				
115	RCFW Head Tank				
116	Winch				

SUBMARINE DESIGN AND DEVELOPMENT

HMS *Superb* (seen here in 1978) is typical of current British SSN practice, with a fatter stern (45 degrees rather then 30-degree tail cone angle), a lower sail and bow planes much farther down on her hull. The fuller stern was adopted for better propulsive efficiency, not in fact gained, but it proved most useful because it provided extra buoyancy to support a heavy jet-pump propulsor.
MoD

abandoned diesel-electric construction. Only very recently has this attitude changed, with a Royal Navy order for the new Type 2400. In this case the advantage of diesel-electric power is very silent operation *when the submarine is nearly immobile*. That makes a diesel-electric submarine attractive as a barrier sensor platform, quiet apart from any weapons it may carry. One might argue that such barriers become more and more important (and more and more difficult to erect) as the Soviets silence their submarines (see Chapter 6) to escape detection by long-range systems such as SOSUS.

THE BRITISH NUCLEAR DETERRENT

In 1962 the RAF, at that time the sole British strategic nuclear deterrent, expected to maintain its viability through equipping its bombers with a US-designed air-launched ballistic missile, Skybolt. When the United States suddenly cancelled the weapon, it offered Britain Polaris instead. The Royal Navy thus came, for entirely external reasons, to maintain British national strategic forces. It built a force of four Polaris submarines for this purpose, always maintaining one or two on patrol.

British and American concepts of naval strategic deterrence differ. The US force was large enough for the boats on station at any one time to destroy a substantial fraction of Soviet urban areas. One might dispute the appropriate figure, but it was a large one. Moreover, the destruction of several boats would not automatically negate the deterrent and in any case US planners believed that

POSTWAR DEVELOPMENT IN THE WEST

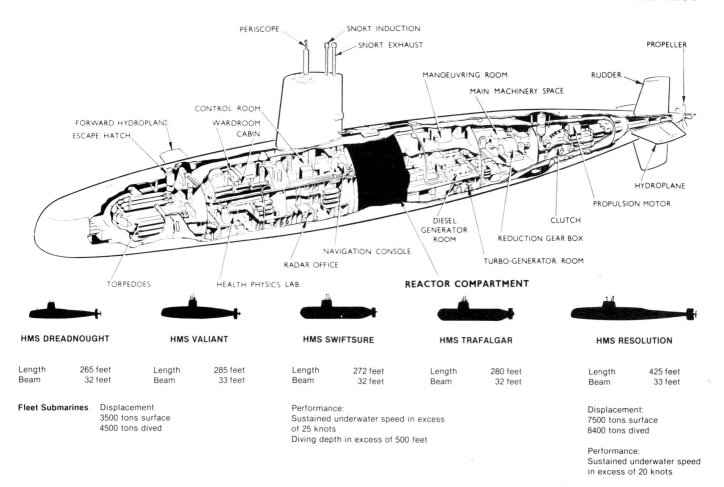

The evolution of Royal Navy nuclear attack submarine classes from the *Dreadnought* (launched 1960) to *Trafalgar* (launched 1981). The cutaway is a *Valiant*-class boat. *Dreadnought* was a hybrid, essentially the British-designed bow with a power section and stern based on USS *Skipjack*, with her S5W reactor. *Valiant* was an all British design including much superior silencing. Studies initially showed that merely joining the British-designed machinery to the *Dreadnought* forward end would have increased displacement from 4000-4600 tons, while reducing reserve buoyancy and stability. In fact the forward hull had to be lengthened and submerged displacement grew to 4850 tons. Note that the forward trim tank and WRT tank were moved inside the pressure hull. *Swiftsure* was significantly faster, deeper-diving, and quieter, with a new reactor core for greater power. The increased drag caused by the improvements was minimised by shrinking the ballast tanks to 10 per cent of surfaced displacement (13 per cent in the two earlier classes); another 1.5 per cent was contributed by internal (50ft) tanks. The sail was considerably reduced, as in the contemporary US *Los Angeles* design; periscope depth was reduced 13 per cent. This class introduced pump-jet propulsion as a standard feature after tests in a *Churchill* class submarine. The current *Trafalgar* is essentially an improved *Swiftsure* with a new long-life reactor core (Core Z rather than Core B). Even so, detail improvements increased submerged displacement from 4950 to 5200 tons.

Polaris submarines would be extremely difficult to detect even in wartime. The British attitude was quite different. They could not, and did not want to, maintain forces independently capable of deterring the Soviets from anything they might attempt. Rather, the objective was to retain some major contribution to overall Allied deterrence power. In extremis, the single British submarine was expected to be able to do substantial damage, for example to Moscow. This strategy's viability depended on a belief that a single submarine could survive for long periods in wartime.

FRENCH NUCLEAR DEVELOPMENT

As for France, the attempt to follow America and develop a domestic nuclear submarine was temporarily abandoned in 1958. The United States refused to share design data, and probably most of the available French nuclear expertise was developing a domestic nuclear bomb. When Charles de Gaulle took office in 1958, he was determined to develop a fully independent national deterrent, which came to include a submarine component. For a time, indeed, the French government tended to emphasise that a strategic submarine could attack targets anywhere (a policy of 'tous azimuths'), whereas land-based medium-range bombers and, later, missiles, were clearly directed only against the Soviet Union. As in Great Britain, the size of the strategic submarine force suffices only to maintain one, or possibly two, on patrol at any one time. Moreover, the French Navy could not claim sufficient of the defence budget to purchase both the new nuclear missile submarines *and* a new generation of nuclear attack craft.

That accorded with French national policy. From about 1960 on, France increasingly relied on nuclear deterrence as virtually her only counter to any type of Soviet attack in Europe. The French Army was expected to function much more as a trip-wire or strategic screen than as a direct obstacle to a determined Soviet attack. It followed that any war longer than a few days would rapidly go nuclear. Thus the primary French naval mission was redefined; classic protection of shipping would be unimportant, and only nuclear attack systems were emphasised. At first that meant carrier battle groups; later it meant submarines. The French replaced their early postwar ASW escorts with the A69 class corvette. Her main function was to keep the approaches to the main ballistic missile submarine base clear of Soviet ASW submarines. The other naval mission is intervention to protect the nations formerly part of the French Empire, for which France maintains defence responsibilities. This overseas role may explain the construction, from the early 1970s onwards, of new classes of diesel-electric, and then nuclear, attack submarines.

The smaller Western navies and the Japanese all continued to build more or less conventional diesel-electric submarines. The two main Baltic navies, those of West Germany and Sweden, deserve special mention. The Baltic is notoriously difficult for ASW, largely because it is so shallow. Baltic submarines can be relatively small (since the sea is not large), and their designers can save weight by limiting diving depth, to

SUBMARINE DESIGN AND DEVELOPMENT

Sjöormen was the first of the modern Swedish submarines, commissioned in 1968 as first of a 1125/1400-ton class of five. She introduced the X-stern and sail planes as well as high speed turbo-charged diesels into Swedish practice. Note the large volume of batteries amidships and the diesels under the main deck, where the power generators are not directly connected to the big electric motor aft. These coastal boats measure 165ft oa, carry four 21in bow torpedo tubes and two 16in stern tubes, with a crew of 23 and have an endurance of 21 days. Top surface speed is 15 knots, underwater 20 knots.
Kockums

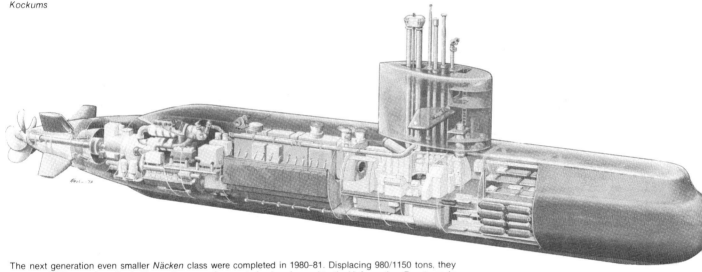

The next generation even smaller *Näcken* class were completed in 1980–81. Displacing 980/1150 tons, they measure 162ft oa and need only 18 crew because of computerised engine and tactical information. Bow torpedo tubes are increased to six and top speeds by 5 knots. The role of Swedish submarines in countering Soviet underwater incursions is one of the many mysteries surrounding these continuing violations of Sweden's neutrality.
Kockums

an extent impossible in truly ocean-going craft. Limited endurance also probably limits the volume required per man, both for living and for stores.

U-BOATS SINCE 1955

West Germany resumed U-boat development when she was permitted to rearm, in 1955. Her craft (as well as many intended for export) are designed by a private organisation, Ingenieurkontor Lübeck (IKL). Most were built by Howaldtswerke in Kiel, Thyssen (Emden) running a poor second. IKL was founded in 1946 by a group of former U-boat designers, returning to submarine design under the leadership of Professor Ulrich Gabler in 1957. U-boats were initially limited by treaty (with the Western European Union) to 350 and then to 450 tons.

The German Navy concept of Baltic submarine operations emphasised low cost, low manning, and relatively low endurance. The first staff requirements were patterned on the late-war Type XXIII, a coastal submarine with two torpedo tubes (without reloads). Two mass-production types were contemplated; an anti-ship attack submarine and a very small ASW submarine. Thus, in 1956, 12 350-ton Type 201 submarines and a series of 58-ton Type 202 coastal midgets were planned. The German Navy began both designs but then handed over to IKL for their development and all subsequent designs. In each case, submarine size was driven up by sensor requirements, so that Type 201 grew to 395 tons (and even then was not fully satisfactory) and Type 202 to 100 tons. As in the Type XXIII, Type 202 had only two tubes and two torpedoes; Type 201 had the eight-tube array characteristic of later IKL export designs. They reflected wartime demands for maximum ready torpedoes, regardless of reloads numbers. This large salvo could be fitted in so small a boat only because each swim-out tube took up relatively little space. The other unusual feature of these and later German Navy U-boats was that they were built of non-magnetic steel, to make detection and attack difficult, even in shallow water.

Even after the tonnage limit had been increased to 395 tons, Type 201 was somewhat cramped. The German Navy wanted to fit a second sonar so the design was expanded to 450 tons as Type 205. The bow array was now fully passive, and an active (transmit-only) transducer was fitted to the sail's forward edge. When it was used, the bow array acted as the associated receiver.

POSTWAR DEVELOPMENT IN THE WEST

When the tonnage limit was raised to 450 tons in 1962, West Germany was also allowed to build six 1000-ton U-boats. The enlarged Type 201 became Types 205 and 206; the larger submarine, Type 208 (not, in the end, built). Type 205 was developed into a Type 207 (*Kobben*) for Norway, a major difference being replacement of the German type non-magnetic steel by American HY80.

The enforced compactness of these designs encouraged technical inventiveness; Gabler and IKL produced the most compact available submarines, with minimum manning levels and the sort of agility particularly important in shallow waters. Gabler has often maintained that the US Navy, for example, has been relatively self-indulgent in a design sense because, blessed with nuclear power and not cursed by any upper limit in size, it can afford a certain margin. Certainly IKL benefitted enormously from US and British suspension of diesel-electric submarine construction, which removed the two leading potential exporters. As a result, it has designed the largest fraction of modern non-Soviet conventional submarines now either in service or on order. Even the British had to adopt an IKL design for boats built by Vickers for Israel (Germany was not permitted to) because their contemporary *Oberon* design was too large.

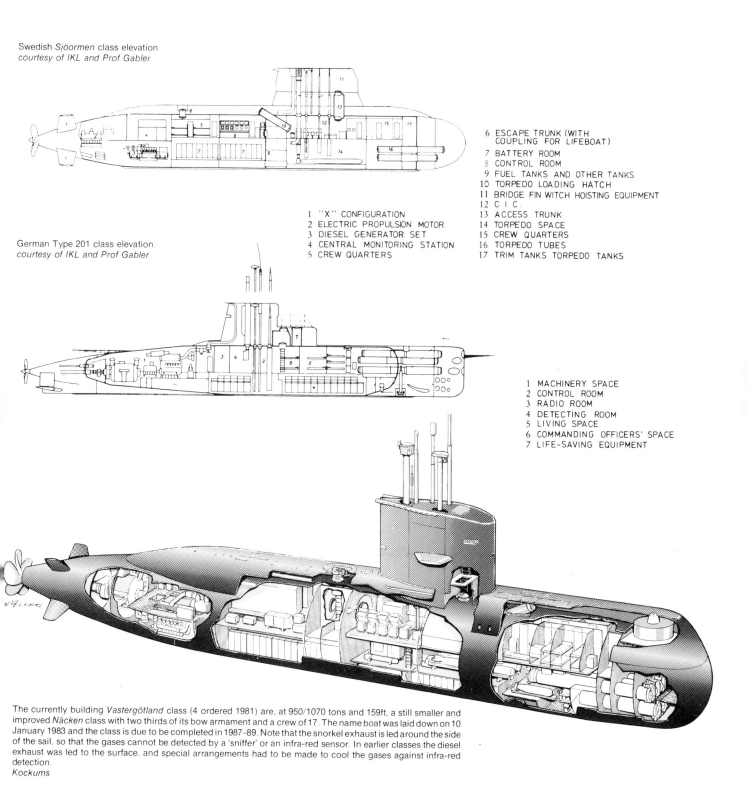

Swedish *Sjöormen* class elevation.
courtesy of IKL and Prof Gabler

1 "X" CONFIGURATION
2 ELECTRIC PROPULSION MOTOR
3 DIESEL GENERATOR SET
4 CENTRAL MONITORING STATION
5 CREW QUARTERS
6 ESCAPE TRUNK (WITH COUPLING FOR LIFEBOAT)
7 BATTERY ROOM
8 CONTROL ROOM
9 FUEL TANKS AND OTHER TANKS
10 TORPEDO LOADING HATCH
11 BRIDGE FIN WITCH HOISTING EQUIPMENT
12 C I C
13 ACCESS TRUNK
14 TORPEDO SPACE
15 CREW QUARTERS
16 TORPEDO TUBES
17 TRIM TANKS TORPEDO TANKS

German Type 201 class elevation.
courtesy of IKL and Prof Gabler

1 MACHINERY SPACE
2 CONTROL ROOM
3 RADIO ROOM
4 DETECTING ROOM
5 LIVING SPACE
6 COMMANDING OFFICERS' SPACE
7 LIFE-SAVING EQUIPMENT

The currently building *Vastergötland* class (4 ordered 1981) are, at 950/1070 tons and 159ft, a still smaller and improved *Näcken* class with two thirds of its bow armament and a crew of 17. The name boat was laid down on 10 January 1983 and the class is due to be completed in 1987-89. Note that the snorkel exhaust is led around the side of the sail, so that the gases cannot be detected by a 'sniffer' or an infra-red sensor. In earlier classes the diesel exhaust was led to the surface, and special arrangements had to be made to cool the gases against infra-red detection.
Kockums

SUBMARINE DESIGN AND DEVELOPMENT

HMS *Repulse* is a 425ft British Polaris *Resolution*-class submarine (7500/8400 tons); she is seen just before being handed over to the Royal Navy by Vickers on 7 October 1968, the second boat of Britain's four-boat nuclear deterrent. Note her folding bow planes. Although the British SSBN programme (1964–69) was an impressive industrial achievement, completed to time and cost, it can be argued that its sheer priority and expense made the run-down of the non-nuclear Royal Navy inevitable, whereas, given approximate nuclear parity between the super powers, more general-purpose warships would be of much more national and NATO use. This argument has been renewed with the current British Trident (Polaris replacement) missile submarine programme.
CPL

CHAPTER SIX

Some Soviet Views

Since the early postwar period, the enormous Soviet submarine fleet has been a permanent feature of Western naval planning. Its sheer size appears to promise a new Battle of the Atlantic, fought against vastly more sophisticated submarines, should war break out. In a more limited conflict, a large submarine force would present the Soviet leadership with interesting options, such as an undeclared or quasi-anonymous anti-shipping campaign, like the Italian one in Spanish waters during the Spanish Civil War (1936–39). The Soviet Union has also exported submarines to many Third World nations thereby greatly complicating the Western navies task. Both Soviet submarine design characteristics and tactics differ substantially from the West's; to appreciate distinctly Soviet ways of operating submarines (and, indeed, other naval forces) is a necessary corrective to the impressions given by numbers alone.

The reader should be aware that the accepted designations of modern Soviet submarine classes are NATO-assigned letters of the phonetic alphabet: 'Whiskey' is W, the later 'Romeo' is R, and so on. The sole exception is *Typhoon* a Soviet designation for a ballistic missile system and submarine. The Soviets designate their submarines and other warships by Project numbers, few of which have been published in the West. Examples include Projects 611 ('Zulu'), 613 ('Whiskey'), and 615 ('Quebec').

The Germans are often credited with teaching the Soviets about submarine warfare. Yet, even before World War II the Soviet Union maintained the world's largest submarine fleet nor had the Russian Imperial Navy neglected to build or buy a great many underwater craft. There were two important reasons. First, throughout the interwar period the Soviets were uncomfortably aware of their industrial inferiority to the West.

They consciously sought 'revolutions in warfare', specifically Soviet tactics and concepts somehow to make up for their material shortcomings. The submarine was a case in point, an inexpensive (if non-traditional) weapon that, even so, could counter the traditional battlefleet the Soviet Navy could not afford. Other examples included an early emphasis on strategic bombers, and the air-armour *Blitzkrieg* tactics of Marshal Tukhachevski. The interest in submarines echoes the French *jeune école* torpedo boat enthusiasts of the last century: relatively inexpensive torpedo craft manned by heroes would destroy any enemy's costly capital ships. Third World navies still acquire submarines as 'equalisers', much as they do missile-armed fast attack craft.

Second, submarines were particularly well suited to the primary Soviet naval mission, homeland defence. In some areas, they were the only warships the Soviet Fleet could support. For example, the Soviets could oppose no major surface ships to the Japanese Fleet in the Far East. The solution, which matched America's and Britain's, was a powerful submarine force. A distinctively Soviet feature was the small (not midget) 'M'

The Soviet Union, the largest submarine operator in the world before 1941, resumed large-scale production postwar, completing 236 'Whiskey' class medium submarines during 1950–57. They were widely advertised as copies of the German Type XXI. However, they retained many prewar features, early units having deck guns and lacking snorkels. This 'Whiskey III' photographed on 26 June 1958 in the North Atlantic, still had twin 25mm AA machine guns forward of her bridge, but her 3.9in deck gun had been landed. Note, however, that its platform, abaft the sail, remained. Nor does this boat show the fixed snorkel exhaust later characteristic of the class. *US Navy*

93

SUBMARINE DESIGN AND DEVELOPMENT

The Soviets continued to operate a relatively large force of elderly submarines for over a decade after World War II. Late in 1957 a US patrol plane photographed this *L-III* class submarine, which had been completed in 1937–39, in company with a much newer 'Zulu' long-range submarine (pennant number 99) in the Sea of Okhotsk. 'L' class modernisation was apparently limited to removal of their deck guns; snorkels were not fitted, and this example appears not to have been fitted with a radar mast.
US Navy

(for Malyutka, 'small one') class of submarine, built in Leningrad and Nikolayev, and shipped to the Far East by rail. Analysis had shown that, for a fixed number of torpedo tubes in place, these craft were less expensive than conventional large or medium submarines. The Soviet Pacific Fleet of this era was also unique in its dependence on long-range (shore-based) naval aircraft.

TACTICS AND COMMUNICATIONS

A distinctively Soviet tactical style also evolved at this time. The Soviet *jeune école* called for the *combined* and centrally controlled use of submarines, naval aircraft, and coastal guns to replace more conventional (and more expensive) surface ships. There was, to be sure, considerable propaganda content in the claim that such specially Bolshevik tactics assured superiority over the conventional tactics (and much superior forces) of any invader, but there were still specifically Soviet features which persist to the present time. Chief among them were the insistence on centralised, generally shore-based, control and the belief that co-operative tactics could make up for deficiencies in individual units. This style of warfare was developed largely because the Soviets tend to subordinate *all* forces, including naval ones, to the local theatre commander; in the case of forces operating off a coast, that will be the local (Army) Front commander. The only purely naval theatres will be oceanic ones, and the tactical style of subordination to a single central commander persists.

Central control in turn assumes that targets will be located (at least initially) largely by specialised sensor systems reporting, not to the forces at sea, but instead to the combined arms commanders ashore. Reliance on such sensors in turn encourages the development of stand-off tactics, in which the target is beyond the horizon of the attacking submarine. An evolutionary form of this idea is for the sensors to dump their data to an oceanic theatre commander aboard a flagship. In Western navies, the guiding principle is control by the man on the scene; the German U-boat arm diverged from it only after considerable soul-searching.

The co-operative idea clearly had ideological attractions. Continuing dependence on central control shows in the enormous attention the Soviets have paid to sea surveillance and to communications between naval HQs ashore and fleet units (including submarines) at sea. In turn, the reach of the surveillance systems largely determines the reach of the Soviet Fleet itself. The major postwar system was high frequency direction-finding (HF/DF), the accuracy of which depends on the ratio of target range to direction-finder baseline; a Soviet fleet dependent on HF/DF could not be effective beyond a radius of perhaps 1000 miles from the Soviet Union. Hence the development of electronic intelligence satellites since the late 1960s, which have a near-global reach, was a major element of the Soviet drive towards a world naval capability. Conversely, *without* the satellites, the Soviet submarine force is unlikely to be able to carry on effective campaigns far overseas, because it will be limited in its ability to find targets except in focal areas – where enemy ASW activity can be expected. One might add that, given the imperative of central control, overseas operation also depends upon reliable communication links ie satellites. Prior to using satellites, the Soviets developed a very reliable HF (high frequency) communications system. They parallel their automatic systems with old-fashioned CW (continuous wave) Morse code transmission, still the most reliable available system in the face of interference or jamming, albeit one of low channel capacity.

External cueing and co-operative tactics change the standards by which submarine sensors must be measured. In the West, sonar operation is judged on the basis of 'unalerted detection', ie detection by an operator who does not know *whether* a target is present. He therefore must deal with the possibility that an apparent target actually does not correspond to a real one; that sets a standard for extracting signals from the surrounding noise. However, *if* the operator knows that a target is present, he can deal with a much higher noise level (or, alternatively, a much

SOME SOVIET VIEWS

lower level of sonar performance). One might describe his sensor as a re-acquisition rather than a search sonar.

Co-operative tactics can greatly improve effective sonar performance, *if* all members of a group can communicate freely and reliably with each other. For example, the usual criterion for sonar detection range is the range for 50 per cent probability of detection. An inferior sonar might have only a 20 per cent probability of detecting the same target at the same range. But three inferior sonars working together will have a joint probability of detection, at that range, of almost 49 per cent.

The Soviet industrial system itself is ill-equipped to produce superior sonars in large quantities. Electronics is a notorious bottleneck, to the point where many Soviet surface warships have had to deploy without important equipment, as can readily be seen from the empty platforms on their masts. Similarly, most analysts of Soviet industry consider quality control a serious problem, yet intense, apparently almost fanatical, attention to detail seems to be required to achieve the high levels of ship silencing required for effective long-range performance. It is not that the Soviets are entirely unable to produce precision equipment, but rather that they cannot do so as part of their conventional industrial system. They must often virtually hand-make such things, at the research and design establishment rather than at the factory level. Other equipment must be imported from East Germany and Czechoslovakia. The Soviet submarine fleet is so large that such techniques are probably entirely inadequate for large-scale improvement; only high priorities can be met.

External control of groups of submarines implies frequent communication. Soviet boats appear to spend much of their time near the surface; that is logical, given their need for externally-supplied information and so they are more willing than their Western counterparts to expose themselves by showing periscopes and radar masts. Overall, they will behave more like the submarine commanders of the past, valuing deep diving primarily as a means of post-attack evasion. Co-operative submarine tactics also place a high value on underwater communication and IFF. The Soviet Navy is often credited with systems superior to those of the West, both in range and in immunity to interception. Further, often there are claims that the Soviets plan to use surface ships as communications relay platforms, receiving long-range radio signals and transmitting underwater signals.

External control also makes high speed desirable, since it allows the quickest concentration of boats against a fast surface target. In the West, the individual submarine is expected to detect the targets it engages. Speed is valuable, since the submarine must close the targets it detects (and must evade their counter-attacks), but there is always an implicit trade-off between speed and sensor range; the latter is determined by the boat's own noise level. Western navies therefore tend to accept a loss in speed as the cost of quieting for greater sensor range. Soviet tactics separate submarine speed from target detection range, since the submarine will not generally be expected to perform the initial target detection.

SILENCING

This is not to deny Soviet improvements in silencing: in April 1983 the US Chief of Naval Operations compared the current 'Victor III' class nuclear attack submarine to the USS *Sturgeon*. That is, the best Soviet submarines are very good indeed. Their construction presumably is of sufficient national importance to merit special industrial

Six 'Whiskeys' were converted to radar pickets in about 1960-61. Unlike their US counterparts, they were not intended to support fleet operations. Rather, they became part of the air defences of the Soviet Union herself, corresponding to a class of converted minesweepers. Note that, unlike the US pickets, this 'Whiskey' has no height-finding capability. Since she was not lengthened, she probably has nothing approaching a US-type fighter control centre. She is, instead, a relatively simple submersible radar station. Her air search antenna folded into the sail when she submerged.
US Navy

SUBMARINE DESIGN AND DEVELOPMENT

attention. However, as noted above, the cost of such attention for the rest of the submarine fleet is likely to be very considerable; there are only so many craftsmen to go around. Western experience suggests that successful silencing often requires the design and production of specialised silent auxiliary machinery. The Soviets can do the same, but only in very limited quantities; their economic system is strongly biased towards procurement of 'off the shelf' equipment, since steady production runs are far preferable to very limited, high-quality ones. Much can be done by good basic design and careful refitting, but there is a limit.

Given Soviet problems in silencing nuclear boats, diesel submarines may be particularly valuable: they can often operate very quietly *without* special production or operational measures having been taken. This is quite aside from their much lower cost or freedom from nuclear production bottlenecks. American proponents of an all-nuclear submarine fleet frequently claim that nuclear craft can be very nearly as quiet as the quietest diesel boat and that the latter are not always at their quietest. But that is only true if a great effort is made to achieve silence, an effort for which the Soviet industrial system is ill-adapted. Thus the Soviets, much more than their Western rivals, must depend upon the *inherent* silencing of diesel-electric submarines for some important missions.

Although Soviet tactics are often the tactics of mass, they have another side. Even before World War II they showed a strong bias towards assuring the survival of their attack boats, even at a high cost in tactical efficiency. In many different tactical circumstances, the Soviets have preferred to attack from maximum stand-off range rather than risk destruction by closing with their enemies. Close co-ordination of fire should, in theory, make up for long range by accumulating rounds on or near the target. Yet much experience shows that it often does not. Both deception and evasion are much easier when the attack is launched from a great distance. The Soviet concern with avoiding counter-attack may well reflect their industrial limitations: they cannot turn out massive numbers of new aircraft or submarines in wartime. They must be husbanded against the requirements of protracted warfare, still the basis of Soviet military planning.

Even before World War II, for example, they developed aerial torpedoes to be dropped from long range and from high altitude, assuring the bomber's escape, even though the targets might well be able to evade them. British naval officers seconded to the 1941-45 Soviet Arctic submarine fleet complained that attacks were too often made from maximum torpedo range. Postwar, the atomic torpedo was described as a means of attacking aircraft carriers from outside their protective ASW screens, and it appears that the SS-N-7 submerged-launch missile (operational from 1969-70) was seen as yet another extension of torpedo range.

Stand-off operation against American submarines is likely to be difficult or impossible, given their generally attributed superior silencing. It appears that, faced with the prospect of ambush, the Soviets have adopted very different tactics. In particular, they have gone out of their way to build deeper-diving submarines better adapted to manoeuvre violently in all three dimensions.

In theory, a US submarine would use its acoustic superiority to get into position, and then fire a Mk 48 torpedo. The torpedo is so noisy that the act of firing cannot be disguised, losing much of the attacking boat's acoustic advantage. There is a growing perception that, once that happens, the Soviets will choose to turn the engagement into a short-range dog fight, in which their acoustic disadvantage will be relatively unimportant. They can, for example, fire two torpedoes back down the line of bearing defined by the Mk 48, turn on their active sonar, and close in, almost as in a World I duel. Under such circumstances, the American preoccupation with stealth turns into a marked disadvantage.

From a design point of view, the more violent the manoeuvre, the more dangerous (since the submarine risks passing through its safe depth), and the more valuable is an automated back-up system. There has been speculation that Soviet tactics, and certainly the new 'Alfa' depends heavily on computer-aided control systems.

OPERATIONS TODAY

Clearly much has changed since the Soviet *jeune école* emerged in the early 1930s. Yet the basic tactical style remains much the same, in all aspects of modern warfare. The object in nearly every form of naval warfare is still the destruction of a specific target ship or formation; screening, the basis of much Western naval tactics, is still largely foreign to the Soviets. Operations are still directed from an external command post, preferably ashore, and are still ideally carried out after external reconnaissance. In particular, the rigid style of command from above persists and, with communication improvements, may even have ossified further. The fascination with stand-off attacks by dispersed units has, if anything, intensified with the development of successive generations of naval missiles.

Thus a typical Soviet naval operation begins with target detection by some long-range sensor; in the case of a NATO carrier battle group in wartime that might be a shore-

Running in an April 1979 exercise, a 'Foxtrot' (improved 'Zulu') displays her ESM mast. Her bow shows sonar domes, their sound-transparent windows unpainted. Note, too, the row of sonar windows (below the bridge windows) on the forward side of her sail. The class remains in production for export, now serving with the Cuban, Indian and Libyan navies.
MoD

SOME SOVIET VIEWS

The 3000/3700-ton 'Tango' class diesel-electric attack submarine of identical length but beamier, replaced 'Foxtrot' from 1972 in production (14 built) for the Soviet Navy, and is itself now being phased out. The extension at the after end of the sail houses the snorkel exhaust of this 1976 example.
US Navy

based HF/DF station or an electronic ferret satellite. The Soviet naval high command and General Staff war room, like that of other nations, maintains a continual plot of important foreign warships, as well as of its own forces. Available attack platforms, surface ships and aircraft as well as submarines, would be concentrated for an attack. Soviet doctrine calls for co-ordination in time and space, although in practice that is very difficult. As the anti-carrier mission developed in the 1960s, one Soviet writer argued that bombers and submarines should attempt to attack together. Both would have nuclear weapons; the bombers' should be airburst, so as to avoid damaging submarines striking with torpedoes.

Perhaps the most fundamental difference between Soviet and Western submarine practice is that the Soviets remain heavily committed to anti-surface ship operations. Some analysts write of a 'bastion' theory: the Soviets wish to keep all Western forces, surface, air, and submarine, out of their Northern and Pacific bastions. Others argue that anti-carrier operations remain Russia's priority partly because carriers have nuclear-capable aircraft. Although Western submarines are quite capable of sinking surface ships, as HMS *Conqueror* proved in the Falklands, they are designed primarily to deal with Soviet submarines.

Soviet naval practice reflects a combination of Soviet grand strategy, which sets the scenarios in which the armed forces are expected to be used, and a variety of internal pressures, such as the nature of the Soviet industrial system and the level of interservice rivalry. Although the Soviet Communist political system brooks no real dispute concerning ultimate goals, it would appear that tactics and short-term objectives are subject to intense controversy, much of it familiar to students of Western bureaucratic politics. The Navy is the junior Soviet service, and as such it has had to justify its high cost again and again; Admiral of the Fleet of the Soviet Union Sergei G Gorshkov's celebrated books are attempts to achieve a stable naval constituency by linking seapower to central Soviet national objectives that cannot be accomplished without it. Whether his concepts will survive the death of his political patron, Leonid I Brezhnev, and the developing Soviet economic and demographic crises is not entirely clear. For a student of Red Navy development, interservice rivalry is an important cause of sharp and apparently unpredictable shifts in naval missions and in the naval building programme.

ECONOMIC FACTORS

Opposing such shifts is the rigid Soviet planned economy, rigidly directed by Gosplan, the State Planning Committee. Economic planning is complex because individual industrial managers cannot themselves negotiate freely with their suppliers and with their customers; instead, everything must be decided centrally by Gosplan. Moreover, individual managers receive bonuses based on fulfilling their quota of the national Plan. They therefore have strong incentives to avoid major production shifts from year to year, so that their own plants can operate on something approaching a steady level. Similarly, Gosplan itself is reluctant (indeed, virtually unable) to make major changes to its economic plan. Both the managers and the Gosplan officials are political appointees, with ties higher up in the Soviet government, and therefore quite capable of exerting indirect pressure on the military to avoid unwanted changes (such as improvements) on its hardware. That is why the Soviets sometimes keep producing clearly obsolete systems, such as the MiG-25 high-altitude interceptor. The Soviets are well aware of this problem. Yuri Andropov announced plans to decentralise authority soon after he assumed power in 1982. The entrenched bureaucracy's strength shows in those plans' frustration; ultimately Andropov had to announce that, somehow, he was increasing local managers' authority and, at the same time, the power of Gosplan.

The economy is notoriously incapable of producing sufficient complex electronic equipment. Although high-quality goods can be produced in very small quantities, most accounts of the Soviet industrial system emphasise the difficulty of imposing quality control. For example, it appears that inertial guidance systems for long-range ballistic missiles could not be provided until the late 1970s. Thus the 'Yankee' and early 'Delta' class submarines are without the Soviet equivalent of the US Ship Inertial Navigation System (SINS). Reportedly the Soviets had to depend on detailed sea-bed mapping for underwater navigation.

Nuclear reactors are almost certainly another production bottleneck. If, as seems likely, there will be more nuclear surface warships and also larger individual submarines (requiring more or more complex reactors), then probably the building capacity for new nuclear submarines will shrink. On the other hand, there is increasing evidence of a 'high-low' mix policy in Soviet submarine building such as 'Deltas' and *Typhoons*. Of the new nuclear attack (torpedo-armed) types, the high end appears to be represented by a new titanium 'Mike', the lower by 'Sierra', the

SUBMARINE DESIGN AND DEVELOPMENT

'Victor III' successor. The Soviets appear to build, in addition, two new diesel submarines per year for their own use. 'Tango' production has just ended at 20 boats with the first 'Kilo' class, apparently of higher performance. Continued diesel boat production is a way of maintaining numbers despite any reactor production limitation, quite apart from such units, very real operational value.

More generally, the production organisation rather than the user dominates the Soviet economy, in the military sphere quite as much as in the commercial. It may have been symbolic, for example, that Stalin ordered his major naval build up at just about the time that he purged his military officers, including his naval high command. When major weapon systems fail, the military leaders usually go to the designers to ask for changes, not the other way around; they know who has the power and sometimes accept quite mediocre designs, a problem much better known in Soviet armoured vehicles than in submarines, but present in both. Submarine problems are reflected in the relatively small percentage deployed at any one time, and in allegations of operating casualties. Alternatively, it has been suggested that the low tempo of deployment can be explained by requirements to maintain a high level of (perhaps paper) readiness: deployments naturally erode a boat's readiness, since it develops minor defects and requires a refit on return.

NUCLEAR ACCIDENTS

The US Secretary of the Navy, John Lehman, has remarked that Soviet nuclear submarine reactors are not sufficiently shielded, and reportedly the well-developed Soviet 'rumour mill' has circulated some rather frightening stories. Given the absence of an authoritative official press, the rumour mill can be disastrous. For example, in April 1970, a fire, not related to her nuclear reactor, broke out aboard a 'November' class attack submarine. Fearing the worst, her crew abandoned ship, and she sank. They may have been right to do so. Although only the 'Golf' lost in 1968 and the 'Charlie' sunk in June 1983 off Kamchatka have ever been openly discussed, the US Department of Defense deleted one 'Hotel' class ballistic missile submarine from the order of battle in the late 1970s, implying that it had been sunk. Another nuclear submarine may have been lost in the Mediterranean about 1970. There have been several well-publicised break-downs on the surface, as in 1980, when an 'Echo' lost power (apparently after a fire) near Okinawa. In addition, the Soviets apparently experienced serious failures in their diesel attack boats. One might estimate that announced casualties are no more than 5 or 10 per cent of the total since 1945.

Rigidity enforces a remarkable degree of standardisation. For example, about 1964 the Soviets designed their first modern ballistic missile submarine, the 'Yankee'. It appears to have been a rather hurried effort, and has been criticised as noisy and generally unsatisfactory. Yet, the next SSBN, the 'Delta', used the same hull and propulsion, with a larger missile compartment, and successive variations on the 'Delta' also used essentially the same components. The next class, *Typhoon*, seems very different, with an elliptical-section hull, but that almost certainly consists of a pair of cylindrical ones, again variations on the original 'Yankee'.

At the beginning of the Soviet production system is the design bureau, an independent organisation responsible for producing a specific type of design on a steady basis. Strong political forces oppose the elimination of any bureau: a production ministry's prestige and power depends in large part on the size of its work force, including the number and size of its design bureaus. Hence a ministry generally will prefer to keep designers in business, even if national policy shifts away from their type of weapon. Sometimes the bureau will be reassigned, but sometimes its existence will prove useful when national policy shifts again. The story of the Soviet seabased strategic missile force, later in this chapter, illustrates the unique role of the bureau system.

STRATEGY

Soviet naval strategy has developed on two planes. First, there is a profoundly defensive mindedness, reflected in large-scale construction of submarines intended to deny the sea approaches to the Soviet Union to

'Kilo' (seen here in July 1982 in the northern Sea of Japan) is now the only Soviet diesel attack class in production for the Soviet Navy. At 219ft and 2500/3200 tons it reverts to 'Romeo/Whiskey' size, and may originally have been intended for export, to replace ageing medium submarines. The bow and stern escape hatches are painted as white roundels to help search and rescue, and the head of a communications buoy can just be seen forward of the after hatch.
US Navy

SOME SOVIET VIEWS

Westerners. Second, even now, the primary Soviet scenario is a war in Central Europe, in which the Red Army objective would probably be the Channel and the Benelux ports. Only in the past 15 years has Admiral Gorshkov tried to shift interest towards more naval, Third World theatres, where the Soviet Union might conceivably engage in limited war. But sea surveillance and naval communications capabilities impose operational limitations on the Soviet Fleet, so that it may be unable to deal with eventualities outside those envisaged by Soviet planners.

In principle, the defensiveness derives from Soviet ideology, consistent since the 1917 Revolution. In theory, as the centre of unfolding world revolution, the Soviet Union is always threatened by (and hence must deter) a West determined to destroy that revolution before it is itself brought down. Many Western observers would describe the Soviet position as paranoid. Paradoxically, this defensive mindedness may engender profoundly offensive actions, as the Soviets may choose to pre-empt a non-existent Western threat. In addition, since they consider the world revolution inevitable, they may choose to defend the evolving forces of 'progress' from Western attack; a Westerner would of course view this as Soviet intervention to undermine a Western ally defending itself.

The pro-revolutionary element of Soviet ideology makes it impossible for the Soviet Union formally to accept the current status quo. As a result, Soviet concepts of nuclear strategy differ radically from the West's. Most Western theories of escalation and the conduct of theatre warfare have an early end to the war, not victory (which would be more costly) as their goal. The ultimate goal is a return to the prewar status quo. Thus some Western arms control advocates have argued that anti-SSBN ASW should be curtailed to avoid threatening the balance of deterrence, even in wartime. Even without explicit agreement, the US Navy does not include attacks on Soviet ballistic missile submarines in its official list of wartime missions. The Soviet view is very different. A successful war is one superior to the prewar status quo, and it is valuable to maintain nuclear superiority throughout the war and the bargaining process. The destruction of enemy ballistic missile submarines is a worthwhile means to that end; the Soviets plan to hunt down US submarines and to protect their own in sanctuary areas, on the assumption that the United States will adopt much the same strategy.

Prewar Soviet naval geography was largely that of the Baltic and the Black Sea, leading to the two primary industrial ports of Leningrad and Nikolayev. The few capital ships were divided among the Baltic and Black Sea Fleets, where they could serve as a kind of mobile coastal artillery to support the naval aircraft, fixed guns, and minefields. Submarines would serve two distinct roles, as seaward pickets, to warn of incoming hostile forces and begin the process of attrition, and as the only means of penetrating hostile base areas to attack enemy forces as they sortied. Aircraft minelayers were to complement the forward-area submarines. In theory, too, the larger long-range boats could attack enemy merchant shipping and, in an emergency, could carry Soviet seapower beyond the enclosed seas.

'Romeo' and 'Whiskey' (right) class boats are shown in drydock before 1973. Their stern planes and circular propeller guards are visible. *US Navy*

STALIN'S SUBMARINES

Submarines were among the first products of Soviet naval shipbuilding; the first Five Year Plan (1928–32) included 31 medium (6 'D' class and 25 'L' class) and 3 larger ('P' class) boats. The 'D' ('*Dekabrist*') was reportedly based on Italian designs, and the 'L' ('*Leninets*'), a minelayer with two stern tracks, is often said to have been based broadly on the British *L-55*, sunk in the Baltic and raised by the Soviets in 1928. Four more classes were developed during the Second (1933–37) Five Year Plan: the medium 'Shch' and 'S', the

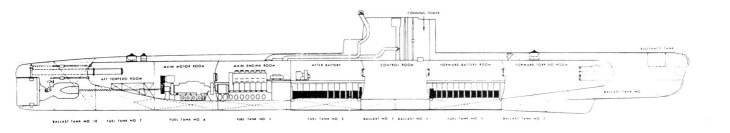
Elevation of the current 'Whiskey V' class with its separate snorkel exhaust at the rear of the sail.

SUBMARINE DESIGN AND DEVELOPMENT

At 183ft and 400/540 tons the smallest of the three Soviet submarine classes begun just after 1945, 'Quebec' (seen here on 5 January 1961) was the only one with a closed-cycle (Kreislauf) powerplant; 30 were built (1954-57), only being operated in the Baltic and Black Sea. The projection at the rear of the sail housed the snorkel. *US Navy*

large 'K' class 'cruisers', and the small coastal 'M' class. Of these, the 'S' class was designed by the German-owned IVS office in 1933-34, just prior to Germany's resumption of U-boat construction, and was closely related to the Type II double-hull U-boat.

Both before and after the war, the greatest stress was placed on the medium category. The 1933-37 Five Year Plan envisaged a total force of 369 in service as of 1 January 1938: 69 large; 200 medium; and 100 small ('M' class). The Soviet industrial base could not support so large a programme; only 150 were actually in service at that time. Even so, the next Five Year Plan (1938-42) called for a total of 341 in service as of 1 January 1943: 15 large (12 'K' and 3 'P'); 192 medium (6 'D', 25 'L', 52 'S', 109 'Shch'); and 134 small.

In fact this programme was never completed:

Class	Laid down by 22 June 1941	Delivered	Cancelled	Programme
'K'	12	6		12
'D'	6	6		6
'P'	3	3		3
'L'	25	19		25
'S'	59	17	2	52
'Shch'	95	77	14	109
'M'	106	78	28	134

On the eve of the German invasion in June 1941, their approximate disposition was:

Fleet	Long Range	Medium	Coastal
Baltic	7	35	21
Northern	2	7	6
Black Sea		25	14
Pacific		48	37

The Baltic long range submarines included the three unsuccessful 'P' class, which saw virtually no war service. The remaining boats were transferred to the Northern Fleet via the White Sea Canal in August 1941, operating in the Arctic and off Norway. Similarly, the six 'K' class delivered in wartime at Leningrad were transferred to the Northern Fleet via the Danish Straits in 1948. In addition, several 'S' class medium submarines under construction were evacuated from Leningrad via inland waterways and completed at Astrakhan (Gorki) or at Molotovsk (now Severodvinsk), serving in the Northern Fleet.

In the main theatre of operations, the Baltic, the Germans attempted to blockade the boats at Kronstadt by minelaying, but from 1942 onwards the Soviets managed to break out into the Gulf of Finland. But the Gulf was so shallow that the Germans managed to seal off its western portion with a net laid early in 1943. They therefore lost no ships in the Baltic until Finland signed an armistice with Moscow in September 1944. Then the Soviet submarine force was able to reach the German Baltic shipping, operating from new ice-free bases through the winter of 1944-45.

In the Black Sea, Soviet submarines proved valuable as transports supplying the besieged Sevastopol. Although no Soviet equivalent of the US cargo submarine was ever revealed, it seems likely that covert naval operations were a feature of postwar Soviet planning. In particular, they had to secure the key choke points of the Danish Straits (Baltic) and the Bosphorus (Black Sea) early in the war, both to protect against attack and to insure the way out for their own forces. The postwar 'Quebec' class closed-cycle diesel submarines would have been capable of reaching both after high speed submerged runs from their bases at Kronstadt and Odessa.

AFTER 1945

Stalin resumed his warship programme after 1945, rebuilding the shattered naval industrial complex even at a high cost to other military and civilian needs. There were two major changes, in naval geography and in naval technology. The Baltic, its southern shores largely in the hands of the Red Army, was no longer the chief axis of expected foreign attack. The new probable enemies, the United States and Britain, would much more probably strike in the North, where there was no natural choke point to close against them. From the Western point of view, the sheer size of the postwar Soviet underwater fleet implied that Stalin planned a new Battle of the Atlantic. Again, because there was no natural choke point, it would best be mounted by the Northern Fleet.

The Soviets built up that fleet to by far their most important in the 1960s. This strategic shift north implied a change in both principal types of submarine. The large boats ('Zulus') would have to be able to operate in mid-Atlantic and off the US East Coast; the medium ones ('Whiskeys') would have to form a barrier in the Arctic, and perhaps in the Norwegian Sea. The pronounced defensive orientation of the Soviet fleet of this period shows in the massive number of 'Whiskeys' (236 in the USSR, as well 21 in China) built, compared with 'Zulus' (26 plus 6 completed as prototype ballistic missile boats). The former, with an endurance of 45 days and a range, snorkelling, of about 6000 miles at 5 knots, was unsuited to the sort of mid-ocean anti-shipping campaign feared by NATO strategists.

Both major Soviet designs reflected the seizure of wartime German technology, as it was applied to existing Soviet preliminary designs for 'S' and 'K' class successors. The Soviets did not adopt the German figure-8 hull. Against all Western expectations, they also did not mass-produce any equivalent of the Walter-powered Type XXVI; they built a single (and unsuccessful) test boat, called the 'Whale' in the West. They did have a closed-cycle diesel system, developed for installation in an 'M' class hull. It appears to have powered the centre shaft of the postwar 'Quebec' class small submarine (which was, however, about the size of a wartime medium 'Shch').

In 1948 a Soviet admiral mentioned a programme to produce 1200 submarines, presumably all of new (and as yet unrevealed) designs. The existing force was no great threat. That November, the US Office of Naval Intelligence (ONI) reported current strength as about 281 units, but that included 13 very elderly boats and 103 coastal units incapable of operating in the North Atlantic. However, the Soviets had obtained four Type XXI submarines in the postwar division of German tonnage. They captured 14 in advanced assembly at Schichau/Danzig, as well as parts for 20 more. However, a later evaluation was that the Type XXIs were used primarily for technical exploitation; no more than four ever operated. No Walter boats fell into Soviet hands, but they did have the central design office at Blankenburg, to which Type XXVI work had been transferred, as well as the Walter turbine plant. ONI believed that the Soviets had captured one 2500shp and one 7500shp turbine there, but without either plans or the necessary auxiliary equipment could not build a Walter submarine very soon.

The one bright spot was that the existing submarine force would not be suitable for conversion to high underwater speed. That would have entailed fitting more powerful electric motors. Soviet submarines employed direct (diesel) drive rather than diesel-electric drive (as in the US 'fleet boat'). Their motors also functioned as battery-charging generators, when they operated on the surface. Motor and diesel power were, therefore, closely related; any improvement in the motor/generator would entail diesel replacement as well. By way of contrast, Western high-speed conversions of war-built submarines entailed simple increases in battery power and in motor (not generator) capacity. The existing diesel generators simply had to work longer to fill the extra battery capacity. Soviet submarines still employ direct diesel drive, but in postwar types it was matched to the new requirement for high sustained underwater speed.

ONI found the future bleak; by 1951 it expected 356 Soviet submarines, including 26 Type XXI or their equivalents, 60 snorkel boats with high surfaced speed, 130 conventional units, and 140 coastal types. Only the Type XXI and the snorkel were really threatening, but they were enough to launch the United States into what amounted to an ASW mobilisation. In fact it took the Soviets about five years after 1945 to begin the mass production ONI feared, and even then most boats appear to have been intended more for defensive than for long-range attack missions. In retrospect ONI magnified the threat, underestimating World War II devastation in the Soviet Union; the naval part of the first postwar Five Year Plan was devoted largely to rebuilding the *means* of warship production, and new ships were laid down only towards its end.

Thus as of 1 February 1950 the only new Soviet submarine was a 'B' class, characteristics as yet unknown, of which eight units were reported. It became the 'Whiskey', (236 built 1950-57). ONI estimated that the Soviets were at pre-war German levels of output, about 20-30 boats per year, but that within five years they could attain the German peak rate of 30 *per month*. In fact production peaked at an annual total of 83 in 1956; by way of comparison, the United States built 73 (larger and more complex ones) in its peak wartime year of 1944. In both cases, the naval programme included large numbers of expensive surface ships; ONI erred by assuming that Stalin would be wise enough to emphasise the weapon the West feared most.

In 1950 the estimated distribution of submarines was:

Fleet	Ocean	Medium	Coastal
Northern	27	4	6
Baltic	41	24	40
Black Sea	2	10	34
Far East	12	26	29

PEAK STRENGTH – 1957

By 1954 ONI credited the Soviets with 47 'Guppy' equivalents (mostly 'Whiskeys') and 9 snorkel ex-U-boats, out of 345 operational units (83 obsolete submersibles), but production rates were thought to be rising, apparently towards an estimated 140-160 per year. In fact production dropped sharply in 1957, as the Soviet naval outlook shifted to conform with Khruschev's 'Revolution in Military Affairs'. At the time, this drop was interpreted as no more than a shift to new models. Even so, the Soviet submarine force reached a high point of 473 boats in 1957. At that time there were 89 long, 268 medium, and 115 short range attack types, the latter ultimately vanishing in favour of long and medium range submarines. There was also the first of a new generation, a strategic attack submarine.

In 1957 both the long and the medium range attack types were being superseded by new designs: the 'Whiskey' was giving way to a new 'Romeo', and the 'Zulu' to a new 'Foxtrot' class. No 'Quebec' successor appears to have been developed, reflecting its rather specialised role. More importantly, Soviet naval strategy was changing radically, due to the 'Revolution in Military Affairs'. This phrase is shorthand for the introduction of missiles and nuclear weapons and, in a larger sense, for a transition from conventional long war to short war concepts.

Until after Stalin's death there was little discussion of nuclear weapons within the Soviet military. From a purely political point of view, it was too embarrassing to admit the concept of weapons so powerful that they might make a surprise attack decisive. Stalin had allowed Hitler to surprise him in June 1941, and Stalin could not be accused of error. His solution was to argue that surprise attack was essentially irrelevant; 'permanently operating factors' such as her sheer size made the Soviet Union unbeatable. Stalin's successors argued that nuclear weapons were qualitatively different, that they could achieve decisive results.

KHRUSHCHEV'S NUCLEAR REVOLUTION

In the West, such comments have generally been taken to mean that the Soviets would be early and massive users of nuclear weapons. However, in the context of their deeply defensive mindedness, the same statements can be read as admissions that the Soviet Union could be defeated *only* through the use of these 'weapons of mass destruction'. Such views cannot be expressed directly in Soviet writing, but they are present nonetheless. Under Stalin, there had been an underlying assumption that war with the West was inevitable; surely it would be fought with nuclear weapons, the only kind that could force a decision. Khrushchev modified this to include the possibility of the threat from *Soviet* nuclear weapons somehow deterring the West. That was enough to make them the basis of his military policy. More recent Soviet doctrine envisages the possibility that the war, if it does come, may never escalate to nuclear use.

Khrushchev really had to choose; the economy was not strong enough to support traditional large non-nuclear forces as well as research, development, and deployment of the new nuclear ones. Some writers have argued too, that the demographic 'echoes' of the poverty and mass killings of the 1930s and of the Great Patriotic War had so reduced military-age manpower pools that Khrushchev could not possibly have continued to expand the enormous Red Army. From about 1956 onwards, he enforced his new policy by cancelling production of many tactical weapons, such as anti-tank attack aircraft and light bombers, in favour of long-range nuclear delivery systems, initially bombers but later the rockets he much favoured.

He also appears to have revised naval strategy. Medium submarine production was cut drastically. Khrushchev is said to have remarked that he had little use for any submarine unable to launch nuclear weapons. He also seems to have called for a shift of coastal defences toward missile-firing patrol craft and bombers. The cut in 'Romeo' production (only 20 were completed in the USSR) is sometimes explained by poor performance, but that is belied by continued building in China and North Korea.

The 'Zulu' successor, the 'Foxtrot' class, continued in production for a decade, well into the 1960s. After a five-year hiatus, production was resumed for export, at the low rate of about one per year, and still continues. Several reasons for its survival can be advanced. First, in the mid-1950s the Soviets were developing a nuclear torpedo partly as a strategic weapon and partly as a means of destroying NATO nuclear strike carriers. Only a long-range submarine could carry such weapons to North America or, indeed, into the Central Atlantic against NATO naval formations. 'Foxtrot' also shared components with missile-firing submarines, so that its production was favoured by the industrial system.

Khrushchev also continued the nuclear submarine programme. The Soviets generally date it from 1953, and the prototype boat was probably begun about 1956; it was completed in August 1958. The first units were torpedo submarines, effectively nuclear equivalents of the 'Foxtrot', codenamed 'November' in the West. As with diesel-

SUBMARINE DESIGN AND DEVELOPMENT

The 3000/3750-ton 'Juliett' (16 boats built 1961–68) diesel and the 5000/6000-ton 'Echo II' nuclear (29 built 1962–67) classes (both photographed by the Royal Navy in April 1979) comprised the second generation of Soviet cruise missile submarines; in each case, the front of the sail houses a massive guidance radar/transponder. The SS-N-3 missile tubes (4 and 6 respectively) are in the casing; they elevate to fire and the cuts abaft them are for the missile exhaust. The guidance radar mechanism can be seen protruding from the top of the sail and the open bridge is clearly well abaft it.
MoD

electric submarines, Khrushchev tolerated a large programme; again, the nuclear torpedo may have been an important factor. Soviet tacticians argued that only a nuclear submarine would be fast enough to gain a favourable attack position on the bow of a carrier, firing from very long range and using the large lethal radius of the nuclear warhead to make up for any fire control errors.

FIRST MISSILE SUBMARINES

The naval leadership of the time badly needed an alternative mission. Khrushchev and his associates had already cancelled much of Stalin's expensive surface fleet, and the Navy had little prestige in the Army minded hierarchy. The new naval mission was strategic missile attack against land targets overseas. At this time the Soviet bomber programme was failing, and the ICBM was not yet really in sight: only a submarine could deliver a strategic weapon against the greatest enemy of all, the United States. There were two parallel programmes: a cruise missile, the SS-N-3, and a ballistic missile, initially a Navy version of the Army Scud, later the SS-N-4. The Scud variant was test-fired by a converted Northern Fleet 'Zulu' in September 1955. Five more 'Zulus' were later converted to ballistic missile submarines, carrying three launching tubes (compared to two in the prototype) in their sails. Early cruise missile tests were made from a converted 'Whiskey' with a single elevatable launching tube, the 'Whiskey Single Cylinder'. Two parallel series of conversions followed: the very austere 'Twin Cylinder', probably intended for tests and training, and the more streamlined 'Whiskey Long Bin', the earliest operational SS-N-3 cruise missile platform.

It is not clear whether the submarine-launched ballistic missile was entirely a product of the post-Stalin naval panic. The Germans had designed such weapons during World War II, of which plans and parts were captured by both Western and Soviet forces. There were also reports of Soviet tests as early as 1951; some work dates from 1946. Certainly Stalin pressed for systems capable of reaching North America, going so far as to form a special aircraft design bureau (under Vladimir M Myasischev) for that purpose. However, the urgency and the special import of the strategic mission was largely a post-Stalin phenomenon. In particular, the first generation strategic submarines were all adaptations of existing types, not altogether new ones.

Meanwhile, specialised strategic submarines were designed and built, in a massive programme. The 'Golf' class diesel ballistic missile submarine was essentially a lengthened 'Foxtrot'; the 'November' nuclear powerplant appeared in the 'Hotel' class ballistic missile submarine and in the 'Echo' class cruise missile submarine. A diesel cruise missile submarine, the 'Juliett', may also have been designed at this time, although it never appeared in a strategic version. The initial ballistic-missile submarines were 'Zulus' converted in 1956–57, but the first 'Golf' was launched in 1958, the first 'Hotel' following a year later. The SS-N-4 ballistic missile was first fired in 1956, and considered operational by 1958.

Like the American Regulus, both early Soviet systems had to be fired from the surface, making their platforms vulnerable. Only in 1961 did the Soviets launch a ballistic missile, the new SS-N-5, from underwater; it also had more than twice the SS-N-4's range. SS-N-5 became operational in 1963, three years after Polaris. The cruise missile was not replaced by an underwater-launch equivalent until 1984 (SS-N-21).

Even before the first submarines had been completed, the Navy strategic programme was in political trouble. The land forces had

The Soviet Navy was the first in the world to build ballistic missile submarines. This is a view of the 377ft, 5000/6000-ton 'Hotel' class (7 built 1959–61) carrying her three missiles in an extended sail that is stepped down. Her 'Snoop Tray' radar mast is flanked by the other antennae.
MoD

SUBMARINE DESIGN AND DEVELOPMENT

The nuclear-powered 'Charlie' cruise missile classes (12 'Is' built 1969–73 and 6 plus 'IIs' since 1973), an example of which is shown before 1975, were direct descendants of Soviet anti-ship attack submarines, missiles (SS-N-7) replacing their torpedoes. Eight external tubes occupy her bow section, forward of her diving planes (note the covered slot).
MoD

always been much more influential, and out of them grew in 1960 the Strategic Rocket Forces (SRF), Khrushchev's particular favourite. The SRF was given a monopoly of overseas strategic attack. For its part the Navy was given the bluewater anti-carrier mission, taking over all existing Soviet Air Force anti-ship missile bombers, and also developing a new family of anti-carrier missiles. The 'Echo'-launched SS-N-3 cruise missile was altered to attack surface ships, using a new radar guidance system. Existing 'Echoes', known as 'Echo I' in the West, could not fire the new anti-ship version, because they lacked the necessary guidance electronics. They were later converted to pure attack submarines. Most 'Echoes' ('Echo II') are adapted to fire the SS-N-3 anti-ship version, recognisable by the massive electronic array (normally housed under retracted, shrouded covers) at the forward end of their enlarged sail.

CRUISE MISSILE TACTICS

SS-N-3 tactics were a good illustration of basic Soviet concepts. The missile could be fired from a range of about 200 miles, well beyond any conceivable ASW screen, but also well beyond the launch vessel's horizon. Moreover, as it approached a large task force, it would have to select the carrier from among her escorts. The Soviet solution was to use co-operative targeting. The submarine would be cued into position by shore-based sensors such as HF/DF nets, but would be unable to give details of the target formation or pinpoint the target itself. A pair of 'Bear D' radar reconnaissance bombers would therefore be sent out. One at least would survive to scan the formation, sending its radar picture back to the surfaced submarine. The latter would launch a missile that also sent back a radar picture. Matching the two, the submarine fire control officer would be able to designate the SS-N-3 missile to the appropriate 'blip'. Only then, several minutes into the flight, could the submarine safely submerge. If it was caught on the surface before mid-course guidance had been accomplished, the attack would be ruined.

The physical emblem of the SS-N-3 anti-carrier system was the massive 'Front Door/Front Piece' radar array at the forward end of the 'Echo II' and 'Juliett' sails. It was not the system's only limitation. The radar reconnaissance plane had to be sent out in time to catch the target force. It could not search; it would be too vulnerable to fighters vectored in on its own radar emissions. Nor could its pilot expect many corrections in flight: HF/DF 'cuts' were relatively ephemeral data. Thus effective 'Bear D' range was a function of aircraft speed, task force speed, and radar sweep width. Strategically, it could be classed with Soviet continental defence systems. SS-N-3 could not be deployed well outside Soviet waters until satellites replaced the shore-based HF/DF net and the radar aircraft.

EARLY BALLISTIC MISSILE TACTICS

The ballistic missile submarines were also, at least nominally, given an anti-ship role, depending upon dead-reckoned prediction of target motion and a big nuclear warhead's large lethal radius. Such attacks were difficult because Soviet ballistic missiles then did not have onboard computers: they had to be hard-wired for a fixed trajectory. Thus the submarine could not fire until its target approached the (fixed) missile impact area; only adjustment in azimuth was possible. Even so, the system was tested, and the abortive SS-N-13 missile of the early 1970s may well have resulted from this shift. It was unique: a ballistic missile with terminal (apparently passive radar) homing able to be fired from a submerged submarine. SS-N-13 must have been difficult to develop; although there were reports that the concept had actually preceded that of the SS-N-6, it was not tested at sea until 1972. Testing ended in 1973, with speculation that the Soviets did not want to sacrifice any of their SALT-limited seaborne missile tubes for purely tactical purposes.

One important argument against the submarine strategic missile force was that it could not survive in the US ASW zones (SOSUS zones) from which missiles would have to be fired to hit strategic targets in North America. The Soviets did not deploy their strategic submarines off North America until about 1966, after conducting a major ocean survey. That would accord with the

SOME SOVIET VIEWS

shift back towards a naval strategic programme, after 1964, which is described below. A major and costly ocean survey was necessary to make up for the lack of an equivalent to the US Ship Inertial Navigation System (SINS); certainly Soviet ballistic missiles of this period suffered from the lack of inertial guidance systems. Given a sufficiently detailed chart of the sea bottom, a submarine can navigate, in effect, by map (but only in conjunction with piloting and celestial navigation).

Once patrols began, the submarines were generally placed in holding areas about a day away from the launch zones, specifically to avoid SOSUS detection. Typically that meant west of the Azores and east of Nova Scotia in the Atlantic, and west of Hawaii in the Pacific; the latter area was where a 'Golf' was lost in April 1968.

Although it was forbidden to re-enter the strategic missile sphere, the Soviet Navy benefitted enormously from industrial inertia. The early missiles, the Scud, SS-N-4, and SS-N-5, were all designed by the Yangel bureau, responsible for most Soviet ICBMs. A parallel V N Chelomei bureau worked on naval cruise missiles such as SS-N-3. In the late 1950s, before the SRF shock, Chelomei began development of an alternative series of naval ballistic missiles, apparently based in part on technology developed for a new land-based medium size ICBM, the SS-11. Given bureaucratic continuity, Chelomei's work continued even after the SRF decisions. Although the SS-N-6 was a very different missile, it could still be fitted in a submarine hull designed to carry the earlier weapons. The evidence is that a 'Golf' was used as the test boat. After the big strategic shift, SS-N-6 technology was incorporated in a new ballistic anti-ship weapon, the abortive SS-N-13.

SS-N-6 could reach about 1200 miles, and so could not overcome the central objection to the underwater weapon. However, the Chelomei design bureau had more powerful weapons in mind. In 1961 Admiral Gorshkov showed Khrushchev models of submarines with 16 or 24 missiles, their ranges so great that they could reach US targets from within Soviet-controlled seas. This was the genesis of the SS-N-8/'Delta' combination, but Khrushchev does not appear to have approved.

NUCLEAR ATTACK SUBMARINES

Khrushchev did allow continued development of attack submarines, presumably as part of the Navy's continuing anti-carrier assignment. The nuclear torpedo allowed a submarine to attack from beyond the carrier's protective screen, but its explosion might damage the launching vessel. The Soviets also declined to fit the short-range 'Styx' anti-ship missile with a nuclear warhead on the grounds that its surface burst would also destroy the missile boat firing. Thus the nuclear torpedo's successor was a 'winged torpedo', the supersonic SS-N-7 missile, fired from underwater and using terminal homing to overcome fire controls errors. Only a non-nuclear version is known. The platform for this weapon from 1969-70, the 'Charlie' class submarine, was lineal successor to the 'November'; it introduced a new nuclear propulsive system. Built at Gorki, 'Charlie' was transported to the Northern Fleet by inland waterway. Canal system dimensions almost certainly limited its length; for similar reasons, only 'Whiskeys' and not the longer 'Zulus' were built at Gorki. The big missile section forward appears to have ruled out more than one reactor, and 'Charlies' reportedly were too slow to keep up with Western carriers.

'ALFA'

Finally, by all accounts Khrushchev was fascinated by new technologies. About 1956 he acceded to Admiral Gorshkov's plea to develop the titanium-hulled submarine now known as *Alfa*. There have been ironic suggestions that this project was inspired by US statements that within the decade submarines would reach 45 knots and 3000ft depths. Reportedly, too, a large titanium industry was built specifically to support the 'Alfa' programme. The submarine has often been described as an 'interceptor of submarines', which would be in line with standard Soviet tactical practice. Late 1950s and early 1960s Soviet ASW envisaged early approximate location of the target, with sub-chasers rushing out to re-acquire, refine location, and then attack. A fast submarine has the advantages of all-weather operation and superior sonar operation; nuclear power would be valued for high-speed endurance measured in hours or days, not weeks or months. The result is said to be very highly automated, probably with an unmanned (hence more compact) engine room. 'Alfa's' technical complexity shows in its lengthy gestation: although a prototype appeared in 1969, it was a failure, and is no longer in service. The current boat emerged only in 1978, but is still the world's fastest, at 42 knots or more, and the deepest diving, at about 3000ft, beyond the reach of most Western weapons. Yet titanium construction is probably much more important as a weight-saver, allowing more weight for very high power.

'YANKEE'

The interlocked Soviet political and industrial systems do not respond well to dis-

The 311ft 'Victor I' class of 4300/5100 tons (14 built 1968-75) is a specialised nuclear-powered ASW submarine, roughly contemporary with that of the ballistic-missile firing 'Yankee'. This 'Victor', photographed on 21 April 1974 in the Malacca Straits on passage from Leningrad to the Pacific Fleet, shows clearly the extensive flat deck and the covered slot (just forward of the sail) into which her port bow diving plane had been retracted. 'Victor' is credited with very high speed (30 knots) and has two 'Charlie'-type reactors. Later versions ('II and 'III') have a longer torpedo room serving the 8 bow tubes (18 torpedoes) and probably more computer fire-control space as well to fit the SS-N-16 Subroc-like ASW missile and now the SS-N-21 strategic cruise missile as well. Note her high freeboard, corresponding to much more reserve buoyancy than is common in Western submarines.
US Navy

SUBMARINE DESIGN AND DEVELOPMENT

ruption, for however noble a purpose, and Khrushchev was probably removed largely for his radical policies. In 1964, then, the Navy saw its opportunity to move back into strategic attack, using the existing SS-N-6 missile and a new, probably crash-designed, submarine, the 16-tube 'Yankee'. The new submarine employed a new powerplant, presumably initially designed with the 'Charlie' in mind. The tactical missile submarine actually *appeared* later (1968) than the 'Yankee' (1967), but is surely explained by the priority the Navy gave its revived strategic arm. This sequence is further muddied by the fact that, according to a Soviet emigré, Admiral Gorshkov was proposing a 'Yankee'-like submarine to Khrushchev in 1961. One might imagine that the 'Yankee' project began about 1960, was suspended for political reasons, then rushed to completion from 1964 onwards.

'Yankee'/SS-N-6 was an interim system, both conceptually and strategically. Like its predecessors, it could not overcome the SOSUS threat; Admiral Gorshkov was reduced to arguing that his submarines would be a valuable reserve force, to tip the nuclear balance after the land-based missiles had done their damage on both sides.

'Yankee' patrols off the US East Coast began in June 1969. Typically one was stationed north of Bermuda, and another south of that island, with a 'Hotel' east of Nova Scotia and a 'Golf' west of the Azores. 'Yankee' patrols in the Pacific, initially west of Hawaii, began in 1970. 'Yankee' patrols continued even after the 1970s deployment of missiles (SS-N-8) that could be fired from Soviet home waters; some American strategists speculated that they were intended to launch minimum-warning attacks against US bomber bases, firing their missiles at short range with depressed trajectories. But no depressed-trajectory tests were ever reported, nor is any such mission in the Soviet literature. That suggests the much more mundane conclusion that the 'Yankees' are available in the event of a capitalist surprise attack. Surely they would not long survive in the SOSUS surveillance zones. Some Soviet accounts suggest that, through the late 1960s, patrolling ballistic missile submarines were assigned primarily to naval targets such as US SSBN bases, to avoid SRF wrath.

'VICTOR'

The 'Yankee' programme appears to have been associated with a new attack (in this case ASW) programme, 'Victor'. Like the ballistic missile submarine, the latter used the new 'Charlie' reactor. Built at Leningrad and possibly long enough to fit two reactors (for high speed); it may have been envisaged as a 'Yankee' escort. 'Victor' may also have been developed with the new SS-N-15 nuclear missile (a Soviet copy of the US Subroc) in mind. By this time NATO strategy included a barrier across the GIUK Gap, which 'Yankees' would have to penetrate en route to North America; SS-N-15-equipped 'Victors' could help them punch through. As with the nuclear torpedo and the SS-N-7, SS-N-15 (and its later successor, SS-N-16) would satisfy the Soviet tactical bent for maximum stand-off range. Although, by this reasoning, a hurried design, 'Victor' appears to have been reasonably successful. It has been built since about 1965 in progressively modified forms though the early boats at least had reduced operating speeds because of severe vibration.

Meanwhile a much more ambitious, strategic submarine took shape. The SS-N-8 missile (4200-mile range) could hit North America from Soviet-dominated waters. It was mated to a slightly modified 'Yankee', the 'Delta' class. There was an associated programme of surface warship development (including the *Kiev* class carrier) to control the new submarine sanctuary zones. 'Delta' became operational in July 1973, the first SS-N-8 having been fired in 1968. The two successor missiles fulfil the same strategy; SS-N-18, in modified 'Deltas', and SS-N-20, in the new *Typhoon*.

CURRENT BUILDING PROGRAMME

As this is written, the Soviets continue to pursue the largest submarine programme in the world, with eight major classes underway: a specialised ASW attack submarine, 'Sierra' ('Victor III' successor); the large titanium-hulled 'Mike'; a new (probably experimental) 'Uniform' class attack submarine referred to in the press as a 2000-tonner capable of 50 knots; the new diesel-powered 'Kilo' class attack submarine; the giant nuclear 'Oscar' class cruise missile launcher (essentially an 'Echo II' successor); the huge *Typhoon*; the existing 'Delta III' or a successor; and an attack submarine conversion of the 'Yankees' the Soviets cannot retain as strategic missile submarines under SALT. 'Foxtrot' production continues for export, and several existing programmes, including 'Alfa' and 'Tango', are ending.

A new strategic cruise missile, SS-N-21, essentially the Soviet equivalent of the US Tomahawk, has also appeared, it will probably be carried by 'Victor III' class submarines. It may be associated with an enlarged torpedo tube required to fire SS-N-16. The latter is likely to have a larger diameter than SS-N-15 because it carries the relatively large (16in) and heavy Soviet ASW homing torpedo, the 21in Subroc could lift the lighter US Mark 44 or 46.

The emergence of 'Oscar' suggests a return to anti-ship emphasis, consistent with renewed Soviet interest in distant Third World operations. Unlike the SS-N-3/SS-N-12-firing 'Echo' and 'Juliett', it need not surface to provide mid-course guidance: the new SS-N-19 missile is so fast that information provided at the moment of launch should suffice throughout flight. Global reach is provided by satellite down-link, also being fitted to some earlier anti-ship missile submarines. At the same time, the new 'Kilo' appears to be a functional successor to both 'Tango' *and* 'Whiskey/Romeo'. 'Tango' is too large to operate in confined waters, such as the Baltic and the South China Sea, yet the Soviets have produced nothing smaller either for themselves or for their numerous clients. The many exported 'Whiskeys' are ageing, and the clients cannot very well turn to the West. Now they have something for themselves.

As befits a mass-production economy, the Soviet Union supports these programmes with a huge naval industrial base, including the large submarine factory at Gorki, the United Admiralty yard at Leningrad, the covered yard at Serodvinsk, and a Pacific yard at Komsomolsk.

The Soviet Navy lagged behind the US Navy by about three years in introducing nuclear attack submarines; the 363ft 'November' class of 4500/5300 tons (15 built 1958–64), one of which is shown in distress off Cape Finesterre on 10 April 1970, was the first. The short sail and mast radome are Soviet characteristics.
US Navy

CHAPTER SEVEN

Submarines in the Third World

Most Western naval analysts probably expect submarine war only in the context of a more general conflict involving the Soviet Union. Yet warfare in the Third World, both among local powers and between local powers and the superpowers, seems far more likely than the NATO/Warsaw Pact struggle studied more intensely than any other scenario. All warfare since 1945 has occurred in the Third World, and there is no reason to imagine that this will change in the future. In most places the stakes are low enough to insure against frightening forms of escalation by the superpowers. In many countries, at the same time, there are strong internal pressures favouring conflict, for example to readjust boundaries set by the former imperial powers. The old practice of fighting to vent internal political pressures survives, as witness the Argentine decision to seize the Falklands from Britain. Submarine warfare is likely to be a feature of many such conflicts, again as in the Falklands.

Third World submarine fleets have two very different kinds of significance for the major Western navies. First, there is every reason to believe that the Third World, already the chief international battleground, will become even more unstable in the future, as the current bloc structure breaks down. The major Western navies can, therefore, expect to encounter small numbers of Third World submarines in the near future, as the Royal Navy did in the Falklands. The experience may be a major shock, as these navies will not resemble the Soviet Navy against which NATO forces have trained. Second, the Third World is the single major arms market. For both the West and the Soviets, sales to its navies keep shipbuilders employed and thus preserve them for any future national requirement.

In 1983 there were about 100 diesel submarines in Chinese Navy service, plus about as many again in 20 other Third World or

Peru was the first Latin American country to operate submarines. These 186ft, 576/755-ton US-export R-class submarines were built by Electric Boat using some components originally ordered for US Navy S-class units. Four were delivered in 1926-28, two more being cancelled. They were refitted in 1955-56 with US search radars and sonars. This photograph was taken in 1959; *R-1* was being scrapped.
By courtesy of Dr Robert L Scheina

SUBMARINE DESIGN AND DEVELOPMENT

When Chile decided to buy new submarines between the World Wars, she bought three *Capitan O'Brien* class boats of 1540/2020 tons and 260ft from Vickers. Equivalent to the Royal Navy's contemporary *Odin* class, this is the name boat which entered service in 1929, as did the others, with a large conning tower incorporating a Vickers 4.7in gun.
US Navy

neutral European navies. These figures compare with 132 diesel submarines in NATO service (13 navies), and (reportedly) 161 active in the Warsaw Pact (4 navies). It is worth stressing that as of 1983 only 40 of the world's 145 navies possessed submarines. Many smaller navies received surplus US and Soviet submarines during the 1950s which now require replacement, but the United States cannot supply new diesel-electric boats: she produces (and designs) none for her own use.

During the interwar period, the greatest submarine exporters were France and Italy. Although she sold many surface craft to foreign navies, Britain's submarine sales were limited to Chile and Estonia. The US Electric Boat Company, which had built the original Holland boats, sold four submarines to Peru; others were built abroad under its licences. Germany maintained her U-boat design capability by designing submarines in the Netherlands (at IvS, the Ingenieurkantoor voor Scheeepsbouw) for construction abroad.

The end of World War II changed the export market in several important ways: first, some of the prewar submarine navies either no longer existed, or could no longer operate such craft. One of the two main pre-war builders, Italy, fell into the latter category. Second, the ranks of potential submarine operators were swelled by de-colonisation: notably India, Indonesia, Israel, Pakistan, and South Africa. Third, the market was flooded by a large surplus fleet left over from the wartime British and US programmes, often provided on extremely favourable financial and training terms under mutual defence arrangements. Finally, any navy wishing to build a submarine in the first postwar decade had to acknowledge that it would probably soon become obsolete, given the rapid progress of submarine design. By the time the direction of submarine evolution had become clear, in the mid-1950s, one of the three main potential builders, the United States, no longer made the diesel-electric craft suited to smaller navies. Her influence was twofold: she supplied modernised World War II ('Guppy' and Fleet Snorkel) boats to many navies, including some which had not previously operated submarines, and she supplied design support to foreign navies. Thus the Dutch *Zwaardvis* (launched 1970) is generally described as a modified *Albacore*, and many postwar Japanese submarines show US features. Actual export construction was left to Britain and France.

Both exported standard submarines developed for their own navies. Britain sold *Oberon*s to the Commonwealth (Australia and Canada), to her traditional customer – Chile, and to Brazil, (buyer of Italian submarines before 1939). France built a simpler and less expensive submarine, the *Daphne*, and sold it both in Europe (Spain and Portugal) and to smaller Commonwealth navies (Pakistan and South Africa). Reportedly the West Germans regard Spain, Portugal, and Pakistan as almost reserved to France, given the strong ties between these countries and the French naval industry. Presumably the large French naval contract with Saudi Arabia should have a similar effect there.

As this is written, however, the centre of Western export submarine building is the Federal Republic of Germany, where most have been designed by Ingenieurkontor Lübeck (IKL), and built by Howaldswerke (HDW) in Kiel, Thyssen (Emden) running a poor second. By 1966 West Germany had largely built the U-boat force allowed her by treaty, and IKL sought foreign customers. It developed a new 1000-ton Type 209 specifically for export to Latin American navies, on the basis that Britain and France had already captured much of the rest of the export market. Although Dr Gabler has tried hard to avoid any increase in displacement, his relatively small craft has grown by about 40 per cent since 1967. Since Britain virtually abandoned building non-nuclear submarines (with the exception of the new Type 2400), IKL has taken over her Latin American markets as well: at the time of writing, two 1400-ton Type 209 were being completed for Chile, and two more were on order for Brazil. The other customers are Argentina (2), Colombia (2), Ecuador (2), Greece (8), Indonesia (2), Peru (3), Turkey (5), and Venezuela (4). IKL also designed the three Type 206 Israeli submarines built by Vickers (1972–77), and very nearly sold Type 209 to Iran.

Type 209 is essentially a coastal submarine.

SUBMARINES IN THE THIRD WORLD

Many of its purchasers appear to want something more flexible in their next-generation boats. That was why Argentina turned to Thyssen in 1979 for her new TR 1700, described as ocean-going. India asked for a new design, a 1500-ton type designated IKL 1500. In 1982 HDW offered to build a larger submarine, the IKL 2000, for the US Navy. Although that offer was rejected, the company apparently sees the design as its answer to the TR 1700. The IKL 2000 is among the contenders for the Australian *Oberon* successor; others presumably include the British Type 2400.

For the immediate future the primary competition is between France, whose *Agosta* has succeeded her *Daphne*, and West Germany (IKL and Thyssen). The French have recently revealed a new export design, the CA 1, whose high degree of automation (hence small crew) is considered particularly attractive to Third World navies. It is reputedly intended specifically to replace existing Type 209s. However, since the French Navy has shifted towards construction of nuclear attack submarines, it is not clear that parallel development of a commercial diesel type will succeed.

The market as a whole will probably continue to expand. In the past, navies have generally progressed from small surface forces towards undersea forces. Saudi Arabia now engaged in an ambitious naval programme, will probably soon be interested in submarines. South Korea and Taiwan have long sought offensive submarines, but they have been thwarted by US policy. Taiwan did receive US craft, but only for ASW training; now she is buying her own attack submarines in the Netherlands. Presumably Korea, with a very strong economy, will soon be buying similar craft. Former Soviet client states include most notably Egypt; Indonesia already falls into this category, with her Type 209s. Iraq, should she recover economically from her war with Iran, would be another.

There is also China, which is in a somewhat ambiguous position. She builds nuclear submarines of her own design, but also still builds obsolescent Soviet-designed submarines ('Romeo'), which she can export; at the same time she is interested in buying new Western naval technology. Egypt recently decided to buy Chinese-built submarines outfitted with Western electronics.

The remaining Soviet client states must rely on Soviet production. That is why the elderly 'Foxtrot' design (of late 1950s origin) is still being built. However, it is too large for shallow water. 'Foxtrots' smaller equivalent, 'Romeo', has not been built for many years, but in 1982 a new medium diesel-electric boat appeared: 'Kilo', with what appears to be an *Albacore*-type high speed hull. Although none has yet appeared in any foreign navy, 'Kilo' may well be intended partly for export. The 'Koni' class frigate, which apparently *was* intended only for export, would be a precedent.

There are, moreover, two new and important trends. The first is the gradual breakup of the two great postwar blocs. More and more of the smaller states are trying to follow more independent foreign policies, as they begin to distinguish their own national interests from those of the blocs to which they nominally belong. In some cases this distinction is so strong as to engender neutralism. Examples of shifting states include Egypt and Indonesia, which foresook the Soviets, and Iran, which dropped the United States deciding that the entire bloc concept was irrelevant. Although up to now the Soviets have not had to operate at sea against any of their former clients, it is certainly a future possibility.

The second trend is the growing wealth of Third World nations, such as Brazil, Saudi Arabia, and Singapore. Many are growing economically considerably faster than the developed states, and may soon reach regional superpower status. Economic growth should entail growth in naval – including submarine – capability, well beyond current standards. This is not an entirely new phenomenon: two prime historical examples are Japan and the United States. Many of the most rapidly growing states are Western-aligned but such allegiance will not necessarily be permanent. Perhaps more importantly, the current bloc structure cannot deter conflict *within* one bloc or the other (or, for that matter, between members of one bloc and many neutrals).

Interior photographs taken in 1943 aboard *Almirante Simpson* of the same class and typical of submarines of that era. To the left of the periscope is the bank of valves controlling ballast tanks. Note the periscope well under the officer's foot.
By courtesy of Dr Robert L Scheina

SUBMARINE DESIGN AND DEVELOPMENT

There was no overriding strategic threat to keep Argentina and Britain, or Pakistan and India, from coming to blows, as there would be in a confrontation between, say, a US-backed Israel and a Soviet-backed Syria.

Submarines have long been an element of the smaller navies, despite their cost. They were initially popular as a kind of 'equaliser', a small and relatively inexpensive warship able to sink much larger and far more expensive ones or at the very least inhibit them by that threat. Once successful submarines were built, they were bought in numbers by the less powerful navies, ranging from France and Germany to the smaller European navies, and also to Latin American fleets such as those of Brazil and Peru. After the Russian Revolution, the new Soviet state saw submarines in just this light, placing them very high on her list of naval priorities.

The submarine remains popular in the smaller navies, with much the same rationale: they cannot afford carriers or, often, even large destroyers; but they can afford the means of destroying those who do. Both before and after 1945, exports to small navies kept several of the specialist Western submarine builders in business.

From the point of view of a small navy, submarines are a mixed blessing. In wartime, they can exert an extremely valuable threat, perhaps even deter invasion. That is the rationale for submarine construction and operation in, for example, Sweden. Conversely, peacetime submarine operation is extremely expensive on a ton for ton basis and maintenance is both expensive and time-consuming. It might, moreover, be argued that the mere existence of the submarine, combat-ready or not, provides a useful degree of deterrent effect.

Further, submarines cannot fulfill many of a small navy's essential peacetime tasks which, practically, may far outweigh wartime ones. The two principal ones are presence and civil action. Presence means exerting naval influence without attacking and that depends upon the appearance of surface ships. Submarines must reveal themselves to 'show the flag', and that revelation in turn drastically limits the extent of power they can project. Civil action is extremely important in the Third World: by bringing supplies and services such as medical care to remote areas, the Navy can help to unify a nation. Again, surface ships are the only rational choice: submarines are relatively expensive to operate and to maintain while operating budgets are small. From a peacetime point of view, which in many small countries is the only rational one, a surface navy is the logical choice.

However, as national resources increase, a submarine force's relative cost declines, and its potential increases. As a minor power moves into regional power status the range of technology it can afford will probably expand considerably. This range may include nuclear power and even submarine-borne nuclear weapons: it is notable both France and China

The planesman, controlling (probably) the stern planes, has a depth indicator (in metres) with a 'bubble' to show the inclination of the submarine. The dial to his right, which he is watching, displays diving plane angle.
By courtesy of Dr Robert L Scheina

succeeded in building nuclear submarines of entirely domestic design.

From a purely military point of view, small submarine forces labour under very severe limitations. Long refits, not to mention combat losses, can have enormous effects. Argentina began the Falklands War with only two modern submarines, one of which was refitting. Individual boats have nothing approaching sufficient sensor range to find targets in the open ocean; even the smallest submarine force requires attached reconnaissance systems, such as long-range aircraft. Otherwise operations are limited to coastal waters and to fixed points. In this sense the Argentinians were fortunate that the British Task Force had to remain within a relatively short distance of the islands. That was mainly due to the Sea Harrier aircraft's limited range; the two British carriers had little real freedom of action.

That they were never effectively attacked underwater illustrates another major small power submarine limitation. The one operational boat, *San Luis*, had been used intensively for crew training, as Argentina was (and is) about to receive a class of six new TR 1700 submarines. Her sister *Salta*, under refit, was rushed to sea trials but had to return to port. Reportedly a torpedo hung up in one of her swim-out tubes, and only two of her four diesel engines were working.

That is not to say that *San Luis* was in very good condition. One of her diesels was inoperable, which lengthened battery-charging times. As part of the intense training programme, submariners had been run through her, so that two-thirds of her crew had joined less than a month before the war. Worse, she had a defective fire control computer. The Type 209 design allowed for such a failure, in that there was a back-up manual torpedo fire control system, in which the operator steered the wire-guided torpedo

SUBMARINES IN THE THIRD WORLD

In the engine room, note the switches for the main motors (in the rating's hands) and the telegraphs overhead; the middle one indicates voltage, and that on the right is set to astern. Taken together, the three seem to indicate that the submarine is surfacing: The captain has just checked the surface through the periscope, the electric motors are being cut out, way has been lost (by going astern), and the tanks are being blown.
By courtesy of Dr Robert L Scheina

with a joystick. But when this panel had been wired prior to installation, two wires had been interchanged, so that commands were misinterpreted, eg right for left. As a result, although she managed to survive within the British ASW defences, *San Luis* was entirely unsuccessful.

Her commander, Capitán de Corbeta (Lt Cdr) Fernando Maria Azcueta, reported that, during his 34 days in the war zone, he made three attacks, each with a single wire-guided torpedo. He was armed with German SST 4 anti-ship weapons and with US Mark 37 Mod 3 anti-submarine torpedoes. The first attack was against British destroyers or frigates, presumably screening a carrier, at an estimated range of 10,000 yards. It was nighttime, and the captain reported that there was little point in using his periscope: he worked entirely by passive sonar. The guidance wire broke about three minutes after firing, and no attempt was made to re-attack. The attack was detected by the British, who counter attacked, dropping at least one homing torpedo from a sonar-equipped helicopter.

On a second occasion, *San Luis* attacked a destroyer and a frigate in San Carlos Water, immediately after HMS *Alacrity* had sunk at midnight the 3900-ton inter-island steamer *Islas des Estados* (10-11 May). Again the wire broke (this time after a 2½ minute run), and re-engagement was impossible because the range was opening rapidly.

Finally, there was a difficult target which Azcueta believes was a British submarine proceeding at 6-8 knots. He fired a Mark 37, and heard a small explosion (probably not a warhead) on the target bearing. The range was short – about 3000 yards – and the target was difficult to classify. With benefit of hindsight, we can conclude that none of these torpedoes ever went anywhere near their targets, and indeed that their eccentric paths may have caused their guidance wires to snap.

The Argentine failure, then, has two roots, both characteristic of a small navy's handicaps. First, resources for maintenance cannot be very plentiful; hence the broken computer and the poorly-repaired backup panel. Second, one must note the Argentine commander's failure to press home his attacks, or even to work out the nature of the failure. Had he discovered the relatively simple problem, he might well have been able to overcome it. This latter failure probably can be blamed on the submarine commander. He did not close his targets to observe the effect of his fire probably because he was overimpressed with the potential and constant activity of the British ASW ships and helicopters. This was a natural consequence of relative inexperience. Thus, although the Argentine commander was able to penetrate the British ASW defences to reach what he considered firing positions, he was not rewarded with success.

SUBMARINE DESIGN AND DEVELOPMENT

Brazil turned to Italy for her pre-World War II submarines. The 1390/1884-ton *Humaita* of 285ft (launched 1927), a modified version of the Italian *Balilla* class long-range submarine, is shown at Rio on 2 May 1945.
By courtesy of Dr Robert L Scheina

Type 209 plan and elevation.
courtesy of IKL and Prof Gabler

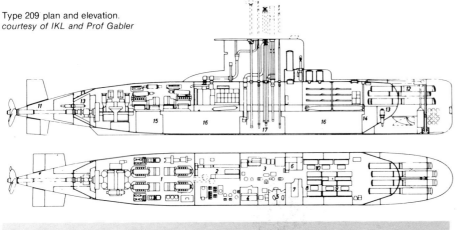

1 MACHINERY SPACE
2 CONTROL ROOM
3 C.I.C.
4 RADIO ROOM
5 SANITARY SPACES
6 COMMANDING OFFICERS' ROOM
7 GALLEY
8 OFFICERS' QUARTERS
9 PETTY OFFICERS' QUARTERS
10 CREW QUARTERS
11 BALLAST TANKS
12 BALLAST TANKS
13 TRIM TANKS
14 TORPEDO TANKS
15 FUEL TANKS
16 BATTERY ROOMS
17 COMPENSATING TANKS

The Argentine Navy saw submarine action, albeit without success, in the 1982 Falklands War, when its Type 209 *San Luis* penetrated the screen of the British Task Force. This is *Salta*, her sister boat, in dockyard hands at the outbreak of war and not refitted in time. Argentina has since taken delivery of her first of six TR1700s (also West German built), the *Santa Cruz*, at present the fastest (25 knots) diesel submarine in service.
By courtesy of Dr Robert L Scheina

Finally, small navies cannot provide their submariners with realistic experience of ASW attack, and therefore with effective counter-ASW tactical training. They are just too small to develop the requisite expertise. That is not such a problem within NATO, where each member of the alliance necessarily benefits from the others, and where one navy's submarines can exercise with another's ships. Regional exercises such as the US-Latin American 'Unitas' series have much the same effect. However, as Third World navies become more independent of one another, they will cease to benefit from the larger navies' experience. Again, the Falklands was an example. Although the Argentine submarine commander was able to evade detection in the islands' favourable hydrography, he was said to be badly shaken by the one vigorously prosecuted attack the British were able to mount on his boat. He came close to giving up, although in the end he persevered. Yet an outside observer of ASW evolution would probably feel that the British had never come close to sinking him. More experience with simulated ASW attacks might have made a considerable difference.

From the Argentine point of view, the few operational submarines did achieve something by their mere existence. The British

Task Force had to mount extensive, and expensive, ASW searches and expend considerable energy in erroneous attacks. Rear-Admiral John Woodward had to shape his dispositions to meet the threat of undersea as well as air and surface attack, at a cost he could ill afford. Presumably, for example, he stood as far as possible to the east of the islands with the two carriers to avoid exposure to submarines sheltering in the area almost as much as to avoid air attack. At one point the British were dropping homing torpedoes so close to their ships that a Mark 46 actually homed on and destroyed the torpedo countermeasure (Nixie decoy) being trailed by the carrier HMS *Hermes*.

From the British point of view, the ASW aspect of the Falklands War may be typical of future Third World operations. British (and other NATO) ASW is designed primarily to defend *moving* formations in relatively deep water against fast nuclear submarines. A high cruising speed forces the submarines to move at high (noisy) speed too. In open water, diesel-electric boats have to be lucky just to come within attack range. That leaves choke point barriers. In the Falklands, with the British Task Force tied to a fixed point, modern diesel-electric submarines were likely to be particularly effective. Virtually any Western intervention in the Third World is likely to require major forces to remain more or less on station for extended periods, but the British were particularly unfortunate in that short Sea Harrier range tied the Task Force relatively close to the islands.

Shallow water also caused difficulty, in that most Western sonars are said to be poorly adapted to the reverberation phenomena typically encountered there. Standard ASW weapons such as homing torpedoes are ill-suited; reportedly the British found theirs exploding as they struck the bottom. The depth bomb mortars, such as Limbo, developed after 1945 specifically to deal with bottomed submarines in comparatively shallow water are rapidly being discarded.

The Royal Navy was apparently able to attack submarine contacts at will. That may not be repeated in future Third World conflicts, where ASW forces may be required, for political reasons, to avoid attacks on neutral submarines in their operating areas. Such rules of engagement may seem impractical, but they are nonetheless familiar to the student of limited warfare. They might easily have been imposed in the Falklands; rumour had it that the Soviets were trailing the Task Force with nuclear submarines. Clearly the Soviet craft would have been neutral observers and the British government would have wanted to avoid any incidents.

For its part, the Argentine Navy was severely limited, Even its modern diesel-electric submarine was not very mobile, and so could not effectively attack the much more vulnerable British supply line leading down to the South Atlantic.

If the future holds more Falklands, it

An HDW-built Type 209 in drydock shows several characteristic features: the nest of eight bow tubes, the extended (curved) bow plane and the single-hull configuration.
HDW

probably also holds a much more sophisticated technology in Third World hands. America and France have already developed anti-ship missiles suitable for firing from torpedo tubes, at targets well beyond the horizon. First class navies can probably counter them, albeit at a high cost, but not current Third World forces. Again, as of 1983 such weapons have not been exported to the Third World. However, surface-launched Harpoons and Exocets have been sold quite widely. It is by no means clear that modification for submarine launch is very difficult.

It is also possible that submarines will be the delivery mechanism adopted by some future Third World nuclear powers. Torpedoes are much simpler than ballistic missiles, and they can reach many of the world's important cities which are seaports.

SUBMARINE DESIGN AND DEVELOPMENT

Reportedly the Soviets developed their early nuclear torpedoes on just this basis. To what extent will the major powers have to maintain continuous surveillance of the growing Third World submarine fleets?

The last submarines built for export in the United States, at least to date, were four for the Peruvian Navy: the lead boat, the 243ft *Tiburon* of 825/1400 tons is shown on 10 February 1954, 10 days before completion. Although they resembled the 'Guppies', these craft were modified versions of the only previous small modern US submarine, the *Mackerel*, which Electric Boat built on the eve of World War II. Six units were originally planned. Note the 5in/25 'wet' gun abaft the sail, which must have been among the last of its kind installed. These submarines were refitted in pairs at Groton, Connecticut, in 1965 and 1968; they were fitted with unstepped sails (as in US 'Guppy IIIs') and the guns were removed from the two later units.
US Navy

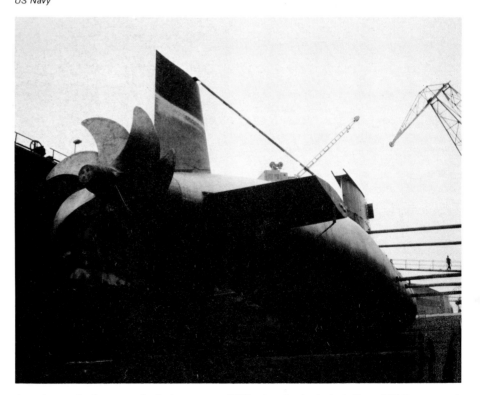

A modern scythe-form propeller is shown on an HDW submarine in drydock. Since 1962 German yards, principally HDW, have delivered or are delivering 97 submarines for 16 countries.
HDW

CHAPTER EIGHT

Diving and Underwater Manoeuvrability

The relative importance of different underwater characteristics depends on submarine and ASW tactics; these issues in turn shape submarine design. During World War II the U-boats were forced towards sustained underwater operation largely because of extended air patrols in their patrol areas. Similarly, the initial impulse towards long underwater endurance was the ASW practice of holding submarines down, hunting them to exhaustion. Very deep diving was also a response to ASW tactics, and also to the inability of existing World War II sonars to maintain contact at depth. Since 1945, underwater manoeuvrability has become more important as sonars and homing weapons have become more effective.

The shift from a submersible balanced primarily towards surface performance to an underwater craft, such as the Type XXI U-boat and its successors, optimised for submerged speed, replaced relatively long hulls (for surface speed) with relatively fat ones (for minimum underwater resistance), as described in Chapter 9. Another major change was in fast diving's relative importance which declined as submarines came to spend more time submerged. This was very much a trade-off issue. First, the size of the floodable superstructure (casing) was determined by surface requirements, especially dryness at high speed. A large casing in turn represented a large air volume to be emptied as the boat dived, and the speed with which it emptied was determined by the number and size of the limber holes in it. World War II practice, then, was to speed diving by enlarging the holes and increasing their number. But these same holes were a major contributor to underwater drag and, potentially, to underwater flow noise. Thus the fast submarines show drastically reduced casings, for reduced underwater drag, but also suffer from slow diving time (for their size), due in part to reduced limber holes.

How easily a submarine can dive depends upon how much buoyancy it must lose before it can sink below water. Since that reserve buoyancy is reflected in freeboard, a sub-

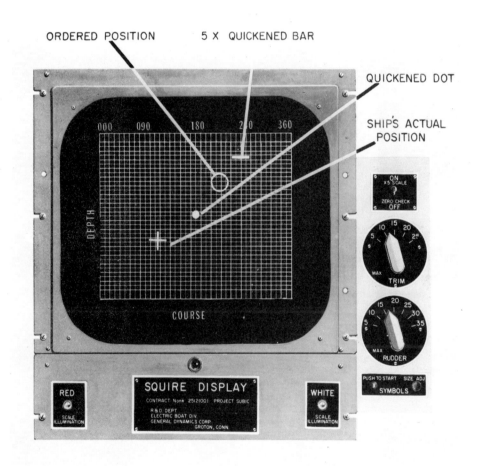

SQUIRE DISPLAY – COMING TO ORDERED COURSE & DEPTH

SUBIC, Submarine Integrated Control, was a US Navy attempt to devise a new generation of submarine control systems capable of meeting the requirements of fast, highly manoeuvrable submarines. One experimental display, SQUIRE, is shown; note the 'quickened' symbols, which showed a planesman or helmsman the likely consequences of current control settings, to allow timely reactions.
General Dynamics Corporation

marine intended for surface cruising requires very considerable reserves, which means large ballast tanks. They in turn contribute heavily to drag when the boat cruises underwater so craft intended for high underwater speed, at least in the West, typically show very small ballast tanks, and therefore very limited freeboard when surfaced.

Soviet practice, on the other hand, is to provide very great reserve buoyancy. Several explanations have been suggested. One is that Soviet wartime experience was largely in diving and surfacing among the islands of the Finnish archipelago: the Soviets still consider the ability to surface rapidly (for example in danger of grounding) valuable. Another is that Soviet boats often operate in icy conditions, when considerable reserve

115

SUBMARINE DESIGN AND DEVELOPMENT

The diving controls of the US fleet submarine *Batfish* (SS 310), shown in May 1945, were typical of World War practice, with separate stern (at left) and bow (at right) planesmen. The diving officer, his eye on the depth gauge above and between the two planes, directs the operation; each planesman has a gauge showing the angle of his planes. Another depth gauge is visible before (actually well to the left of) the stern planesman; unlike the main gauge, which reads to 600ft, it is calibrated only to about 160ft. The valves were controlled from another panel. *US Navy*

buoyancy is an assurance of survival in the face of collisions with small ice floes. Yet another is that the Soviets may not be entirely confident of their powerplants, a claim believable in view of the string of publicised submarine casualties. Also, the continued use of double hulls (for massive ballast tanks) contributes some protection to Soviet submarines. That is, a lightweight torpedo exploding against the outside hull is less likely to do immediately fatal damage than one exploding directly against the pressure hull of a Western-type submarine. It can, however, be argued that any severe hull damage would force a Soviet submarine commander to return to base, presumably passing through a Western barrier en route there.

DIVING DEPTH

Then there is diving depth: for every 100ft down, water pressure increases by 44.45lb/sq in in standard sea water (43.5lb/sq in for fresh water). Departures from circular cross-section become more and more expensive at greater diving depths. Similarly, attempts to build larger-diameter submarines become more difficult, since stresses increase with diameter at a fixed depth. But hull diameter is ultimately limited, not by structural strength, but by channel depth in harbours, and by

DIVING AND UNDERWATER MANOEUVRABILITY

drydock capacity. Modern submarines have very limited reserve buoyancy in their limited freeboard. Thus most of their diameters go into draft, and the harbour limit is probably about 40ft. An alternative upper bound is imposed by the risk of collision with surface vessels. With the advent of super-tankers (VLCCs), this is an appreciable depth of water. The Soviet choice of paired side-by-side pressure hulls, rather than a single elliptical-section pressure hull, for *Typhoon* may reflect this concern, as well as inherent limits on pressure hull diameter.

Increased diving depth adds other problems as well. Every hull penetration, such as a propeller shaft of a periscope, is a potential point of weakness, and requires special design procedures. Nuclear submarines, with their extra hull openings for coolants, present particular design snags. Unlike diesel submarines, they must keep their hull penetrations open to the sea, even at very great depths. One might imagine an alternative class of submarine designs in which hull penetrations were minimised by using sealed electrical servos outboard, connected to the inside of the pressure hull only by wiring. In theory, even the usual periscope might be replaced by a floating lens or television, the former connected to the interior of the submarine by optical fibres. In the past, such radical concepts have generally been rejected by the submarine community as far too risky: the underwater environment, with its crushing pressures, is extremely demanding, and unforgiving of error.

There might appear to be a considerable factor of safety in any stated diving depth; wartime submarine memoirs are filled with accounts of dives well below design depths, to escape depth charging, or as a result of damage. But a submarine designer has pointed out that the typical factor of 1.5 (US), 1.75 (British), or 2.0 (German) is well below that considered acceptable in most engineering practice. For example, most commercial codes call for a safety factor of 4 in pressure tanks, and there have still been explosions. The Picard bathysphere, which descended to the bottom of the Marianas Trench, had a safety factor of 2.5. Moreover, a submarine descending at anything like a steep angle may quickly pass through its 'safe' operating band, particularly if travelling at high speed. With the advent of fast deep-diving submarines, there is now considerable interest in emergency means of recovery from accidental dives, particularly those due to jammed or loose stern planes or to accidental flooding. The faster the submarine, the narrower the safe band of depths in which it can travel, limited above by the range at which propeller cavitation (with its attendant noise) begins, and below by the depth from which it will not recover in time from a stern plane or flooding casualty.

This last point is somewhat controversial. At high speeds, where a large plane angle would cause real problems, submarines generally limit themselves to very small angles. It might, then, be argued that the big excursion can somehow be neglected. That is not, however, current practice.

Typically there are three diving depths: a normal operating or test depth (Deep Diving Depth in Royal Navy parlance), the published figure; a 'safe excursion depth' or Maximum Permitted Depth, which the submarine can safely reach only a very few times in its operating life; and a crush or collapse depth. Typically the number of excursions to Maximum Depth have to be recorded for fatigue history. Normally the margin between Deep Diving Depth and collapse depth is so large that fatigue is a relatively minor problem, as long as the designer can reliably calculate stress concentrations, and apply an adequate factor of safety. The relation between the three is somewhat arbitrary, depending in part on the fatigue life a navy expects of its submarines. US fleet submarines were initially designed to dive to 200ft, but on occasion commanders trying to evade Japanese depth charge attacks went to twice that depth without permanently damaging their boats.

UNDERWATER CONTROL

From a control point of view, a submerged submarine reacts to two different sets of forces, static ones due to its positive or negative buoyancy, and dynamic ones due to the flow of water over its hull, sail, rudder, and diving planes. The latter are analogous to the aerodynamic ones an aircraft or an airship feels. In both cases, it is useful to distinguish

The Austrian submarine *U-2* (1909-20) blows out her ballast tanks while diving. Note that she has almost stopped in the water, typical procedure for pre-1914 submarines. War experience soon made crash-diving, using considerable speed to drive the submarine under, the rule rather than the exception. The early submarines tended to stop, close down their surface engines, go awash (as here), and only then start their motors to submerge.
US Navy

SUBMARINE DESIGN AND DEVELOPMENT

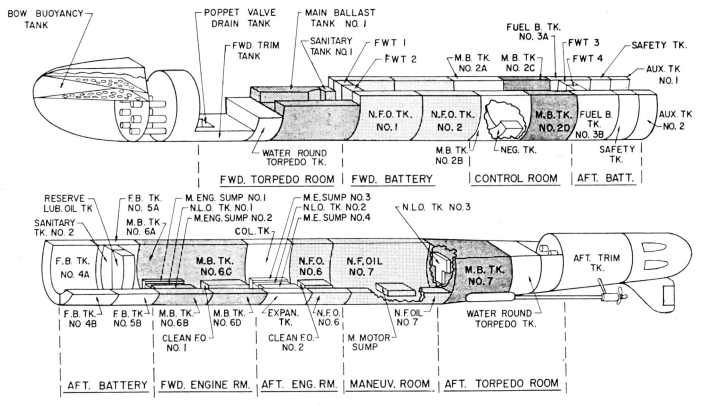

TANK ARRANGEMENT

Tankage of a typical double-hull submarine, in this case a US 'fleet boat'. Note the negative tank amidships (O tank in British parlance).

net or total forces pushing the submarine bodily up or down (or sideways) from moments, or turning forces. The turning effect of a force depends on both its magnitude and on its lever arm, its distance from the submarine's centre of gravity. In the case of the planes, relatively small control forces can make themselves felt largely because they are exerted at the ends of relatively long lever arms. Similarly, errors of trim, ie weight imbalances, at the boat's ends are more important than those nearly amidships. That is why the trim tanks are located as far fore and aft as possible. Moments explain why the detailed balance of weights aboard a submarine, as well as the totals, are so important, and thus why both design and operation call for intense attention to such details.

For example, when a torpedo is fired, and the torpedo tube fills with air, the balance of weights aboard the submarine changes, and in a particularly unfortunate way, since the changed weight is generally at the bow or extreme stern. Special compensating tanks are required to maintain both weight and trim (fore and aft angle or moment) balance, and proper compensation is both essential and relatively complex. Matters are further complicated by the fact that torpedoes cannot be fired at very high speeds, so that static (weight) rather than dynamic (and more easily controlled) forces may dominate. The near-midships placement of torpedo tubes aboard modern US nuclear submarines greatly reduces this trim problem.

The ideal is to maintain the submarine in a neutral condition, neither rising nor falling in the water (except on command), and on an even keel fore and aft, with no tendency to take a trim in either direction. In principle that requires both perfectly neutral buoyancy (zero net force), the submarine weighing precisely as much as the water it displaces; and perfect trim fore and aft, every weight being properly compensated. In practice the dynamic forces exerted by the diving planes (and, sometimes, by water flow over the hull itself) can compensate for considerable imbalances. The extent of imbalance, in fact, dictates a minimum operating speed (ie minimum plane effect), below which the submarine is unmanageable. True hovering, by pumping and blowing tanks, is the only condition in which purely static measures suffice for control.

Note that a submarine underwater has nothing like the static stability a surface ship enjoys. There is no waterplane, whose intertia acts to resist forces causing the boat to roll or to pitch. Rather, there is a relatively fine equilibrium, easily disturbed by the movement of weights (such as crew) within the boat. Hence the vital importance of the planes even in a slow submarine.

BALLAST TANKS

In a World War II submarine, ballast tanks might account for up to 30 per cent of total volume of the submarine; current figures in single-hulled types are generally far lower, since the external ballast tanks of the past greatly increased wetted area and, therefore, underwater resistance. Such tanks were either slotted below (ie open to the sea), or closed below by valves (Kingstons), and are closed by vent valves above. It was standard practice, at least until the mid-1930s, to use Kingstons, which increased a boat's potential buoyancy on the surface by making maximum use of the ballast tanks' volume. Open slotting, later standard, limits the volume of air in the main tanks to that which, compressed, can balance the pressure of the water below it. With the vent valves shut, air in the tanks keeps out the water and the tanks contribute to the buoyancy of the submarine. When they are open, the air escapes, the tanks flood, and the submarine dives. The number and size of these vents determines how quickly the tanks can be flooded. They also contribute heavily to underwater drag, since the drag of a slot is four to five times the drag of a flat plate of similar size.

From World War I to the mid-1950s *Albacore* hull form (in the diesel-electric *Barbel* and in the nuclear *Skipjack*), US practice, like other navies', was to use wide saddle tanks for ballast. Among their advantages was a considerable increase in the waterplane inertia, and therefore in stability, in the surfaced condition, a reflection of that mode's importance. The stability initially built into a submarine was particularly important because virtually every modification, if it added weight, had to be compensated for. The usual compensation was solid ballast, within 2ft of the keel, so that

DIVING AND UNDERWATER MANOEUVRABILITY

FUEL BALLAST TANKS
3A, 3B, 4A, 4B, 5A, 5B

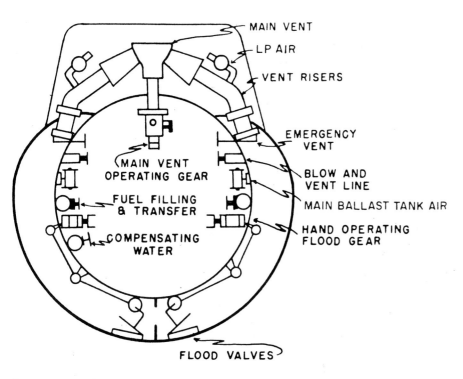

Ballast tank valves in a US 'fleet boat' showing flooding and blowing valves.

topweight problems were more intractable in submarines. That is, unlike a surface ship, every weight added (even if below the centre of gravity) results in a loss of stability, because solid ballast has to be removed to maintain the equation between weight and buoyancy. A US Bureau of Ships designer, Captain E S Arentzen, claimed that unusually rigorous demands for initial stability 'enabled [the Navy] to operate submarines for many more years without major enforced alterations than those nations which accepted lower values [of metacentric height]'. In a modern 'body-of-revolution' submarine (one completely symmetric round its revolving axis), the metacentre does not move as the submarine heels: it is approximately on the centreline of the hull. As a result, the submarine has positive stability over a 180 degree range, and the designer can accept a considerably smaller metacentric height. Moreover, he no longer need be nearly so concerned with extended operation in rough seas on the surface.

The US Navy switched to 'wrap-around' tanks completely surrounding the pressure hull when it adopted the *Albacore* shape for nuclear submarines. Claimed advantages at the time were that such tanks provided more reserve buoyancy for the same wetted surface (partly since they did away with free-flooding superstructures or casings); that they provided a better structural transition to the pressure hull proper; that they reduced structure-generated noise as water flowed over them; and that they improved protection against depth charging. At the same time spring-loaded covers were introduced to seal the flooding slots when the submarine was submerged and to reduce noise.

A submarine can operate in several very different conditions of buoyancy. On the surface, with ballast tanks fully empty, it rides with maximum freeboard. That was originally standard submarine practice, but it made diving relatively slow. During World War I it became common practice to operate with the Kingstons open, so that the main tanks were partly full, and would flood completely as soon as the vents above were opened. In an alternative 'ready to dive' condition, complete filling of the main ballast tanks will just submerge the boat, giving it the proper trim (by the bow) to go under. A condition still nearer to submersion is obtained by flooding all but one or two of the main tanks, so that the boat is awash, with only the sail and perhaps part of the main superstructure above water. Flooding the remaining tanks will take the submarine down. Finally there is the submerged condition, in which the boat is nearly at neutral buoyancy. In some cases there may be a slight excess buoyancy (perhaps one pound per ton of total displacement) that can be balanced by the diving planes' dynamic forces.

In classic submarine practice, the ballast tanks were concentrated around amidships, to reduce any trimming effect they might have. Smaller trim tanks fore and aft, and compensating tanks amidships, were used to maintain the submarine as close as possible to neutral buoyancy and to stable trim. The consequences of severe trimming errors could include a down angle so great that the battery fluid would begin to spill; poor buoyancy control could drive a submarine to the surface in the midst of an ASW force. Errors closer to proper buoyancy could be made up for by the use of the planes, but that required some minimum speed, ie a minimum drain on the batteries. The better the trim, the lower the minimum speed and the longer the underwater endurance of the submarine. Wartime memoirs show almost an obsession with preserving the charge in the batteries, which was the only guarantee of a submarine's underwater mobility. Similarly, a standard ASW tactic was to keep a submarine down until it ran out of battery power, after which it would have to surface to face gunfire or ramming.

It is necessary to compensate for consumption of stores, fuel, and torpedoes, by flooding appropriate tanks to match the boat's changing weight. Diesel oil is lighter than sea water, and in many submarines it is carried in tanks open to the sea underneath, floating on the water. As the oil is consumed, the tanks fill with the heavier water that has to be balanced by flooding a compensating tank.

Tankage affects the submarine's underwater stability. Since there is no waterplane, with its inertia opposing pitching or rolling, underwater, the surface ship concept of metacentric height is no longer valid. But there is an equivalent, the distance between the centre of buoyancy (B) and the centre of gravity (G), which must be located below B for positive stability when submerged. When submerged, G must be sufficiently far below B to provide an adequate righting moment to balance disturbances in pitch and roll from a dynamic point of view. That is, the submarine is equivalent to a weight suspended from a point at B. When it pitches or rolls, the moment arm resisting that motion is proportional to BG.

Note that static measures, such as filling tanks by opening valves or blowing them with compressed air, affect trim and net buoyancy much more slowly than dynamic ones. Thus, even in slow submarines, the planes are the best means of attitude (trim) control. They can overcome a slight excess of negative buoyancy, as long as submarine speed is sufficient. The use of negative buoyancy to accelerate diving was an index of increasing confidence in underwater submarine propulsion.

Pure buoyancy control underwater is impossible because water density generally does not vary significantly directly (or linearly) with depth. If it did, the same volume of water not able to support a submarine at one depth might be able to do so farther down, where the water would be heavier. Indeed, when there are density layers in the ocean, a submarine can float on them. However, the choice is much more usually either to rise to the surface (positive buoyancy), maintain depth, or sink. Indeed, as a submarine sinks, its hull compresses slightly with increased water pressure, so that its volume (and therefore its buoyancy) actually decreases slightly.

WATER DENSITIES

Details of sea water density can critically affect submarine operation. That is, the lifting effect of a cubic foot of empty tank varies with density of the water around it, by as much as 2.5 per cent between, say, fresh and salt water. Similarly, water density varies with temperature, and in many cases temperature dependence may be even more important than the fresh-saltwater difference. To take the latter, a submarine designed for saltwater operation will ride deeper in freshwater, which is not as dense. When diving, it will submerge before the main tanks are full. An auxiliary tank must be provided to balance off this difference, as submarines generally have to operate under a great variety of circumstances. The water in great river estuaries, ie off major ports, may be much closer to fresh than to salt. At the other end of the scale the Baltic is saltier than many oceans, and therefore denser. In some places, such as the Strait of Gibraltar, there are density layers in the water, so that a submarine can sink through the top layer and then float on the denser one.

In 1939-40 British submarines hurriedly dispatched to the relatively freshwater areas of the Skaggerak found it difficult to jettison enough weight to operate: they had been ballasted with saltwater operation in mind, and none of the lead in their keels had been removed before they left. Later in the war, as emergency equipment and fuel multiplied, the margin of variable weight was so far reduced that the Royal Navy found it difficult to operate in the outflow of the great Asian rivers, since its submarines had also to be able to operate in the surrounding salty seas.

DIVING

The early submarines dived with slightly positive buoyancy, as a safety feature: they were driven down by their diving planes, and kept underwater by power. If the power failed, they would automatically rise but quite soon it was appreciated that a slight negative buoyancy would give a much faster dive. With enough power, even a heavy boat could maintain itself at constant depth by means of its planes, and regain neutral buoyancy by pumping or blowing tanks. This practice became widespread during World War I, when the true value of very quick diving became apparent. Submarines were, therefore, fitted with Q (quick-dive) or Negative (buoyancy) tanks. Originally they were tanks with buoyancy equal to that of the conning tower, so that with all ballast tanks flooded, the submarine would run awash, with only the conning tower exposed. If the Q tank were then flooded, the vessel would take on a negative buoyancy, sinking by a combination of its weight and its planes. The Q tank would then be blown when the desired depth, usually periscope depth, was reached. Typically it then provided some small reserve of positive buoyancy. From this point of view, the Q tank was best located immediately below, or slightly forward of, the conning tower, so that flooding it would give the boat a slight down angle.

In the early Holland boats, the submarine normally trimmed by the stern when surfaced. When preparing to dive, it was flooded to an 'awash' condition, with 3-5in of water over the hull, and only the conning tower visible; in this state buoyancy was reduced to about 300lb. Power was switched to the electric motors, and the planes put to about 8 degrees down when the submarine had attained 5-6 knots; the boat then dived at about 10 degrees, and had to maintain speed to remain underwater. That is, speed was used to overcome reserve buoyancy. The entire process was cumbersome; first the submarine had to stop in the water, and then it had to flood down very precisely. If it flooded too fast, it could develop a downward momentum overcoming the small buoyancy reserve. One early British submarine, *A-4*, was nearly lost this way, diving to 90ft with a ventilator open before she could be brought under control. A contemporary US paper gave a diving time, from an initial condition with all tanks empty, of 29 minutes. However, once the submarine had accelerated in the awash condition, it could dive in about 8 seconds. By way of contrast, later submarine diving times were of the order of 30-60 seconds, although some very large submarines, such as the British 'K' class of World War I, could take as long as 5 minutes.

As submarines grew larger, the idea of diving with a small reserve of buoyancy became less attractive, and the dive at an angle was seen as dangerous: the submarine might well build up far too much momentum to level off at depth. In the Royal Navy it was the practice from the 'D' class onwards to dive without positive buoyancy, although it appears that American design practice retained some reserve of buoyancy through World War I. In many cases maximum operating depth was less than one submarine length underwater. Bow diving planes were added as a means of keeping the boat horizontal while changing depth; the British maintained that they also improved navigational qualities submerged. Later, however, as confidence in submarine machinery increased, dives were again on an incline, so that one criticism of the above-water diving planes on interwar British submarines was that it took so long to get an angle on the submarine. Design practice did not really fundamentally change again until the advent of the very fast submarine, in which bow planes sometimes made for underwater instability.

World War I experience showed how important fast diving could be, and the British investigated this issue during the 1920s. It was assumed that on a war patrol the submarine would be trimmed down as far as possible, to reduce its silhouette and diving time; the calmer the water, the deeper it would be trimmed. The minimum acceptable diving time would be the time taken to shut off the engines and close the conning tower hatch, which would not be less than 10 seconds. Tests showed, too, that it was unlikely that a submarine would sink much faster than 2ft per second after the conning tower was awash. In HMS *Seahorse*, a small 1932 boat for example, from full buoyancy on the surface with Q tanks flooded with planes hard over, the submarine passed from 20-35ft in 8 seconds, with Q tank not blown until passing periscope depth. It followed that time to periscope depth could be as short as 20 seconds, for a boat with 34ft periscopes.

The definition of diving time varied from navy to navy. In the Royal Navy the *first* man down the hatch pressed the diving alarm (klaxon), whereas in US practice it was the last; British submarines began their dives *with their hatches open*, a typical comment being that 'there was something wrong if water did not come down the hatch as she dived'.

SURFACING

Surfacing is also a combination of dynamic and static forces. In a slow submarine, the chief surfacing force would be buoyancy, with tanks blown by compressed air; but in fast submarines the forces that can be exerted by the control planes may be much stronger. Moreover, in many modern submarines with relatively small ballast tanks, the buoyant force they can exert is very limited. As a result, they must rely more and more completely on their engines, and the consequences of engine failure become more severe. In 1963 the USS *Thresher* reportedly was unable to recover from a combination of flooding and engine problems.

Submarines carry a compressed air supply, often stored at a pressure of 4000lb/sq in, for blowing main ballast, for discharging torpedoes, and, after reduction to lower pressures, for a variety of auxiliary services. Traditionally, HP (High Pressure) air reservoirs (flasks) were sized to allow the submarine to surface several times before they had to be recharged. Recharging air bottles is a lengthy process, accomplished by an HP air compressor drawing air from the surface either through the conning tower hatch or through the snorkel intake. For diesel boats surfacing frequently, particularly when there was a danger of being forced to dive before fully recharging the bottles, it was common practice to economise on the use of HP air by using either the diesel exhaust gases, or a low pressure air blower, to complete the blowing of ballast tanks as soon as the submarine was safely buoyant.

Since a submarine's buoyant ascent from depth is difficult to control, due to the

DIVING AND UNDERWATER MANOEUVRABILITY

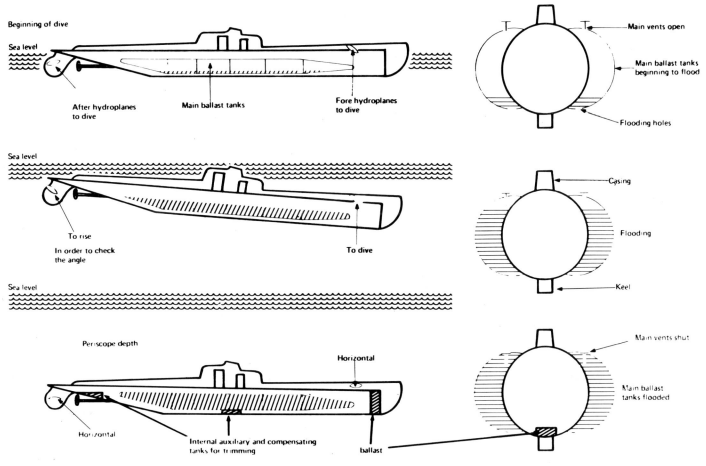

Diving a conventional submarine. At higher speeds, the effects of the planes predominate and ballast tankage is often much reduced.

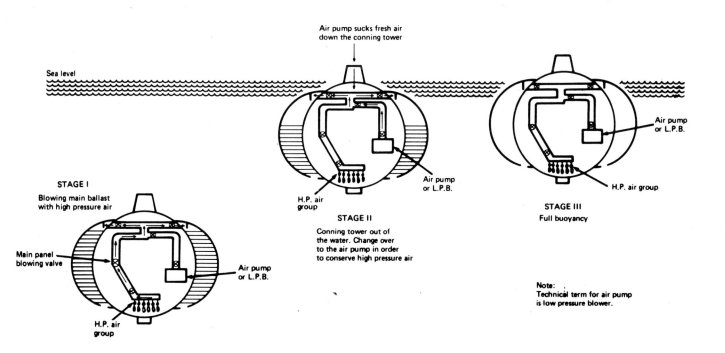

Surfacing a submarine by means of compressed air bottles normally from periscope depth.

SUBMARINE DESIGN AND DEVELOPMENT

expansion of air blown into its tanks, and surfacing at a rush risks collision with surface shipping, it is normal practice to blow the tanks at periscope depth. The amount of precious HP air used is very dependent on sea conditions. It is important, especially for boats with saddle tanks, to pass rapidly through the low stability state that applies when the superstructure (casing) contains trapped water. For then there is still a free surface of water in the ballast tanks, and only a small waterplane to provide stability.

As a countermeasure to accidental flooding, blowing main ballast is increasingly ineffective as diving depth increases because, for a fixed volume and pressure of compressed air, the volume of water that can be ejected from the ballast tanks is halved for each doubling of depth. For example, the total compressed air capacity of the British 'A' class (launched 1944-47) was sufficient to blow 176 tons of water at 200ft and equivalent to the main ballast tank (MBT) capacity. Had the submarine been capable of diving to 800ft the same compressed air system would have been capable of ejecting only 44 tons.

The US Congressional Committee investigating the *Thresher* disaster concluded that '...the design, and limited blowing capability of the deballasting system, which might have been adequate for World War II and postwar conventional submarines was inadequate as an emergency system for the large, deeper diving, high performance nuclear submarines'. This led to the fitting of large bore emergency blowing systems connected to dedicated air bottle groups, always maintained at full pressure under the SUBSAFE programme. Even so, there is a limit to the weight and volume that can be given to emergency bottle groups. The emphasis has therefore been on prevention rather than cure, with a heavy investment in quality control and improved fabrication techniques to safeguard the integrity of seawater piping systems. Flood alarms and separately operated hull valves are also fitted. But the most immediate and effective countermeasure is to increase speed to drive the submarine to the surface by means of hydrodynamic lift on its hull and planes.

In early submarines, compressed air was not always a reliable safety measure. Typical alternatives were a detachable lead keel, the loss of which could provide enough buoyancy to surface, and a special 'safety tank' within the pressure hull. The latter was always filled when the submarine was underwater, but sufficient compressed air was kept aboard to blow it even at considerable depth.

DIVING PLANES

Diving planes perform three very different functions; diving, surfacing, and depth and trim control. The latter must be quite precise at or near periscope depth. At greater depths, it is more important for manoeuvring, so that the rate of changing depth is more important than the ability to *maintain* a particular depth. The moments, or turning forces, they exert are proportional both to the direct forces up or down due to their angles and areas, and to their distance (movement arm) from the boat's centre of gravity (CG). In this they are exactly analogous to rudders; initially, in fact, they were often described as horizontal rudders. Note, too, that when the submarine turns, particularly at high speed, the forces on its rudders, sail, and planes interact, sometimes in a complex way.

Typically they are set fore and aft, as far as possible from the boat's CG, exerting turning forces (moments) in proportion to their distances from that centre. Like wings, their lift is proportional to their angle of attack. Thus a down angle on the bow planes pushes the bow down, and an up angle pushes it up.

One of the two helm/plane stations of the newly completed US nuclear attack submarine *Los Angeles* (1976) with the diving control panel in the background. The vertical gauge is marked 'flood' and 'blow'. Note the clear plastic safety cover over the emergency blowing switches. The compact panels shown replace the combination of two planes, one helm, and several valve stations (compare, for example, the photographs in Chapter 7). *US Navy*

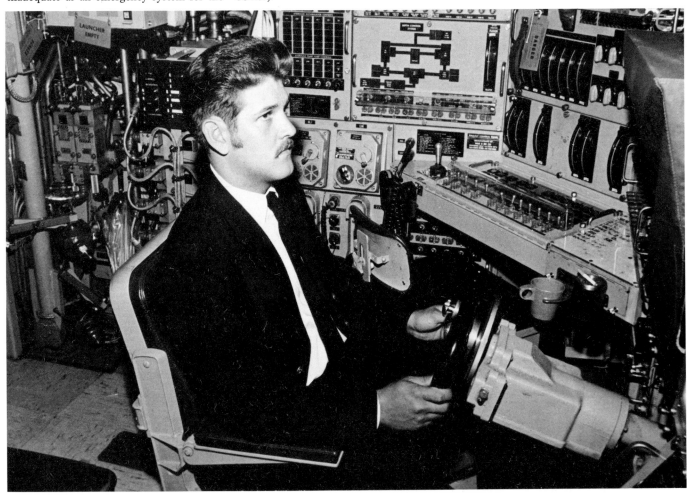

DIVING AND UNDERWATER MANOEUVRABILITY

Since the stern planes are at the other end of the submarine, they have the opposite effect. In theory, a submarine could operate entirely with one set or the other, and Holland equipped his early boats only with stern planes. They therefore dived at an angle. Bow planes were initially added to permit submarines to dive on an even keel, although that has not been standard practice for many decades.

In most submarines plane control is exercised by tilting the planes, varying their angle of attack and therefore their lift. But in modern IKL-designed diesel submarines, the bow planes' angle is fixed relative to the hull, the control forces varying in proportion to the area exposed, the planes pivoting in and out of the casing above the pressure hull. In consequence, separate planes must be provided for diving and climbing. The IKL solution is to rig only one plane at a time, the planes on opposite sides of the submarine being provided with opposite (but fixed) angles relative to the hull axis. The only earlier class with a similar system was the French *Narval* (launched 1954–58) in which separate pairs of planes were provided for each function.

At high speed, the bow planes destabilise a submarine in the vertical plane. The Germans first discovered this when they designed fast U-boats during World War II, finding that they pitched above about 12 knots, ie above the underwater speeds formerly attainable. The solution then was to provide special stabilising surfaces aft, and such surfaces still feature in the current IKL designs. The first US 'Guppies' had their shaft bossings filled in for the same reason, but it appears that 'Guppies' without this extra surface encountered no difficulties. That may have been because the US submarines typically housed their forward planes both on the surface and at speed underwater. Professor Gabler, the IKL designer, has argued that by housing bow planes above 12 knots, he can eliminate much of this directional instability, and so greatly reduce the fixed horizontal fin area (and, consequently, the appendage drag) of his submarines. This drag reduction equates to a 4 per cent reduction in battery power for a given underwater performance.

That can result in a very considerable saving in submarine cost, both for construction and over the full life-cycle. Typically a submarine battery lasts about seven years, so that most submarines will have theirs replaced two or three times (or more) over a 20-30 year life. Note, incidentally, that some 'Guppies' are now about 40 years old. Battery weight accounts for much of a diesel boat's surface displacement, a typical figure in a large IKL design being about 22 per cent of 2700 tons. Any weight saving is reflected in a saving in total submarine size and therefore cost. One might also argue that reductions in fixed fin area are reflected in better manoeuvrability, in this case better ability to change depth rapidly. Submarines generally do not steer as violently as possible in peacetime, as their operating lives are fatigue-limited. British submarines carry counters which indicate how many times they reach maximum pressure.

Bow planes located underwater (when the submarine was fully surfaced) would be effective as soon as they were inclined, and so would (in theory) make for fast submergence, but they were also a source of resistance, making for reduced surface speed. Planes

The Royal Navy adopted aircraft-style controls for its postwar submarines. This is the steering and hydroplane console aboard HMS *Dreadnought* in September 1963, her first year in service. The planesman (depth control) sits on the left, helmsman on the right, with the trimming officer between and behind them. In front of each console are three instruments: plane angle (foreplanes to right, aft to left), rudder angle, and depth. The depth controller also has a digital indicator of set depth and a scale showing the angle of the boat; note that the former has two digits covered for security, so as to avoid suggesting how deep the submarine can dive. The digital indicator on the right indicates the course to be steered, and there is a revolution counter next to the engine-room telegraph, with rpm and speed dials (the latter covered up) above.
CPL

SUBMARINE DESIGN AND DEVELOPMENT

above the waterline would not slow a submarine, but they would not take effect until it reached the awash condition, ie until some considerable flooding had occurred. Bow planes were also notoriously subject to damage when coming alongside or docking. One compromise was folding planes, employed by many navies. However, it was argued that the extra mechanism increased their chance of failure. Although not adopted for that purpose, US style fairwater planes are not subject to damage when coming alongside ships and piers, since they do not extend beyond the maximum beam of the hull. Even so, they have sufficient surface area to make for good submerged control, facilitate the periscope depth keeping without pitching the submarine, and avoid flow noise near the bow sonar.

This is a trade-off. Bow planes far forward provide a more effective movement for low speed control when submerged and can therefore be made smaller to reduce drag. To further reduce drag, and noise, at high speed they can be retracted – at a cost in mechanical complexity. Paradoxically, at high speed they need to be kept extended if they are to counteract any stern plane jam. This is a captain's decision, depending upon the circumstances.

The planes carry their own hazards. Since they are mechanical, they can jam. The worst such casualty would be a jammed stern plane, since the stern plane has the greatest effect on submarine diving angle. If the jam occurs at high speed, the submarine can be driven down very rapidly, to its collapse depth. Recovery depends in part on the moment that can be generated by the unjammed bow planes.

Particularly since the *Thresher* sinking, there has been great interest in control designs which make inadvertent dives difficult or impossible. The experimental *Albacore*, for example, was fitted with what amounted to an aircraft-type dive brake abaft her sail. There is also the X-type stern plane configuration, in which all four planes combine rudder and normal plane functions. It seems unlikely that all would accidentally jam, since they must generally be powered independently. Swedish submarines have used this configuration for some years, partly because, for a given total fin area, it minimises fin projection beyond the side of the submarine. Because fin motion is complex, the Swedish submarines generally employ computers to translate helm and diving commands into appropriate fin motions. The X-stern was particularly attractive for the Swedish Navy, which operates in the shallow Baltic, because it maximises tail fin area without projecting the fins beyond the keel line; the submarine can, therefore, bottom without damaging them. The US Navy also considered the X-stern, and rejected it in the late 1960s. The computer may well have been the reason why: US submariners have consistently preferred what they consider much more reliable manual systems. More recently, the Dutch Navy adopted the X-stern for its currently building *Walrus* class, and some accounts of the prospective US 'Next Generation Submarine' design indicate that it, too, will have an X-stern.

Turning illustrates the action of the dynamic forces. From above, a submarine resembles a crude wing, so that it generates a lift force (in this case sideways) if the hull is yawed, ie turned at an angle (drift angle) to the direction of its forward motion. The sail is often a more efficient wing, from this point of view. In aircraft terms, the drift angle is the angle of attack: within limits, the greater the angle (or the speed), the greater the effect.

The Royal Swedish Navy now used integrated helm and plane controls (single operator control) as illustrated here aboard a *Näcken*-class submarine (6 December 1979). *Kockums*

When the force is applied away from the boat's CG, there is also a turning moment. Thus the sail effect will be particularly pronounced if, as in current US submarines, it is well forward of the CG. Even the hull's centre of lift is often forward of that, producing its own yawing moment attempting to increase the drift angle. But any submarine rotation of (ie increasing drift angle) produces other dynamic (rotational) forces that resist it. When the submarine turns, there is also a centrifugal force. Directional stability demands that the forces tending to damp out increased yawing dominate over those tending to promote it, ie

DIVING AND UNDERWATER MANOEUVRABILITY

Modern US control room design is exemplified by the new ballistic missile submarine *Ohio* in October 1981. The diving control panel is at the left, with the planesman in the centre of this photograph, and the helmsman to his right, obscured by the diving officer who supervises both. The plane/helm control panels are identical, and are set up so that one man can operate both planes and helm as an integrated control system. However, two-man operation is standard US practice. Many foreign navies have gone much further with automation, and at times the US Navy is accused of over-manning, of excessive preference for men over automation. The standard reply is that, as long as automation can be avoided, human control is far more reliable.
US Navy

that the rotational forces' lever arm (the difference between the force opposing static yawing and the centrifugal force) is longer than the lever arm of the pure drift force. That is not the case in a simple aerodynamic body, in which the force opposing yawing is not large in any case. The usual solution is to add a control force in the form of a vertical fin aft. The longer its moment arm, the more effective it can be, so that the best location for the vertical stabilisers is right aft, as in an arrow. Similarly, the way most powerful turning force can be supplied is by a completely moveable vertical fin as far aft as possible.

The fin area of the sail also affects turning. Since it is close to the CG, it cannot generate much of a movement arm, but it does produce a side force causing the submarine to roll, since that force is exerted *above* the centre of gravity. When the rudder is first turned, the boat sideslips slightly, and also rapidly changes heading. It tries to persist in its original path, and hence has a large drift angle. That in turn increases the force on the sail, a more efficient wing than is the hull as a whole, and the submarine tends to 'snap roll' hard over. It then comes onto the turning path, with a much reduced yaw angle, and a much gentler heel. It is sometimes suggested that this phenomenon is aggravated in US submarines by their forward placed sails. Certainly the larger the sail, the more efficient it is as a wing.

The German firm of IKL proposes to utilise this type of motion for recovery from an inadvertent dive. If a boat goes hard over, the heel it takes on will cause the sail to generate a degree of lift, and at high speed it

125

SUBMARINE DESIGN AND DEVELOPMENT

will gradually spiral upwards.

In each case, as soon as the boat is no longer on an even keel, its diving planes and rudders begin to interact, since neither any longer controls either depth or heading completely. Even without rolling, there is some interaction due to cross flows and because the submarine is not symmetrical top and bottom.

Vertical motion is analogous but more complex, since there is also a moment due to the boat's static stability seeking to overcome any pitch angle. Thus there are net up or down forces due to lift (drift angle) and to control surfaces, and there are moments due to the control surfaces, to lift (due to drift angle or angle of attack) and to static stability. The moment of a control force exerted at the appropriate point along the hull (the Neutral Point) just cancels out the static stability and hull lift moments, allowing the submarine to rise or fall through the water without changing trim. Similarly, there is a Critical Point (corresponding to the centre of pressure in aerodynamics) at which the control force just cancels out the positive or negative lift due to the drift angle on the hull itself, so that it can change pitch angle but not depth. As in the case of a turn, drift angle creates its own moment because the centre of vertical force does not match the boat's CG.

Typically the Neutral Point is about halfway between the bow and amidships. One claimed advantage of current US sail planes (fairwater planes, in current parlance) is that they are near the Neutral Point and thus can permit the submarine to change depth without pitching. Note that the *only* Soviet submarines with sail planes are the 'India' diesel class submersible carriers (see below) and ballistic missile boats before the *Typhoon*s.

The position of the Critical Point depends on speed, since that in turn determines the size of the lift force due to pitch angle. It moves aft, away from the Neutral Point, with decreasing speed. At the Critical Speed, generally about 3 knots, it is at the stern planes' position, where they cannot control depth, although they can still control pitch angle. Below this speed the Critical Point is abaft the stern planes, and a dive (up) angle on the planes produces a bow down pitch, although the boat still rises. Hence the traditional practice, developed for slow submarines, of controlling depth with the bow planes (which experience no Critical Speed phenomenon), and the pitch angle with the stern planes.

As speed increases, the Critical Point moves forward towards the Neutral Point, and the bow planes become less and less effective in both depth and pitch. That is why the bow planes can be folded in in many modern fast submarines; *Albacore* even operated without them altogether, avoiding the low-speed regime around the Critical Speed.

Because a submarine running at or near periscope depth is generally at low speed, traditional practice still prevails there; the bow planes are still the primary means of depth control. Dive angle on them not only increases depth, but also gives the boat a down trim angle. The stern planes maintain a trim angle suitable for the boat's speed and overall weight balance, so that the bow planes need not carry a mean rise or dive angle if the vessel is heavy or light. However, at moderate or high speed and greater depth, the bow planes become relatively ineffective, and in some cases they are even destabilising. Not only are they closer to the CG (with, therefore, smaller movement arms), but it is also sometimes claimed that hydrodynamic interaction between them and the hull reduces the forces they can exert.

MODERN CONTROL SYSTEMS

Submarine control practice has changed considerably as speed has increased. As noted, at high speed flows over different control surfaces interact more and more, so that changes in depth can produce changes in heading, and vice versa. In addition, it can be argued that steering decisions are more difficult to make, since the outcome of particular plane or rudder movements may be more difficult to grasp. Hence the development of more and more integrated control systems, so that ultimately a single man can 'fly' a submarine in three dimensions, to make the greatest possible use of its inherent manoeuvrability. Many modern boats have this capability, although it is by no means universally used. The use of aircraft-type controls appears to have originated with the dynamically- (rather than buoyancy-) controlled Walter submarines of 1939–45.

Until that time, submarines generally had three separate control positions: forward and after planesmen, and a helmsman. It was possible, in effect, to divide up depth control (forward) trim (aft), and heading (helm) only because the submarine moved so slowly that the watch officer had time to compensate by pumping trim tanks. In such craft there was no direct communication between helmsman and planesmen, but there was little effective interaction between movement in the two planes. As speeds increased, so did dynamic forces; moreover, the safety factor of time decreased sharply. Many postwar fast submarines employed aircraft-type joysticks controlling both sets of planes: a wheel quadrant at the top of the stick controlled the rudder. On the basis of seagoing experience, joystick motion was imparted proportionally to the planes, one-third to the foreplanes (housed at high speed), two-thirds to the after planes. One man could then 'fly' the submarine, although in practice two are sometimes used. From the *Oberon* class (launched from 1959) onwards, British submarines (except for ballistic missile craft) have been fitted for One Man Control. All British submarines from *Oberon* onwards have autopilots, which are regularly used. The typical division of labour still reflects earlier practice, in that one man controls the rudder and the other the planes. Thus even current systems (often with autopilots) do not appear to take account of interactive effects such as yaw, although in practice an experienced 'pilot' can generally anticipate cross coupling effects.

That really requires computer assistance. In 1963 the US Navy introduced a computerised 'road in the sea' display for both helmsmen, to translate directional and depth commands into appropriate plane and helm commands. In theory this system is superior to the dials of classic submarines because it responds much more rapidly. Yet there are many who feel that the need for very rapid response has been overblown, and that such elaborate systems are not worthwhile. In particular, computer errors or malfunctions can have fatal results, whereas depth gauges and gyro compasses tend to be much closer to the relevant physical phenomena. Feeling within the US Submarine Service ran so strong that this CONALOG system was not incorporated in the current *Los Angeles* class.

ESCAPE AND RESCUE

No discussion of submarine operation underwater can exclude the issues of escape and rescue. Escape is taken to mean unaided departure from a bottomed submarine; particularly during the past decade, rescue by an external vehicle has been an alternative. The submarine operating environment can be divided approximately into three regions: shallow water, down to about 600ft, from which unaided escape is possible; deeper water, down to collapse depth, from which rescue is worthwhile; and the deep ocean, which will crush a submarine long before it hits bottom.

Escape is generally by means of special breathing apparatus; the escapee is effectively unprotected from the sea pressure around him. If that pressure is too great, then too much carbon dioxide will be absorbed by body tissues, and, upon reaching the surface, the escapee will suffer from the 'bends'. The US Mommsen Lung exemplifies escape equipment. It is a self-contained short-endurance breathing device; the British Davis Submarine Escape Apparatus (DSEA) was similar. More recently, the Royal Navy has developed a technique of 'free ascent', in which the escapee merely breathes out steadily while he shoots to the surfce. His buoyancy is provided by an inflated rubber hood covering his entire head, apart from his face. The current British Hooded Escape Apparatus has been tested to 600ft and a theoretical limit of about 675ft has been predicted. Both figures are far above the test depth, let alone the crush depth, of many modern submarines; hence the development of a variety of rescue vehicles.

From a submarine design point of view, escape equipment requires some (albeit limited) provision. There must be special escape trunks (air locks), and specially strengthened internal bulkheads allowing the submarine crew to concentrate while pressures are equalised prior to escape.

DIVING AND UNDERWATER MANOEUVRABILITY

When the escapees reach the surface, they are subject to all of the usual hazards facing swimmers in the open sea. For example, when the British submarine *Truculent* sank after a night collision with a Swedish ship in the Thames in January 1950, many of her crew members successfully rose to the surface, but were swept out to sea on the outgoing tide. Current German practice, which recognises this problem, is to provide an inflatable raft in a pressure-proof container.

Although a major hull penetration at depth would swiftly destroy the interior (and, therefore, the crew) of a modern submarine, there remains the possibility that relatively minor damage might disable a submarine which, bottomed, would still be largely intact. In the past, diving bells have been used for such rescues. Typically a diver would guide them into position atop a submarine's escape hatch. For example, one saved 33 survivors of the sinking of the USS *Squalus* in 1939. The US McCann Rescue Chamber, suspended from a rescue ship, is rated down to a depth of 850ft. By the late 1950s submarine test depths exceeded its capabilities. Moreover, divers in flexible diving suits could not operate really effectively at such depths.

After the *Thresher* disaster in 1963, it became evident that the US Navy had no means of dealing with such circumstances. The Deep Submergence Rescue Vehicle (DSRV), a small submarine, was designed to solve this problem. In theory, DSRVs would be stored at strategically located bases, and attack submarines fitted to carry them out to the disabled craft for rescue operations. Reportedly they can operate at depths as great as 5000ft, far in excess of current test (or, probably, collapse) depths. This figure presumably reflects US interest, in the early 1960s, in much deeper-diving craft. At a total weight of 37 tons, the DSRV can even be flown aboard a C-141 Starlifter or C-5A Galaxy transport, a capability tested in 1978–79. As a test of DSRV capability, in 1979 a DSRV based at San Diego was flown to Glasgow, then trucked to the Clyde Submarine Base at Faslane and mated to the British missile submarine *Repulse*, which steamed out to a simulated submarine

Although SQUIRE was not adopted, another automated display, CONALOG (Contact-Analog) was; it is the 'road in the sea' on the control panel aboard the nuclear-powered USS *Queenfish* (SSN 651), shown nearing the North Pole in August 1970. In theory, the display shows the helmsman and planesman what they must do in order to come to the required depth and heading. It received mixed reviews within the submarine force, and was not incorporated in the *Los Angeles*, partly on the grounds that it represented an unnecessary (and quite possibly unsafe) degree of automation.
US Navy

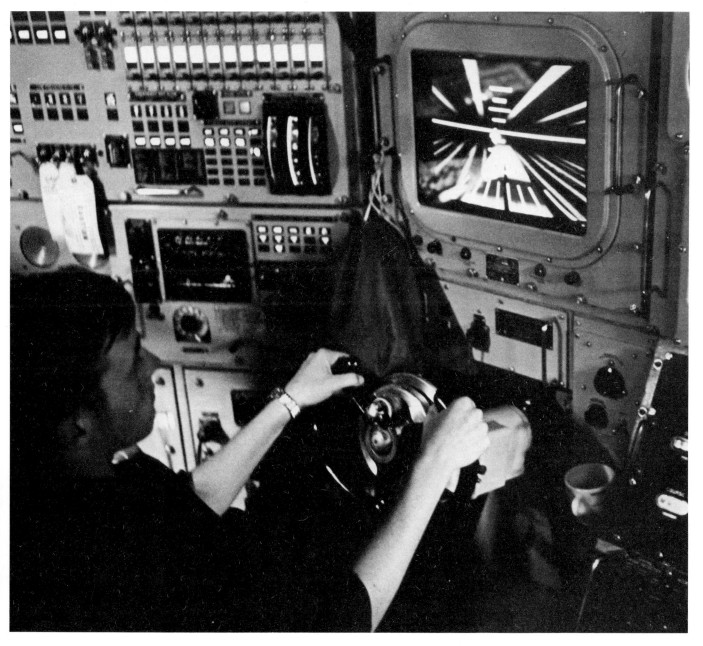

casualty, HMS *Odin*, bottomed at about 400ft off the Isle of Arran. The DSRV was launched and recovered at a depth of about 250ft. In this case the elapsed time from San Diego to embarkation at Faslane was about 47 hours.

Since submerged submarines are not continuously in contact with their bases (and, indeed, since submariners try to avoid communicating), some considerable time will pass between a submarine casualty and notification. That became evident in the May 1968 loss (with all hands) of the nuclear boat USS *Scorpion* SW of the Azores en route home from the Mediterranean. Second, it will be vital for the submarine to be able to give some indication of just where it has bottomed. In the past, submarines have been provided with signal buoys for this purpose, but there is a natural fear the the buoys themselves will be somewhat noisy, and that they will become dislodged under the stress of wartime attack. In the US Navy, for example, they were welded down during World War II.

The American programme initially called for construction of 12 rescue craft, each to be able to carry 12 survivors; later the number was cut to six, and passenger capacity doubled. Ultimately only two DSRV were built. They were completed in 1971 and 1972, but declared fully operational only in 1977. As this is written, the DSRV is usable by both US and British submarines. The Royal Navy has also experimented with adaptations of existing and commercial submersible craft that exist in considerable numbers around the British Isles, for work in connection with North Sea oilfields. The Swedish Navy has its own rescue craft, the URF, designed for road transportation to the coast. More recently the Soviets have built a special submarine transport, codenamed 'India' in the West, carrying two submersibles in tandem deck-wells.

IKL in West Germany has proposed an alternative particularly well suited to navies operating in relatively shallow water: a rescue craft integral with the submarine hull. IKL reasons that its craft may well hit bottom well above their crush depth, and that internal pressure-proof bulkheads may save their crews, for escape via special 'Gabler Spheres' built into the hull structure proper. For this reason, IKL submarines, unlike most others designed in the West, still incorporate pressure-proof internal bulkheads.

That is, other Western designers tend to assume that pressure hull penetration at any substantial depth is likely to be disastrous. As long as ballast tank volume must be limited in the interest of speed, the ability to surface despite damage is limited as well. Thus no modern Western submarine has even a one-compartment standard of survival when it is submerged. That is why US (and presumably most other Western) submarines no longer incorporate very strong internal bulkheads: once the pressure hull has been penetrated they are sure to sink, and they are unlikely to hit bottom before exceeding crush depth. IKL is an exception because it designs relatively small submarines to operate in shallow seas such as the Baltic. Reportedly the Soviets also still contemplate survival after hull damage; they compartment their submarines quite extensively. That may reflect an expectation that they will more frequently operate at or near the surface, where flooding would indeed be controllable.

CHAPTER NINE

Propulsion-Conventional and Nuclear

A powerplant can be visualised as a combination of stored energy (usually, for a submarine, in a nuclear reactor or in batteries and fuel tanks) and a means of converting that stored energy as efficiently as possible into propulsive power. The submarine aspect is that, at least part of the time, energy conversion must be accomplished underwater. Apart from nuclear fuel, the most efficient means of storing energy appears to be fuel which must be burnt in combination with an oxidiser. Thus a conventional submarine powerplant can be visualised as a means of very efficient energy storage (fuel oil), a means of conversion to less efficient storage (such as a diesel generator), and storage and conversion systems well adapted to underwater operation (batteries and electric motors).

For a modern diesel-electric submarine, the goal is to minimise exposure to detection, ie to minimise time spent snorkelling as a fraction of overall running time, the greater the battery capacity and the faster the charging rate, the better. That is quite apart from any desire for high surface or subsurface speed. Requirements for sustained underwater speed are one (but not the only) factor determining total battery capacity, which determines in turn the total energy that must be supplied per charge. Diesel power and battery characteristics in turn determine how quickly the charge can be applied.

These concepts contrast with earlier requirements for high surface speed, ie for high propulsive power to be derived from the high-efficiency engine. Diesels have always suffered from limitations on their maximum power. At any particular level of diesel development, power per cylinder is limited, so that a single engine can be made to develop more power only by multiplying the number of cylinders. This generally means lengthening the unit and is difficult to do in a space (length) - critical design. Because each piston moves in jerks, stopping and starting several times during its cycle, a diesel crankshaft tends to twist (ie to vibrate torsionally). The longer (and faster-running) the engine, the worse the vibration. This type of trouble was encountered, for example, in the World War I British 'J' class, in which power was maximised, by enlarging the earlier Vickers eight-cylinder diesel ('E' class) to 12 cylinders, in an attempt to reach fleet speed. Extra engine length also consumed space: machinery spaces took up 36 per cent of a 'J' boat's overall length. Machinery space became particularly critical in post-1945 submarines, both because length itself had to be minimised and more of it was needed for batteries. The US Navy, for instance, developed a series of radial diesels that proved unsuccessful. In the multi-deck *Albacore*-hull submarine *Barbel* of 1958, three engines were arranged on two levels, ie in the length which is another boat might have sufficed for only two.

Several navies tried to connect two diesels end to end on each propeller shaft, but they could not easily be synchronised, and vibration worsened. The only really satisfactory arrangements appear to be either a single engine per shaft or a diesel-electric plant in which the engines are only indirectly connected to the shafts. In most pre-1939 installations, both the diesel and the motor/generator were clutched or geared to the same propeller shaft. When batteries were being charged, the motor/generator was disconnected from its shaft, which was then unpowered; underwater, the diesel was declutched. Surface power was thus limited to one or two (if there were three in all) shafts while batteries were charged. Soviet submarines still employ this system.

The alternative was to run *all* electrical power through the batteries while the diesels were running on the surface. Each diesel ran its own generator that fed into the batteries.

France adopted steam surface propulsion for many of her pre-1914 submarines. This is Maxime Laubeuf's *Narval* of 1899, their prototype and also the first double-hull submarine. Note her resemblance to contemporary French surface torpedo boats and her two visible torpedo dropping collars (the frames beneath her conning tower and left of the ensign). Diving was very slow because it was necessary not only to shut down the boiler but also to dissipate its heat before submerging.
Popperfoto

SUBMARINE DESIGN AND DEVELOPMENT

A typical current nuclear propulsion system.

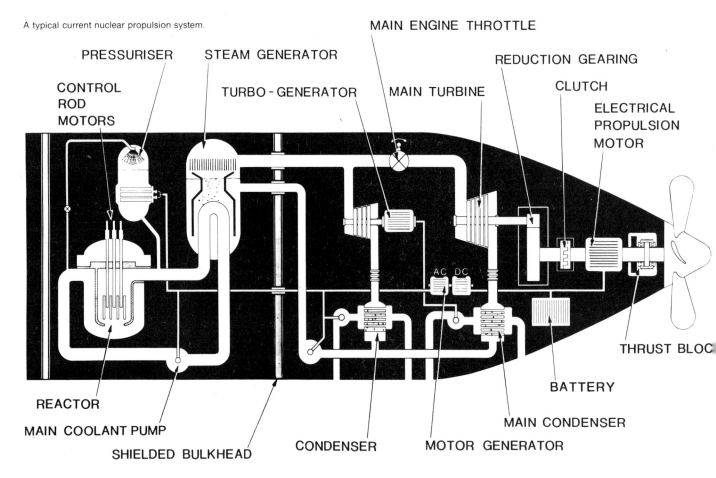

The batteries in turn were always connected to motors driving the propeller shafts. This was a much heavier arrangement, but it was also much more flexible, and it made for higher surface speeds when charging. It was used by the US 'fleet type' submarine, and many postwar craft, in which underwater (motor) power actually exceeds surface (diesel) power.

Efficiency can be measured both in terms of energy loss in conversion (eg the thermal efficiency of a diesel) or in terms of weight or volume efficiency (engine weight per horsepower). To some extent the two can be traded off: a heavier but more energy-efficient engine can be paired with a smaller quantity of stored energy in the form of fuel oil. The latter is a much more efficient means of storing energy: a diesel achieves about 2 horsepower-hours (hph) per pound of oil, even allowing for snorkelling inefficiencies. That compares with about 0.013 – 0.027 hph/lb for typical lead-acid or nickel-cadmium batteries, and with 0.04–0.08 hph/lb for the most efficient batteries (silver-zinc) though they are severely limited in the number of charging cycles they can survive. The batteries themselves are only about 50 – 80 per cent efficient in their use of charging energy.

During the early 1970s in connection with studies of small non-nuclear submarines, several US analysts studied an alternative form of energy storage, a solid carbon (graphite) block which might be heated electrically to 5000°F. The induction coils heating the block would be protected from melting by helium cooling, and by being on the outside of the block. Thermal energy would be extracted directly by passing the working fluid of a Brayton-cycle (see below) engine through the carbon block. In theory, the hotter the block, the more efficient the entire cycle. Proper insulation would limit heat leakage, one study assuming a rate of 0.45 per cent per hour and a charging efficiency of 80 per cent. Net efficiency (electrical energy in/thermal energy out) was predicted to be 57.2 per cent, including heat leakage. No such system was ever tested in full-scale, but it may be relevant to note that, in the past, submarine steam engines (nothing like as hot) proved hazardous when their heat leaked into submerged submarines. It is not clear from the little published whether the thermal sink designs took the whole submarine's thermal balance into account.

The open-cycle (snorkel or surface) diesel saves weight by obtaining its oxidiser (oxygen) from the atmosphere. A closed-cycle diesel would obtain about 0.5hph/lb of combined fuel oil and oxidant. That is because 3.5lb of oxygen must be burned for every pound of fuel oil. These figures, taken together, show that the air-breathing diesel is by far the most efficient of the lot, and explain why battery endurance, however long, is far more limited than diesel endurance. The closed-cycle figure shows why the Walter and Kreislauf systems are better than batteries, but are still confined to brief bursts of power. That is, on a fuel basis a Kreislauf diesel is about three times as efficient as the relatively heavy lead-acid batteries. Hydrogen peroxide was better. The 1600-ton Type XVIII U-boat was to have had an underwater endurance of about ten hours at a full speed of about 24 knots. The new Thyssen TR 1700, the fastest diesel-electric submarine in the world, is credited with a *one-hour* sustained speed of 25 knots.

In theory, exotic fuels and oxidants can better these figures. When burned in air, hydrogen has about three times the energy per unit weight of conventional fuel oil, although it is much less dense. Metals such as beryllium and aluminium can contribute over twice the energy per unit weight of a fuel oil-liquid combination. Beryllium-oxygen has about 60 per cent of fuel oil's energy content available for burning in air. That in turn suggests that an appropriately-fuelled closed-cycle submarine might approach a conventional snorkeller's endurance.

CLOSED-CYCLE ENGINES

The choice of fuel and oxidant determines depth performance. If the combustion products are gaseous, then they must be discharged against water pressure. This phenomenon limits the depth performance of both current US torpedoes, the Mark 46 and Mark 48. Mark 50, the Advanced Lightweight Torpedo (ALWT) designed specif-

PROPULSION – CONVENTIONAL AND NUCLEAR

ically for high speed at great depth, employs a reaction the products of which are not gaseous: lithium/sulphur-hexafluoride. In the mid-1970s the same reaction was suggested as a heat source for a closed-cycle submarine engine. It was extremely intense and could not easily be throttled, but that was acceptable for a high-energy sprint or burst propulsion system.

The first closed-cycle plants were the Walter steam-gas turbine and the Kreislauf diesel. After 1945, the US Navy planned six 7500shp submarine powerplants: five more or less conventional types intended to provide ten hours of burst speed, and their successful competitor, the first nuclear plant. All five closed cycles could use either hydrogen peroxide or oxygen. Project Alton was the Walter cycle. Ellis was a pressure-fired steam plant, ultimately used in surface ships. Gentry was a diesel-cycle gas turbine, and Gumbo was a closed-cycle (Kreislauf) diesel. Wolverine was a closed-cycle gas turbine. All five were cancelled in 1953; they required nuclear-size submarine hulls, and seemed to offer no particular advantages.

More recently there has been interest in two closed-cycle external combustion plants, the Brayton and Stirling. In each, a source of heat is applied to a working fluid. Thermal efficiency is measured by the temperature difference between the heat source and a cooler, equivalent to a steam engine's condenser engine. The Brayton cycle employs a two-stage turbine; typical working fluids are argon, helium, and xenon. This fluid is expanded into a vapour in a heat exchanger, passed through the first turbine stage, exhausting through a recuperator or heat exchanger into a heat sink. It is then compressed by the other turbine stage and pre-heated in the recuperator before reentering the heat exchanger. A Brayton cycle engine was an unsuccessful competitor for the ALWT torpedo engine. On a larger scale, about a decade ago rough estimates showed that a 5000 ton Brayton-cycle (liquid oxygen-oil) submarine could travel 2000 miles at 9 knots, spend 40 days on station at 3 knots, and sprint for 40 hours at 26. This was hardly nuclear performance, but it was much better than diesel-electric, being achievable entirely without snorkelling.

The other choice is the Stirling piston engine, capable of about 40 per cent thermal efficiency, and comparable in size to a diesel. Unlike a diesel, a Stirling experiences no noisy explosions during operation. The Swedish Navy actually planned to install it in a submarine, but apparently it is not quite mature enough technically.

Somewhat more distant are thermal converters or thermionic generators, which convert heat directly into electrical power. Thermionic effects have been known for many years, but used only on a small scale. At least in theory they should attain high efficiencies. This class of systems includes battery-like generators which draw their energy from heat flow across them.

A new German MAN diesel engine is shown shortly after its installation aboard the US submarine S-20 (SS 125) at Mare Island in 1932. The neighbouring engine has not yet been fitted, which is why the normally cramped engine room seems spacious. Diesel problems plagued the US World War I submarine fleet because surface performance required a combination of compactness and high power; hence the adoption of foreign equipment. Within a few years a new generation of domestic high-speed diesels had appeared, partly funded by railway developments in the field and these engines served through World War II.
US Navy

SUBMARINE DESIGN AND DEVELOPMENT

HMS Submarine K 26

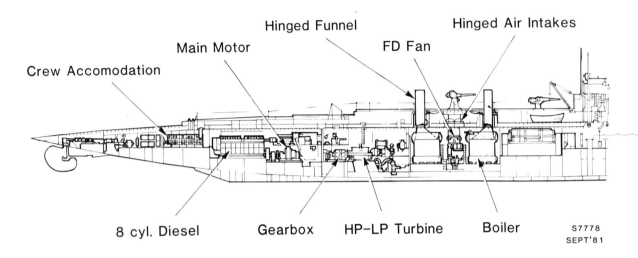

The last pre-nuclear British steam submarine powerplant as fitted in HMS *K-26* (1919).
By courtesy of the Institution of Mechanical Engineers

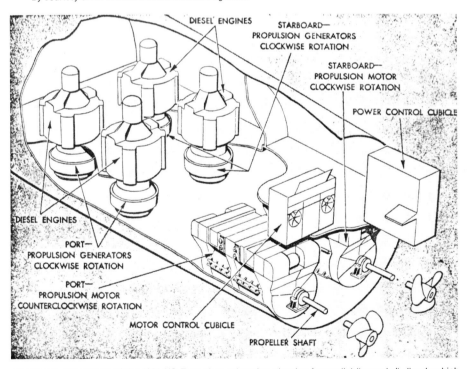

Machinery arrangement of the 1951 US *Tang* class submarine, showing four radial ('pancake') diesels which proved unreliable and had to be replaced.
US Navy

Perhaps the major design challenge in all of the fuel-burning closed-cycle engines, aside from having sufficient oxidant in compact form, is exhaust disposal against the immense external pressure of great depths. That generally requires some form of gas compression, at a cost in power. Some metallic fuels are exceptions as they produce solid end products. From time to time hybrid systems are proposed, capable of closed-cycle or snorkel operation – such as Walter's original concept.

FUEL CELLS

The other major competitor for non-nuclear, non-snorkelling operation is the fuel cell, in which an oxidant and a fuel are combined chemically, producing electricity directly. Efficiency can be very high, and (unlike a thermal engine) imposes no great problem of heat dissipation. The fuel cell concept has been known for about 140 years, and the development of practical plants began in 1958. Efficiency figures as high as 70 – 80 per cent are quoted. In theory they should make for minimum fuel and oxidant storage. In many cases the reaction product is pure, drinkable, water. Fuel cells are already used for land-based utility energy production, and the DSRV rescue vehicle (see Chapter 8) is powered by an alkaline fuel cell (oxygen and hydrogen fuels). A typical utility cell, using gasoline, diesel oil, or JP-5 as a fuel, is under development by United Technologies, in packages of up to 26MW (almost 34,000hp). Unlike the acid cell, it is quite complex, requiring a turbocompressor to supply the air oxidant and also to help convert the fuel into hydrogen and carbon dioxide. Such a cell operates at 390°F, with over 56 per cent efficiency claimed. Other fuel cell technologies include a lithium-seawater cell (which, however, produces gaseous hydrogen as a reaction product) and a lithium-peroxide cell (which produces water). Fuel cells seem likely powerplants for any future generation of non-nuclear submarines, but probably not before the early 1990s.

At the moment submarines are limited to

PROPULSION – CONVENTIONAL AND NUCLEAR

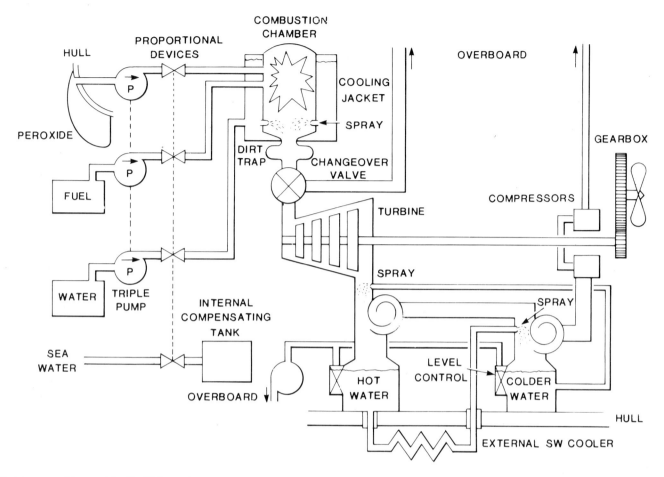

Hydrogen peroxide propulsion/the Walter cycle.
By courtesy of the Institution of Mechanical Engineers

diesels and to lead-acid batteries similar in principle to car batteries. The diesels are specially adapted to charging. Modern lightweight units are resiliently mounted for silencing, and charging capacity is maximised by running several simultaneously. They are designed specially to exhaust against water pressure when snorkelling. A diesel exhausting into the air will produce more power, but will also emit far more tell-tale exhaust products. Snorkelling requirements are reflected in design capabilities for quick starting and stopping. Modern IKL submarines have sensors in their snorkels which shut down their diesels when waves close the air intakes, thereby avoiding the handicap of earlier installations, whose diesels tended to suck the air out of the boats when their air intakes were temporarily closed by wave action.

Superchargers are now being used to boost power further without any great increase in weight. But snorkelling introduces its own problems. Conventional turbochargers extract their energy from diesel exhaust. In most modern submarines that same exhaust must fight its way out against water pressure, and much less energy can be extracted.

Mechanical superchargers have also been tried, but in only a few cases.

BATTERIES

The usual lead-acid batteries are very heavy, but relatively cheap, and they remain standard. Alternatives are silver-zinc and silver-cadmium, both are lighter and more compact, but they are more costly, and less tolerant to the normal usage cycle of lead-acid batteries. Silver-zinc does not behave well if recharged from a partially discharged condition; to retain its capacity, it must be fully discharged first. All present gas hazards. A lead-acid battery being charged evolves hydrogen, which can be explosive. If seawater enters it, poisonous chlorine gas is released. Discharged at high rates, they also evolve heat that must be removed. Fast charging may poison the electrolyte, which must be circulated mechnically to bring hot electrolyte to the top of the cell for extraction.

Postwar lead-acid battery development has been spectacular. If the British late 1950s installation in the *Oberon* is taken as a basis, German batteries of the late 1970s showed about 60 – 70 per cent more energy per unit weight at high discharge rates, and about 20 per cent at lower rates. At the same time designers such as IKL could devote unusually high percentages of total displacement to batteries, 20 – 25 per cent being typical. By contrast, the wartime Type VIIC fraction was about 8 per cent, and even the 'electro-U-boat', the Type XXI, devoted only about 15 per cent. Current batteries discharge much less of their energy at high (eg 1 hour) than at very low rates, and future improvements may well be in this direction. A typical battery can deliver about 0.013 hph/lb at the 1-hour rate, but 0.033 hph/lb at a 100-hour rate. These figures respectively represent 20 and 50 per cent of the theoretically possible rates. There are alternative battery materials. Sodium-sulphur batteries are currently being tested in cars. By 1990 they may be able to achieve about 0.07 hph/lb at a high discharge rate, and slightly more at low rates. Applied to existing submarine designs, that might buy a 450 per cent more in high-speed underwater endurance.

Two techniques have been proposed to extend battery endurance. One is external stowage of battery acid. As each cell discharges, its electrolyte gradually poisons. If fresh acid is supplied, this poisoning effect

SUBMARINE DESIGN AND DEVELOPMENT

can be overcome. The other is a hybrid drive, in which a closed-cycle engine is used to keep batteries charged underwater. They would not replace diesels, but supplement them when snorkelling was tactically impossible.

NUCLEAR REACTORS

The other great theme of modern submarine propulsion is the nuclear reactor. It provides virtually unlimited underwater endurance at high power, but at considerable cost in overall submarine size and, apparently, complexity. Submarine reactors generally employ much more highly enriched fuel, virtually weapon-grade, than commercial ones, to achieve higher energy densities. During the early 1950s US submarines competed directly with US nuclear bombs for much the same fissionable material. As U-235 (oralloy) production increased, submarine reactors could be provided with more highly enriched fuel. Thus reportedly the original *Nautilus* core was 18 – 20 per cent enriched, but the boat was refuelled with a 40 per cent enriched core, and the hotter *Seawolf* reactor (S2G) used 90 per cent; the higher the enrichment, the more compact the reactor.

Even in the early 1960s, the American S5W was credited with about 140,000 miles submerged endurance, or 3500 – 4000 steaming hours. Clearly even 50,000 miles would be well beyond anything needed on one patrol; fuel efficiency is more a determinant of how often a submarine must be refuelled, ie removed from service for a substantial period. How long that must be depends in part on the design of the fuel itself. Reportedly the *Nautilus* cores were relatively poorly designed for replacement, and her first refuelling took several months. In later designs the fuel elements can be removed and replaced as a unit; in 1959 a refuelling time of three to four weeks was reported.

The process of fission requires relatively slow ('thermalised') neutrons, which represent only a fraction of those produced by fission reactions. The fuel rods are therefore surrounded by a *moderator*, whose atoms slow down the fast colliding neutrons to a usable energy level. Energy is typically extracted in the form of heat, via a coolant circulating through the core. American and British pressurised water reactor (PWR) plants use water as both moderator and coolant. Sodium was tried unsuccessfully in the USS *Seawolf* (launched 1955). The very high power density of the current Soviet 'Alfa' class submarine is generally attributed to a liquid metal coolant.

In these systems, a *primary* circuit or loop extracts heat from the radioactive core, giving it up in a heat exchanger or steam generator. To take reactor size, efficiency depends in part on how many passes the coolant makes through the reactor core; that determines how much coolant must flow to transfer a given amount of heat. Although the original US plants employed only a single pass, the more compact, and much more powerful, S5W, employs a triple pass. The *secondary* loop carries steam to and from a turbine. Most potential coolants become more or less radioactive within a reactor, and hence must be included within the shielded portion of the plant. Water, the usual coolant, is only moderately affected, and its radioactivity decays rapidly after a plant is shut down. Sodium is much worse, but it was tried because of advantages to be described below.

Helium, lead, bismuth, and hydrocarbons do not become radioactive at all, if they can be kept free of impurities. These latter substances therefore can be used directly for power generation. Shielding, which in conventional plants accounts for 20 – 30 per cent of total weight, can be limited to the reactor itself. In particular, it is often claimed that a nuclear gas turbine (presumably using helium as the working fluid) would be the lightest conceivable nuclear plant. Reportedly a lightweight fast-neutron nuclear gas turbine was proposed for the 1957-58 US *Skate* class. A conventional PWR was substituted because of insufficient time for development. The principal (and crushing) design problem of such systems is apparently leakage. For a time a hydrocarbon-cooled plant was under development for destroyer use. It would have been roughly similar in design to a pressurised water plant, but the coolant would not have corroded the fuel elements. But this system was abandoned, partly because the coolant tended to decompose inside the reactor.

Thermal efficiency in the system's steam portion (and therefore its compactness) depends on the temperature drop between heat exchanger and condenser (which is at sea water temperature). Maximum temperature within a conventional reactor is set somewhat below the boiling point corresponding to coolant pressure. The coolant cannot be permitted to boil within the reactor, as its temperature would fall. Coolant actually leaving the reactor will be somewhat cooler than this maximum. Pressure is maintained within the reactor container by inserting another large vessel, a pressuriser, in the primary loop. Steam filling the top of the pressuriser compensates for changes in coolant volume as the reactor inlet and outlet temperatures change. The greater the range of temperatures, the larger the pressuriser.

How much heat the coolant can transfer to the steam side of the system depends upon how much hotter it is than the steam. Thus there is a benefit, in terms of heat transfer rate and heat exchanger size, in *reducing* steam temperature. That increases turbine size, but it also limits the size of the radioactive heat exchanger. Since shielding is a major fraction of total plant weight (20 – 30 per cent in early examples), that is often a net weight saving. For these reasons US nuclear plants use saturated steam at relatively low temperatures, whereas non-nuclear steam plant practice has gone in the opposite direction since the 1920s. For example, the prototype civilian power plant at Shippingport, (Pennsylvania), developed during 1953-57 on the basis of naval experience, experiences a temperature rise of only 34°F in the core's coolant with an inlet temperature of 508°F and an outlet temperature of 542°F. These temperatures correspond to a pressure of 2000 lb/sq in, at which saturation (boiling) temperature is 636°F. Reportedly early US nuclear plants employed the type of saturated-steam machinery common in the 1920s, which implies operating temperatures of about 300°F.

In a 1957 article, the then Rear Admiral Hyman G Rickover (Head of the Bureau of Ships' Nuclear Power Division) claimed that this very limited temperature range (with average coolant temperature constant) made control more effective over the wide range of possible operating conditions. That is, large changes in power plant load correspond to relatively small changes in temperature, so that rapid manoeuvring does not entail large thermal stresses that might otherwise present trouble, and perhaps add considerably to the system's overall weight. A very limited temperature range also minimised pressuriser size; since the latter had to be shielded as part of the primary loop, reducing its size reduced shield weight.

Control is also simplified by the reactor's basic stability. For example, as more energy is demanded in the secondary loop, more heat is extracted from the primary, and coolant temperature falls slightly as a result. That in turn slightly increases coolant density, and therefore its ability (as a moderator) to thermalise neutrons. The reactor power level therefore rises to compensate. Similiarly, if power demand is reduced, coolant temperature rises (as less energy is being extracted), scattering cross-section declines slightly, and energy output follows. All of this occurs entirely without reference to the control rods that can shut down the reactor altogether.

The only escape from low-temperature steam technology is to raise maximum coolant temperature. Liquid sodium was a proposed solution; it promised a tenfold temperature rise through the reactor, and therefore several hundred degrees more temperature in the steam generator. Graphite was used as a moderator. The mid-1950s *Seawolf* operated with superheated steam, and in this respect was much closer to non-nuclear naval plants. Heat transfer was much more efficient, and a liquid metal plant could achieve a given horsepower level with only 85 per cent of a pressurised-water unit's thermal power. But the *Seawolf* reactor suffered a superheater leak, and the plant was ultimately abandoned in 1959 as unreliable. In a more general sense, liquid metal systems have the important drawback that the working fluid must be kept heated to avoid freezing. This added complexity makes human error much more likely.

Even so, liquid metal probably offers the only way really to reduce reactor plant weight and volume. The Soviet 'Alfa' is reportedly highly automated, and may employ an

PROPULSION – CONVENTIONAL AND NUCLEAR

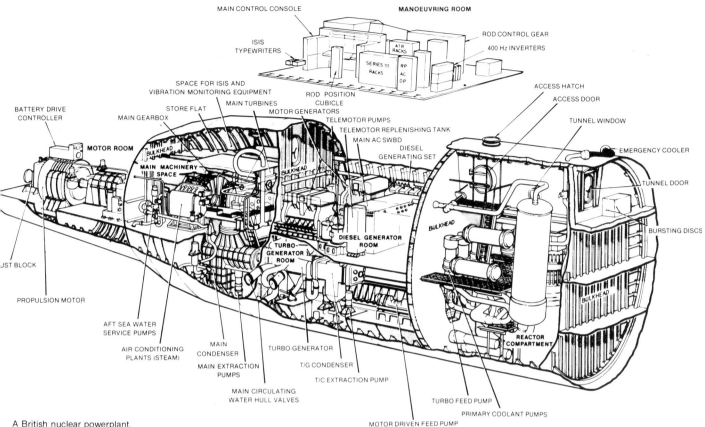

A British nuclear powerplant.

unmanned engine room. In that case its reactor shielding may be considerably lighter than in US plants, not least because there is much less need to provide access. A liquid metal cycle based on non-radioactive materials such as lead and bismuth would further reduce shielding costs, since the steam generators could be outside the shield. Turbine weights would fall because high steam conditions could be employed.

All current US plants employ water, and there is said to be no current interest in any return to liquid metals, whose supporters feel that they were abandoned prematurely. Certainly the US Navy made a conscious choice in favour of a proven technology rather than various theoretically better alternatives. One reason may have been the immense cost and complexity of developing wholly new plants. The US programme's history shows that their number has declined. Two plants, the *Nautilus* PWR and the *Seawolf* sodium type, were developed virtually simultaneously, work also proceeding on carrier, cruiser, and large destroyer reactors. By the late 1950s the Naval Reactors group had also produced a smaller *Nautilus* plant equivalent for the *Skate* and *Halibut* submarine classes (S3W and S4W); an advanced (high-power) reactor for the huge *Triton* (S4G); a small reactor with about a tenth the output for *Tullibee* (S2C); all before devising the standard 15,000shp S5W that powered the *Skipjack*, *Thresher/Permit*, *Sturgeon*, and ballistic missile submarines. By contrast, the only really new system developed during the 1960s was the natural-circulation type (S5G)

of the *Narwhal*, which appeared in enlarged form in the new *Ohio*. The current *Los Angeles* plant is reportedly a modified version of the existing and much-improved destroyer reactor (D2G, now S6G). Again, it has recently been reported that Naval Reactors has only one major new start in mind, a single reactor plant powerful enough (at 48,000 – 56,000shp) for a destroyer. This project actually dates from the early 1960s and has already been the basis for the carrier *Nimitz*'s large reactor (A4W). It will probably form part of the FY 89 'new generation submarine' now in the early design stage. British experience appears to mirror American, in that it is increasingly difficult to improve the early designs, and new plants are taking much longer to develop. That may be related to much stiffer noise and shock requirements.

In his 1957 article, Admiral Rickover, who was responsible for the US programmme, remarked that nuclear plants were likely to be operated virtually continuously at the upper end of their power curves, because there was little or no point in economising on fuel. Thus they would not enjoy the effective safety margin inherent in conventional machinery. Nor could they be maintained easily underway, as access to radioactive spaces would be extremely limited. Admiral Rickover was also very sensitive to reactor safety. It has also much preferred manual, or at least manual-monitored, systems to automated ones. This attitude extends to other aspects of the US submarine programme, such as intense dislike of CONALOG (see Chapter 8). A manned machinery compartment must, in

turn, be heavily shielded. By contrast, the Soviets who are said to apply rather relaxed radiation safety standards throughout their fleet, appear to have opted for unmanned machinery spaces in the 'Alfa' class. That saves more than shielding weight, since much less access space around the system is required. Presumably the cost in reliability seemed acceptable for a relatively short-endurance submarine 'interceptor'. Note that even a considerable relaxation in actual shielding requirements does not save greatly on weight, since the difference between relatively complete shielding and the absolute minimum to prevent rapid death is not very great.

PWR operation requires considerable auxiliary power, primarily to operate the primary loop's circulation pumps. As long as the reactor operates, these pumps must run to remove the heat that otherwise would soon melt the pressure vessel. The pressuriser needs electrical heaters to maintain sufficient steam within it. The pumps and turbo-generators are, in turn, sources of noise. Thus, no matter how slowly it is steaming, a submarine powered by a PWR cannot be completely quiet. However, in an appropriately designed reactor, the water circulates partly because of the thermal gradient set up by the nuclear reaction itself. At low enough power, then, coolant pumps can be turned off altogether, as in the natural circulation reactor designs of the *Narwhal* and *Ohio* classes. At higher power levels, pumps must be switched on. It is also possible to provide a conventional PWR with several sets of

135

SUBMARINE DESIGN AND DEVELOPMENT

COMPARISON OF VALIANT AND SWIFTSURE MACHINERY SPACES

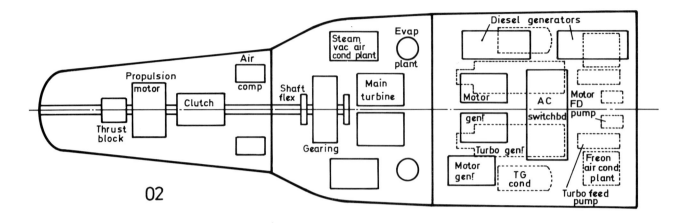

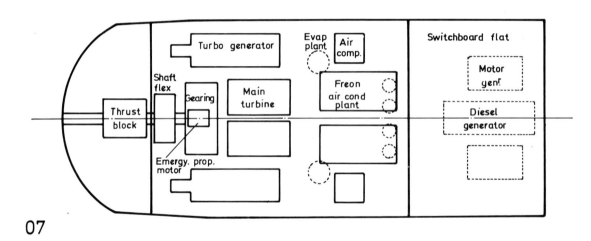

The machinery spaces of the British nuclear attack submarines HMS *Valiant* (SSN 02) and HMS *Swiftsure* (SSN 07) compared. Silencing is obtained by noise isolation, which in modern nuclear submarine practice means placing machinery on a raft sound-isolated from the hull proper (right p 137, looking aft).

pumps, some not being switched on until higher power is required.

Another reactor system peculiarity shared, incidentally, with the closed-cycle types previously described) is its need for a condenser through which seawater must flow to provide a heat sink. The condenser in turn may employ either pumps and/or the natural seawater flow as the submarine moves. At very low speeds pumping is required, again a source of noise. Moreover, the need for a condenser can make bottoming difficult, as sand may be sucked in. Recent drawings of the British submarine *Swiftsure* appear to show condenser ducting in the horizontal tail fins, well clear of the bottom.

SUBMARINE NOISE AND SILENCING

No discussion of submarine machinery can be separated from the issue of noise, most of which is machinery-generated. A submarine produces discrete 'lines' or frequencies (narrow-band noise) superimposed on a continuous spectrum (broad-band noise). There are three general sources: machinery, the propeller, and flow noise along the hull. Unbalanced diesel 'thumping' can be quite loud, and gearing emits a distinctive whine. Even fluid flowing through piping can gurgle. Rotating machinery and pumps, moving at steady rates, contribute lines. Liquid flow is generally broad-band noise. Propeller noise is a continuous hiss modulated by beats at the blade rate (sometimes used to help target classification). Broad-band noise increases faster with speed, largely because it is due to flow over the hull and propeller blades. When discrete lines are due to nuclear components, they may well be detectable no matter how slow the submarine.

From World War II on, suppressing underwater noise has been a constant task. Diesel engines are inherently noisy, but can be muffled through isolating them from the hull proper by means of resilient mountings. Recent electric motors are designed to run at propeller speed, so that no noisy reduction gearing is needed.

Silencing is also a major consideration in propeller design. Blade-rate noise is due to interference between the flow from individual moving blades and disturbances, either upstream or downstream. It was most common in pre-*Albacore* submarines, which generally had their rudders and stern planes abaft the propellers. Modern surfaces well forward of the propeller cause much less trouble, except during sudden manoeuvres. The Swedish X-stern carries these surfaces particularly far from the propeller. Propeller blade skewing helps too, in that the transition (in the slipstream) from one blade to the next is softened.

Recent British submarines employ pump-jets instead of conventional propellers (as apparently will the new US FY 89 submarine) apparently to reduce further noise reduction, at a considerable cost in weight at

PROPULSION – CONVENTIONAL AND NUCLEAR

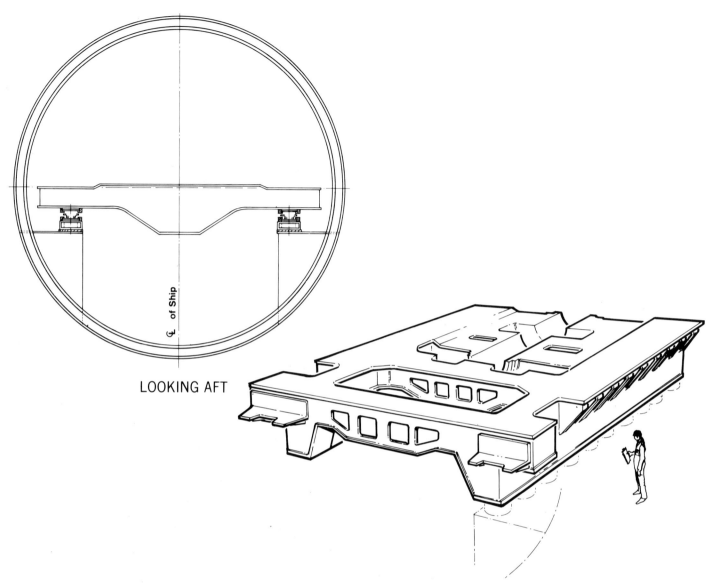

LOOKING AFT

the very end of the propeller shaft. Pump-jets (already used in torpedoes such as the Mark 48) consist of a single multi-blade rotor turning relatively slowly against stator vanes in a duct. In effect it is a high-pitch, low revolution propeller. The major design problem is energy loss to the slipstream, but it is solved by the stator.

The early nuclear submarines were much harder to silence, having two major noise sources, the reactor (including turbo-generators), and an even noisier turbine reduction gearing. Early US attempts at silencing appear to focus on the turbine. The first was the 1960 ASW submarine *Tullibee* with turbo-electric drive. When the corresponding fleet submarine, *Thresher*, was designed, the first sketches showed a turbo-electric plant, but after a few months it became clear that an entirely new power train design would take too long. Instead, the turbines and their gearing were sound-isolated from the hull, a level of quieting approximating to a non-isolated turbo-electric plant.

Such sound isolation entails a rigid 'raft', flexibly supported from the hull proper, to carry the machinery, and in theory its supports deaden their noise. Such flexibility carries its own problems; all piping connecting the steam generator (*not* on the raft) to the turbine must be able to flex as the raft moves on its resilient supports as must the propeller shaft at the other end. When it adopted this technique, the Royal Navy encountered problems at high power; its rafts can be locked in place if necessary. Silencing is much more complex than this indicates; it includes hull linings to deaden the great variety of internally-generated noises. World War II submariners rigged for quiet running by stopping in their tracks, not daring, for example, to drop tools to the steel deck. A modern nuclear submarine is so well sound-insulated that even a grenade explosion probably would not escape its hull.

The raft technique was supplemented, during the 1960s, by two experimental power trains on modified *Thresher* hulls: a new turbo-electric plant in *Glenmard P Lipscomb*, and a direct-drive (ungeared) turbine in *Jack*. In the latter the designers had to accept a much larger turbine (machinery spaces were 10ft longer than in others of the class), but minimised its growth by having its two elements (conventionally the rotor and stator) counter-rotate, each driving a contraprop. At the same time a natural circulation reactor was tested in *Narwhal*. None of these approaches has been adopted in more recent US attack submarines, although *Ohio* does have a natural circulation reactor.

Perhaps nuclear power's single most important effect was to relax enormously many previous submarine design constraints in auxiliary machinery as much as in propulsion. Submarine internal atmosphere determines its endurance quite as much as engine capacity. Oxygen must be supplied and gases such as carbon dioxide swept out. In a conventional submarine, the snorkel is the principal oxygen source and, when the boat is continuously submerged, special oxide 'candles' are burnt. Special absorbent material (soda lime) can be spread to purge various gases. Endurance, then, is often more limited by candle supply than by battery charge. If all of the candles are exhausted during one period between exposure, later

137

snorkel cycles will be limited by the boat's own air capacity, its internal volume.

Nuclear practice is radically different. Since the engine works indefinitely without contact with the atmosphere, the objective is to create a self-contained, or nearly self-contained, atmosphere within the pressure hull. Fresh oxygen can be obtained from seawater by electrolysis, without limit as long as the reactor continues to supply power. Similarly, gases can be purged by electrically-powered catalytic devices. Perhaps this solution's greatest achievement was detailed analysis of trace substances from the artificial atmosphere. Extensive air conditioning is provided, not merely to deal with the great heat generated by the reactor, but also to keep the crew relatively comfortable, and hence relatively effective.

DIESEL OR NUCLEAR?

Inevitably, nuclear and conventional powerplants have been widely compared. Nuclear power was so much the answer that at first it appeared beyond comparison. Any navy which could afford it would have to go nuclear. That was certainly the Anglo-American position in the late 1950s. More recently, advocates of diesel-electric submarines have found important points in their favour. First, the difference in cost *is* important, particularly to provide enough boats for barrier or blockade operations. Current diesel-electric submarines are generally smaller, cheaper, and require many fewer crew. But all of these advantages are relative. A US study of a diesel-electric submarine, SSX, estimated, in August 1982, that a lead boat would cost $612 million, with $310 million for follow-ons, when a new *Los Angeles* class nuclear attack submarine cost about $700 million. SSX characteristics were not revealed, so it is not clear to what extent the paper submarine was either 'gold-plated' or relatively incapable. After the reactor, the weapon system is the most expensive single item in the submarine, whether diesel-electric or nuclear.

Second, diesel-electric submarine advocates can point to superior silencing, at least when running on electric motors. It is true that their rather austere silencing treatment is imperfect, but surviving US diesel-electric submarines have often successfully ambushed alert surface forces. Like their World War II predecessors, they are essentially very effective manned mines, but to what extent will submarine operations be barrier patrols? For a diesel-electric submarine is truly silent only when nearly motionless. Although first-generation nuclear submarines were extremely noisy, current carefully silenced ones are very quiet even *while proceeding at high sustained speed.*

Third, there is sheer size and handiness. Nuclear power generally appears to require a fairly large submarine. Even the American attempt to build a small one, the *Tullibee,* ended with a craft as big as the largest earlier US postwar diesel-electric types. Much of this growth was blamed on the powerplant. Diesel-electric submarines supporters argue that small size is necessary for a boat operating in relatively shallow or constricted waters. The larger the submarine, the longer it takes to answer its helm, or to manoeuvre underwater. Moreover, the smaller the submarine, the smaller the sonar target it represents. But it can be argued that, at least for a large navy, even a diesel boat needs so much equipment that it cannot really be very small. When the German HDW company tried to sell the US a modern diesel-electric attack submarine, it had to set displacement at a far from minute 2000 tons. As for sonar, it can be argued that high burst speed and a large internal capacity make evasion and countermeasures matter more than size.

Fourth, there are manning issues. Diesel-electric submarines need relatively few crew. Current nuclear submarines are heavily manned, partly, at least in the US Navy, because automation is so deeply distrusted. The US Navy maintains an elite corps of nuclear reactor operators and engineering officers, who expect ultimately to command all of the nuclear submarines and surface ships. At least until very recently, its morale was reportedly relatively low, due to a combination of very rigorous management and by having to serve very long unbroken periods at sea. The two were connected, in that low morale led to a low re-engagement rate, which in turn reduced the number of officers available to fill the existing commands at sea.

In FY 83 Congressional Testimony, the Navy stated that 79 per cent of submarine commanders and junior officers were assigned to sea duty, and these could expect to spend 14 of the first 20 years of service at sea. This was considered a great improvement on an earlier average of 16-18 years out of 20; the goal was to reduce these figures to 11 years at sea and 9 ashore or on staff. To what extent other navies have avoided creating such a specialist officer corps is not clear; they may not be encountering the American problems. One might argue, too, that *if* diesel submarines had to make long patrols, their relative lack of crew comfort would soon tell in terms of keeping sailors.

The two propulsion systems make for two very different design philosophies, typified by the German IKL submarines and by US nuclear practice. No matter how sophisticated, a diesel-electric plant is always very limited both in available power and in endurance. The IKL designs therefore show extraordinary attention to detail. For maximum cost-effectiveness, IKL introduced unmanned machinery spaces, to save several watch-keepers their living spaces and provisions. It reportedly adopted swim-out torpedo tubes at least partly because they do not use much torpedo-launching energy. The bow planes of IKL boats house at high speed to reduce resistance, and their sails are relatively small for the same reason.

The senior IKL designer, Ulrich Gabler, is said to regard US nuclear submarine design as extremely sloppy; any excessive volume or resistance can always be compensated for by the reactor's enormous sustained power. The Americans would presumably reply that only so much design time is available for any particular submarine, and that nuclear power's great virtue is to free attention for the most important issues, such as high-speed silencing and appropriate very long-range sensor arrays, which do not really concern a designer of small offensive diesel submarines.

The US Navy has generally argued that, given a limited budget, it is much better to buy general purpose submarines able to reach operational areas rapidly in a crisis. The alternative would be forward basing at a sacrifice of strategic flexibility. Post-1945 experience certainly shows that crises have rarely occurred in the expected places. For example, although an Indian Ocean Fleet was often proposed before 1979, it was not taken seriously, yet the United States now finds herself operating one. Even now there is no appropriate supporting base for forward deployment. It is true that bases exist for forward deployment into the classic choke points in the event of general war, but stationing forces there in peacetime would be quite expensive.

There is little doubt that, in some important circumstances and for many navies, diesel-electric submarines remain the ideal answer, but not universally. It was not Admiral Rickover and his 'nukes' alone who pushed the United States into her current 95 per cent nuclear fleet. Perhaps that fleet's one great defect, from a defensive point of view, is that, when it has no diesel submarines of its own, the US Navy could ignore their unique capabilities and cease practising appropriate countermeasures. But Navy spokesmen often argue that exercises with NATO's many diesel submarines overcome this potential problem.

HULL FORMS

Submarine hull form reflects the central choice of underwater or surface performance. On the surface, resistance comes from hull friction and waves; a longer hull, reduces the latter, which is why high surface-speed boats, such as the World War II US fleet type, were so long. Waves persist when a submarine is only shallowly submerged, but vanish at more than three hull diameters below the surface. A fully submerged boat undergoes hull friction, turbulence (eddies) due to hull projections, and hull form drag. All of these effects can be separated into bare-hull and propelled-hull parts, the propeller making either a relatively small or a massive contribution depending on its size, power, and position.

High speed submarine hull design began in Germany during World War II very much on an ad hoc basis, although Walter did test hull forms in a wind tunnel. Thus the Type XXI and its relatives had figure-8 hulls only for additional battery or fuel capacity. No alternative appears to have been investigated, even

PROPULSION – CONVENTIONAL AND NUCLEAR

though the German hull forms were known to suffer from dynamic instability at 10-12 knots, and so needed stern stabilisers, both horizontal and vertical, as well as ordinary rudders and planes. A fast U-boat's very wide speed range (2-26 knots) was itself a problem; dynamic forces increased as the square of the speed, so that maximum forces were about 169 times the minimum. The Germans found themselves developing autopilots to overcome such instabilities as a characteristic slow pitch of up to 5 or 6 degrees up or down.

After 1945 the US Navy began work on 'bodies-of-revolution', symmetric, like a torpedo, around their long axis. Apparently, this was more to avoid dynamic instabilities than to achieve unusually low underwater resistance. The new hull form family was based on blimp and dirigible (airship) practice, with spectacular results, both in drag reduction and in improved propulsive efficiency. At 1799 tons, the wartime conventional Type IXD U-boat required its entire 1100hp to attain 7 knots. Type XXI had about half as much drag: at 1820 tons, it could achieve 7 knots on 540hp, and the earlier U-boats 1100hp gave 10.8 knots. The US project's 1953 outcome, *Albacore*, required only 136hp to make 7 knots, and on her full installed power of 15,000shp, she could make 33.5. Earlier submarines, with a propulsive efficiency of about 0.6, generally had two propellers angled out aft, as in surface ship practice. With a single propeller right aft, abaft the stern planes and rudders, (as well as her hull form) *Albacore* reportedly attained a propulsive efficiency of about 0.9.

Compared with earlier American submarines, the *Albacore* hull form represented a drag reduction of about 40 per cent. As applied to the nuclear *Skipjack*, it gave about 7 knots more than *Nautilus*, at roughly equal power. That is, for equal speed and displacement, a *Skipjack* hull would require 37 to 39 per cent less power than a *Nautilus*. For equal power and displacement, it would achieve 10 per cent better speed.

In theory, you can best reduce friction by limiting a submarine's wetted surface, for a given internal volume (displacement). That would make a spherical hull ideal. Form drag depends on the rate of sectional area changes along a hull; it is lowest for a long slender body, and highest for a short fat one. In practice submarine hull forms are a compromise. A typical plot of total resistance (form plus friction) against slenderness (length divided by diameter) shows a minimum at a ratio of about 7:1, about that in *Albacore*. If the bow and stern are properly designed, it is more efficient to increase internal volume by adding a parallel (tubular) mid-body than by altering the form of the hull ends. That is one reason (albeit hardly the only one) why submarines like *Los Angeles* tend to be closer to torpedo than to *Albacore* shape.

Hull shape details help determine frictional resistance, because water flow over the submarine hull is not smooth (laminar); friction increases over portions subject to turbulent flow. The bow design must delay the onset of turbulence, and elliptical bow forms appear to work very well. The actual transition is a function of Reynolds Number, and takes place only 1-3 ft from the bow at high speeds. Water flow accelerates as the submarine's cross-section increases, but there must come a point in the hull where this is no longer the case. Matters again change aft, where the sections begin to decrease, and the flow must decelerate. The flow can separate from the body of the submarine, creating additional drag. The German World War II reaction was to tackle this with a very fine stern, its lines only gradually closing in; that meant losing after torpedo tubes. The Type XXI's characteristic knife-stern introduced its own snags, such as a magnified 'wall-suction' effect tending to pull an alongside boat into a dockside.

The propeller influences effective hull drag, since it can overcome some of the afterbody shape's effects. One might imagine an almost conical hull, delaying turbulence until almost the stern. The short stern, abruptly tapering, might create considerable drag, except that the propeller would balance off the hull form's deceleration effects there. Such a hull form would be very extreme, and much would depend on the very careful matching of propeller and stern form. Yet, the idea suggests that there are alternatives to the slender stern of *Albacore* and the fast U-boats, and may explain the full-stern hull forms of modern British attack submarines.

During 1939-45 aircraft designers sought to achieve fully laminar flow over wings; one might imagine a similar goal in submarine design. That is, for a non-laminar flow, the separated boundary layer creates its own 'form drag', typically an order of magnitude greater per unit area than the skin-friction drag associated with full laminar flow. For the best streamlined non-laminar bodies, such as the NACA Series 58 used for *Albacore*, flow separates within 5 per cent (in length) of the body nose. That compares with 50-75 per cent in a laminar-flow body, representing a reduction in hydrodynamic drag of 60-80 per cent.

During the late 1960s US hydrodynamicists began to experiment with laminar-flow hull forms, initially for torpedoes but later for manned craft. Model tests suggested that drag reductions as great as 65 per cent were theoretically possible, albeit only in relatively small hulls. Typical hull forms were gradually tapered forward, and necked in relatively sharply just aft of their maximum diameters. For a given total

USS *Nautilus* (SSN 571) was the first nuclear submarine, 323ft oa and displacing 3533/4092 tons, and this official 1:48 cutaway model illustrates some of her design features. The reactor and steam generator are indicated only in a stylised way, but note that they are very close to amidships, where unexpected changes in weight (between design and construction) would have the minimum impact on the boat's trim. Note, too, that the steam turbines abaft the reactor take up more of the boat's length than does the S2W reactor itself. Recent US Navy claims that massive reductions in reactor weight would have little impact on overall design suggest that, although the reactor may be the densest object in the submarine, it is much lighter than the other machinery. Although the emergency diesel is not clearly shown here, a snorkel is evident (the after-most mast in the sail), and other sketches show that its piping was led up from the engine room and under the casing, as in a fleet submarine. The dark areas under the control room and the mess are batteries, also for emergency use. Note that she is single-hulled, and has no conning tower, only a tube leading to the bridge in her sail. Nor has she stern torpedo tubes.
US Navy

hull volume, they were somewhat fatter than typical submarine hull shapes.

One result was a series of proposals for very small high-speed submersibles, to operate in conjunction with larger conventional submarines. The submersibles would, in theory, benefit from a new generation of closed-cycle powerplants. A 'Hi-Technology (Underwater) Fighter', a 30-ton, three-man machine, was sketched. It would have had a 24-knot cruising speed and a 30-knot dash speed; on an energy storage of 12,000 hph it could (in theory) cruise 3500 miles at 24 knots. Laminar flow would also greatly reduce noise and much improve sonar performance to a range of over 20,000 yards. For a time it appeared that laminar flow might initiate a submarine revolution as radical as that of *Skipjack*. Then it was discovered that true laminar flow was impossible with the numerous impurities common in seawater, and so conventional submarine hull forms remain the rule.

REDUCED 'SAILS' AND STREAMLINING

Nor can the effects of hull appendages be discounted. A large but streamlined sail (as in *Skipjack*) may contribute up to 30 per cent to total resistance, and a fully-appended hull may have 20 or even 60 per cent more resistance than a bare hull. From time to time it is proposed to eliminate the sail altogether. More recent modern submarines, such as USS *Permit* of 1961, have relatively small sails which contribute no more than 8-10 per cent to total resistance. Wartime U-boat design is indicative. A Type VIIC's big conning tower-bridge structure accounted for about 60 per cent of total submerged resistance. A Type XIV's flood openings absorbed about 1000hp underwater at full speed. As for the streamlined Type XXI, although 18 knots was predicted from model tests, the first boat could not exceed 15.7 knots; decreasing the area of flood openings increased this to 16.5, but increased diving time from 21 to 27 seconds.

This experience was typical of the minute attention to detail required. For instance, the passive bow sonar (Balkon, or 'balcony') cost 0.2 knots. There was intense pressure to reduce the size of the streamlined sail; Walter calculated that using the Type XXI sail in the smaller and faster Type XXVI would cost about 4 knots. He therefore virtually eliminated the conning tower previously standard in U-boats, reducing fairwater or sail resistance to only 15 per cent of its previous (already relatively small) value. As a result, the Type XXVI's sail accounted for only about 7 per cent of resistance, compared with 23 per cent in Type XXI. The open bridge standard in earlier U-boats was almost eliminated; model tests showed a gain of 20 per cent if the bridge were plated in altogether. On the other hand, very small boats needed relatively large bridges, proportionate to their human occupants, not to the hull as a whole. Thus the coastal Type XXIII's bridge added about 38 per cent to overall resistance.

On a subtler level, hull smoothness can make a major contribution. That is already evident from advances made in surface ship hull paints. For submarines, there are periodic proposals that special polymers be released into the flow around the hull, to reduce drag. The results, at least in theory, can be dramatic, and can reproduce the Walter turbine's tactical consequences: that is, a load of polymer should be able to boost submarine speed by up to about 10 knots, for a limited period.

Given the vast changes in submarine hull form since 1945, it is striking to what extent simple streamlining, as opposed to a total redesign, could contribute to underwater performance. The most prominent example was the US 'Guppy' programme. Fleet submarines, originally capable of only about 8 knots underwater, could make up to 19 when properly streamlined and provided with high-capacity batteries (but not with new electric motors). It appears that the later choice of a much shorter hull in the *Tang* class was motivated as much by underwater manoeuvrability as greater propulsive (hull) efficiency. The *Albacore* hull was a very different concept, growing out of extensive theoretical and model studies after World War II.

Last but not least there is propeller design. Submarine propellers, unlike those of surface ships, have to operate efficiently under several radically different sets of conditions. For example, a pre-World War II submarine ran at high speed and power on the surface, and at a much lower speed and power underwater. Modern submarine propellers are optimised for deep high speed runs. Depth is important because it decides the extent to which cavitation is possible. The deeper the submarine, the more power that can be passed through it before cavitation, with its attendant noise, begins. The other major modern feature is very large diameter, possible when the propeller is on the centre-line, clear of any obstruction. Larger diameter means slower rotation and greater efficiency.

CHAPTER TEN

Sensors and Communications

To a submariner, sensing means seeing without being seen; seeing well enough to attack targets and to evade ASW craft and navigational obstacles. Originally that appeared to be impossible: the same laws of nature which make a submerged submarine invisible also block its view of the surface, and light is absorbed so quickly underwater that there was little point in trying to see the underwater features of nearby ships. The first submarines were provided with vision ports in their conning towers. Typically they ran just below the surface, exposing their ports momentarily to give their commanders glimpses of their surroundings. By about 1903 periscopes were standard; they gave a much less satisfactory view, but could be used while the submarine remained entirely submerged.

PERISCOPES

Through the early part of World War I it was assumed that the periscope was the only way a submerged submarine could sense its surroundings. Although supplemented by sonar, it remained the principal means through World War II. Since it had to be exposed to be used, and since it made a very visible wake, or feather, the periscope could also be used by alert observers as a point of aim for ASW weapons. Even if the submarine were nearly dead in the water, the daytime glint of sunlight reflected off the lens could be seen. Submarine commanders soon learned to minimise such exposure, forming a mental picture of nearby ships from a few glimpses. Typically they were trained on an 'attack teacher', a periscope looking out over a collection of small model ships arranged by an instructor, who could gauge the accuracy of the student's mental picture.

The two primary quantities in periscope design are the size of the lens and the length of the tube. Size determines how well a lens can

Submarine passive sonars were developed during World War I as an ASW measure, allowing a submarine to remain completely submerged while in ambush. A Y-tube hydrophone, consisting of three microphones at the vertices of a triangle, is shown aboard the US submarine *H-5* (SS 148) at San Pedro (California) about 1919. The seaman is bending the rubber enclosure of one of the microphones. Electronic equipment inside the submarine could rotate the beam formed by the microphones, to achieve some limited sense of the direction from which a sound came.
US Navy

SUBMARINE DESIGN AND DEVELOPMENT

The simpler alternative to electronic rotation was physical rotation of a directional hydrophone: this is a C-tube, aboard the US submarine *H-5*, at San Pedro about 1919. Each bulb enclosed a microphone attached to a headphone, and the operator turned the device until the sound level was equal in both his ears. This device operated at relatively low frequency, and therefore its 5ft baseline gave it only poor directionality. During the interwar period both the US and Royal Navies turned to 'supersonics', ie to much higher frequencies, for both active and passive sonars, to achieve better directionality with devices of similar size. Ultimately they had to return to lower frequencies for their passive systems, because water absorbs higher-frequency sound too well. *US Navy*

gather light, and also the diameter of the periscope as a whole, which in turn determines the size of the tell-tale wake. As in virtually all sensors, there is a trade-off between a wide field of view (with limited precision) and a narrow but highly precise (in this case, highly magnified) view. Generally periscopes are specialised in this way; the former for search, the latter for attack. In some cases submarines were also fitted with an air search periscope, or with air search optics incorporated into another instrument.

Tube length determines periscope depth, in turn a measure of how secure the submarine can be while it observes. Also, the deeper the boat, the steadier it will be in a seaway; hence the initial American and German practice of placing the periscope eyepiece in a conning tower above the main pressure hull. This had to be abandoned because the conning tower contributed too much underwater resistance and too much additional equipment (such as radar and sonar output consoles) was needed near the eyepiece for efficient attack.

Periscope length, or stroke, is limited by vibration, which typically begins at 8-9 knots. As the submarine moves through the water, eddies form on the periscope, and it tends to vibrate. The massive supporting structures so evident in pre-streamlined submarines were intended largely to suppress vibration and, thus, to permit observation at somewhat higher speeds. Given the need to observe several times during the approach to a target, a submarine commander would hardly wish to slow down each time.

The periscope was supplemented by sound systems during and after World War I, navies differing in their willingness to abandon optics. The US position was probably the most extreme, in that 'single ping' sonar was to be used to find the range. In theory (which proved incorrect), a combination of passive sonar and the single ping rangefinder would suffice to develop fire control data. British practice emphasised the periscope, which after a time incorporated an optical rangefinder. During World War II compact rangeonly radars suitable for periscope-head installation were developed, appearing aboard US submarines as ST. Both the US and Royal Navies also developed surface-search (including ranging) radars able to operate when the submarine ran at periscope depth; their principal defect was their size, which made their wake more detectable.

These radars solved the problem, unless their own emissions were detected by escorts. Navies therefore differed after 1945 in their willingness to employ such sensors. Electronic Support Measures (ESM) are the inverse of radar; interceptors that detect radar (or radio) signals. It was discovered that water vapour over the ocean frequently forms a microwave 'duct' which channels signals well beyond the horizon, within a narrow zone just above the sea. Submarine radars were frequently within this zone, whereas surface ship masts rose well above it. Thus submarines in exercises were sometimes able to detect surface ships well beyond the range at which they themselves could be observed. Moreover, radar emissions can often be detected beyond the range at which their echoes can be picked up, so that ESM range may greatly exceed radar range.

More recently, periscope developers have added such refinements as infra-red detection and image intensifications (for passive night operation), optical stabilisation, and even automatic target-tracking. Hybrid optical-electronic systems are generally described as *optronic*.

SOUND DETECTORS

The great 1914–18 discovery was that sound detectors, properly used, could substitute for the light detector (the eye at the periscope). Sound does have major limitations. Its wavelength is so much longer than that of light that objects detected by their sounds are necessarily relatively ill-defined. That is, a lens or other receiver can distinguish objects in different directions in inverse proportion to its

SENSORS AND COMMUNICATIONS

own size in wavelengths. A typical light wavelength is measured in thousandths of a millimetre, so that a lens 3in across might be almost a hundred thousand light wavelengths across. By contrast, a typical sound wavelength might be measured in fractions of a foot, so that even a receiver extending over the beam of a submarine would be quite crude by comparison.

However, sound has the critical advantage that it is the only kind of signal the sea freely transmits, and therefore the only kind of signal a submarine can employ without piercing the surface in some noticeable way. Current sonars are divided into *passive* (receive only) and *active* types. The latter send out pulses ('pings') and, like radars, detect objects by the echoes they return; distance is measured by the time delay between emission and return. Thus sonar theory and practice are largely like radar's. In both cases, actual performance is modified by environmental factors, particularly refraction. In the case of radar, refraction creates shadow zones. Refraction is stronger in sonar, and shadow zone phenomena are even more significant. There are sonar parallels to all forms of radar signal processing and beam steering; only some of them can be described here.

In theory, the passive systems provide bearing but not range; however, as noted in Chapter 4 and below, there are ways of converting passive data into ranges for fire control. Active systems automatically give range data much more readily, but their 'pings' reveal the sending submarine. For this reason many underwater systems are designed to track targets passively, then send out a single ping to obtain a fire control range.

Sound frequencies range from the audible range (zero to perhaps 20,000 cycles per second) up to the inaudible or 'supersonic' range of early sonars (15,000 – 30,000 cycles per second, or 15 to 30 kiloHertz, KHz, or kilocycles, kc). Wavelengths, which determine how well a device of a given size can distinguish direction, are inversely proportional. Since the speed of sound in water is about 4500ft/second, a 10kc signal has a wavelength of abut 4/10 of a foot, a one kilocycle signal, 4.5ft. How narrow the beam is and how accurate it is generally depends, then, on the size of the transducer, the device which converts sound into usable (generally electrical) signals and vice versa.

It was known well before 1914 that some sounds could carry through seawater for long distances. That was the basis of the 'submarine bell', rung underwater near lightships and lighthouses, to warn surface ships in foggy weather. Similar bells were used in peacetime manoeuvres as a means of signalling between surface ships and submerged submarines. But it was only in January 1915 that the Royal Navy began to experiment with hydrophones, first for submarine detection and then as a means by which a submerged boat could also use the sounds of surrounding

The former US radar picket submarine *Rasher* (SS 269) displays typical antennae in this 10 November 1960 photograph. The ST-1 (14) radar is a range-only device mounted just below the window of her attack periscope. Her communications and ECM masts were much more extensive than those of other fleet submarines, dating from her service as a radar picket. Note, too, that unlike an attack submarine of this period, she had no air search radar.
US Navy

143

SUBMARINE DESIGN AND DEVELOPMENT

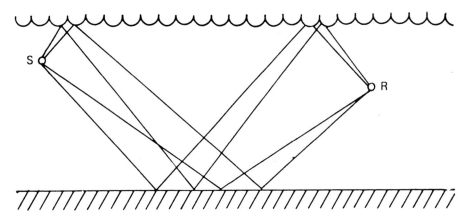

Multiple transmission of sonar signals can be used to determine target depth. These are the alternative paths from source (S) to target (R) using one bottom-bounce. They all show virtually the same transmission loss, since differences in bottom-bounce, surface reflection and path length are small. There are also paths for two, three etc bounces, each entailing greater losses. The effect of multipath is to split the echo, and the extent of the splitting measures target depth. The APS-125 radar of the US Navy's Grumman E-2C Hawkeye current carrier-based airborne early warning aircraft has a similar technique to measure target altitude.

shipping to form a picture of its environment, without ever exposing its periscpe. It would not be nearly so precise, but the submarine could take time to refine it, since it was not placing itself in danger.

Although hydrophones were originally designed for surface ships to detect submarines, they worked equally well in the other direction. The British *B-3* appears to have been the first submarine so fitted, in March 1916. With a fixed unit on each bow, she was able to swing to within two degrees of the precise bearing of any propeller noise. Many submarines were fitted with a variety of hydrophones by 1919, the anti-submarine 'R' class receiving a particularly sophisticated type, permitting, in theory, submerged attacks with little or no periscope exposure.

These first (passive) sonars or hydrophones operated at audible frequencies; they were little more than microphones placed in the water to listen for sounds. By comparing sound intensity among several such instruments in an array, an operator could estimate the direction of a sound source. Long wavelengths and limited system dimensions made for very limited directional accuracy. Because they gave only a direction and not a direct range, hydrophones were only of limited value.

Towards the end of World War I, Paul Langevin in France suggested a solution to both problems. He devised an active system based on the piezoelectric effect: an alternating current passed through a quartz crystal would cause it to vibrate. Conversely, when the crystal vibrated, it generated a weak varying voltage that could be amplified. This primitive transducer operated at what were then considered extremely high frequencies, about 25kHz, and could therefore achieve appreciable directional accuracy. For the first time it appeared that purely underwater systems could 'see' with reasonable definition. World War II sonars were all direct descendants, using a variety of transducers to achieve a range of supersonic frequencies at various power levels. This asdic (later sonar) was advertised at the time as the answer to the underwater menace, since a surface ship equipped with it could expect to detect, attack and sink submarines. However, like the hydrophone, it worked both ways, and from the late 1920s British and American submarines were generally fitted with such devices.

Experience later showed that active sonar was far less effective against surface ships than against submerged, since surface reflections create many false targets. Passive sonar is a very different matter, since only the target is radiating noise signals. Effective active or passive sonar range depends upon three factors: the way in which the sea bends the signals; the extent to which they are absorbed by the sea itself; and the extent to which the sonar and its associated signal processor can distinguish relatively weak signals from among the random noises always present.

SOUND BEHAVIOUR UNDER THE SEA

At relatively short ranges, out to about 10,000 yards (just under 5 miles) or less, sonar beams generally behave almost like light or radar beams, following a 'direct path'. At greater ranges the teams' natural bending must be taken into account. Under relatively rare circumstances, direct-path performance out to about 20,000 yards is possible, which is why the current big SQS-26/53 American surface ship sonar is sometimes credited with such a range. Since sound velocity varies with depth (and with location, for that matter), beams of sound are bent as they pass through water, just as light rays are refracted as they pass through different kinds of glass. The detailed structure of the water determines how a sonar will operate, and it varies from place to place and from season to season. Moreover, sonar operation in much of the ocean is limited by the sea bottom's geography; submarines can be expected to hide in the shadows generated by undersea ridges and other features.

Sound velocity is determined primarily by water temperature, density, salinity, and pressure; a density layer, formed when one current passes over or under another, will reflect sound like a mirror. The same is true of areas off the major river mouths. More generally, in the deep ocean, wind and wave action mix the surface with water farther down, forming a layer of approximately constant temperature. Below this layer is the thermocline, in which water temperature decreases with depth, towards the constant temperature of the deep sea. Typically the thermocline is divided into two levels, a seasonal one affected by surface conditions, and a deeper one which is not. At constant pressure, sound velocity decreases with water temperature, so that it is roughly constant in the surface layer, and decreases in the upper portion of the thermocline. But velocity *increases* with water pressure, so that at some (considerable) depth the trend reverses. If the water is deep enough, then, there is a depth of *minimum* sound velocity.

Any level of sharp change in sound velocity acts as a mirror, as long as sound waves approach at a sufficiently glancing angle. The surface layer, then, acts as a kind of duct, carrying signals generated in it over long distances; it also tends to prevent sonar signals generated at the surface from penetrating below. In the Atlantic, storm and wind are so violent that the layer extends as much as 300 – 600ft below the surface. Only relatively late in World War II, then, could submarines normally operate deep enough to hide beneath it.

As in the case of refracting glass, there is always an angle of incidence beyond which a signal will penetrate rather than reflect. A submarine under the layer, then, is not entirely invisible to a surface sonar, but because the sonar beam must be pointing down at a relatively steep angle, it can be detected only at a relatively short range. Therein lies the importance of variable-depth sonars.

Sound generally bends towards regions of lower velocity. Thus, below the layer, as velocity decreases, a beam tends to bend towards the horizontal, until the depth of minimum velocity is reached, when it bends over and begins to point back towards the surface. The effect of the deep sea, then, will be to refocus sound signals at a great distance from their source, in a *convergence zone*. The range at which re-focussing occurs depends on water conditions, and about 35 miles is typical for the North Atlantic. Convergence zone range is considerably shorter, about 10-25 miles in the Mediterranean. The Mediterranean is special in several ways. Because it is much shallower than the Atlantic and Pacific (1500 fathoms in the major basins, compared with a nominal 2500 in the oceans), it makes for much stronger bottom bounce signals. On the other hand, since the signals cover shorter paths, bottom bounce range is about 40 per cent less than that to be expected in the oceans. Its nearly closed basins act as

SENSORS AND COMMUNICATIONS

reverberation chambers for low frequency sound, amplifying ship-generated noise, which in turn is trapped in the unusually shallow 'deep' sound channel (at about 400ft during most seasons). During April to December there is a very shallow surface layer that conventional surface ship sonars cannot penetrate (they are limited to a range of about 2000 yards), hence the popularity of variable depth sonars in the Mediterranean. However, convergence zone conditions are nearly ideal. By contrast, during the rest of the year powerful sonars can achieve very considerable direct path ranges, even beyond 20,000 yards. Convergence zone phenomena were first predicted after World War II, and were first detected in the late 1940s. Refraction can also trap sounds in a 'deep channel', about 4000ft down, which makes for extremely long listening ranges. In theory, a very deep-diving submarine would be able to exploit this phenomenon.

The same sound beam, projected at an even steeper angle, will pass right through the layers and strike the ocean floor, from which it may be reflected, in a 'bottom-bounce'.

SONAR PERFORMANCE

In the late 1950s as the US Navy sought to increase effective sonar range, it turned to both convergence zone and bottom-bounce modes of propagation. In theory, if the sonar's angle of depression can be varied continuously, it can sweep most of the blank zone between the direct path and the convergence zone, so that targets can be detected and tracked as far away as 70,000 yards (34.5 miles). The big spherical sonars incorporated in US submarines from *Thresher* and *Tullibee* (1960) onwards were intended to exploit just these phenomena. Both were effective only in relatively deep water. In depths much less

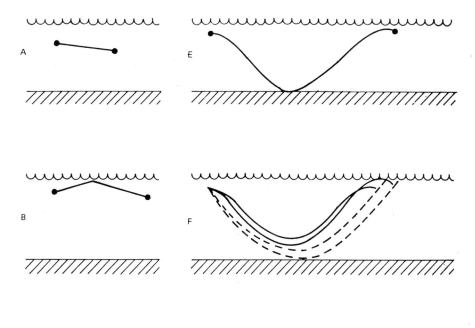
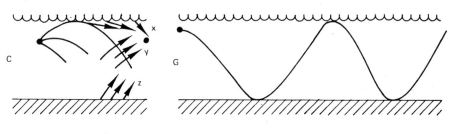
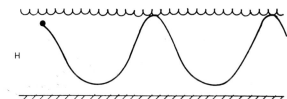

than 1000 fathoms, a signal strong enough to be detected after bouncing off the bottom may also be detected after *multiple* reflections, in which case it will be impossible to determine target location. That is why, for example, sonar operation in shallow waters such as the Falklands was so difficult. Convergence zones are not formed in water less than about 1000-2000 fathoms deep, precise figures depending upon the particular area's sound velocity profile.

Such exotic forms of operation were possible only if sound absorption by the sea itself could be overcome. At any given frequency, absorption is a percentage effect, so that the higher the power, the greater the tolerance of absorption. Increases in active sonar power are, however, limited by *reverberation*. The stronger the sonar signal, the further it carries and the greater the energy available for random reflection and re-radiation: from impurities in the water, from the surface, from the bottom. Reverberation is a major

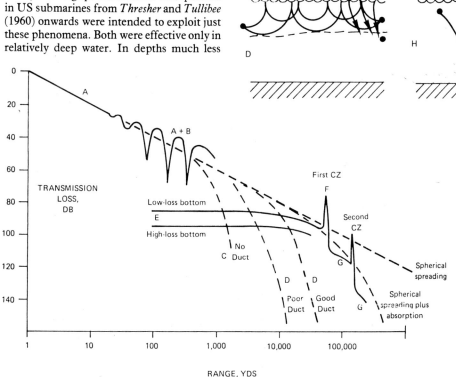

Modes of sonar signal propagation from a shallow sonar, such as that of a submarine. A is the direct path, B and G reflection off the surface, D is ducting, in which shallow signals are trapped near the surface. F and H show the operation of the convergence zone. Much depends on the roughness of the sea bottom. Signal strength in a duct falls off more slowly than outside it, since the signal cannot then spread vertically.

145

SUBMARINE DESIGN AND DEVELOPMENT

limit on sonar performance in shallow water. The lower the frequency, the lower the absorption, ie the further the sound will carry.

The combination of high power and low frequency accounted for much of the increased range of postwar sonars. Thus World War II sets operating at supersonic frequencies were generally credited with a 3000 yard range; 1500 being considered typical. The 8-12kc American SQS-4 could often reach out to 10,000 or even 20,000 yards, and 5000 was typical. Roughly halving the frequency to 5kc doubled reliable range to 10,000 yards (SQS-23), and a further decrease to about 3.5kc (SQS-26) brought reliable or nominal range to 20,000 yards, albeit only under very good conditions; that appears to be the maximum for direct-path sonar. SQS-4 was actually installed in many American submarines during the 1950s. The next major US Navy submarine sonar, the spherical BQS-6, corresponds roughly to SQS-26 in frequency and in technology. Signal propagation from deeply submerged sonars is easier than from surface sonars; in 1960 BQS-6 range was estimated as 80,000-100,000 yards (40-50 miles), which figures do not match convergence zone range. They could be compared with 6000-8000 yards for existing active submarine sonars. Like its surface counterpart, after two decades BQS-6 and its descendants are still the standard.

The other major variables in sonar performance are directionality, signal processing, and self-noise. The first determines how far the sonar can concentrate the signal, reflected or emitted, from the target and exclude nearby noise sources. Since target dimensions are fixed, it is desirable actually to reduce the sonar beam's size as the range increases. That increased precision is also, of course, vital for the control of longer-range weapons. Hence the pressure for very large transducers, compounded by the trend towards lower frequency (ie longer wavelength). That in turn required the development of a new technology after World War II.

Before 1945, Anglo-American sonars employed single transducers that rotated to change bearing. They were called 'searchlights'; operating at the short wavelengths of 'supersonic' signals, they could form relatively well-defined beams. At 24kc a 17in transducer produced a 22-degree beam, considered sufficiently precise during World War II. By contrast, the US wartime JT, a 5ft line hydrophone operating at 100 cycles to 12kc, was credited with only the same beam width. These levels of directionality became less and less acceptable as sonar ranges, both passive and active, increased. SQS-4 and the related BQS-2, with about twice the wartime sonars' range (at lower frequency), had about half the beam width. Mechanical rotation also carries its own noise sources, which limit sonar sensitivity (and, therefore, range). It was possible to silence training mechanisms

British antennae and masts aboard HMS *Aeneas*, a modernised (one of 14, 1955-60) 'A' class attack submarine. From left to right they are a whip (radio) antenna, snorkel, search radar, search (left) and attack periscopes, and an ESM mast. Note that the search periscope is binocular, for optical range-finding.
C & S Taylor

for rotating transducers, but the American view, after 1945, was that such silence was very difficult to maintain in practice.

The alternative was to keep the sonar fixed, forming beams in various directions by adding the transducers' inputs in the appropriate phases. Such systems of this type were developed during World War II by both the US and German navies, for very different reasons. Unlike the Anglo-American navies, the Germans had been relatively unsuccessful in developing 'supersonic' systems, and had had to turn to the intrinsically much larger lower-frequency type. Not wishing to sacrifice directionality, they had extended their arrays across the bows of their later U-boats. Their type of electrical rotation was not altogether a new idea; it had, for example, been applied to subchaser hydrophones as early as 1918. When it was rediscovered after World War II, it became the basis of the large US passive submarine sonars BQR-2 and BQR-4.

Following a very different path, the US Navy found that its searchlight sonars missed many potential contacts because they had to search each direction in sequence. Their operators had to train them, 'ping', and wait for echoes before looking in another direction. At 4000ft/second, a search out to 3000 yards could take more than four seconds. That in turn greatly limited search rate, so much so that active sonar operators, unalerted to a target in a particular direction, were unlikely to detect it. Surface ships tended to use their sonars to maintain contact with submarines that had revealed their whereabouts by attacking. Even so, the war-time sonars required relatively wide beams in order to achieve anything like a fair probability of target detection.

The solution was to build a sonar that could look nearly simultaneously in all directions. It consisted of a fixed circular array of transducers, all of which would be energised together to send out a 'ping' in all directions. In early scanning sonars an electrical commutator scanned, in effect, through a sequence of possible receiving beams, ie through combinations of time delays among the transducers. By scanning rapidly, the scanning sonar could come close to looking in all directions simultaneously. Scanning technology was suited to the larger sonar dimensions needed anyhow to handle lower frequencies.

Omni-directional transmission clearly limited the amount of energy in any one direction, and therefore the sonar range. Modern US surface ship and submarine sonars therefore have an alternative rotationally directed transmission (RDT) mode, in which the individual transducers of the array transmit in phase to produce a single beam. In fact only those within 60 degrees to each side of the beam direction effectively contribute, so that modern RDTs generally produce three beams simultaneously, all three rotating together.

The big fixed passive systems encountered problems of their own. The bow of a submarine could not be perfectly, or even nearly, circular, requiring special compensation at some bearing angles. It was also difficult, at least in the early postwar period, to manufacture large numbers of sufficiently similar hydrophones or of sufficiently precise delay lines. Thus the first US BQR-2 showed bearing precision at least equal to the earlier JT (BQR-3) (with a far narrower beam), but there were large systematic errors in the bearing itself. These problems may explain why the Royal Navy preferred rotating transducers for its surface ship and submarine radars through the 1950s, the submarine attack Type 187 (the dome above the bow) being a primary example. But, as this is written, fixed array sonars, at least in the West, have completely replaced the earlier mechanically-trained type in production.

The West German and American array sonars all consisted of arrays of vertical assemblies of hydrophones. Their beams could be steered only in the horizontal plane, ie in bearing. Although they could detect loud signals at great distances, ie at several convergence zones, they clearly could not take full advantage of 'bottom-bounce' and convergence zone propagation, since their beams could not be tilted. They were also limited in effective range because they operated at relatively high frequencies, in the 500-2500Hz region.

The next step was a new type of non-directional (spot) transducer built into a large sphere, whose beam was steerable vertically as well as horizontally. The technology which made the sphere possible also enabled transducers to be spread along a submarine hull surface. The larger the array, the lower the frequency at which it could operate, albeit with much reduced directional accuracy.

Both the active and the passive systems searched each direction in sequence. In an active sonar that sampling could be relatively rapid. The receiver had to dwell in each direction only long enough to be able to distinguish an echo from the background noise. The situation for passive reception was much more problematic. That is, successful passive detection depends upon *integration*, ie upon listening for a time so that the desired signal, repeated over time, can be distinguished from the random background. In theory, the longer the integration period, the greater the probability of detection. However, the longer the integration time, in such a system, the longer the system must 'stare' in each direction before shifting to the next – and the less chance of detecting a target that shifts from direction to direction relatively quickly. Mechanical switching from beam to beam was also relatively noisy.

MULTI-TARGET TRACKING

By the late 1950s electronic data storage made it possible to 'stare' in all directions simultaneously. All the transducer output was processed to form signals and equivalent to those associated with the series of beams the earlier type of sonar would have formed sequentially. All of these 'pre-formed' beams are formed simultaneously, and their signals can be displayed and analysed together. Because adjacent beams are continuously monitored, a fast-manoeuvring target is relatively easy to detect. This digital multi-beam steering (DIMUS) is much faster, quieter, and more precise than the earlier electro-mechanical system, and is the key to multi-target tracking.

DIMUS was even worthwhile in very long range active sonars. Their coded signal pulses are relatively lengthy. By staring continuously in each direction, the sonar receiver can gain the full benefit of that coding. DIMUS was invented in the late 1950s. In 1960, for example, theoretical studies of a BQR-2B passive sonar equipped with it showed detection range against a snorkelling submarine increased from 50 to 70 miles, assuming a very quiet listening boat. But DIMUS was first applied only to surface ship sonars, initially the big SQS-26. It was not tested aboard submarines until 1968. Later it was applied to the BQQ-5 and BQQ-6 of the *Los Angeles* and *Ohio* classes, respectively. BQR-21 is a DIMUS passive sonar that replaces the mechanically-scanned BQR-2s of pre-*Thresher* attack submarines; it is credited with the ability to track five targets simultaneously, with sufficient accuracy for fire control. DIMUS is also an essential element of the towed array.

The ultimate limit on conventional sonar transducer size is the submarine hull itself. In the 1950s both the Royal and US Navies developed conformal arrays spread along the hull. The integrated sonar developed for *Thresher*, and adapted for subsequent classes, includes BQR-7, a 50ft row of spot hydrophones three high, for passive search and target classification. In 1956 an experimental system of this type was credited with a range of up to 100 miles against a snorkelling submarine, and an ability to localise such a target within 2 degrees. The British system, which may have preceded the American one, was Type 186, a series of groups of hydrophones operating at about 1kc, and forming a series of overlapping athwartship beams. A submarine so equipped would search for targets either by circling at low speed or by turning back and forth across the expected course of an approaching target.

TOWED ARRAYS

The next step was to go beyond hull dimensions altogether by towing a series of hydrophones in the form of a linear array. In theory the array can achieve impressive range simply by increasing effective transducer size while reducing frequency. No details of US submarine towed arrays have been released, but the initial surface escort type, the Edo SQR-18, is probably not very different. It consists of 32 sound-isolated hydrophones, probably operating at frequencies below 1kc.

Towing conferred other important advantages. First, the array could be suff-

SUBMARINE DESIGN AND DEVELOPMENT

USS *San Francisco* (SSN 711), a *Los Angeles* class attack submarine, stows her towed tactical array passive sonar in the fairing running aft along most of her 360ft hull, and visible in this 15 March 1981 photograph of her in the James River during sea trials, (just prior to completion by Newport News Shipbuilding of Virginia). There is too little space in her ballast tanks to stow more than the associated winch and cable; the array is deployed from one of her tail fins, so as not to foul her propeller. In theory, a thinner array might be stowed inside her hull, and so could be made substantially longer, for better directivity.
US Navy

iciently streamlined to reduce water flow noise, so that it could operate even at relatively high speeds. Even so, flow noise remains a serious limitation, and long-range operation much above 12 knots is rare. It was relatively isolated from ship noise, and, since it was towed in the relatively calm water well aft of the submarine propeller, it could look well aft.

Each hydrophone is virtually omni-directional, but beams are formed by appropriately adding and subtracting their outputs, as in the large fixed sonars. The array is most sensitive to broadside sounds, but its array of beams extends to directions much closer to its axis. Relatively ill-defined beams can even be formed along the direction of the array. Probably the array's greatest disadvantage is that, because being symmetric around its long axis, it cannot distinguish left from right.

Towed arrays are largely passive in operation (some have an 'active adjunct' mode), and they did not become really practical until the cost (and size) of signal processing could be brought down. In addition, it is only in the last decade that individual transducers have shrunk to diameters permitting high-speed towing without great water resistance.

Array performance appears to be quite impressive. Although submarine array performance is highly classified, we do know that comparable arrays seem to have made a considerable difference in surface ship sonar performance. It appears that the LAMPS III helicopter was purchased specifically because the new tactical towed arrays (roughly parallel to the tactical submarine systems) were capable of reaching the second convergence zone, and perhaps the third. One might assume that submarine performance would be comparable, since submarine and surface ship arrays are presumably towed at about the same depth.

There are, of course, drawbacks. The array's sheer size makes it relatively difficult to handle. Two approaches have been tried. The array can be stowed aboard the submarine; for example, the current US type is in a tube running along the outside of the pressure hull. It is not that the array must be kept rigid, but rather that, because American submarines are largely single-hulled, there are so few places to stow the towing cable. It appears that the US choice has been the main ballast tank forward of the pressure hull and abaft the bow sonar. The Soviet 'Victor III' submarine is credited with a towed-array stowed in a large fin nacelle; presumably there is plenty of space between its outer and pressure hulls for the associated winch and cable. In both cases the array must be led out a fin so that it does not foul the propeller. Alternatively, the array can be clipped to the submarine as it leaves port.

Each has advantages and disadvantages. The stowed or retractable array can be deployed at will, and in relatively shallow water can be retracted to avoid damage. It was supposed to be towed arrays that imposed a depth restriction on British submarines in the Falklands. On the other hand, the retractable array is quite expensive. A clip-on array can be simpler and less expensive. Moreover, it can be procured in more limited numbers, as there is no need to provide one per submarine. The US Navy appears to have fluctuated between these two positions. British attack submarines appear to use clip-on arrays, although ballistic missile submarines have stowable ones.

There is also the question of length. At least up to a point, the longer the array, the better. It can be argued that beyond some fixed length the array no longer represents a coherent receiver, so that the length advantage is lost. The longer the array, the more difficult to stow. In theory, the thinner the array, the easier it is to stow a given length. Hence current US interest in a Thin Line Array, even though a thinner array should be more subject to flow noise.

The other problem is that, if the submarine is to use data from the array, there must be some way of maintaining array heading and depth relative to the towing boat. That is difficult because both the towing cable and the array proper are (and, indeed, must be) relatively flexible. To some extent the array heading and even flexing can be monitored and compensated for.

SIGNAL PROCESSING

Signal processing sophistication really began in World War II. At that time sonar beams were much too broad to provide sufficient precision for fire control, but a transducer could be arranged to transmit or receive two overlapping beams, their centrelines at a slight angle. The echoes in both would match only when the transducer was pointed directly at a target. This split-beam technique was first employed for contact-keeping, since the sonar could automatically detect a growing difference between the two echoes, which in turn would indicate target motion out of the beam. During 1939-45 this was called Bearing Deviation Indication (BDI); the same technique was also used to achieve very high bearing precision in both rotating (eg JT, Type 187) and fixed (BQR-2, BQR-4) passive sonars. In its contact-keeping mode, and applied to a large fixed array, it is Automatic Target Following (ATF).

Another major signal processing issue is distinguishing a signal, either a returning ping or the emission of a target, from the surrounding noise. Active sonars frequently code their pings, and then match the sounds they receive against the coded format. For example, many sonars send 'FM slides', long pulses during which the sonar frequency changes noticeably. If a returning ping is shifted in frequency, that indicates that it has been reflected by a moving target. This doppler shift thus can be used to distinguish a moving submarine from a feature of the sea bottom.

For a passive sonar, one key point is that target noise has a well-defined and characteristic frequency spectrum, whereas the background is relatively flat and featureless. Many passive systems therefore display signal strength at a range of frequencies. As the system continues to sample incoming sounds, it can display integrated intensities, ie the products of signal strength at each frequency and the proportion of the time that particular frequency has been heard. No matter how weak the systematic signal, it should rise above the noise, given a sufficiently long integration period. The random components of the spectrum should cancel out. In theory, the longer the integration period, the more sensitive the system. But targets move and over a long period of integration the sound source may move so far that nothing useful can be extracted from a single beam. Hence the value of DIMUS' simultaneous processing.

Signal processing has two aspects: detection and classification. Bare detection is the process of extracting an (unidentified) systematic signal from background noise. Once the signal has been detected, it must be classified by matching its details against possible target details. Much depends upon the target noise spectrum's details. It is customary to distinguish narrow-band from broad-band signals. The former consist of very sharply-defined frequency lines. If the lines are stable over time, integration can be maintained for a considerable time, and a faint signal distinguished amid much noise. If spectrum details are known, doppler shifts indicative of target motion are relatively easy to measure.

Narrow-band low frequency signal processing was developed during the late 1950s for both submarines and sonobuoys. For example, the BQQ-3 component of the BQQ-2 submarine sonar was a narrow-band processor for target classification. The new concept required operation at frequencies below those for which many existing sonars had been designed. However, low-frequency components of the submarine spectrum mix with (modulate) the higher-frequency ones, and in the late 1950s a de-modulation technique, DEMON, was developed to permit the application of the new processing (for target classification) to those earlier systems.

Broad-band processing is more difficult, but as long as the target signature remains stable, the same concepts apply. Submarine machinery is the major source of narrow-band noise, but flow noise over the hull contributes to the broad-band part of the spectrum. Sources of machinery noise were discussed in some detail in Chapter 9.

Narrow-band signals are clearly the ideal means of target classification, but not of initial detection. A passive receiver might be imagined as a series of receivers, each operating over a limited frequency range. The narrower the range per receiver (ie the better the narrow-band definition), the more receivers are needed. Alternatively, one might imagine a smaller number of receivers

SUBMARINE DESIGN AND DEVELOPMENT

The US fleet submarine *Grouper* (SS 214), at Mare Island on 17 July 1945, displays her late-war electronic equipment: air and surface search radars (larger and smaller antennae, respectively for SV and SS) and a DF loop. Early war experience showed that the latter could pick up fleet HF broadcasts when the submarine was at periscope depth; it replaced earlier antenna systems, and (in effect) remains in current service in streamlined form. The white outlines indicate changes during this refit; the significance of the wire antenna alongside the fairwater is unknown.
US Navy

scanning continuously over relatively wide frequency bands. The wider the scan width, the less time the receiver can spend at any particular narrow band of frequencies, and the less its chance of detecting a narrow-band signal. Matters would be relatively simple if signal details were known in advance, but they are not.

Fire control needs made for particular ingenuity in signal processing. Before 1939 matters were simplified by the target always being on the surface; modern submarines must often operate in a complex three-dimensional battlefield. They must, therefore, attempt to determine depth as well as range and bearing, all with minimum exposure by active pinging. The goal has always been totally passive fire control. That was impossible before World War II, since submarines generally carried only a single passive instrument. In 1942, however, the Columbia University Laboratory at New London, Connecticut, USA, developed Passive Triangulation Ranging, in which two 5ft JT line hydrophones, almost at the ends of the submarine, were used to obtain ranges. Bearing accuracy was assured by a form of BDI, but effective range was limited by the boat's length itself. It was quite acceptable given effective torpedo ranges limited to about 3000 yards. But postwar homing torpedoes could do much better, and a variety of tactics, described in Chapter 4, were devised.

The next stage was a much more sophisticated use of the form of incoming signals. Any point source of sound under water sends out circular waves, which expand outwards as they travel. A measurement of their wave-front curvature is a measure of the radius of the circle, ie of its distance from source. In 1953 the US Naval Ordnance Laboratory developed PUFFS, initially the Passive Underwater Fire Control Feasibility Study. Three vertical arrays were arranged in a straight line along the submarine's hull. The time delay between reception of a signal by each of the three could be used to measure the direction and curvature of the wave front. This was still a form of triangulation, and PUFFS, like TLR, was limited in range by baseline (ie submarine) length; the more distant the target, the smaller the relative angle between hydrophones, and the less accurate the range. It is still, however, probably the best available purely passive system, still mounted, in modified form, aboard current American underwater craft. The French DUUX series is reportedly analogous, and the new Wide Aperture Array (WAA) is a direct development.

Techniques like PUFFS are important because they permit rapid passive ranging. The alternative is a lengthy stalking, using TMA, and it may be entirely impractical. But PUFFS range is limited by hull length. With the advent of the towed array in the mid-1970s, some submarine commanders adopted, on an informal basis, a new technique: they used the array itself as one

SENSORS AND COMMUNICATIONS

end of a ranging triangle, with the hull sonars as the other. Inaccuracies in array heading made such a procedure difficult, but it still provided greater ranges than existing fixed hull sensors. Since the two sensors did not receive at the same frequencies, there was a very real possibility that the higher frequencies received by the bow sonar travelled a different path through the sea than did the lower ones received by the towed array.

Really long range operation, with its alternative sound paths, made even more exotic concepts possible. Under the right circumstances, there are four distinct sound paths between a submarine and its target: the direct path, the two-way bottom-bounce path, and two alternative combinations of bottom-bounce and direct path, or three distinct time delays between transmission and reception. Each returning 'ping' splits into three, and the time difference measures target depth. In general, there are many more than four paths, including several involving surface reflection. Like most other exotic sonar techniques, this one works only under limited circumstances. The airborne early warning radar in the Grumman Hawkeye aircraft employs comparable method of height determination. Similarly, it can be argued that a passive sonar can estimate range partly by such multi-path splitting of the structure of received sounds. The listening submarine can observe the change in signal structure as it varies its own depth, just as, using TMA (see Chapter 4) it could observe change in a target bearing and bearing rate while manoeuvring.

Sonar location is an important submarine design issue. Arrays can be large, and they have to be kept clear of turbulence as far as possible. Hence the US preference for bow domes, and the decision to move the torpedo tubes and bow planes, both noise sources, abaft them. Given the transducers' position, it is necessary to transmit their outputs to sonar signal processors with minimum loss. Sonar equipment rooms must therefore almost adjoin some types of arrays, although much has been done over the past decades to reduce internal signal transmission losses.

The US Navy is alone in its willingness to devote the bow's entire volume to a 15ft search sonar. Other navies appear to prefer GHG-style arrays either above or below a nest of torpedo tubes. The Royal Navy mounted its Type 187 *above* the bow at the same time that the US Navy mounted its BQR-2 below. One can speculate that, operating in shallower waters, the Royal Navy envisaged sometimes bottoming its attack submarines.

WORLD WAR II SONARS

We can briefly compare submarine sonar suits at various dates. On the eve of World War II most US submarines were equipped with a single passive sonar, such as JK or JP, on deck, and a combined active/passive sonar and sounder such as WCA (QC and JK) under the keel. In theory, a submarine could use the passive unit to make a sound-only attack, obtaining a 'single ping' range with its active sonar. Note that such ranging required a relatively broad beam, to insure that the target would be caught in it on the first attempt. For example, the postwar BQS-2 scanning sonar operated with a 12 or 13 degree beam in the scanning mode, but with a 42 degree searchlight beam in the single-ping mode. Only during the war did it become clear that listening ranges were far greater with sonic than with supersonic equipment, and the lower-frequency JT replaced the earlier types. Some submarines had two, for TLR. Some were also fitted with the very high frequency QLA mine-detection sonar.

Like the United States, Britain installed sonar (asdic in British parlance) in her submarines before 1939. Reportedly the original intent was to provide a means of engaging submerged submarines, the transducer being placed atop rather than beneath the hull. There was also interest in sound attacks, but ultimately the Royal Navy appears to have preferred to employ submarine asdics passively, as highly directional hydrophones. Although many accounts of US submarine war operations mention single-ping ranging, British accounts appear to emphasise use of the periscope.

The Germans had failed to develop effective supersonic systems, and from 1935 onwards they equipped all U-boats with various forms of the lower-frequency GHG, consisting of receivers built into the skin of both sides of the lower bow. Electrical compensators effectively steered the resulting beam. By 1943 something better was needed, and 48 receivers were relocated into a chin ('balcony') array in a Type IXC submarine. It formed the basis for the advanced types employed in later U-boats, including those captured by the Allies. The Germans claimed that they could detect single ships at about 12 miles, and convoys at about 60 miles. By contrast, early attempts to develop an active 'pinger' failed because insufficient power was developed; the U-boat tended to give itself away. The Type XXI, operating entirely underwater, required some type of rangefinder, and efforts resumed. Ultimately a swivelling transducer was mounted inside the Type XXI sail; tactics resembled those developed prewar by the US Navy. Thus, in a Baltic convoy exercise off Bornholm Island in 1945, GHG was used for initial contact, and the active transducer, operating passively, turned towards the direction indicated by the GHG. When the range was short enough (as measured by the intensity of propeller noise), the active set was keyed. In contrast to American single-ping operation, the Germans found that, under favourable circumstances, they needed three pings to establish course, speed, and range.

US AND BRITISH SONARS 1948 TO DATE

One US sonar developer remarked that the decision to build a new submarine class was usually the impetus for major new sonar developments. Thus the BQR-2 was first specified in April 1948 for *Tang*, the postwar attack submarine; the BQR-4, in June 1949, for the new SSKs; and the big spherical

USS *Sea Cat* (SS 399) tested the first American towed radio buoy, which can be seen with its cradle on deck. Note *Sea Cat's* small whip antenna. The sail carries a streamlined VLF loop forward of her surface-search radar. *US Navy*

SUBMARINE DESIGN AND DEVELOPMENT

sonar, which became the BQS-6, was part of an integrated system begun in mid-1956 for a new nuclear FY 58 SSK, and then incorporated into what was to have been the last of the *Skipjack*s, *Thresher*. The new *Tang*s carried their BQR-2 sonars in chin sonar domes, supplementing them with BQR-3, a modified version of the wartime JT, in a topside dome. There was also an active sonar, BQS-2; some boats of this period had surface ship type SQS-4s instead.

The first postwar British attack submarines, the *Oberon*s which were designed somewhat later (about 1951-52), had Type 186 conformal arrays down their sides, and Type 187 searchlight transducers above their bows. Claimed accuracy, using split-beam (BDI) techniques, was half a degree. Type 187 could be used in an active mode for mine detection. Finally, there was a sonar intercept and (limited) direction-finding set (Type 197) atop the sail.

All current US systems are descended directly from the type designed for the FY 58 SSKN, the BQQ-2 of *Thresher*. It comprised the BQS-6 spherical bow transducer, primarily passive but capable of single-ping ranging; a conformal passive search and classification array (BQR-7); and three PUFFS ranging transducers on each side. The current *Los Angeles* system adds a towed array and better signal processing, and the entire integrated active/passive system is designated BQQ-5

RADIO COMMUNICATIONS

Effective submarine operation requires not only some covert means of sensing surroundings, but also a means of two-way communication. That same opacity of the sea, which conceals the submarine, also makes it very difficult for signals of any type to penetrate in either direction. The chief exceptions are sound signals, which can, under the appropriate conditions, travel vast distances underwater, very- and extremely-low frequency (VLF and ELF) radio signals, and blue-green laser signals. Tactically, the physical limits on submarine communication practically determine that submarines will operate largely as solitary units, communicating only from time to time either with the surface fleet or with other boats. More active cooperation would require unscheduled two-way contact, under current circumstances difficult at best.

In particular, the systems in use since about 1930 generally allow a shore station to contact a submerged submarine for one-way traffic. Except for ELF, each requires the submarine to limit its operations while receiving. For example, VLF reception is possible only when the antenna is near the surface. The surface fleet relies increasingly on satellites, which operate at super-high frequency, but to benefit a submarine must put its satcom antenna (atop the periscope mast) through the surface. Thus the submarine must periodically sacrifice some measure of stealth in order to receive messages. Sending is worse; the submarine has to surface, or at least to expose an antenna, to reply. The US Navy, for example, transmits fleet messages continuously on frequencies submarines can be expected to read. Each submarine periodically deploys a VLF antenna and copies all the messages, noting those addressed specifically to it. In this system, deployed fleet units, which do not have a VLF capability, can communicate with even a relatively nearby submarine only by sending messages to shore stations (by HF), for retransmission on VLF as part of the fleet (Fox) schedule.

Similarly, one submarine can communicate with another by transmitting to the shore station, then waiting for its message to be rebroadcast on VLF. ELF radio, the only type really effective throughout all submarine operation, has so little information content that it must act instead as a 'bell ringer', warning a deployed submarine to come to a depth at which it can receive VLF radio. Short-range communication between submarines and surface ships, or between submarines themselves, is possible, but only at a great cost in stealth.

The existing system has one major defect: the submarine is available for communication only on an intermittent, scheduled, basis. The more often it makes itself available, the more vulnerable it is. However whenever it co-operates with other naval forces, it may become necessary to contact it immediately. Some form of alerting signal is required; ELF is an attractive possibility, because a submarine can receive it continuously, even while deeply submerged and at fairly high speed. However, as yet the United States has only a rudimentary ELF system, and one must assume that other 'bell ringers', such as explosive signal charges, are currently used. For the future, blue-green lasers, which can penetrate well into the water, may be an effective 'bell ringer'. Such 'bell ringing' has important operational consequences, in that a submarine answering by exposing a tactical antenna (currently UHF or VHF) is also exposing itself. An enemy might, therefore, choose to duplicate the bell-ringing signal to assist his ASW forces.

The *information content* of radio signals increases with increasing frequency. Below High Frequency (HF), for example, there is insufficient band width to support voice communication. The higher the frequency, the greater the amount of information it can carry in a limited period of time. During World War II, the German U-boat arm suffered because its long-range HF communications were being intercepted and DFed (direction-found) by the Allies. One solution was burst or squirt transmission (*Kurier*), in which a message was compressed for very rapid transmission. There was no way to avoid *some* exposure, but *Kurier* kept it to a minimum.

High frequency has been the standard means of long-range fleet communication in all navies since the 1920s. During World War II VHF and then UHF became standard for tactical communication within a fleet. This changed only with the advent of satellites, some of which operate at super HF. The great advantages of SHF are tight beams, which are difficult to intercept, high information capacity, and channel capacity that permits an individual satellite to carry many separate messages simultaneouslsy.

Each method has major limitations. As will be clear from the discussion of sonar, sound transmission through the sea is uncertain at best. The most effective path, the deep sound channel, is not directly accessible. In theory, a submarine could suspend a hydrophone into it, but that would be cumbersome at best. At ranges similar to sonar's, similar signals can be used for underwater communication; they actually form the basis for modern underwater telephones. One official writer went so far, in 1966, as to claim that the active feature of the big BQS-6 submarine sonar was valuable for communication with surface ships during direct support operations. But any form of pinging is likely to betray the submarine's presence. The solution, a low-probability of intercept (LPI) system, has been eagerly sought almost since 1945. In theory, it would employ coding to bury usable signals within the background (ambient) noise of the sea; both sender and receiver might synchonise systems that would shift frequency very rapidly, so that no sustained signal would be detected. Some modern fast-frequency-hopping airborne radio communication systems, such as the US Joint Tactical Information Distribution System (JTIDS), employ this approach. Another technique is spread-spectrum: the signal is split up and spread among a variety of frequencies. There is not enough of it on any one channel to alert a listener. This concept is applied to radio as well as to acoustic signals. Alternatively, VLF signals, which are not very directional, could be used; here the radar analog would be the relative immunity of lower-frequency systems to anti-radar direction-finding and attack. Again, data rate would suffer badly.

Sound may, then, be an effective means of relatively short-range communication, but it is unlikely to be reliable over very long ranges. At present that leaves radio. Until after 1945, it was assumed that submarines could neither transmit nor receive radio signals while submerged. Typically they would surface, generally at night, at scheduled times to receive fleet broadcasts, sending at the same fixed times. However, several navies discovered, apparently independently, that a submarine at periscope depth could receive low-frequency radio signals. These fleets built massive installations, such as the Royal Navy's 15kc transmitter at Rugby and the US Navy towers at Annapolis. At first it appeared that long wire antennas were required aboard the submarine, but both the British and, during World War II, the Americans discovered that relatively compact insulated loop antennas

SENSORS AND COMMUNICATIONS

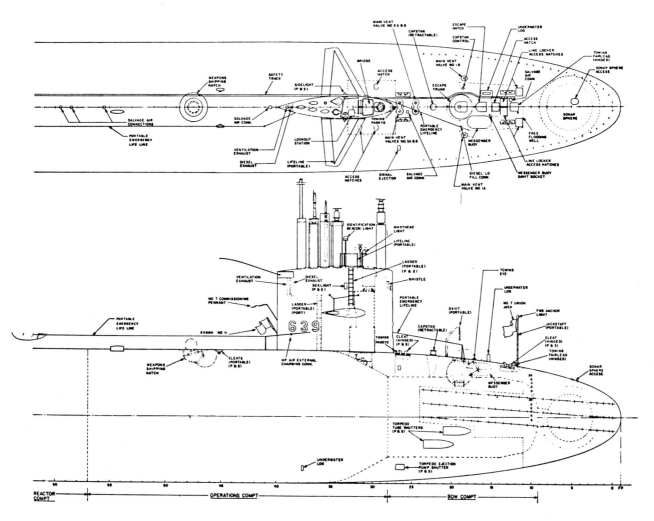

Exterior forward installations on the US *Sturgeon* class nuclear attack submarine *Tautog* (SSN 639).
US Navy

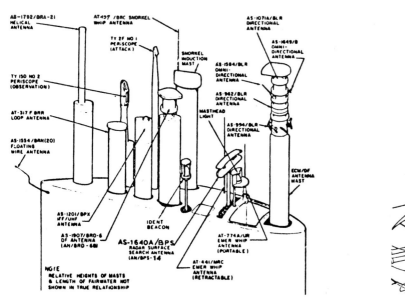

Antenna and mast arrangement for the same boat.
US Navy

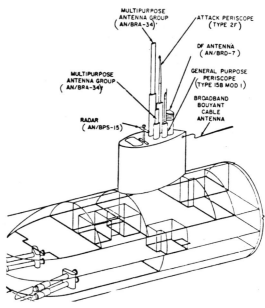

Antenna and periscope arrangement for the US *Los Angeles* class (SSN 688).
US Navy

153

sufficed. The US antenna, for example, was the device initially fitted as a radio direction-finder.

The only defect here was that the submarine had to come so close to the surface, where it might be relatively easy to detect. Current US submarines, for example, have trailing buoyant cable antennas. A submarine several hundred feet down can still receive VLF signals. That appears to suffice for most applications. But the speed, course, and depth restrictions inherent in the trailing wire appear to be unacceptable for strategic submarines. That is the official American rationale for developing ELF communication links to their SSBN fleet. No submarine could expect to *transmit* VLF signals over any appreciable distance. Like a sonar hydrophone, a radio antenna is a transducer, and its efficiency depends upon its size in wavelengths, half a wavelength being the minimum. The radio wavelength corresponding to 15kc is about 6 *miles*. Thus submarines were always limited to medium and higher-frequency radio transmission. Even so, until well after 1918, antennas were relatively large. Radio range was determined by mast height, and submarines were therefore severely limited. That is why fast surface ships, such as light cruisers, generally had to accompany submarine flotillas to sea: they functioned as radio relay ships. After World War I, as British and US attention turned to the Far East, limits on submarine radio range were particularly vexing. The British did not expect to achieve much more than 1000 miles; they could barely hope to receive signals from the Sea of Japan in Hong Kong. HF range gradually improved, and by World War II quite compact antennas, usable from periscope depth, existed.

In the early 1950s the US Navy became concerned that submarines communicating in this way would be exposed to attack, and asked the Naval Research Laboratory to develop a means of maintaining communication from greater depths. The result was a towable buoy carrying its own antenna, which could be streamed from a depth of 110ft while the submarine ran at 8 knots. One advantage of such systems, demonstrated during the Cuban Missile crisis of 1962, was that a submarine in a barrier could report without having to surface out of the barrier. Many current Soviet submarines carry communications buoys in fairings abaft their sails.

More generally, any sustained transmission *by* a submarine invites direction-finding, as the U-boats discovered to their cost during 1939-45. Their solution was the first LPI transmitter, *Kurier*. This system took a signal, and compressed it into a short 'squirt' which, in theory, a direction-finder scanning over a frequency range would not detect. In fact the Allies had beaten the existing version of *Kurier* by the end of World War II, but the necessary intercept equipment was much too massive to place aboard ship. Thus, at the least, *Kurier* eliminated the problem of shipboard HF/DF. Presumably the same principle applied to later submarine signal transmitters.

CURRENT COMMUNICATION SYSTEMS

The current view appears to be that emergency HF transmission is unlikely to be very important, whereas a submarine cooperating with air and surface forces should be able, in an emergency, to transmit VHF and UHF signals while submerged. Two methods have been developed. SLATE and SLOT are expendable American submarine buoys that can be launched from the standard 3in countermeasures tube. SLATE is a two-way link, containing a UHF transceiver and antenna. Signals are transmitted between submarine and buoy by a cable that can be cut from within the submarine. SLOT is launched to transmit a pre-recorded UHF message as long as its battery lasts.

Two other communication systems deserve mention here. For some years it has been known that intense blue-green laser signals can penetrate sea water in detectable form down to 400ft or more. As problems developed with the proposed ELF strategic submarine communication system, there were several suggestions that blue-green lasers be substituted. They could be placed aboard satellites or aircraft, or even reflected from ground stations off passive satellites. Although in theory a laser might carry enormous amounts of information per unit time, in fact the laser spot is so small at the surface of the water that is has to be scanned very rapidly in order to have a reasonable chance of hitting the submarine, whose location is (in theory) unknown. Thus the message must be repeated very rapidly, and its effective information content is very limited: like ELF, the blue-green laser would probably be a bell-ringer.

The other relatively new system is the fleet communciations satellite. Satellites cannot transmit at VLF or ELF, and thus are limited to communication when the submarine is at or near the surface. However, at the high end of the frequency range, a satellite can transmit data so rapidly that exposure is minimised. Recently the US Navy developed a SHF antenna specifically to be mounted atop attack periscopes. Presumably it was, in part, a means of achieving the sort of data rates implicit in long-range targeting systems such as Outlaw Shark (see Chapter 11).

One other sensing issue deserves discussion here: navigation. Many types of submarine operation require relatively precise navigation while the submarine remains entirely submerged. Because underwater IFF is so poor, submarines are generally assigned to individual patrol areas. For example, submarines occuppying a barrier avoid attacking each other by limiting themselves to targets crossing their own patrol areas. Such a tactical practice is possible, in turn, only if the submarines can easily determine whether, in fact, they are within those well-defined areas, without exposing themselves to detection. In theory, a submarine's safety operating in direct support of surface ships depends upon a mobile version of the same practice: a moving sanctuary zone, within which the escort submarine operates, is defined. Ballistic missile submarine navigation, for precision shooting, imposes similar requirements. In theory, ballistic missile shooting requires an extraordinary degree of precision, far beyond the demands of, say, a submarine barrier. Stellar update systems, in which the missile corrects its position by checking several star positions as it emerges from the atmosphere, somewhat alleviates such requirements.

None of this is very new: in the winter of 1940, for example, British submarines on submerged station off the French coast found it impossible to remain in their assigned patrol areas, or to regain those areas. They could not navigate effectively in daylight, because that would have required exposure, nor could they depend upon star sights at night, so close to the enemy. Some early (and exotic) postwar solutions to the problem are mentioned in Chapter 4, in connection with SSK operation.

For the US Navy, the solution was SINS, an inertial navigation system that sensed submarine motion by measuring submarine accelerations, integrating them to estimate speeds. Since the accelerations are measured relative to the earth, the submarine can (in theory) navigate independently from them. In practice, however, the SINS is a computer with a finite degree of accuracy. The longer it runs, the greater its accumulated error. Therefore it is standard practice to update SINS whenever possible. All of the updates require the submarine to lift an antenna above the surface: LORAN, OMEGA, and navigation satellites. Except for satellites, all of these systems lose accuracy as the submarine moves farther and farther from their transmitters. That is one reason why satellite networks such as NAVSTAR are ultimately likely to displace them. By comparison, because Soviet ballistic missile submarines tend to operate in home waters, they should achieve improved positional (and therefore hitting) accuracy even with relatively primitive navigational aids, far short of SINS.

CHAPTER ELEVEN

Weapons and Tactics

Submarine tactics are shaped by a combination of weapon characteristics, sensor characteristics, and the attempt to operate concealed from enemy sensors, both surface and submerged. Until after 1945, the targets were surface ships, and surface ship and airborne sensors were the primary dangers. Moreover, except for HF/DF and radar, there were no very long-range anti-submarine sensors. Specialised submarine tactics, then, were confined to the tactics of dealing with localised screens and barriers. A careful commander could expect to detect surface ships well before he risked detection, and could choose either to evade or to risk detection by attacking. This theme was developed in greater detail in Chapter 3.

Submarines have never been blessed with the kind of clear presentation of their surroundings common in surface and air warfare. A few quick glances through a periscope, for example, had to suffice to give a World War I or II commander a picture of the tactical situation. Modern passive sonars are better, because their operation is continual, but their outputs are incomplete at best, and misleading at worst. Compared with optical sensors such as periscopes, they are much easier to confuse or to decoy. Nor do they give the same kind of 'solid' detection: sonars with rated ranges in the tens of thousands of yards sometimes do not detect targets until they have closed to well within 10,000 yards.

Postwar, at least in the West, submarine tactics changed radically. In submarine v submarine warfare, long-range acoustic detection is a constant threat. The submarine

The essence of the torpedo (and, for that matter, of the anti-ship missile) is that high performance is packed into the weapon, allowing economies in its platform. Thus even relatively small submarines could sink capital ships. This is the torpedo room of an early US submarine, the *A-4* (SS 5, ex-*Moccasin*), at Manila, about 1912. The single torpedo tube breech is in the centre, and the rails and pallets for moving the 845lb 18in Whitehead Mark I torpedoes (range 800 yards at 26.5 knots) are not too different (at least in concept) from torpedo-loading systems in current US submarines.
US Navy

SUBMARINE DESIGN AND DEVELOPMENT

Specialist minelaying U-boats of 1914–18 were equipped with vertical free-flooding chutes as illustrated by 6 (one minus its grill) aboard this UC III-class boat (capacity of 14 mines) surrendered at Cherbourg about 1920. Note the breeches of the external 19.7in torpedo tubes with reloads alongside the mine chutes.
US Navy

itself is very limited in its ability to sense signals coming from astern. It is said to have 'baffles' over the arc which its sonars cannot cover. A careful submarine commander turns every so often to 'clear baffles', ie to look astern over that dead angle, and thus to make stalking more difficult. Sonar range performance is irregular: under some circumstances it may greatly exceed weapon range, whereas under others the opposite will be true. When it does exceed weapon range, the submarine commander must approach his target in such a way that he does not alert it, so that he does not risk counter-attack.

Unless he uses active sonar, a submarine commander cannot expect to determine target range (hence speed) with any great precision, at least outside triangulation range. He must, therefore, try to refine his estimate of target motion as he closes, and that in turn requires complex manoeuvres such as those described in Chapter 4 (TMA). Active pinging solves this problem, at least under favourable acoustic conditions, but most submariners would argue that it gives away their position to an acoustically inferior enemy. It can also be argued that the sonar 'ping' itself can be so shaped as to make information extraction difficult. If the submarine is operating in direct support, the target may assume that the ping has been made by a surface ship. Attacking on that basis, it will be open to submarine attack.

Time is also a factor. If great detection range is not matched by weapon range, then the engagement can be protracted. Even though the target may be much noisier, and even though its sensors may be less sensitive,

156

WEAPONS AND TACTICS

there is still some probability that it can counter-detect before the stalker can attack. The longer the stalk, the greater the danger.

Moreover, the greater the disparity between detection and engagement (weapon) range, the greater the importance of sufficient *sustained* quiet high speed, to enable the stalker to 'convert' his detections into attacks. Once the stalker gets near the target, he must determine its location, speed, and course well enough for fire control. Hence the efforts to obtain Rapid Passive Localization (RAPLOC) of submarine targets, first by PUFFS and its derivatives, and then by triangulation using towed arrays. In the absence of such devices, a single ranging ping may be inescapable. For example, the US Mark 45 nuclear torpedo was guided and fuzed by wire. The firing submarine had, therefore, to determine target range quite precisely, by pinging; the weapon was unpopular partly because of this requirement. It is not clear whether PUFFS ranges were ever considered a viable substitute.

Each submarine mission has its own tactics. Examples in US service include barrier patrols, both fixed and moving; 'lane sanitisation' (clearing the path) for a convoy or battle group; alerted interception (in which the submarine follows up on a long-range contact, such as a SOSUS detection); ocean areas search; and the integrated escort of a formation, in which the escorting submarine operates directly with the other ASW escorts.

In the barrier case, the target is a transiting boat attempting to pass through at minimum risk. If the barrier merely forces the transiter to move very slowly and quietly, it is reducing its time on patrol station and thus its effectiveness. A submarine on barrier patrol will, therefore, operate passively, moving as slowly as possible to remain on station. If the conformal and towed arrays are the most effective onboard long-range detectors, then the submarine will also probably have to weave back and forth across the direction from which the transiters will probably have to come, since these sensors are most effective when broadside-on.

A fast moving submarine, on the other hand, may often generate enough self-noise to swamp incoming signals. It may, therefore, have to 'sprint and drift', alternating periods of high and low (quiet listening) speed. It may also have to use its active sonar from time to time, perhaps sprinting from the place at which it pings. Speed may be required to close targets which are not approaching; that might, for example, be the case with an intercepting submarine. In each case, much depends upon weapon range and also upon weapon acquisition range, a measure of how much inaccurate target data can be tolerated.

The central theme of submarine weapon development is the attempt to attack ships and submarines while paying a minimum price in stealth. That is, a submarine which, submerged, is effectively invisible must necessarily reveal its presence every time it strikes; the closer the target, the more dangerous that revelation. On the other hand, the greater the range, the greater the chance of missing the target, and so perhaps revealing itself without even achieving a hit in return. The meaning of all of these terms changes with evolving anti-submarine surveillance technology. Thus a 10,000 yard torpedo would have assured the survival of a boat from either World War. In 1983, however, a torpedo that can be detected at 10,000 yards can be evaded, and firing it probably invites counter-attack. For that matter, some surveillance systems make it dangerous to fire a ballistic missile from under water.

TORPEDOES

The torpedo was (and remains) the natural submarine weapon; submarine design and tactics reflect its virtues and faults. A torpedo is, in effect, a small unmanned submarine. It achieves higher than submarine speeds because more of its volume can be devoted to propulsion; since its endurance is extremely limited, it can expend its energy much faster. The first torpedoes were propelled by compressed air, and their performance depended on the pressure built up in their air flasks. Later heaters were added to boost air pressure, and by World War II the standard method of propulsion was steam (in fact, steam-boosted air). It had the virtue of relative reliability and simplicity. But any air torpedo left a wake of bubbles behind it, and many submarines were counter-attacked by escorts following the wake back to them. Moreover, the wake alerted the target ship. If the latter was fast enough, it could hope to evade an incoming weapon.

During the 1930s, several navies sought major improvements in torpedo performance, either for greater range, greater speed (to reduce the possibility of evasion), or for compactness to increase warhead size in a weapon whose dimensions were fixed by the existing torpedo tubes. Examples include the Japanese oxygen torpedo (effectively wakeless) and attempts in the United States to use hydrogen peroxide. Several navies tried to develop electric (ie wakeless) torpedoes, but only the Germans actually employed them early in World War II. Later in the war the US Navy copied the German propulsion system, for use by submarines in the Pacific War.

All of these torpedoes were intended for use against surface ships, and therefore

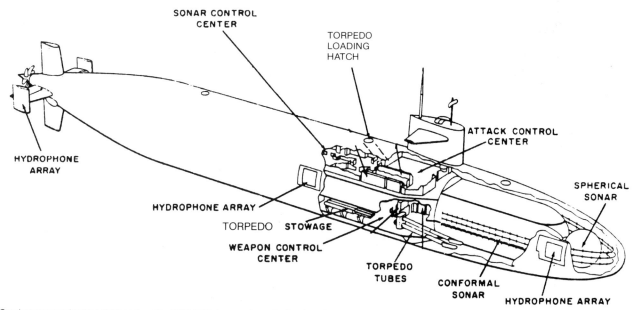

Combat systems for the USS *Los Angeles* (SSN 688) class nuclear attack submarine
US Navy

SUBMARINE DESIGN AND DEVELOPMENT

operated near the surface, under conditions of relatively low external pressure. Conventional air-steam torpedoes, for example, had to exhaust against water pressure. The greater the pressure, the greater the percentage of propulsive energy expended in fighting it. After 1945, when torpedoes were developed for submarine v submarine ASW, they had to be able to operate against very considerable pressures. Three approaches have emerged. The first is electric propulsion, using more and more sophisticated batteries. Such a system is essentially immune to water pressure, but the energy storage of a battery is limited (see Chapter 9). The second was internal combustion, as in the US Mark 46 and Mark 48 torpedoes. Both, however, produced exhaust products (gases) that must be dumped overboard, against water pressure. Both therefore lose power at great depths. Hence the third solution, an internal combustion plant whose waste is compact enough to remain within the torpedo body. The new Mark 50 Advanced Light Weight Torpedo (ALWT) is an example. When it is fired, electric squibs melt a block of lithium, which reacts with sulphur hexafluoride to produce heat, which in turn boils water for the steam to power the torpedo. This system is complex, but it is effectively depth-independent, and it is quite energetic. One might argue that, although the chemical fuel is much more energetic than a battery per unit weight or volume, the complexity, weight, and volume of its engine more than balances off that apparent advantage. Hence, for instance, the British decision to use battery power in the lightweight Stingray.

Presumably the weight of energy storage counts for more in a larger, longer-range torpedo; hence the semi-Otto powerplant of the new British Spearfish. As this is written, a lithium-sulphur hexafluoride plant is reportedly being developed for later Stingrays.

Beside the fact that it can be fired, while a submarine is at its most invisible (ie submerged), the torpedo's first great virtue lies in combining great explosive efficiency with minimum demand on the launching craft. That is, pound for pound, explosives are most effective against ships when they are detonated underwater. Second, because it is self-propelled and largely self-guided, a torpedo imposes few requirements on its launching platform: a relatively small torpedo boat or submarine might expect to launch a weapon sufficient to sink a capital ship at a considerable distance. The latter carries over to modern self-propelled anti-ship missiles, and explains the efficacy of fast missile boats.

In each case, the bulk of the investment required to achieve high performance is concentrated in the disposable missile. By contrast, much more of that investment is reusable in a gun system. As long as relatively few reloads are required, the self-propelled system is much more compact. However, as the number of rounds rises, the redundant investment in each becomes a greater and greater burden on the whole system, and reusability saves a great deal in space and weight.

The greater the burden on the individual round (in this case, on the individual torpedo), the larger and more expensive it must be. For small submarines, the great size of each torpedo means relatively few can be

Full-length torpedoes are large even compared with naval guns. A 21in US Mark 18 electric torpedo (based on the German G7E and weighing 3154lb including a 575lb warhead: range 4000 yards at 29 knots) is shown alongside the 5in/25 'wet' gun (unique because the bore did not have to be sealed underwater) of a US fleet boat 1944-45. The circular ports atop the torpedo mark its batteries which occupied most of its 20ft length.
US Navy

carried. Even modern large submarines still suffer from limited magazine space. On the other hand, the torpedo weapon system incorporates just enough of a fixed investment, in the form of a torpedo tube, to limit weapon size quite severely. American submarines still fire torpedoes designed within parameters (21in diameter, less than 21ft long) set before 1914. That is, submarine torpedoes designed in the 1930s, such as the Mark 14, had to fit the tubes of earlier submarines still forming the bulk of the US fleet at that time. Conversely, the tube dimensions of new submarines were determined by the size of existing standard torpedoes. These dimensions then survived radical shifts in the US submarine force's role. A submarine completed in, say, 1942 with 21in torpedo tubes would retain those tubes through up to four decades of radical weapon and mission evolution. In the American case that meant, first, the change from steam to electric torpedoes within the standard anti-shipping mission; then the change to the ASW mission, prosecuted by means of homing and wire-guided torpedoes launched at much greater depths; then the wire-guided nuclear ASW torpedo (Astor). Moreover, because later submarines had to be able to stow and fire the earlier torpedoes, *their* tube dimensions did not differ significantly from those of the earlier boats, and thus entirely new classes of weapons were affected.

Thus, after a brief flirtation with specialist minelaying submarines, the US Navy decided to develop mines that could be laid from standard torpedo tubes and stowed in standard torpedo racks. Mine dimensions were fixed at torpedo tube diameter, and at about half standard torpedo length. When tactical submarine missiles were developed during the late 1960s and early 1970s, their size, too, was limited by torpedo tube dimensions. The size of the Harpoon anti-ship missile was actually set by other launchers, such as the Mark 13 missile launcher, but Tomahawk cruise missile dimensions match those of the still standard torpedo tube. Any alternative required new launching tubes and, it appeared, a much larger submarine to carry them.

WORLD WAR II TORPEDO TACTICS

Probably the torpedo's single greatest flaw was its limited effective range, a function of torpedo speed, guidance, and submarine fire control and sensor performance. Until well into World War II, all torpedoes were straight-runners, effectively equivalent to very slow artillery shells. Running time was the time during which a target might evade, either accidentally or after detecting an approaching torpedo. It was also the elapsed time during which the gyro had to keep the torpedo on course. For example, a British World War II submarine commander, Rear-Admiral Ben Bryant, claimed that torpedoes rarely strayed less than one degree off course. At a range of 3000 yards, that was a 50-yard error. The faster the torpedo, the better chance that a correct fire control solution would suffice for a hit. Almost the same might be said of more reliable gyros.

A submarine commander had to estimate target course and speed on the basis of a few quick glimpses through his periscope. Each exposed him to detection, since his periscope made a very visible 'feather' wake in the water. On the other hand, more observation time made for better estimates and so for a better fire control solution. In theory, target bearings could be plotted, and (at least by 1939) periscopes sometimes incorporated range-finders. Target speed could be estimated from propeller turn counts, or by plotting rate of advance, given an estimated course based, perhaps, on the target's apparent angle of inclination, based on the line of masts and funnels. The combination of an observed rate of change of bearing and an accurate range would also yield target speed. It was even possible for a submarine fire control party to analyse the zigzag course of a target so as to choose the appropriate firing solution.

Periscope exposure seemed so dangerous to the pre-World War II US Navy that it sought an alternative: the sound attack. The new high-frequency ('supersonic') passive sonars were credited with sufficient angular accuracy to make them usable for fire control, much as a periscope might be used to measure bearings. They had the advantage of being continuously usable. In theory, a single 'ping' would complete the fire control data. In practice, sound approaches generally failed because the existing sensors were inadequate, but similar passive fire control concepts were applied after 1945 to submarine v submarine ASW.

The combination of limited fire control accuracy and limited torpedo performance determined effective range. Thus, according to Bryant, although British torpedoes had a magnificent nominal range of 10,000 yards, it was best by far to fire at about 600 yards; beyond about 1500yards, too much depended on the accuracy of target course and speed estimates. For example, torpedoes had to lead the target to make up for the distance made good while the torpedo was in motion. Bryant considered about 2000 yards the practical limit for attacks on individual ships. Greater ranges were better suited to 'browning' shots, ie to semi-random attacks on groups rather than individual ships.

Torpedoes also had a minimum effective range. Bryant reported that standard Royal Navy World War II types initially dived, coming up to running depth only at about 400 yards. Inside that range, they would tend to dive under their targets. This corresponds to the minimum range of modern guided missiles, prior to which guidance is ineffective because they are not flying fast enough.

Navies differed in the sophistication of their torpedoes. The US Mark 14 had an adjustable gyro, so that it could adopt a preset course after leaving the torpedo tube. It was usually automatically (mechanically) set by the Torpedo Data Computer (TDC). Several British writers have suggested that this early example of automation was not altogether beneficial, as, like more recent machines, the TDC operated on the principle of 'garbage in, garbage out': that it converged towards *a* solution hardly guaranteed that it was the correct one. Input accuracy greatly improved when periscope ranging radars came into use during the war.

The Royal Navy made do with a variety of hand computers, such as the 'is-was' and the 'Greek slide rule', and showed little interest in angled fire. Thus although British torpedoes in use in 1939 could, in theory, be set at a 90-degree gyro angle, anything other than a straight shot was considered unreliable. In consequence a British submarine commander had to swing his boat until he came onto the proper torpedo course, which he would calculate and set on his periscope.

The time lost swinging to achieve firing angle sometimes allowed targets to escape. For example, typically a 90-degree swing required about four minutes, even if the submarine were not evading escorts at the same time. The closer the target, the faster it would cross that angle. For example, at 2000 yards (about a mile) a 15-knot target would cover 60 degrees in four minutes. Nor was a submerged submarine fast enough to catch up. It had to approach from ahead, with the shot lined up in advance, so that the target crossed the preset line of fire. That was impossible if the target was passing astern: Admiral Bryant particularly regretted his lack of stern tubes, as a 180 degree swing was prohibitively slow.

The standard tactic was to fire a spread, or salvo, spaced around the estimated future target position to compensate for random errors. The greater the range, the denser the required spread, ie the more torpedoes per salvo, to cover a greater area around the estimated target position. Ultimately spread density was limited by the number of torpedo tubes and then by the number of torpedoes aboard. Conversely, any attempt to limit submarine size must mean fewer torpedo tubes, fewer torpedoes per salvo, the greater the range, the larger the spread. Thus Admiral Doenitz, designing a U-boat force intended specifically to attack British trade, tried to reduce individual boat size to a minimum to increase his numbers. That in turn reduced the torpedo load (and the salvo size) aboard each boat. Doenitz concluded that salvoes were impractical, and that his captains would have to close to such short ranges that single torpedoes would almost certainly hit.

A typical 1914-18 submarine fired a salvo of two 18in torpedoes to a relatively short range; up to 1916 there was no recorded case of a British submarine hitting a moving warship at a range beyond 1000 yards. Typical British submarine salvoes in 1939-45 were four 21in torpedoes of much greater range and explosive power, although even then ranges beyond 5000 yards were rare. A US

SUBMARINE DESIGN AND DEVELOPMENT

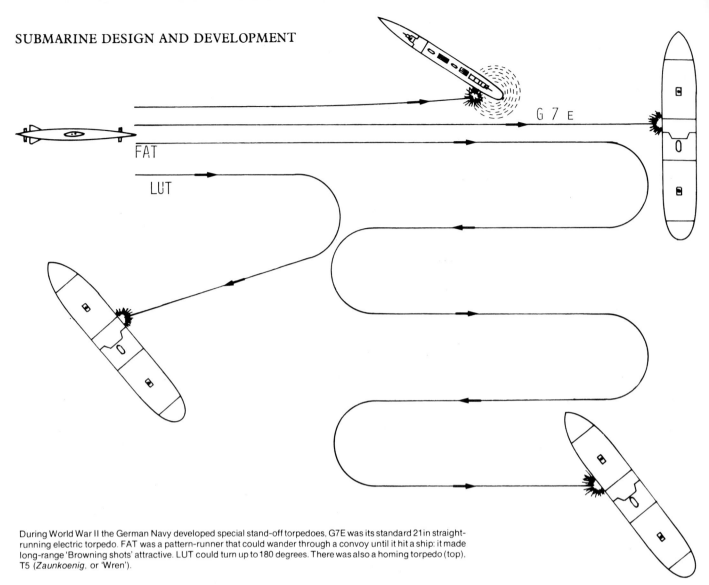

During World War II the German Navy developed special stand-off torpedoes. G7E was its standard 21in straight-running electric torpedo. FAT was a pattern-runner that could wander through a convoy until it hit a ship: it made long-range 'Browning shots' attractive. LUT could turn up to 180 degrees. There was also a homing torpedo (top), T5 (*Zaunkoenig*, or 'Wren').

postwar analysis showed three torpedoes per salvo, and about one in three hit. Homing torpedoes were generally fired singly; they, too, made about one-third hits.

All of this explains the great torpedo developments of World War II, pattern-runners and homers. Both greatly increased effective range by compensating for fire control inaccuracy. The Germans introduced pattern-runners, which they designated LUT, in 1943, to permit U-boats to fire at convoys from beyond their escorts' sonar range. They would weave in and out among a formation of targets, exploding when they hit. Submariners had always been willing to fire long-range 'browning' shots into groups of ships on the statistical chance of making a hit, but LUT greatly increased the odds. There was no simple countermeasure, other than expanding the screen to exclude the longer-range attacker. Postwar, the Royal Navy evaluated greatly increased torpedo range (which increased the attack area around a convoy by a factor of about three) as almost as important as the new fast submarine technology.

ACOUSTIC HOMING TORPEDOES

The Germans and the Allies introduced acoustic homing torpedoes roughly simultaneously in 1943. The German FAT or T-5 or *Zaunkoenig* (Wren) (GNAT, German Naval Acoustic Torpedo, in Allied parlance) was an anti-escort measure. If a submarine under attack did not have to solve a complex fire control problem, but instead could fire a homing torpedo back at the attacker, then its chance of evasion would greatly improve. Even from an offensive point of view, high-speed ASW craft were difficult targets. Similar technology was incorporated in the contemporary US FIDO, or Mine Mark 24, an air-dropped ASW homing torpedo, and in the Mark 27 anti-escort and Mark 28 long-range anti-ship submarine-launched torpedoes developed for the US submarine offensive in the Pacific.

All operated passively, homing on propeller and hull flow noises. Several more elaborate homing systems were later developed. Many current acoustic torpedoes are passive/active. They acquire their targets passively, heading for the propellers. However, once they reach a preset range, they steer to attack amidships, homing from abeam by means of an active sonar. Anti-ship torpedoes are often wake-homers. They are intended to sense the turbulent wake a ship makes, crossing it at an angle and then turning to cross again closer to the ship. In theory a properly programmed zigzag course will bring them into the ship's side, although a fast enough ship will still escape.

Homing torpedos generally ran out to a preset (enable) distance before their seekers were turned on, so that they were unlikely to circle back. Moreover, their acquisition ranges were not so great that they had any chance of picking up their targets at the moment of launching. Effectiveness was limited because it was impossible to correct torpedo aim for target motion during run-out. The usual solution is a form of mid-course guidance, in which the torpedo trails a wire as it runs out. The current US Mark 48 is an example. Since it runs out on the basis of submarine sonar data, it can move very fast, generating considerable self-noise until it reaches acquisition range. That high speed, at least in theory, increases the chance of sucessfully attacking fast Soviet submarines. On the other hand, the torpedo may be detectable at very great distances, and, like the visible wake of early anti-ship torpedoes, its noise reveals the attacking submarine. Wire guidance imposes another limitation as well. The wire is generally led out through the torpedo tube, which cannot be reloaded until the torpedo has run out. This limitation is particularly serious for a submarine which, like most US attack types, has few torpedo tubes. For example, a 40-knot torpedo would take 15 minutes to run 20,000 yards (just under 10 miles). Although the Allies defeated T-5 by means of acoustic decoys (Foxers), similar anti-escort weapons seem to have been very attractive. The final US wartime submarine design showed fixed broadside anti-escort torpedo tubes under its bridge. The postwar *Tang* was initially designed with a pair of countermeasures-launching tubes aft, but they were ultimately replaced by two 'swim-out' tubes for acoustic, presumably anti-escort, weapons. Postwar Royal Navy practice appears to have been similar: attack submarines carried their anti-ship torpedoes forward, for offensive action, and their anti-escort (defensive) torpedoes pointed aft, to be fired as they fled. Reportedly the Soviets did the same, often with 16in homing weapons.

TORPEDO FIRE CONTROL

The other major attempt to overcome fire control and guidance error was to make the torpedo lethal even if it missed by a small distance, by exploding it under the target's keel. That could break a ship in half. However, it is most difficult to arrange, as the British, German, and US Navies each independently learned during World War II about under-the-keel hits after each devised a proximity (magnetic) firing pistol for this purpose. Each then discovered just how difficult such fuzing could be, the American experience being the most notorious. Ironically, at least in their case, the device was never properly tested precisely because it was considered so lethal: better to test it once, then keep it highly secret. The Germans ultimately developed an active (as opposed to passive in the US case) magnetic fuze, which the Soviets captured, and, apparently, adopted.

For the Allied navies, undersea tactics and weapons changed radically as the emphasis shifted to ASW after 1945. The objective was generally to ambush a submarine attempting to penetrate a barrier; that in turn implied dependence on stealthy, ie passive, sensors for the entire fire control solution. As compared with US prewar sound attack practice, matters were somewhat improved because homing torpedoes tolerated relatively inexact solutions. At first the assumed target was a cavitating, snorkelling submarine, which meant a submarine exceeding about 4 knots at periscope depth. The ambushing submarine generally had to lie nearly or completely dead in the water to reduce self-noise and thus to increase its own sonar range. It could estimate the approaching boats' speed from its propeller turn count. Speed, bearing, and the rate of change of

Subroc, a submarine-launched ASW rocket, (emerging from the Naval Ordnance Laboratory pressure chamber at White Oak, Maryland October 1964) was the most futuristic of the US underwater weapons deployed in the early 1960s. It was associated with the new generation of very long range, VLF spherical sonars in the *Thresher/Permit* class attack submarines, and is credited with a range of about 20 miles. By contrast, the contemporary surface ship weapon, Asroc, operated in conjunction with the much smaller, higher-frequency, SQS-23, was effective only out to about 10,000 yards. Although a torpedo-armed version of Subroc was proposed, it was never developed, on the theory that aiming errors at very long range would much exceed the acquisition range of any homing torpedo. A typical sonar beam might be about 11 degrees wide, which at 10,000 yards (Asroc range) would correspond to an uncertainty of about 2000 yards; at 40,000 yards (Subroc range), that would increase to about 8000 yards. A very large nuclear warhead could, however, make up the difference. The yields of US weapons have never been published, but destructive radius is roughly proportional to the cube root of the yield, so that the Subroc warhead is probably at least 64 times as powerful as that of Asroc. Subroc is to be replaced by a new stand-off weapon, now under development by Boeing and Gould.
US Navy

SUBMARINE DESIGN AND DEVELOPMENT

The major US non-nuclear submarine ASW weapon of the late 1950s and the 1960s was the 1430lb electrically-propelled 11ft 3in Mark 37, which existed in both free-running and wire-guided versions. It has now been replaced in US service by the Mark 48, but is still widely used abroad. Note the runners; it is a 19in swim-out weapon. Reportedly it suffered operationally from its batteries' limited energy content; shots often failed because the torpedo did not have sufficient endurance (13,000 yards range at 16 knots). Northrop Corporation is now offering to rebuild Mark 37s with internal combustion powerplants and new homing devices.
US Navy

bearing yielded a range and a course, and thus a fire control solution, at least in theory. In practice, accuracy costs precious time because bearings change relatively slowly and their accurate measurement is a lengthy process. This is a very general defect of all purely passive systems. As for weapons, a snorkeller was very nearly a surface target, and SSKs of the early 1950s generally planned to use either a spread of Mark 14 straight-runners or a single homer.

Within a few years, sonars such as the BQR-4 had extended SSK ranges to tens of miles. Torpedo ranges were still much shorter, and it was often necessary to obtain a quick approximate range to see whether a target could be engaged at all. One solution, proposed by the then Lieutenant Commander J E Ekelund, USN, was change the target bearing rate by changing the *listening* submarine's speed or course. Always assuming that the target was moving at a steady course and speed, the change in target bearing due to a specific change in listening ship speed across the line of sight gave the range. The new technique was simple, and it did not depend, like the earlier one, on knowing the relationship between target propeller turns and speed. Moreover, it remained useful after the targets ceased to be cavitating submarines; the Ekelund idea applied equally well to a nuclear submarine. Later the concept was elaborated: the listening submarine carried out a series of precise manoeuvres, measuring changes in target bearing. The general technique is sometimes called Target Motion Analysis (TMA).

All passive techniques are limited in their accuracy. As long as the standard weapon was a homing torpedo, that was no great problem, as their seekers could make up for range and bearing errors. However, in the late 1950s the United States introduced Astor (Mark 45), a nuclear torpedo. Although it was wire-guided to the vicinity of the target, it had no terminal homing. Moreover, in accordance with standard US nuclear policy, it was command-detonated. That in turn required fairly precise target location; typically a submarine would emit a single ping to obtain an accurate range. A similar technique was probably used by submarines firing the longer-range Subroc anti-submarine missile. Most submariners much prefer the stealth of fully-passive fire control, one reason why the non-nuclear Mark 48 replaced the much more lethal Astor.

TORPEDO TUBES

The torpedo tube is needed to guide the torpedo while it is accelerated; once it is running at high speed, its own gyros can keep it on course. Some early submarines had external dropping collars instead of tubes, and suffered badly in torpedo accuracy. Until after 1945 torpedoes were ejected by pulses of compressed air. Systems used during 1914-18 tended to emit large bubbles of air which were visible when they reached the surface. The next stage of development was to suck back the air pulse as it reached the muzzle of the tube. Even so, the force of torpedo ejection was air, and that limited the depth at which torpedoes could be fired. This limitation made little difference as long as submarines were intended to attack only surface craft, but when ASW became an important submarine function, different means of launch had to be provided.

One was 'swim out', in which the torpedo propelled itself out of the tube. Space had to be provided around the torpedo, to allow water to flow back as it swam out. The US Navy is said to have adopted swim-out launching for its Mark 37 ASW torpedo so that war-built fleet boats with pneumatic tubes could fire it. That in turn required the new torpedo to be limited to 19in diameter to permit it to swim out of existing 21in tubes. Presumably the current Soviet 16in ASW torpedo can swim out of standard Soviet full-diameter tubes. From time to time there are reports of small-diameter tubes aft in Soviet submarines, and one wonders whether they may not be standard-diameter swim-out installations. The first practical swim-out installation was developed for the Type XXIII coastal U-boat. Swim-out imposes special requirements on the torpedo, which must be dynamically stable even at the very low speed, perhaps 8-10 knots, at which it leaves the tube. Moreover, at least ideally, the submarine bow must be designed for minimum hydrodynamic interference with the tube muzzles, to avoid deflection of torpedoes running free in these relatively wide spaces. Hence, for example, the wide bulbous bow shape of the German IKL submarines, which (at least in theory) avoids cross-flow across the nest of eight tubes.

Swim-out tubes are extremely compact and simple; hence their adoption for IKL's relatively small submarines. Similarly, the US *Tangs*, which had relatively fine lines aft, had a pair of swim-out tubes there, to save space. Swim-out is also considerably quieter than any other form of ejection. However, such a tube cannot launch the wide variety of non self-propelled mines and missiles submarines now employ. For example, the German IKL submarines must carry any mines they lay in external cannisters. In addition, because there is so much space around the torpedo, there is always the possibility that it will go off course as it is launched, perhaps even becoming lodged in the tube.

WEAPONS AND TACTICS

For a small submarine, external weapon carriage is always an alternative to torpedo tubes. The 398/550-ton *Pluviose* class French submarine *Ventose* (built at Cherbourg 1907 in a class of 18 double-hulled boats 1906–11) prepares to dive and shows two of her 18in torpedoes and Drzwiecki dropping collars (she carries 6 externally with only one tube and reload). They were relatively unsuccessful because they could not impart a steady course to the torpedo, but the idea was revived for World War II midget submarines and is the basis for several current small submarine designs.
US Navy

The more expensive and space-consuming alternative is water pulse ejection, effective at any depth. Before firing, the tube is flooded and the muzzle door opened to the sea, so that water pressure is equalised. When a hydraulic pump forces a water pulse into the tube's breech end, the torpedo is forced out. Firing rate depends on pump capacity and size. A submarine with only one pump can fire only one torpedo at a time. Both air-driven hydraulic rams and gas turbines have been used as pumps. The latter appear better suited to rapid re-firing.

During World War II the Germans developed an intermediate system, a piston inside the torpedo tube that shoved the torpedo out without releasing an air bubble. It was adopted postwar by the French Navy. Like air discharge, this system is limited in depth.

Each time a torpedo is launched, its tube fills with water. The weight equivalent to the torpedo volume compensates for the weight of the torpedo, but the remaining WRT (Water Round Torpedo) adds weight that must be compensated for. To avoid a trim by the bow upon firing, the submarine generally carries equal amounts of water in special WRT tanks. The only alternative would be to carry the torpedoes wet, with the tubes flooded. That is not really practicable at present.

Torpedo reloads are generally stowed immediately adjoining the nest(s) of tubes, and the reloading rate determined how many targets a submarine could engage during a single attack. Although torpedoes are extremely large, there was, until the advent of fast submarines, insufficient space for any kind of power loading system. The Type XXI was provided with a power system specifically to increase the number of targets it could attack per convoy.

When the US Navy had to reduce the standard torpedo battery from six to four tubes in *Thresher*, special efforts were made to increase the firing rate to compensate. But wire guidance was introduced at the same time. Since a tube cannot be reloaded while the wire pays out (it takes 10 minutes for a 10,000-yard run at 30 knots), rapid reloading of each tube became less valuable. It could also be argued that the higher single-shot probability of kill of a guided, homing, torpedo made multiple-torpedo salvoes much less valuable. On the other hand, particularly with the advent of DIMUS, a submarine can, in theory, engage multiple targets simultaneously. That in turn should require more tubes (see Chapter 13). But supporters of fewer tubes will argue that running several simultaneously fired torpedoes risks of mutual interference, either acoustically or

The French Navy is currently unique in using hydraulic rams to launch torpedoes. The housings of the rams can be seen protruding from some of the 8 bow torpedo tube breeches aboard the French *Daphne*-class diesel submarine *Doris* (S 643, completed 1964). This system is effective to greater depths than the air ejector previously standard, but not to the depths reachable by water ejection (as in the US and Royal Navies) or swim-out (as in IKL practice). Unlike swim-out, it provides positive ejection, and hence can be used to launch unpropelled weapons such as mines and encapsulated missiles. France is also unique in holding to her pre-1939 torpedo calibre of 550mm (21.7in).
French Navy

SUBMARINE DESIGN AND DEVELOPMENT

Modern submarines generally employ power to handle their large torpedoes. This is the torpedo room of the ballistic missile submarine USS *Ohio*, (SSBN 726), showing a 21in Mark 48 torpedo (range 35,000 yards at 55 knots) strapped down for transfer. Note that both the pallet *and* the individual cradles carrying the 3480lb torpedo can move laterally, and that the entire pallet can move forward, the 19ft-long torpedo entering its tube over the roller visible near its nose. A second torpedo, in shadow, is visible immediately beneath this one. Power transfer systems allow for very tight packing in torpedo rooms; even so, because of heavy torpedoes' size, modern submarines do not carry more weapons than their predecessors.
US Navy

even by crossing guidance wires. In addition, the submarine sonar may be unable to distinguish multiple torpedoes. Confusing weapons destined for different targets, then, it may cause the submarine fire control system to issue incorrect steering commands. These considerations will become much less relevant as 'fire and forget' missiles become more prevalent.

TORPEDO STOWAGE

Stowage itself has always been a problem. The old single-deck submarines could devote their entire hull diameters to a forward torpedo nest. Although modern craft have considerably greater diameters, they also generally break that diameter into several decks. Typically the tubes must fit above or below a large bow sonar transducer. In American boats, they are confined to a single deck depth abaft the transducer, and this design feature reduced the torpedo salvo from six to four tubes. Deck height in turn determines the number of reloads, since generally there is only a single bank of reload torpedoes abaft the tubes, with one or more per tube. Published figures suggest that there are rarely as many as 30 per submarine, including torpedoes in the tubes. In modern US submarines sketches show two layers of torpedoes in a space less than 25ft across. Each probably occupies a net width of about 2ft, so the total must be about 25 weapons.

Space must, moreover, be left to shift weapons from tube to tube, since the submarine carries several very different types. A modern US attack submarine can carry Harpoon and Tomahawk anti-ship or anti-shore missiles; Subroc ASW stand-off weapons; Mark 48 torpedoes for anti-ship and anti-submarine attacks; a variety of mines; and torpedo-size decoys (mobile submarine simulators). Also, until recently, there were Mark 45 nuclear ASW torpedoes and straight-running Mark 14s for anti-ship attack. Typically there will be one Subroc and one Harpoon ready in the tubes at all times. The situation is complicated somewhat by the fact that Subroc, developed in the late 1950s, requires analog data, whereas the newer weapons, such as Harpoon and SOW, are digital. As this is written, Subroc is being modified for digital operation as part of a modernisation programme. That leaves very little space with which to realise the enormous tactical versatility that these weapons can provide.

The alternative is to use the submarine purely as a sensor platform, with other craft, such as aircraft, attacking the relatively distant target it detects. This is one version the direct support (intergrated escort) role and it is also the SSK/VP tactic described in Chapter 4. If, for example, a submarine armed with a 10,000-yard weapon detects a target at 110,000 yards, it must cover a relative distance of 100,000 yard, (50 miles) before it can engage. Even at a high closing speed, 25 knots, that is two hours without allowing for imperfect target location. If a submarine on barrier patrol can effectively

WEAPONS AND TACTICS

stalk only one target at a time, engagement time and sensor range define the percentage of transiters it can hope to attack. Massing the transiters can become an attractive anti-barrier tactic.

Ideally, the torpedoes should be 'wooden rounds', capable of long storage in a ready condition, but in fact they are too complex, and live in too hostile an environment. Many submarines built up to 1945 had external torpedo tubes, and even carried extra torpedoes in pressure-tight containers outside their pressure hulls. Such torpedoes tended to deteriorate badly during a war patrol, to the extent that British submarines were expected to fire theirs off, whether or not against targets, on their return from patrol. Interwar French submarines were a variation on this theme; they mounted relatively large numbers of trainable external tubes atop their pressure hulls. One argument was that four-torpedo salvoes should be available in all directions. Conventional stern tubes were also provided.

MISSILE SYSTEMS

Attempts to escape from tube dimension limits are costly, as they require new types of tubes (or other weapon launchers). Strategic missiles such as Polaris are the most obvious example. Sixteen Polaris, each with a single warhead, roughly doubled the size of a submarine quite capable of taking rather more than 16 standard torpedoes. Among these tubes' indirect costs were heavier hull framing, to make up for the many pressure hull penetrations. Similarly, an attempt to add 20 tactical cruise missiles (STAM) helped make the Advanced High Performance Nuclear Attack Submarine (APHNAS or 'Mid-Seventies Attack Submarine') into a 14,000-ton monster quite beyond even US naval budgets. In both cases, the tubes had to penetrate the pressure hull, presumably to allow for maintenance and for last-minute adjustment. When such access was foregone, tubes could be added *outside* the pressure hull, as in the later *Los Angeles* class boats, in which 12 vertical tubes for Tomahawk are to be added between pressure hull and sonar transducer, at no great cost in net size.

Quite possibly the future submarine anti-ship weapon will not be an underwater weapon at all, but a much faster missile, launched underwater and impacting either above or below water. In this sense a 45-knot torpedo fired at a target 5000 yards away is equivalent to a 450-knot missile fired at a target 50,000 yards (25 miles) away.

Fast submarines were such difficult targets that, by the mid-1950s, the US Navy was willing to employ nuclear weapons against them. This is the 18ft 9in-long ASTOR, or Mark 45, the 2330lb nuclear torpedo (seen during test runs in June 1959 at the Naval Torpedo Station, Keyport, Washington), electrically powered, with a reported range of 12,000 yards at 40 knots. The propeller has a shroud ring for quieter running. It was wire guided, and, following the positive release doctrine of nuclear weapons, was detonated on command. That in turn required the submarine to obtain a precise range, by sonar pinging. As a result, Mark 45 was never altogether popular. Moreover, many within the submarine community believed that it had a kill probability of 2 – one for the target and one for the firer. Mark 45 was the first US nuclear weapon to be retired (1976) without a direct successor; in effect its successor is Mark 48. Note the guides along the side of the torpedo. The US Navy adopted 19in calibre from 1956 for Marks 37 and 45 so that they could be fired by fleet submarines at any depth, by swim-out. The guides kept the torpedo in line as it left the 21in tube.
US Navy

SUBMARINE DESIGN AND DEVELOPMENT

Eurydice shows four of her eight bow torpedo tube shutters and the prow dome of her DUUA-1 sonar. The lower bow dome housed a lower frequency active/passive sonar.
E C Armées

WEAPONS AND TACTICS

Submarine-launched anti-ship missiles, like the US Harpoon, should transform the submarine threat. Unlike wire-guided torpedoes, they are 'fire and forget' weapons and therefore can easily be fired in salvoes at several targets. There is, therefore, a new emphasis on rapid firing and reloading. The Soviets solved this problem in their 'Charlie' class nuclear-powered cruise missile submarine by providing one tube for each oversize SS-N-7 or -9 missile. Such Western torpedo tube size weapons as Harpoon, Tomahawk and Exocet (SM 39) can be carried in greater numbers, but require more complex handling arrangements. They also require positive ejection from the submarine. Harpoon is launched from the torpedo-size capsule shown, which breaks open on reaching the surface. Encapsulation in turn reduces the usable volume of the torpedo tube. Thus Tomahawk, which is carried in the same tube and so has about the same volume, but is not encapsulated, is a much larger missile with an effective anti-ship 'range' about four times Harpoon's.
McDonnell Douglas

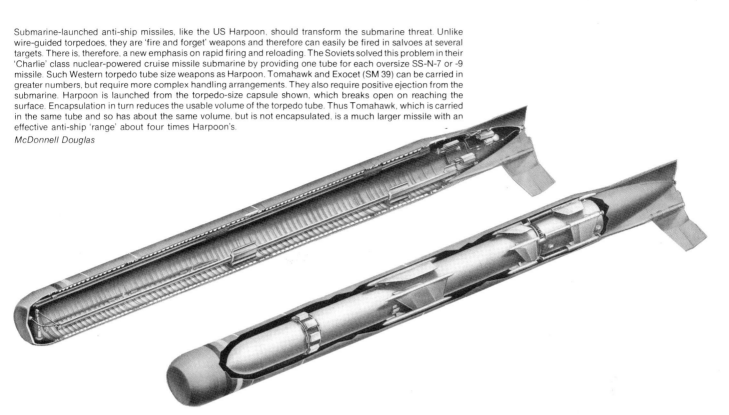

Eurydice (S 644), of the 869/1043-ton French *Daphne* 190ft class, displays her four external 21.7in/550mm stern tubes while building at Cherbourg. Note, too, her extra set of stabilising fins, fixed to her hull at the inboard end of the propeller shaft. She disappeared off Toulon on 4 March 1970.
E C Armées

SUBMARINE DESIGN AND DEVELOPMENT

Deck guns retain some value, even in a missile age, since they alone can be used to threaten small craft short of sinking them. The Royal Navy, conscious of its policing role East of Suez, retained provision for such weapons aboard its modernised submarines. HMS *Andrew* (S 63), the very last British gun-armed submarine displays her 4in/33 calibre Mark XXIII gun in March 1974, her final year of service. She made the first underwater Atlantic crossing (by snorkel) in June 1953.
C & S Taylor

Torpedo lethality is often less than might be expected. These photographs show an attempt by a Japanese Maritime Self-Defence Agency submarine to sink the large derelict tanker *Yuro Maru* in the North Pacific during November 1964. Both show the tanker after one torpedo hit, in the fourth of four attacks. She had already been hit repeatedly by 5in shells, by 250lb bombs and 5in rockets from jet fighters, and by 500lb bombs and 5in rockets from Lockheed P3 Neptune maritime patrol aircraft, over a period of three days. Of three torpedoes fired, only one hit. Another failed to run, and a second ran deep. Even after all of this damage the tanker remained afloat for another three days. A second submarine attack was, therefore, cancelled.
Japanese Maritime Self-Defence Agency

In fact the two situations are not at all equivalent, since the submarine can obtain quite good initial data at 5000 yards, whereas at 50,000 it is subject to many inaccuracies, balanced only by some form of terminal homing. On the other hand, if the torpedo is a homer, it may have an acquisition range measured in hundreds of yards. Missile radar ranges against surface ships are measured in miles. Thus a homing missile may be able to tolerate much more target movement than a torpedo, so that from the probability of hitting, the missile might be able to fly perhaps ten times as long. Moreover, from the point of view of survivability, a submarine 25 miles from its target is much less likely to be detected than one operating only 2.5 miles away. These remarks do not, of course, apply to underwater targets.

The greater the missile range, the more the submarine must depend upon external sources of information. A US system called Outlaw Shark was developed specifically to support the Harpoon, a 60-mile underwater-launched cruise missile. The view was that a submarine commander needed an accurate image of the ships within a set distance, probably about 100 miles, of his submarine. He had to be able to obtain it passively, insofar as possible. The Soviets use active-radar ocean surveillance satellites for this purpose, dumping their data to submarines lying nearly awash. The US Navy chose instead to seek the data in the mass of information normally collected by the national-level intelligence agencies, 'fuse' it by computer into a picture of the sea around the submarine, and transmit it by special channel. A computer aboard the submarine reconstructs the necessary information from the more general data on the submarine force link. Tests in the Sixth (Mediterranean) Fleet were apparently quite successful, and a successor system is now entering service.

Outlaw Shark, and indeed any system of externally supplied intelligence, places a great burden on submarine navigation. The same might be said of ballistic missiles, target intelligence for which is, at least in theory, provided with reference only to geographical co-ordinates. The strategic mission requires minimum submarine exposure, ie minimum reference to any traditional navigational

WEAPONS AND TACTICS

reference, such as the stars or even the sea bottom. The American solution was a missile-type inertial navigational system. It could be expected to drift slightly over time, and the submarine could update at a small cost in exposure. In some missiles, such as Trident and the Soviet SS-N-8, the missile itself refers to stars overhead as an additional navigational corrective.

What is perhaps more interesting was the US Submarine Force's reaction. Reportedly both Harpoon and Outlaw Shark were cordially disliked. The submariner psychology was and is the loner's, dependent only on his own sensors, and definitely unwilling to risk exposure either by coming to periscope depth to receive the special information, or by firing a missile through the surface of the water, where it might be picked up by radar.

At the moment the efficacy of cruise missiles is still a matter of some dispute. French-built Exocets did sink two British ships in the Falklands, but in each case the warhead was apparently a dud, starting a fatal fire through its secondary effects. Presumably navies reading that war's lessons properly will not be nearly so vulnerable to such weapons in future. Moreover, the cruise missile, unlike the torpedo, can be shot down by close range terminal defence weapons such as Seawolf and Phalanx.

GUNS

One other submarine weapon deserves mention here – the gun, which survived until the end of the submersible era. Running primarily on the surface, a submersible needed some insurance against being surprised by light surface craft in bad weather; guns first appeared aboard such boats about 1910. They were defensive weapons, definitely secondary to torpedoes.

War experience in 1914-18 showed that even these weapons had important virtues of

Torpedoes have always been troublesome, partly because they are so slow. One solution is a projectile that travels at much higher speed through the air. The Royal Navy conceived and laid down in 1916 a class of four double-hull heavy-gun (12in) 'monitor' submarines, capable of surfacing rapidly in 25 seconds to fire a single 850lb battleship shell (40 carried) at short range. These 296ft leviathans of 1601/1950 tons had 30ft periscopes for rangefinding and gun control but M-1 saw no action in World War I (although intended to bombard Constantinople) and was lost with all hands in 1925 as was M-2 in 1932 having had her giant gun removed as had M-3. When fitted, the 12in weapon could train through 15 degrees and could be fired while the submarine was submerged to about 15ft, but had to be loaded on the surface.
US Navy/cutaway model in Science Museum, London, photographed by author

their own. In many cases a submarine could attack individual merchant ships on the surface, with little or no fear of retaliation. Under such circumstances the stealth of a submerged torpedo attack was not needed. With a gun, the submarine could force a merchant ship to stop for scuttling, or could even sink her. Although a submarine was a poor gun platform compared with any conventional surface ship, with little or no provision for range finding or conventional fire control, it could expect a fair percentage of hits at the very short ranges involved, requiring much less elaborate fire control than in the case of a torpedo. Moreover, no submarine ever had a very large number of reload torpedoes, so they had to be conserved. Gun calibres in all navies increased through the war, so that at the end German U-cruisers mounted 5.9in weapons. The US Navy mounted high-velocity 5in guns in some of its flush-deck destroyers specifically to deal with such craft.

There was also an alternative gun concept, much more closely allied to current cruise missile ideas: the British 'M' class submarine

SUBMARINE DESIGN AND DEVELOPMENT

monitor (launched 1917). The concept of this heavy-gun submarine was that relatively slow, erratic torpedoes could not be expected to hit rapidly-manoeuvring warships, such as light cruisers. On the other hand, a heavy gun fired at torpedo range, about 1000 yards, should be certain of hitting. The 'Ms' carried a single 12in gun that could be fired when the craft was on the surface or at shallow depth. It could only be reloaded on the surface. As an illustration of the lesser volume required when much of the weapon system was reusable, the 'M' carried 40 12in shells, but only eight 18in torpedoes. The concept was never tested in combat, two of the three submarines of this class being completed only in 1920. No other navy tried to duplicate these craft, although the French designed one of their own in 1919, and the US Navy also sketched such craft.

World War II experience showed the value of guns in dealing with small ASW ships, particularly if a submarine had been forced to the surface by underwater damage. Both British and American submariners were encouraged to surface and sink such craft by gunfire, far more economical than torpedoes in terms of ammunition expenditure. Some commanders actually preferred quick gun actions, the submarine surfacing at point-blank range, the crews pouring up through the hatches, and the target rapidly and conclusively dispatched.

Throughout the 1939-45 war there was considerable pressure for greater gun power, even at a cost in underwater performance. British submariners in the Mediterranean found their 3in guns far too weak for the purpose, and suffered accordingly. In the US Navy, fleet proposals for 5in guns in submarines had actually been refused prewar for fear that they would encourage submariners to fight on the surface. Instead, the standard fleet submarine was armed with a single 3in/50 calibre dual-purpose gun, although the gun foundation was strong enough to take the larger weapon. The next step was a 4in/50 adapted from destroyers, and then there was a heavy 5in/51, a weapon originally developed for battleship secondary batteries. Ultimately the Bureau of Ordnance developed a 'wet' 5in/25, and in 1945 some submarines carried two of them, as well as automatic anti-aircraft guns.

The gun could not well survive into an era of submarine streamlining, although a few US 'fleet snorkels' carried 5in/25 guns for a short time. Yet guns could often do what torpedoes, like modern anti-ship missiles, could not. Thus the Royal Navy, with its long-established mission of keeping order among the small craft of the Far East, tended to retain provision for mounting deck guns aboard its diesel-electric submarines, and actually did mount them at least during the Indonesian confrontation of the early 1960s. A shot across the bows was a warning which no torpedo or missile could equal.

CHAPTER TWELVE

The Submarine's Enemy – Modern ASW

Traditional concepts of submarine operations concede a great deal to the enemy's ASW forces. Thus submariners often seem to equate undetectability with bare survival. It appears to be a cardinal rule of peacetime submarine training exercises that any submarine detected and tracked for any period of time is as good as sunk. Yet experience in both World Wars appears to show, first, that it is relatively difficult to convert submarine detection into ASW attack and, second, that submarines themselves are tough, highly resistant to what might have been considered fatal battle damage. Again, in the past it might be said that any counter-attack by the submarine would merely make its identification and location more definite, so inviting further attack. However, from time to time submariners chose instead to strike back, either to frustrate and confuse pursuit or actually to destroy the pursuer.

Perhaps the most fundamental issue is the ASW forces' mission, since that determines how successful a submarine's countermeasures may be. One simple answer, used by several navies in the past (sometimes to their detriment) is that ASW is successful to the extent that submarines are destroyed faster than they can be built. Clearly this is a sufficient condition for their defeat, but it may not be a necessary one. For most of World War I, submarines were being built faster than the Allies could sink them, yet the U-boat arm was clearly defeated in 1917-18. In U-boat terms, the targets, the merchant ships, were appearing faster than they could be sunk. In this sense, success or failure could be measured, not directly in terms of the submarines' fate, but rather in terms of how well they could engage their targets. Although a submarine commander could successfully evade Allied forces, he might still fail to operate effectively.

In a shipping campaign, the true measure of ASW success is the survival of merchant ships. If the submarines can be prevented from sinking their targets, their own losses are very much a secondary issue. Merely avoiding enemy submarines may suffice to accomplish minimum ASW goals. Thus wide-area intelligence collection can be of decisive importance, as in convoy routing during both World Wars. The submarine force's objective is always to place a relatively small number of boats close to a limited number of truly important targets. It is, of course, impossible to evaluate here the potential current or future contribution of the major powers' national intelligence systems to any future shipping campaign.

In more modern terms, then, the oft-repeated statement that surface ASW forces would be unable to locate submarines in the open ocean might still be irrelevant, as these same submarines would still have to announce their presence by attacking targets. Thus, as in 1914-18, convoy might be the ideal strategy should current long-range submarine detectors, such as SOSUS (the system of long-range bottom hydrophones), lose effectiveness. Strategic submarines add a new dimension, in that they *are* effective so long as they can exist undetected within range of their targets. Presumably a strategic submarine reveals itself as soon as it fires, but by then its further existence may no longer be very relevant.

Submarine destruction is always the more attractive ASW measure. *If* submarines can be detected efficiently in the open ocean, then it is much more efficient to hunt them down, with forces roughly proportional to their numbers than to await their assaults on convoys, using forces proportional to the number of ships that must be protected. The difference is evident in the evolution of US ASW policy after 1945. It appeared to many that the wartime long-range detectors, HF/DF and the associated prediction of U-boat dispositions by codebreaking, would not be available in any war against the Soviets. Moreover, the new submarine technology, typified by Type XXI, would frustrate wartime-type air ASW forces, dependent as they were on radar detection of surfaced submarines. In effect, the situation reverted to something approaching that of 1917 with the battle back underwater.

US ASW STRATEGY AFTER 1945

Enormous numbers of convoy escorts would be needed. An American 1948 projection called for about 25 high-quality ASW light cruisers or destroyers, 526 destroyers, and 25 aircraft carriers, as well as 250 submarines, all to deal with about 350 Soviet submarines. The situation was saved only by the appearance of the Sound Surveillance System or SOSUS, which (in theory) made hunter-killer operations practical. *If* Soviet submarines in the important operating areas could routinely be detected and tracked, then relatively few patrol aircraft could find and destroy them. In fact SOSUS detection was statistical, so that on the whole a submarine would have a rising probability of detection as it spent more time on Atlantic and Pacific sea routes. Thus the SOSUS strategy was one of attrition: over a period of months, the Soviet submarine force might be destroyed. Attrition could be increased by means of barriers across the choke points.

There was little apparent alternative. The forces required by the 1948 plan could be fielded only because of the enormous wartime US building programme. In 1950, for example, the US Navy possessed 28 light and escort carriers suitable for ASW employment; 9 anti-aircraft cruisers comparable to large destroyers; 351 destroyers; 244 destroyer escorts; and 167 submarines. Most would need modernisation or reconstruction, but even so they represented an important reserve for mobilisation. A decade later, much of this immense force had either been discarded or was clearly no longer worth maintaining. The FRAM programme did keep many *Sumner* and *Gearing* class destroyers (and some fleet type submarines) effective through the 1960s, but the destroyer escorts and the earlier destroyers were too limited to modernise, and even the FRAMs had relatively little remaining life. Yet there was no massive shipbuilding programme to replace this fleet. Ships were far too expensive. Vietnam was the final straw: it wore out the FRAMs without paying for their replacement.

171

SUBMARINE DESIGN AND DEVELOPMENT

The new SOSUS attrition strategy reduced the need for convoy escorts. Merchant ships have always been considered relatively replaceable: as long as submarines were being sunk quickly enough, losses in the first weeks or months of a war could be tolerated. Warship task forces were much more important, and therefore still required a much more intense, directly protective screen of surface escorts. On the whole, then, the number of expensive escort ships could be sharply reduced to screen only the absolutely vital targets.

The SOSUS-based ASW strategy was also attractive because, unlike traditional screening concepts, it could deal with the new threat of strategic missile attack submarines. SOSUS itself was originally bought as a means of strategic defence, since it would warn the United States of Soviet submarines entering their missile launch areas. It became ineffective for this purpose as the Soviets moved their own seaborne strategic missiles into sanctuary areas, but remains important to US tactical ASW. The SOSUS system's mere existence presumably discourages the Soviets from moving their long-range submarine missiles closer to the United States.

The new strategy's impact is evident in a comparison of a US 1950 study of the practicality of maritime transportation, the Hartwell Report, with an ASW Readiness Executive (Op-60) estimate of August 1961. In 1950 the perceived threat was 200-300 Type XXI submarines, emerging at the rate of 100 a year. Existing surface ship active sonars were considered grossly inadequate, and radical measures were demanded. Recommendations included SOSUS itself; dipping sonar; building US nuclear submarines; further development of SSK concepts (given a listening range of 100 miles or more against snorkellers); and the development of nuclear underwater weapons, expected to have kill radii of a mile or more. It was assumed that the Soviets would use their own nuclear weapons against ships and ports, and in mines. At this time direct nuclear attacks against Soviet submarine bases were a major element of American wartime ASW strategy.

By contrast, a decade later Op-60 estimated that without using either nuclear weapons or strikes against Soviet bases, the United States could expect 'to defeat any submarine operations which the Soviets are capable of mounting, in reaction to reprisal or other operations at sea by US forces, commencing on or about 1 January 1962.'

'In the circumstances considered, the most damaging use of Soviet submarines, at least risk to themselves, would be in a ship-sinking campaign against unescorted merchant ships in areas near vital European/Far Eastern terminals. In the situation deemed most probable in the context of reference (a) [Op 60 memo of 7 August 1960], namely appropriate US anti-submarine deployments in advance, and of Soviet reaction without benefit of a pre-planned long stand-down [ie taking their boats off patrol before hostilities], resultant merchant ship losses could be as high as 88-100 per month, or slightly over one-half of one per cent of Free World merchant totals. In exchange, US barrier and killer-submarine operations would sink 36 per cent of all submarine sorties on a sustained basis, or initially 25 submarines per month, a rate considerably above what [Soviet] Bloc submarine effectiveness is believed able to withstand. Successful open-sea VP [patrol plane] and HUK [SOSUS-directed hunter-killer] operations, kill rates not calculated but estimated as of the order of not less than 10 per month world-wide, would further increase Bloc submarine losses. Weapon inventory and production will sustain this campaign...

'In the unlikely [case] of full Soviet and zero US initiative, the foregoing merchant losses could be as high as 100-150 ships per month, or slightly under one per cent per month of the Free World total, declining to the figures of the preceding paragraph in not

Convoy was the major ASW invention of World War I: one of US merchant vessels is shown approaching the British coast. It had a twofold effect: first, it reduced losses by saturating the U-boats attacking it, presenting them with more targets than they could handle, so that, even were they successful, they could sink only a fraction of the ships. Second, it increased the risk inherent in any such attack, because ASW ships were always present when they were made. Because convoys attracted U-boats into the presence of the ASW forces, they provided both a killing-ground and a deterrent. Moreover, because convoy operations concentrated shipping into a very limited fraction of the ocean, them made it more difficult for the submarines to locate targets in the first place. In World War II, Admiral Doenitz attempted to counter this tactic by providing a corresponding strengthened attack in the form of the wolf pack.
US Navy

THE SUBMARINE AND ITS ENEMY: MODERN ASW

over two months. Other situations including different Soviet choices of submarine objectives, Soviet reinforcement by other Bloc submarine forces, US use of nuclear in addition to conventional anti-submarine weapons, and assistance by Allied anti-submarine forces, would all accelerate the destruction of the effectiveness of the Bloc submarine inventory.'

ACTIVE OR PASSIVE DETECTION?

It may be relevant that, at least up to now, all very long-range submarine detectors have been passive, picking up some signal generated by the submarine itself. For example, HF/DF operated by detecting submarine radio transmissions. If the submarine did not transmit, it would blend into its background. During World War II, the Germans developed a burst transmitter, *Kurier*, specifically to defeat HF/DF, on the theory that its signals would be too short to detect. SOSUS and the tactical towed arrays, which share similar technologies, pick up sounds generated by a moving submarine. If the submarine can operate silently enough, it can avoid detection. In theory, high submarine speed should correspond to noisiness, and appropriate surface ship tactics may force a submarine to reveal itself that way, as it manoeuvres to reach an appropriate attacking position. Note, too, that many nuclear plants are *inherently* noisy, due to machinery such as coolant pumps and turbo-generators. Systems such as SOSUS may be able to detect them even when the submarines attempt to operate quietly.

Reliance on passive systems is inherently dangerous, in that the target submarine may be able to eliminate the signature in question. From time to time there are fears that SOSUS will become ineffective, as the Soviets silence their submarines faster than its own signal-processing can improve; and it is also suggested that the Soviets would do something more direct, such as attacking SOSUS arrays and stations. They might also deliberately explode nuclear depth bombs to bury their own boats' sounds underwater with noise reverberating through ocean basins.

One alternative would be an active detector. About 1960 the United States tested a large active sea-bottom sonar, capable of reaching out to several convergence zones. It failed because SOSUS could detect submarines at much greater ranges. It was also feared that a very powerful active sonar's reverberations, reaching across an entire ocean basin, would tend to mask any targets in that basin. The active sonar might overcome noise masking, too, although it would probably be too massive to evade the nuclear sabotage threat.

NON-ACOUSTIC DETECTION

From time to time, too, there are proposals for entirely non-acoustic long-range systems. The ultimate goal is a wide-area system suitable for employment from space. One surprise from recent ground-mapping radar satellite tests was that the sea bottom, rather than the wave profile, was mapped when the satellite was over the oceans. In fact the satellite was detecting *surface effects* apparently due to hydrodynamic phenomena associated with the bottom. The sea surface actually appears to rise over sea mounts, and to be depressed over the great trenches. In theory, then, there should be detectable surface disturbances corresponding to submerged submarines.

Most non-acoustic techniques are based on the idea that submarine disturbance gradually rises to the surface. The water through which a submarine moves is not at the same temperature as the surface, and (in theory), some of it is pushed upward, to form a wake or 'scar' detectable by infra-red. In 1951 US scientists claimed that infra-red wakes could be detected as much as 20,000 yards (10 miles) astern of a submarine at night. A submarine also leaves a trail of ions or condensation nuclei, some of which rise to the surface where (at least in theory) they can be detected from the air. In 1951 such trails were sometimes detected at ranges as great as 11,000 yards. Then there is the wake itself, in the sense of a disturbance in the water, that presumably gradually rises to the surface, where (perhaps) it can be distinguished from the random motion of the waves. In all of these cases, it might be argued that a slow, very deep submarine would leave little signature behind. Any disturbance it made would take some considerable time to rise to the surface. Thus such systems would provide only a delayed image of submarine position and course.

Non-acoustic systems in general are highly classified, so that there is always a fear that some exotic sensor, entirely unknown to all but a few specialists, will revolutionise ASW. There is some feeling within the US intelligence community that the Soviets may be following approaches so different as literally to be incomprehensible. For Soviet experiments, particularly in the early stages, may not even be perceived as ASW exercises. This type of uncertainty makes non-acoustic ASW a fertile ground for speculation and for misunderstanding of much less dangerous Soviet developments. All that really can be said is that, after over three decades of intense work, neither the United States nor the Soviet Union appears to have deployed anything approaching a wide-area non-acoustic ASW sensor. Moreover, both navies continue to build and to operate large numbers of submarines, both strategic and tactical. It might reasonably be concluded that such expenditures would cease or at least decline as soon as either navy came to believe that a true ASW revolution was imminent.

The classic sequence of ASW operations proceeds from *detection*, which places the submarine within some large but well-defined area; to *classification*, in which the target is confirmed as a submarine, to *localisation*, in which the submarine is located

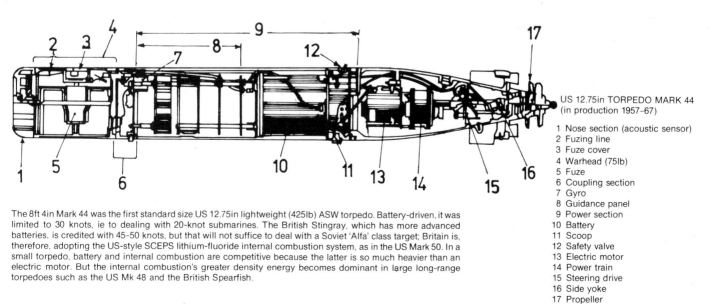

US 12.75in TORPEDO MARK 44 (in production 1957–67)

1 Nose section (acoustic sensor)
2 Fuzing line
3 Fuze cover
4 Warhead (75lb)
5 Fuze
6 Coupling section
7 Gyro
8 Guidance panel
9 Power section
10 Battery
11 Scoop
12 Safety valve
13 Electric motor
14 Power train
15 Steering drive
16 Side yoke
17 Propeller

The 8ft 4in Mark 44 was the first standard size US 12.75in lightweight (425lb) ASW torpedo. Battery-driven, it was limited to 30 knots, ie to dealing with 20-knot submarines. The British Stingray, which has more advanced batteries, is credited with 45–50 knots, but that will not suffice to deal with a Soviet 'Alfa' class target; Britain is, therefore, adopting the US-style SCEPS lithium-fluoride internal combustion system, as in the US Mark 50. In a small torpedo, battery and internal combustion are competitive because the latter is so much heavier than an electric motor. But the internal combustion's greater density energy becomes dominant in large long-range torpedoes such as the US Mk 48 and the British Spearfish.

173

SUBMARINE DESIGN AND DEVELOPMENT

The US 12.75in Mark 46 lightweight (568lb) torpedo (in service since 1963 and seen here in the bay of a US Sea King H3 helicopter on 5 January 1971) is typical of the most widespread class of Western ASW weapons, an 8ft 6in weapon launched from surface ships, dropped from aircraft and carried by stand-off missiles such as Asroc and Ikara. Its range is 12,000 yards at 45 knots and 50ft depth (at 1500ft it is half the range at 40 knots). The Italians even carried its predecessor, the Mark 44, in the nose of a wire-guided electric torpedo (modified German G6E) as the Canguro (Kangaroo) submarine ASW weapon. Limited in diameter by its many carriers, the torpedo can only operate at short wavelengths ie at a high sonar homer frequency, comparable to that employed by World War II surface ship sonars. It therefore has a very limited acquisition range, perhaps 1500 yards at best. Since a 30-knot submarine moves about a 1000 yards per minute, accurate placement is crucial. The other limit is torpedo diving depth. Since the Otto-fuel internal combustion engine exhausts into the water, it must fight back-pressure. The deeper the torpedo, the slower it can run. The British Stingray attempts to solve this by using batteries and an electric motor; the new US Mark 50, by closing the cycle, its exhaust products remaining within the torpedo hull. In all three cases there is concern that the limit on total torpedo weight holds down warhead weight to the point of impotence.
US Navy

sufficiently well to be attacked, and then the *attack*. Each phase presents problems, and opportunities for evasion or counter-attack. In the past submarines were often detected only when they themselves attacked, because detection was (indeed, is) relatively difficult. Long-range systems such as HF/DF (as during World War II) and SOSUS complicate matters, in that submarines can be detected in the open ocean far from their prospective targets. From the submarine's point of view, if it can be detected (and attacked, primarily by aircraft) at any time, its behaviour must be shaped by the need to avoid, or at least to minimise, such detection.

After 1945 the US and British navies developed 'sniffers' to detect snorkel exhaust products, and airborne radars sensitive enough to detect snorkels at a considerable range. Given this combination, any diesel-electric submarine was at considerable risk any time it snorkelled, and snorkelling tactics had to be shaped primarily to minimise the chance of detection. It was later discovered that industrial pollution downwind of any major city would mask snorkel products within about 50 miles of the shore, and that diesel merchant ships would often mimic snorkellers, so that sniffers are not as dangerous as they were two decades ago. Even so, snorkelling is risky, to the point of severely limiting a diesel-electric boat's mobility in the open ocean. One former American diesel submarine commander went so far as to argue that diesel-electric submarines are thereby effectively limited to a coastal role. He believed he could survive in the open ocean, but bare survival, particularly against aircraft, would make him relatively ineffective.

Apart from the long-range systems, the principal submarine detector is sonar. There is a considerable gap between maximum possible sonar range performance and average performance. Under very favourable conditions a powerful low-frequency sonar, such as the US SQS-53, can probably detect and track a submarine out to the edge of the first convergence zone, at about 70,000 yards. Under more nearly average conditions, the sonar would get to about 10,000 yards by direct path, and there would be a Convergence Zone annulus at about 70,000. The area between, swept in theory by 'Bottom-Bounce' operation, would be nearly blank; Bottom Bounce performance has not been nearly so successful as Convergence Zone. When such sonars first appeared, many in ASW believed that the maximum would be the norm, and tactics and weapons evolved to match. In particular, it was no longer at all reasonable to imagine bringing the attacking ship to the submarine, given the lengthy time involved: at 15 knots a ship moves about 500 yards a minute.

Perhaps more importantly, a surface ship is unlikely to be able to *hold* a modern submarine in her sonar beam for 20 or 30 minutes, while she closes the range. Nor is

174

THE SUBMARINE AND ITS ENEMY: MODERN ASW

she likely to wish to; it is too easy for the submarine to counter-attack with guided torpedoes. Hence it becomes important to attack as soon as the submarine is definitely detected. Current stand-off weapons include both missiles (such as the Anglo-Australian Ikara, the French Malafon, and the US Asroc), and helicopter-borne torpedoes (as the US LAMPS system). The helicopter is preferable to the missile in two important ways. First, at extreme ranges (such as at convergence zone), sonars do not have a narrow enough beam to be suitable for missile fire control. Either the missile-borne torpedo will have to search a considerable volume, or, better, the helicopter will go out and relocate the submarine more precisely. Second, at least in theory, the helicopter can filter out false alarms. An escort ship can carry only so many missiles (which may often be fired in multi-weapon salvoes). She can support many more helicopter sorties, and the helicopter can return to the ship whenever it fails to confirm a reported submarine presence.

COUNTERING SONAR

A submarine can turn surface ship sonar's inherent limitations to its advantage in several ways. In shallow water, sonar pulses reflect off the bottom and the sea surface, and it becomes more and more difficult to pick a target out of the echoes. In deeper water, there are often thermal layers which reflect sonar signals. Thus a submarine in very shallow water may be almost undetectable, at least by sonar. Shallow-water reverberation may explain the apparent failure of British ASW in the Falklands. The only solution is sophisticated signal processing that may be able to distinguish among the different reflective paths.

The classic submarine tactic in shallow water is to lie on the bottom, with engines stopped, to minimise noise; in deeper water, submarines sometimes lie atop density layers. The bottomed submarine is a particularly difficult sonar target because the sea bed is covered with so much debris, such as sunken ships and even rocks. Inshore submarine tactics became a problem towards the end of World War II, when snorkel-equipped U-boats were able to operate relatively freely in British coastal waters. As a result, the Royal Navy developed a special imaging sonar, Type 162, to distinguish large objects on the bottom. The US Navy has no equivalent, presumably because it expects to fight primarily in the much deeper waters of the North Atlantic. The only applicable US sensor would be a high-definition mine-hunting sonar, such as SQQ-14 or the new SQQ-30 and SQQ-32, but high definition is bought at the cost of very short range and hence a very slow search rate.

Thermal layers are usually encountered well below 300ft, and therefore were of relatively little interest until after 1945, when submarines were designed for much deeper running. The layers are not perfect mirrors: a sonar beam striking at a sufficiently oblique angle (corresponding to a relatively short range) will penetrate. Thus the primary effect of hiding under a layer was to cancel out the long-range performance of postwar low-frequency sonars, reducing them to (or below) typical wartime levels. That could be enough to bring a submarine through a screen: if the escorts were spaced on the basis of a 10,000-yard sonar (such as SQS-23), which was effective only out to 2000 yards, then perhaps 80 per cent of the screened perimeter of a formation would be open. On the other hand, a submarine under the layer would be as limited as the surface ship, and might suffer accordingly. Nor is the layer an absolute haven. For example, variable-depth sonars, as well as many types of sonobuoys

The nuclear submarine threat seemed in the early 1950s to be too much for homing torpedoes, let alone depth charges. One American response was to develop nuclear (air dropped) depth bombs; a 1243lb 'Betty' (in service 1956–63) is shown on display at the Washington Navy Yard. The object at its tail is a parachute case and its size can be gauged from the 'Fat Man' A-bomb case behind.
Author's photograph

SUBMARINE DESIGN AND DEVELOPMENT

that deploy suspended hydrophones, operate beneath it.

There are also local geographical limitations, due, for example, to differences in water salinity. For example, the Baltic Sea is notoriously difficult, which explains (in part) the numerous Swedish failures to deal with Soviet submarine intrusions.

Deterrence is another factor. Any active sonar announces its own presence every time it pings. It is, therefore, a beacon inviting attack. To the extent to which a penetrating submarine can be expected to attack an active sonar, the ASW forces will have to resort to passive operation, which in turn will make silencing more effective.

Perhaps active sonar's greatest virtue is its ability to overcome considerable noise, at least at short range. No listening sonar placed very close to a formation of heavy ships is likely to be able to distinguish a submarine from the noises they generate. Yet a screening ship will probably be able to use her active sonar, since its pings will be quite distinct and also obtain range data instantly. Accurate ranges are difficult to extract from passive sonar operation, and often require lengthy manoeuvres (see, for example, Chapter 4 on ASW submarine operation).

Localisation is particularly important when submarines are detected by relatively long-range sensors, such as SOSUS, towed arrays, or even conventional sonars operating at convergence-zone range. In each case, the initial detection is not nearly precise enough to permit an attack. The typical procedure is to send out an aircraft or helicopter to re-detect and then to localise, with sonobuoys. Thus the SOSUS weapon system is best described as a combination of SOSUS detectors, command centres ashore, and P-3 Orion attack aircraft.

False alarms are so common that *classification*, ie the determination that some echo or sound really represents a submarine, is a major, and difficult, step in any ASW attack. Without some form of classification, weapons would soon be expended fruitlessly. Even with classification, Allied World War II experience was discouraging; a postwar study showed that, of every ten ASW attacks in 1943-45, only about one was made on a real target. The same word is applied to sonar signal processing, as in a torpedo guidance system. The usual sonar technique is to seek evidence of target motion, in the form of a doppler shift between the outgoing and the returning (echoed) 'pings'. A passive sonar system may classify a particular signature, or the perceived doppler shift of a particular frequency in that signature, or on a systematic apparent change of bearing.

Of all of these passive and active techniques, only the passive detection of a characteristic signature would be useful against a submarine lying stopped, either on the bottom or atop a density layer. Moreover, only a nuclear submarine generates a signature under those conditions, since there need be little moving machinery in a stopped diesel-electric submarine.

The other major means of detection is magnetic. A submarine is a large metal object in a non-metallic sea. Even so, its magnetic field can be detected only at relatively short ranges. In US practice, a helicopter or patrol aircraft prosecuting a contact first detects and classifies it by means of sonobuoys, and then makes a final localising pass, with a magnetic anomaly detector (MAD), before dropping a torpedo or depth bomb. The precision of MAD detection is necessary because these weapons have only relatively short effective (or, in the torpedo's case, acquisition) ranges.

Very few initial ASW attacks during either World War were successful. It was much more usual for a submarine to evade an initial attack, and then to be re-attacked again and again before either being destroyed or being forced to the surface, where its crew would surrender and scuttle their boat. Battle damage assessment was particularly difficult; the experience of both World Wars shows that it is almost impossible to tell whether a submarine, once attacked, has been sunk. Again and again, submarines, leaking oil, managed to survive heavy depth-chargings and then, after the hunters had departed, struggle home. In doing so, they proved that they were far tougher than prewar experts had imagined. They also proved that the hunters could often be misled. After all, they badly wanted to believe that their long hunts had been successful, that oil slicks or debris really did indicate the end of the submarine they had been fighting.

This experience remains relevant. No one really knows how effective modern homing ASW weapons are. In the Falklands the Royal Navy expended many lightweight homing torpedoes without effect, in at least one case hearing explosions (which turned out to be the torpedoes hitting the shallow sea bed). Apart from the Indian Navy's attacks on Pakistani submarines in December 1971, that is the only known combat experience since 1945. Moreover, the number of weapons per ship is only a fraction of what was standard four decades ago, even when that is measured in attacks, taking into account the modern systems' supposed much greater effectiveness. Thus we cannot say whether modern aircraft and surface ship submarine hunters would be more or less credulous than their predecessors. We do know that inexperience was on the submariners' side early in the war, since submarine hunters tended to be more optimistic then than later. If any future war is destined to be a short one, then such inexperience may characterise the entire conflict, not merely its beginning.

'DEAD TIME' AND 'WARNING TIME'

The key concept in the attack itself is 'dead time', the time between the last possible fire control adjustment and the weapons' arrival at the (expected) submarine position. Until the end of World War II, sonars generally projected a beam that slanted down at an angle. The deeper the submarine, the greater the range at which it would be detected. Conversely, there was always a range *inside* which a submarine could no longer be detected, as it would be inside the cone defined by the sonar beam. It was a rule of thumb for US ASW craft that submarine depth was one-third of this minimum range. Depth charges had to be released roughly vertically over the supposed position of the submarine. The time spent steaming from the point at which contact was lost to the release point was dead time, as was the time during which the depth charges themselves sank. Surface ships generally accelerated after losing contact, so as to minimise this dead time; a submarine commander could tell that he was about to be attacked by the sound of that acceleration, and he could attempt to evade during the dead time.

The standard late war fast-sinking 250lb depth charge had to burst within 6 yards of a submarine to sink it. A 15-knot submarine at 600ft would move 220 yards as the charge sank. That is why depth charges were always dropped in large patterns to compensate for the individual weapons' limited accuracy. But that enormous leeway for the submarine effectively eliminated the depth charge as a viable weapon.

There is an associated 'warning time', between an unambiguous warning of an attack and the arrival of the weapons. In the case of depth charge attack, it might be defined by acceleration or by the sound of the charges themselves striking the water. In the case of the modern Asroc stand-off weapon, it is probably set by the sound of the rocket booster striking the water. In the case of Subroc, the US underwater-to-underwater ASW missile, the primary indicator would be the sound of the missile engine igniting. The developmental US ASW Standoff-Weapon (SOW), which is to succeed Subroc, neatly reduces warning time by rising to the surface by buoyancy alone, igniting only when it emerges, and thus greatly reducing the degree of warning afforded its victim. In each of these cases, warning time either coincides with or is less than dead time, and it is the time during which a submarine can hope to evade.

There were several attempts to reduce dead time. One was the team attack, in which one ship maintained contact with the submarine target while another dropped depth charges. Since there was no lost-contact dead time, the attacker did not have to accelerate. Another was a narrow sonar beam that could change its angle of depression, so that contact could be maintained even at close range. The depth charges themselves were streamlined, so as to minimise the dead time during their descent. This became particularly important as U-boats came to dive deeper. There were also ahead-thrown weapons such as Hedgehog, Squid, Weapon Alfa, and Limbo, essentially depth charges that could be fired before contact was lost. In several cases surface ships

176

were equipped with long-range homing torpedoes. If wire guidance could be provided, the torpedo could be controlled by the surface ship sonar out to its enable, or acquisition, range. That would (in theory) eliminate dead time altogether.

The same concepts apply to submarine v submarine ASW. Dead time for a conventional (free-running) homing torpedo begins when the weapon is set, just before launch. Warning time is defined by the relatively noisy high-speed run out to the enable point. In the case of a wire-guided weapon, such as the US Mark 48, warning time greatly exceeds dead time, in that the prospective victim can hear the initial, relatively noisy, phase of the torpedo run, while the torpedo is still under a launching submarine's positive control. Some would argue that this type of warning makes counter-attack attractive, since the target submarine can determine the *direction* from which the torpedo is coming.

Dead time and warning time can be equated to probable miss distance, but the weapon may miss and still come within lethal distance of the evading submarine. Thus one answer to more evasive submarines has been more lethal weapons. Examples include the British Mark X one-ton depth charge, designed specifically to deal with deeply submerged U-boats, and nuclear depth bombs. During World War I, when submarine detection was imprecise, the Royal Navy dropped torpedoes designed to circle at depths of 40ft and 80ft, covering an area roughly the size of a U-boat. This, too, was a means of increasing a weapon's effective lethal area.

ASW HOMING TORPEDOES

An alternative formulation is to drop the weapon within *acquisition* range of the submarine, and then let it home, destroying the submarine by the contact explosion of even a relatively small warhead. In this case advanced electronics and torpedo power balance off much reduced lethal range. The lightweight homing torpedo, originally conceived as a depth charge replacement, is the primary example. Guidance is a mixed virtue. If there are no countermeasures, then a guided weapon is far more accurate than an unguided one, to the point where one may take the place of many. That has certainly been the trend with homing torpedoes, as they have replaced depth charges and such ahead-thrown depth charge weapons as Limbo and Weapon Alfa. But guidance can be led astray. Where a destroyer's experienced human sonar operator may be able to distinguish a decoy from a real submarine, a torpedo, with its very limited intelligence, may not.

Thus the advent of the guided torpedo greatly increases the value of the submarine equivalent of ECM. There is even an underwater equivalent of the new 'stealth' radar-absorbent material: anechoic, or echo-absorbing, rubbers, that can be spread over a submarine hull. Both the Germans and the Japanese experimented with such coatings during World War II. They are unlikely to make so large an object as a submarine effectively disappear, but may well thwart the homing torpedo. Most modern (at least US) homers are primarily active, with passive operation as a secondary option. Given size limitations, a torpedo cannot operate at the low frequencies needed for very long-range acquisition. For some years the US Defense Advanced Research Projects Agency (DARPA) has proposed that torpedoes tow or be guided by a small array that would be optimised for lower frequencies, for passive target acquisition. The array might float in the water, connected to the running torpedo by an optical fibre, but clear of the torpedo's

Nuclear depth bombs did not become really useful until small enough to be carried in small aircraft or even helicopters. Two 2016lb, 7ft 8in × 18in 'Lulus' occupy the extended bomb bay of a Grumman S2F Tracker ASW plane on 17 January 1961. 'Lulu' (in service 1958-71) had the W34 nuclear warhead, also common to the Astor Mark 45 torpedo, and could be triggered hydrostatically or by a timer (backup). Its development, 'little Lulu' (B37), was even smaller, but is no longer in service. Too many restrictions hedge about the use of any nuclear ASW weapon.
US Navy

flow- and self-noise. However, the current homing torpedo can concentrate considerable energy in a high frequency active sonar, the frequency of which is determined, in effect, by the accuracy (beam-width) required for effective operation. The higher the frequency, the shorter the wavelength, the greater the effectiveness of a relatively thin hull covering. At the very least, the torpedo designer may have to improve sonar signal processing to regain his former degree of success, and that in turn may intrude on warhead weight in a weapon already tightly designed.

In other cases, initial acquisition is passive, but the torpedo avoids homing on the submarine propellers by swinging around to

SUBMARINE DESIGN AND DEVELOPMENT

Aircraft may be the most potent ASW weapon, at least in the open ocean. This Grumman S2F Tracker (over the Atlantic near Long Island on 30 December 1960) shows both its bomb bay and main sensors: a snorkel-detection radar in a retractable radome, sonobuoy dispensers (at the rear ends of its nacelles) and MAD in the tail 'stinger' or boom. The latter is essential for precise placement of weapons but has so short a range that its user must fly very low, subject, perhaps, to future submarine launched anti-aircraft weapons. Note also the searchlight (in the starboard wing) used to illuminate submarines surprised on the surface and the inboard rocket pods for attack flanked by homing torpedoes. Such aircraft also carry two other detection devices: ESM, the direct descendant of World War II HF/DF and 'sniffers' capable of detecting snorkel emissions. Submarine designers counter 'sniffers' by emitting exhaust underwater, and infra-red detectors by artificially cooling the exhaust.
US Navy

approach the target from the beam, re-acquiring its target actively. Again, that re-acquisition must be carried out by a high frequency sonar.

Guidance so reduces the probability of missing that much smaller explosive charges become acceptable, at least in theory. That in turn so reduces weapon size that it can easily be carried by aircraft, helicopters, and even by acceptably small missiles. Such was the rationale for the current US 500lb Mark 46 torpedo, whose warhead weighs only about 100lb. It is now frequently argued that so small a weapon, even if it hits, cannot effectively disable a double-hulled Soviet nuclear submarine, particularly a giant such as an 'Oscar' or a *Typhoon*. But, having built up a series of weapon systems that themselves limit the size and weight of this particular payload, the US Navy is ill-equipped to accept any great increase in torpedo dimensions, either to accept a much larger warhead or much more propulsive power. In this context the development of an 800lb Advanced Lightweight Torpedo (Mark 50) is extraordinary though it probably offers the ultimate in performance for its size.

NUCLEAR ASW WEAPONS

Some would suggest abandoning homing torpedoes in favour of a much more certain weapon, the nuclear depth bomb. Certainly, like any other nuclear weapon, a nuclear depth bomb has a very high probability of destroying any target *which comes within its lethal radius*. But, like any other nuclear weapon, it is hedged about with political limitations to the extent that some Western governments refuse port facilities to allied warships even suspected of carrying them in peacetime. And there is the perpetual fear that *any* wartime use of a nuclear weapon will lead to unacceptable escalation. Moreover, an underwater nuclear explosion effectively deafens all acoustic detection systems within some considerable distance. Thus many would argue that, as long as a modern submarine can deceive its pursuers as to its precise location, even nuclear weapons may not be accurate enough.

The US Navy first bought nuclear ASW weapons in the mid-1950s, when it was feared that nuclear submarines would be able to out-run projected homing torpedoes. First there were nuclear depth bombs; later there were Astor, a nuclear torpedo (Mark 45), and the ballistic Asroc and Subroc rockets. Astor was retired some years ago, the first US nuclear weapon to be given up, and until quite recently it appeared that Subroc, too, would have to go. In November 1983 the *New York Times* reported that the United States had the following ASW nuclear weapons (approximate numbers in the US/at sea): depth bombs 560/45 (plus 190 in Allied hands in Europe and 100 in storage in the Pacific); Asroc 225/350; Subroc 110/175. These figures suggest that deployed submarines and surface ships each carry four nuclear Asroc or Subroc.

In each case, the submarine's ability to evade, ie its speed, manoeuvrability (in both vertical and horizontal planes), and depth capability determines how effective a given weapon system may be. It is a rule of thumb in torpedo development that the weapon must be able to run 50 per cent faster than the target submarine, so that a 45-knot Mark 46 is well-adapted to deal with a 30-knot target. Presumably a 60-knot torpedo is needed to attack a 40-knot 'Alfa' class Soviet submarine. Current operational Western torpedoes are generally credited with no more than 55 knots, which probably testifies to the inherent difficulties of combining high speed and endurance within very restricted dimensions. The US Navy abandoned un-guided weapons (such as Weapon Alfa) altogether after experiments showed that agile submarines such as *Albacore* could expect to evade them relatively easily.

EVASION TACTICS

The standard 1939-45 submarine evasion tactic was to go as deep a possible to minimise depth charge accuracy and effectiveness. When, as in the Mediterranean, the surface ships were equipped primarily with hydrophones (ie with passive sonar), it was considered far better to go deep and quiet (ie slow) than to try to run. The standard surface ship tactic was to force a submarine down, then keep it down until its battery ran flat, when it would have to surface and surrender. A typical U-boat could not run more than about 60 miles fully submerged and could not remain down more than about three days. Contemporary Allied ships and aircraft could keep a 60-mile circle under surveillance long enough to catch the U-boat when it surfaced to recharge batteries. The better the battery, the less effective the tactic; current Soviet diesel-electric submarines are credited with extraordinary battery capacities, sufficient to frustrate such hold-down tactics by exhausting the surface ships themselves. At low speeds, modern battery systems (as in a 'Foxtrot') can provide diesel-electric submarines with underwater endurances on the order of a week. The 'Tango', having a much greater internal volume (hence battery space), can probably operate at low speeds for more than a week without having to recharge.

From the submarine's point of view, a great deal depends on its ability to determine when it has been detected, and when an attack is imminent. The sequence is familiar from many World War II accounts: the submarine makes its attack, which reveals its approximate position, then goes deep to evade the inevitable counter-attack. It hears sonar pinging, but the crew know that an attack is coming only when the escorts shift from 'long' to 'short' scale, ie from search to fire control precision in sonar operation. Then the boat hears 'high-speed screws' closing in. Because the sonar beam is a downward-directed fan, it loses contact when the surface ship comes close enough; the submarine commander must judge that moment to evade violently, to spoil the escort's fire control solution. If the boat is deep enough, and the escorts optimistic enough, the depth charges may miss, and it may be able to slip away so quietly that its survival is not detected.

The major wartime refinement on this theme was the decoy, which a submarine could release as it evaded. If the boat was quiet enough, and its evasion violent enough, then the attackers might fasten on the decoy instead of on the submarine. Wartime US decoys were essentially sub-calibre torpedoes, generally fired from the after tubes. Postwar US submarines had special small-diameter countermeasures tubes.

The smaller the submarine signature, the more effective the decoy. In the face of passive sonars, the quieter the submarine, the better the chance that a relatively noisy decoy dominates enemy attention. Anechoic (echo-absorbing) hull coverings reduce the apparent size a submarine presents to active sonars, and thus make decoy devices more effective. Decoys can even record incoming sonar pings, returning them in amplified form to make the decoy appear larger, or to give it apparent motion (via the Doppler effect). Decoying is of course most useful if the submarine itself can put on a burst of speed (without a concurrent burst of noise) to move out of the search area while its pursuers are occupied with the decoy.

The alternative is counter-attack. Late in the Pacific War, several US submarine commanders chose to fire back 'down the throats' of oncoming Japanese escorts. They reasoned that the ASW commanders could survive only by turning away. Moreover, if they did not turn quickly enough, they would be sunk. Either way, the submarine would escape from anything short of a highly-coordinated ASW attack. This tactical practice was reflected in the last US submarine design of World War II, which had six broadside tubes for anti-escort torpedoes. Postwar American, British, and possibly Soviet submarines all had special tubes firing aft, for anti-escort torpedoes.

SUBMARINE AIR DEFENCE

Now, however, ASW attack is far more likely to originate either with an aircraft, a helicopter, or a submarine. Even a submerged submarine can detect an oncoming aircraft or helicopter, since at low altitude the aircraft projects a great deal of noise into the water [One reason why the airship is being re-evaluated the very successful ASW role it played during both World Wars]. It may, therefore, be attractive to provide submarines with some means of counter-attack. At the least, if a submarine can place at risk an aircraft or helicopter making a MAD pass, then such tactics may be abandoned and the rate of false or spoiled attacks greatly increased. That in turn will decrease the stock of weapons available for attacks against real targets.

This is not to say that the submarine will become a great threat to ASW aircraft. Unless a great deal of precious space and weight is devoted to anti-aircraft defence, any future submarine SAM system is likely to be limited to weapons roughly equivalent to current man-portable, short-range heat-seekers, such as Stinger and the Soviet SA-7. They have limited fields of engagement, and are unlikely to account for many attacking aircraft. Much would, then, depend upon their mere existence protecting the submarine; the reader may recall that, quite generally, anti-aircraft weapons are most effective as deterrents, rather than as means of actually destroying aircraft.

The requisite technology already exists. In November 1972 Vickers completed trials of an anti-helicopter weapon, SLAM, aboard the diesel submarine HMS *Aeneas*. It was a cluster of six Blowpipe command-guided anti-aircraft missiles grouped around a television camera, and mounted in a pressure-proof cylinder in the sail. Presumably SLAM was intended as a means of protection during snorkelling; a submarine would be well aware of an approaching aircraft or helicopter, working either from ESM or from sound data. Reportedly its range was too small for it to be effective, and it was never fitted operationally, either in Britain or abroad.

More recent technology can do much better. Current versions of both the US Stinger and the Soviet SA-7 hand-held heat-seeking missiles can home on the 'glint' from the nose of an aircraft or helicopter. Whereas the submarine firing SLAM had to remain at periscope depth throughout the engagement, it would be able to submerge after firing a comparable heat-seeking system. Such a system might be extremely simple with no fire control sensor needed to guide the heat-seeker after launch, the weapon might be fired on the basis of a standard air search periscope or radar.

The heat-seeker would still probably have to be fired from the submarine itself, rigidly connected to the aiming sensor. But aircraft can attack a submarine several hundred feet below water, and the submarine, if it has a sensitive enough sonar, can detect them at some distance. It can also, at least in theory, strike back. The US Defense Advanced Research Projects Agency developed a self-guiding missile, SIAM (Self-Initiated Anti-Aircraft Missile), with dual-mode guidance from a radar array on the missile's sides and an infra-red terminal system in its nose. In theory, a submarine would release a buoy containing a SIAM missile. Its radar would search for the incoming aircraft, and the missile would launch itself at the appropriate moment. Given the relatively low performance of existing ASW aircraft, and their need to approach very closely for that terminal classification pass (and, in many cases, for accurate weapon delivery), SIAM would probably be an effective countermeasure.

As this is written, there is no evidence that SIAM is anywhere near engineering development, let alone production. Nor is there any published evidence of a Soviet equivalent, although the Soviets must be well aware of NATO dependence on ASW aircraft and helicopters. It would, therefore, be unwise to assume that no such weapon will appear within the next few years. As long ago as 1959 the then Bureau of Naval Weapons (just formed by the amalgamation of the Bureaus of Ordnance and Aeronautics) forecast just such a system, and called for a countermeasure in the form of a long-range aircraft-launched ASW weapon (presumably nuclear), to be fired on the basis of sonobuoy data.

As for the ASW submarine, clearly a submarine lying in ambush, using passive sensors alone, will be extremely difficult to detect (at least passively), until it attacks. Then it will have to make noise as torpedo tubes cannot fire entirely noiselessly. The torpedo itself may be detectable by its own propeller noise, at least as it runs out to its enable range.

A submarine commander under attack then has several options. He can try to evade the oncoming torpedo, promptly and violently so that he will be outside acquisition or search range when the torpedo reaches its enable point. However, he must reckon with the possibility that the attacking submarine can still track him and thus command the torpedo, through its wire command link, to follow. He must therefore upset the tracker. There are two options: he can drop noise-making decoys (submarine simulators) while breaking to evade, and he can fire his own homing torpedoes back along the bearing from which torpedo propeller noises are coming. Hearing those torpedoes coming, the attacker will presumably be too busy evading them himself to continue the engagement. Thus means of evasion (violent manoeuvre and noisemakers) and counter-attack operate together. This example also explains part of the attraction of very long-range stand-off weapons: if there is no noise 'strobe' pointing back at the launching submarine, then the counter-attack option is virtually impossible to execute, and the attacked submarine may have insufficient warning time to evade.

COUNTERING MINES AND UNDERWATER EXPLOSIONS

The other modern submarine-killer is the mine. As long ago as 1917 the British considered mining German home waters an effective ASW measure. Mine barriers, such as the Northern Mine Barrage, were also laid as a strategic measure, to channel the U-boats into patrolled areas. During World War II, ASW mines were more commonly employed defensively, for example to block the entrances to the Sea of Japan. These were effectively contact weapons, and the chief submarine-borne countermeasure was a high-precision mine-evasion sonar, such as the QLA mounted aboard US submarines operating in Japanese coastal waters.

Such high precision tends to require very high sonar frequency, and therefore tends to be available only at very short range. Mines themselves have effective ranges: the greater the mine sensor's range, the more difficult it is to evade. Current mines may operate on a submarine's acoustic, magnetic, or even electric (underwater electric potential) signature, or on a combination of signatures that makes decoying difficult. The most sophisticated example publicly revealed is Captor, a US bottom mine that fires a homing torpedo at a passing submarine. In theory, weapons such as Captor are particularly effective because they have very wide lethal radii, and because they can be very rapidly placed by air, for example across choke points. They can, then, cause losses before the much slower-moving barrier submarines and surface ships get into position.

The submarine designer must provide against two very different classes of attack: nearby explosions, like those of depth charges, and contact charges, such as those of homing torpedoes. The chief damage mechanisms are shock and actual hull rupture. Shock has a much greater effective range, and some writers have argued that the psychological effect of near-misses, none of them even remotely fatal, may be decisive during a long ASW hunt. It seems likely that sound-isolation measures, such as the resilient mounting of machinery, also protect against shock. After all, shock is a sound-like pressure wave propagated *into* the submarine from outside, whereas sound isolation is intended to prevent similar pressure waves from escaping the hull. Even so, some now suggest that shock is the primary means of damage by relatively small contact weapons, such as lightweight homing torpedoes.

The blast of an ASW weapon striking a submarine hull can break it open. In effect it adds to the static pressure of the water surrounding the hull, temporarily straining it (locally) beyond the breaking point. A capability to dive deeper thus translates, at shallow depths, into greater resistance to underwater explosion. However, it can be argued that other hull-breaking mechanisms, such as shaped charges, can overcome the hull strength usually associated with great test depths, *if* they can be incorporated in viable torpedoes.

Much depends upon hull structure. Clearly the outer shell of a double-hulled submarine will absorb much of the blast of any underwater weapon. But double-hull construction is wasteful of hull volume, making for greater surface area (per unit pressure hull volume) and thus for lower speed for a given powerplant. The two extremes are represented by American and Soviet designs. Almost the entire pressure hull surface of a *Los Angeles* is exposed to attack. On the other hand, the Soviets have always preferred double hulls, and as a consequence their large submarines may actually be proof against immediate destruction by lightweight torpedoes.

CHAPTER THIRTEEN

Future Possibilities

The United States has shown great faith in the future survivability of submarines by building the massive 560ft, 16,000/18,700-ton *Ohio* class: in future, the *number* of US strategic submarines will have to decline, since each *Ohio* carries 50 per cent more missiles than her Polaris/Poseidon predecessor. In that case the underwater deterrent's viability will rest, more than at present, on each individual boat, rather than on the statistical probability that no enemy can deal with the entire force over a short period. The name boat of the class is shown in drydock at the new West Coast Trident operating base, Bangor, Washington State, early in 1983, before her first patrol. Note the fairing for her towed array sonar, and the end-plates of her stern fins, which house passive sonar arrays.
US Navy

For the major navies, perhaps the overwhelming fact of submarine development since 1945 is that costs, even for relatively limited capability, have risen to the point where each submarine must be considered a major warship. At least in the West, great numbers no longer seem attainable, without enormous sacrifices in capability. In 1982 a *Los Angeles* class attack submarine was priced at about $722 million. By comparison, an Aegis cruiser was expected to cost about $1.04 billion, and a *Perry* class frigate $333 million. The submarine cost was presumably exclusive of some nuclear components customarily not included in the US naval budget. At this time, too, an *Ohio* class ballistic missile submarine cost $1.2 billion, and a nuclear carrier, $3.4 billion. The mere use of large-city names, previously borne by heavy cruisers, for attack submarines suggests how highly these craft are now valued, and how expensive they have become.

There is a view in some quarters that submarine capability has not risen in proportion to costs. Critics of *Los Angeles* say that too many sacrifices were made to achieve her very high speed while she is so expensive that sufficient numbers (only 24 commissioned between November 1976 and July 1983 with the dollar cost of each boat rising almost five fold in the same period) can probably never be built. Even so, it would appear that technological pressures for larger nuclear submarines probably cannot be contained. Chief among them are the conflicting requirements for speed, combat system detection/fire control range, weapons load, and quieting. Virtually every combat system requirement can be satisfied only through enlarging the sonar transducers, both to achieve greater directional accuracy and to operate at lower frequencies. Inside the submarine, more elaborate signal processors require more volume in an already cramped hull. Matters are further complicated by demands for larger torpedo salvoes and even for larger torpedo magazines.

Unless there is some dramatic improvement in reactor and power-train design, every

SUBMARINE DESIGN AND DEVELOPMENT

The Soviet *Typhoon* class ballistic missile submarine (in this 1981 Pentagon artist's impression) is by far the largest ever built (25,000–30,000 tons submerged and almost 552ft long); some would say so large that no single torpedo can account for her. Her unusual hull form is apparently the result of Soviet standardisation; it consists of two side-by-side cylinders, with a double row of 20 missile tubes between them. It is not clear whether the additional volume serves a useful purpose: hull steel is, after all, the least expensive part of a warship, and the Soviets are particularly sensitive to the demands of production continuity, as demonstrated in their earlier SSBNs.
US Department of Defense

Soviet SSBNs are a remarkable demonstration of the effect of industrial inertia. There is considerable evidence that the original 'Yankee' was developed very rapidly (34 built 1967–74); its pressure hull diameter was just less than the 33ft length of the SS-N-6 missile. 'Delta', in its three versions (36 built since 1972), consists of a 'Yankee' hull, suitably lengthened with a hump raised sufficiently to take SS-N-8 and then SS-N-18 missiles. Presumably the process could not be continued with the *Typhoon*'s SS-N-20 because the holes for the new much larger (49ft) missile would have weakened the pressure hull too badly. The existing hull may also have lacked sufficient volume for the fire control system associated with the MIRVed SS-N-20. 'Yankee' class ballistic missile submarine (426ft oa and 8000/9600 tons) in or before August 1976. One of her sail mast hatches is opened.
US Navy

demand for better silencing must entail an increase in powerplant volume per horsepower. Even if speed is to be held more or less constant overall size tends to grow, to fit the larger engine and combat system spaces. Speed itself is a subject of great controversy, being extremely expensive. Once high speed and silencing had been combined successfully in the *Los Angeles* design, there was pressure for even greater speed in a larger submarine (the AHPNAS) proposed in the early 1970s. One argument made at the time was that the higher the maximum speed, the higher the greatest quiet speed.

There was also a suggestion that high speed would carry tactical advantages in barrier operations – the faster the submarine, the better she might be able to apply 'sprint-and-drift' listening tactics, covering a patrol area. If firing a Mark 48 torpedo carries the risk of a return, snap-shot along the line of torpedo propeller noise, then a very fast submarine might be able to move aside sufficiently quickly after firing to avoid such a reaction. Quiet speed might even improve passive fire control techniques such as TMA, in that, the faster the process, the less the chance that the target manoeuvres radically while its position is being determined.

Yet non-nuclear submarines operating on battery power are inherently quiet, and, since sustained high speed is virtually impossible for them to attain in any useful way, they are much less subject to such pressures for growth. Several new propulsion technologies promise substantial reductions in battery weight and volume for a given level of energy storage. But such craft are no less subject to pressures for combat system improvement than are their larger sisters. Most current diesel-electric submarines have relatively simple combat systems, not because of some inherent limitation, but because the navies

FUTURE PROJECTS

The Soviet 'Alfa' is another pointer to the future: smaller, deeper, faster, using a new hull material (titanium), automation and a more compact powerplant, probably based on a liquid-metal nuclear reactor. Both the US and Royal Navies sought greater diving depths in the 1960s; at one stage HMS *Trafalgar* was to have dived twice as deep as *Swiftsure*. The US research boat *Dolphin*, reportedly capable of reaching 4000ft, was advertised as the forerunner of operational deep divers that were never built. Extremely deep operation is costly because of the need to develop a new generation of hull-penetration seals. Both the major Western navies have concluded that, at least for them, extremely deep diving has only limited appeal. The 'Alfa' (267ft oa and 2800/3680 tons; 7 in service since 1979), on the other hand, gains immunity from many ASW weapons with its reported top underwater speed of 45 knots and a diving depth of 2000-3000ft. This example, in or before July 1981, shows (left to right) attack and search periscopes, a radome mast and a HF radio mast.
US Navy

which build them are primarily concerned with anti-ship warfare, rather than with the more complex stalking of submarine v submarine ASW. It would seem to follow that, when the large ASW navies, such as those of Britain and the United States, build nonnuclear submarines, they will be forced to accept craft of quite substantial size. The new British Type 2400 would seem to be a case in point.

Future submarine evolution will occur in the context of world politics probably quite different from that of the past two decades: it seems less and less likely that nuclear weapons will ever be used in East-West conflict, and the simple polarity of the post-1945 world has arguably already vanished. It seems probable, that within a decade, states such as Brazil and South Korea will no longer need foreign-built warships or weapons, and will even possess their own nuclear weapons and nuclear-powered submarines. Submarine operations will surely be a major feature of any future war; the only question is whether some new detection technology will overcome submarine stealth.

Both East and West, submarine silencing is becoming much more effective. Virtually all existing long-range detectors, including those aboard submarines, are passive. For many years signal processing and transducer sensitivity have competed with the silencers, and it would be foolish to declare any final victory on either side, but it is interesting to contemplate the effect of a victory for silencing.

That would probably mean silencing at relatively low speeds; a submarine at high speed, particularly if it is nuclear, probaby cannot ever be completely silent, because substantial flow noise must be created as it displaces large volumes of water by moving. Yet there may be very few (if any) situations in which very high speed is necessary, at least within range of enemy sensors. For example, a submarine equipped with underwater-fired anti-ship missiles need rarely manoeuvre at very high speed to close with its target. Truly silent submarines would be able to penetrate any *passive* barrier. They would probably be detectable only by the act of missile-firing, which would bring ASW back full circle to the techniques of 1917, updated only in terms of the necessary surveillance range. Moreover, active hunting for enemy craft by submarines in sanctuary areas might seem impossible, since they would be detectable only by active pinging - which would be suicidal.

Under these circumstances, high submarine speed would still have two potential benefits. First, in most cases the highest *quiet* speed is directly related to the highest speed; high undetectable speed would clearly remain valuable. Second, submarines spend at least part of their time out of range of enemy sensors, although that fraction may decline with the wider deployment of such long-range sensors as SOSUS and the towed surveillance arrays (SURTASS). Fast movement towards missile-firing position would remain valuable.

Note that silencing would not represent a total victory for submarine stealth: it would shift attention back to active and also to non-acoustic systems. In recent years active sonar, particularly aboard submarines, has been avoided for two reasons. First, a ping can be detected at a much greater range than an echo: the sonar may act more as a beacon than as a sensor. Second, really large fixed active sonars have been rejected because, if enough power is transmitted into an ocean basin, reverberation buries the signals. But there is an increasingly attractive, if as yet somewhat impractical, middle ground: bistatic operation, in which the pinger is physically separated from the sonar receiver.

This is not a new idea. When submarine silencing seemed about to negate early 1950s passive sonobuoys, the US Navy introduced explosive echo-ranging (EER), in which a small signal charge produced sound that echoed off submarines, and could be picked up by existing sonobuoys. EER suffered from reverberation, and within a few years a much superior generation of passive buoys replaced it. But, one can easily imagine a more sophisticated system, in which a powerful expendable pinger was dropped or fired into an area seeded with passive sensors. All could be monitored by satellite, and the results fed to a submarine via a high-density data link. As an ASW attack platform in the forward area, the submarine, even were it unable to achieve much in the way of passive detection range, would still be superior to an aircraft or helicopter because it would be far more survivable. Non-acoustic systems would have a similar impact on submarine tactics; in both cases the ability to transmit data from the externally-monitored sensor would become very important. The US Navy already uses satellites to monitor some ASW sensors: the outputs of the big surveillance arrays (SURTASS) towed by small T-AGOS and AGOS ships are transmitted by satellite data link back to shore-based central computers for processing.

The other case, in which submarines become much more vulnerable, seems less likely at the time of writing. The current generation of sensors, the arrays, is the end result of about two decades of work. About five years ago they showed such promise that many within the surface fleet felt that the relative positions of the surface and submarine navies were about to be reversed, that they had finally regained the acoustic advantages enjoyed in, perhaps, World War II. That may still be the case, but is no longer nearly so certain. Nor is the future of exotic non-acoustic sensors clear, at least as far as unclassified accounts are concerned. Even so, should some of these systems succeed, submarine operations might become extremely difficult.

It is not certain that, even then, the submarine would vanish. One might argue that

SUBMARINE DESIGN AND DEVELOPMENT

Under-ice operations are increasingly important. Soviet submarines lying under the Arctic ice pack would negate many current US advantages. Ice formations break up long sonar trasmissions paths so that virtually all engagements would be at short range. Aircraft would be very limited in their capabilities, nor would submarines be able to employ stand-off ASW missiles as Subroc. Thus under-ice ASW is essentially submarine v submarine, a special requirement for which is the ability to turn sail planes vertical to help break through the ice. The current *Los Angeles* class, its sail shortened to minimise resistance, cannot do so. Here the *Sturgeon*-class USS *Whale* (SSN 638) is surfaced at the North Pole on 6 April 1969 in her first year of operation. US interest in under-ice operations is again growing, reportedly in response to intensified Soviet activity. *US Navy*

even if some new sensor could establish with near certainty that a submarine were in a sea area, that would leave the major task of actually pin-pointing and attacking it. Weapons would still have to travel from launcher to target in a sea that makes them relatively slow, thus giving the submarine a chance to evade. High submarine speed and great manoeuverability might be vital. Thus a strategic submarine – even a relatively visible one – might be far more viable than, say, a fixed missile silo on land, as long as it could operate within some sort of local sanctuary. The Soviets appear already to view *Typhoon* in this way. Yet the anti-ship attack submarine would lose much of its value if its commander had to concern himself almost exclusively with avoiding attack. The best illustration of such behaviour is current diesel-electric tactics, concerned largely with minimising the exposure inherent in snorkelling.

The diesel v nuclear issue is now particularly heated in the United States, where many members of the Military Reform Caucus in Congress appear to believe that the US Navy should purchase a large force of relatively inexpensive diesel-electric submarines. They have argued that the decision to rely exclusively on nuclear power was not reached on militarily or economically rational grounds, but instead was a direct consequence of Admiral Rickover's ambitions and political power. Certainly many of the US nuclear programme's characteristics can be attributed to the Admiral's personal views: the primacy of the powerplant in submarine design, the absolute unwillingness to entertain trade-off analysis, what some would consider an obsession with safety and reliability leading to design conservatism. Admiral Rickover's personal style of operation made him many enemies, and there was a widespread belief that they would break up the nuclear reactor establishment after his retirement. As this is written, that development is still in the future.

Even without the Admiral, it is not too difficult to argue in favour of an all- or largely-nuclear US submarine force. Nuclear power clearly makes for great operational flexibility, particularly in a navy which must habitually steam thousands of miles to its operational areas. Diesel-electric submarines can carry out many important missions, such as barrier patrol, but only if they are forward-based. That in turn requires accurate contingency planning or the submarines will be in the wrong place when needed. Yet the burden of the earlier part of this chapter was that both post-1945 experience and reasonable projections of the future show US participation, not in a major war with the Soviets, but in a Third World local conflict, generally with little warning. One might argue that it was the strategic mobility and endurance of the British nuclear submarines that enabled them to reach and stay on patrol stations off Argentina so soon after the Falklands emergency began. The first of them, HMS *Spartan*, spent 150 days at sea.

In these ways the US Navy differs from considerably from its allies. Only three Western navies come close to any major role outside the NATO area: the British, French, and US Navies. The others, which operate large numbers of diesel-electric submarines, have well defined emergency scenarios in mind: the enemy is relatively nearby, and the forward base is the home base. Even the British and French Navies can generally expect to fight nearby; for them, the diesel-electric submarine is by far the most economical and rational solution.

The other major argument against nuclear submarines is that they are so large as to be unsuited for operation in coastal or narrow waters. It is clearly impossible to exclude such areas from American interest, as so much of the Third World can be so described. One might, therefore, argue strongly in favour of building a relatively small number of US diesel-electric craft. The usual counter-argument is that the US can expect to fight in alliance with other nations, many of which have diesel-electric submarines. It also seems that the ultimate constraint on US submarine forces is numerical, not financial: Congress chooses numbers first, not total costs. Hence each diesel submarine would displace one nuclear boat, and even now the nuclear inventory of 90 attack boats is insufficient.

For over two decades, the official US Navy requirement has been 100 attack submarines. But, there are often hints that the Navy considers this inadequate, and about 150 would be a realistic figure. In May 1983, for example, an Atlantic Fleet spokesman observed that his war plan alone, which must include the GIUK Barrier, required the services of about 90 nuclear attack submarines. According to the current Five Year Defence Plan, by FY1989 the United States will have, either completed or under construction, 62 *Los Angeles* class attack submarines. In service then will be 98 nuclear boats in all, of which the large force of *Permit*s and *Sturgeon*s will be nearing or exceeding the 25-year replacement age. The current proposal is that they be replaced, not by an improved *Los Angeles*, but by a 'Next Generation Submarine', the first of which is to be build under the FY 89 Program.

US naval spokesmen generally suggest that the need for diesel-electric submarines will be filled by the large allied fleet. That would certainly apply in a NATO contingency, but it is by no means certain that NATO navies would be available for other kinds of emergency which the United States is likely to encounter. In the past, for example, most have shown very little interest in Indian Ocean operations. Nor are the other NATO

WEAPONS AND TACTICS

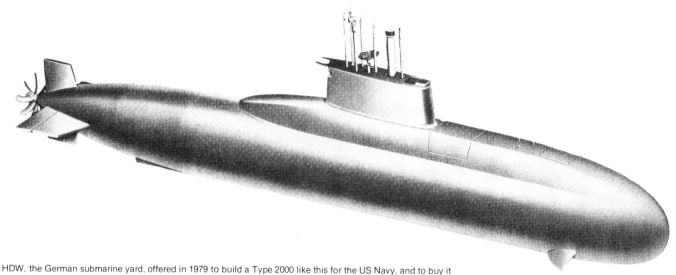

HDW, the German submarine yard, offered in 1979 to build a Type 2000 like this for the US Navy, and to buy it back after a year if it proved unsatisfactory. It was rejected: US naval spokesmen do not deny the diesel submarine's potential value, but argue that, given the need for greater numbers of first class nuclear craft, their limited funds are best spent on the *Los Angeles* class or equivalent. Characteristics: 221.1ft (oa), 217.1ft (hull) × 24.3ft (inside diameter) × 21.3ft (mean) × 42.3ft (height oa); 2182 tonnes surfaced. Propulsion from 1200hp diesels, 8 groups of 120 battery cells each, one 10,000shp motor; crush depth 2000ft, max diving depth 1200ft, max operating depth 1000ft; max submerged speed 25 knots, max snorkelling speed 15 knots, max surface speed 13 knots; submerged ranges 510nm/4kts, 290nm/8kts, 77nm/16kts, 42nm/20kts, 23nm/25kts; cruising range 25,000nm/4kts, 15,000nm/8kts, 6000nm/16kts, 4350nm/20kts; indiscretion rate of 2 hours a day at 6kts submerged (4kts; provisioned for 60-90 days (7 tons of food, 4250 gallons of fresh water, 2650 gallons of drinking water 290 tons (90,000 gallons) of diesel oil; 8 torpedo tubes for up to 26 Mk 48 torpedoes/Harpoon/Tomahawk; crew 30. The design was offered with an optional external forward missile 'belt' able to take 18 Tomahawk cruise missiles or 24 mines.
HDW

powers likely to supply forces to support the United States in the Caribbean, or in the Far East. Ironically, some of these relatively shallow areas are the ones best adapted to diesel submarine operation.

This is actually only one aspect of a much wider problem. Since the formation of NATO, the primary contingency for US defence planning has been a Soviet attack in Europe. American forces have been designed on the assumption that they would benefit from European contributions in areas such as mine countermeasures, ASW – and submarines. But, if the world becomes increasingly multi-polar, then that last specialisation may prove extremely costly and dangerous. This question also arises in contexts such as mine countermeasures, where the United States has come to rely very heavily on allied navies.

Mobilisation is a related issue. If in fact the US Navy cannot hope to maintain sufficient maritime forces in peacetime, is it possible to prepare to expand those forces very rapidly in a period of increasing tension? Mobilisation was a fixture of pre-1941 defence planning, but it appeared increasingly irrelevant as atomic and then hydrogen weapons were introduced. But, if stategic parity effectively cancels out those systems, then long wars and even long approaches to war may once again be the rule.

Again, a conventional view is that diesel-electric submarines are relatively easy to mass-produce, whereas nuclear reactors are so complex that any rapid expansion of nuclear submarine production would be difficult at best. Modern sensor and fire control systems would also represent important production bottlenecks. Certainly a much simpler and less capable type of nuclear submarine (probably considerably noisier) would have to be accepted. Perhaps the most interesting effect of any successful mobilisation of nuclear submarine production would be a change in the balance of the naval officer corps. Current nuclear officers are veterans of an exacting selection process, and were trained first as engineering officers and only second as submarine tacticians. In an emergency, much of the nuclear training would presumably have to be foregone. To what extent would that affect the psychology of the submarine commanders, which was so important in the two World Wars?

Current US thinking is very far from such considerations. The US Navy is attempting to decide on a successor to the *Los Angeles* class, the first boat of which is to be ordered under the FY 89 Program. Despite published claims that the new submarine has been 'designed', it would be more appropriate to say that studies of alternative configurations have begun. The situation recalls that of the experimental destroyer DDX, work on which nominally began about 1977, towards a firm *Arleigh Burke* class design (DDG 51) in FY 84. A cynic would observe that there is almost nothing in the DDG 51 design directly traceable to decisions arrived at so painfully about seven years earlier. The 'design' for the FY 89 submarine is much more closely held, and the notes that follow cannot be definitive.

There is every indication that the FY 89 concept has been motivated by an increasing ambition for tactical independence and an expanded role on the part of the US submarine force. Details of the proposed design reflect both dissatisfaction with existing US submarine designs, and also a very positive view of Soviet submarine designs, apparently particularly the 'Victor III'. Although there has been very little concrete disclosure of the FY89 design, enough has been said to make comparison with the earlier AHPNAS relevant. In each case, large size makes for a large and varied weapon load, with emphasis on long-range cruise missiles capable of striking inland targets. To some extent the attack submarine's ability to carry a significant load of conventional (or even nuclear) land-attack cruise missiles close to key Soviet maritime shore facilities early in a war compensates for the increasing vulnerability of the carrier battle groups currently assigned to this role.

US commanders complain that existing sensor systems are limited in range and in their ability to develop fire control solutions on the basis of fully passive sensors. For example, in May 1983 it was reported that, during exercises, US submarines missed about 40 per cent of possible detections, and about 20 per cent of possible firing opportunities. The new submarine (and *Los Angeles* class units from FY 83 onwards) will be fitted with a new combat system, SUBACS, expected to reduce these figures drastically. It will also have a new generation of sensors, such as the Wide Aperture Array (WAA), which replaces the current PUFFS (BQG-2), a new conformal array, and a new type (Thin Line) of towed array. The new submarine will probably have a pump-jet, for higher-speed passive operation: conventional propellers are said to contribute greatly to noise above about 12 knots.

The other complaint is insufficient torpedo tubes and weapons. There is also intense dissatisfaction with the current torpedo tube configuration, in which the tubes angle out and down abaft the sonar bow. Sketches of

SUBMARINE DESIGN AND DEVELOPMENT

the new design therefore show a much more powerful salvo, eight tubes arrayed across the bow itself in two rows. It appears that there will be two full rows of reloads behind each tube, which probably implies capacity for about 40-60 torpedoes altogether. There is also talk of a few (perhaps two) large-diameter (30in) tubes, as a hedge against requirements for much larger torpedoes. That leaves only the space under the nest of tubes for a big active/passive sonar to replace the current sphere.

Then there are performance issues. The standard complaint - insufficient speed - may be answered by a new PWR plant with about twice the output of the present one. That would allow for about 70 per cent displacement growth at the same speed, or for some considerable increase in both speed *and* displacement. Perhaps more important, the greater the maximum speed, the greater the maximum 'quiet' speed; higher speed becomes more valuable as submarine silencing and signal processing improve to make better use of it.

For many years US submariners have complained of 'snap roll', which they often attribute to the size and position of the sail. The new design therefore shows a much smaller sail, more like the Soviet than the earlier US type. This requires the bow planes to be relocated, and from FY 83 onwards US attack submarines are to have them in the conventional forward position. Presumably that also reflects much reduced reliance on the spherical or hemispherical bow sonar, due, perhaps, to the efficacy of the towed array.

Reportedly the new bow plane location will also make operation in ice easier; the current *Los Angeles* is not considered ice-capable. That will change in the FY 83 craft.

Other changes are to include the first US anechoic coatings and probably an X-stern. Although the FY 89 submarine is to have a US-style single hull, it will have a new beamier hull form, with a lower length-to-beam ratio reminiscent of the fast *Skipjack*.

This is a very large submarine, almost certainly much costlier than any repeat *Los Angeles*, let alone any of the smaller submarines (such as the 'fleet attack' or 'Fat Albert') proposed from time to time. In many ways its proposed design appears to reflect a view that American designers have been far too conservative, and have been overtaken by developments in Europe and in the Soviet Union. Some would go so far as to describe it as an Americanised (if grossly enlarged) 'Victor'.

As for the deep-diving 'Alfa', there is no real hope of building up a domestic titanium industry (a $2 billion investment) capable of reproducing its hull, so that any near-future US attack submarine is likely to be built of steel. A new HY-100 is available to replace the existing HY-80; its successor, HY-130, at one time was expected to appear in the 1970s, but has not been fully qualified for submarine construction, and is not now funded. There is some current interest in non-magnetic hull materials, given the Soviet tactic of using MAD for search across choke points.

Much can and will occur between now and about 1987, when contract plans will actually have to be drawn. The current reform caucus, should any of its members gain further political power, will probably try to cut the size and cost of any new submarine, particularly as the submarine community comes to demand the numbers nearer those of the war plans. They will, however, have relatively few alternatives. Reactor development is so complex a process that only one new plant will probably be developed between now and the 1990s. Its sheer size will dictate something of about the size of the current sketch designs. It probably incorporates quieting features that cannot be duplicated in earlier plants, such as the S5W, short of total redesign. Thus the frequently advanced alternative to the *Los Angeles*, a new submarine with a *Sturgeon* powerplant and a new front end with six torpedo tubes, is probably less and less viable. A more feasible approach might be a modified repeat *Lipscomb* or *Narwhal*, ie an attack submarine for extremely quiet ASW operation. Reduced speed might be traded for an increased weapon load.

It is already clear that there is insufficient funding for any radically new type of reactor or power train. The naval nuclear programme is not large enough to make such a programme profitable, and the prospective benefits are not sufficiently clear to make the investment seem essential to the national interest. And with the current steep decline in the civilian nuclear programme, net US nuclear design capacity is probably diminishing. The Navy currently relies on General Electric and Westinghouse for detailed reactor designs, and neither company will be able to maintain its nuclear staff on Navy business alone. This situation may reverse about a decade hence, as oil once again becomes expensive, and as the current environmental movement wanes, but that will be far too late for the submarines of the 1990s. The other source of new design concepts is the system of Federally funded laboratories, such as Los Alamos and Lawrence Livermore. They have reputedly developed some lightweight PWR ideas, but it is not clear to what extent they can begin engineering work on them.

Nor does it seem likely that the United States will soon be buying non-nuclear submarines. Two years ago the German builder Howaldtswerke offered to build a 2000-ton boat for the US Navy, outfit it to US standards, and then buy it back for the purchase price if the Navy was dissatisfied after a year. Howaldtswerke showed that the 2000-ton submarine had quite adequate transit speed and patrol endurance for a variety of missions in areas such as the GIUK Gap, the Caribbean, and the Western Pacific, particularly if it was forward based. This analysis is reminiscent of Admiral Thomas C Hart's 1930s argument in favour of the 800-ton *Mackerel* and against total reliance on the 'fleet boat': there are many places where something much smaller will suffice, and will even perform better. In Hart's time the submarine officers refused to accept such a craft, and the current US position is the same. The Howaldtswerke offer was rejected altogether, and it seems unlikely that the 2000-ton diesel submarine will be built for any alternative customer. That decision seems increasingly rational in a world moving rapidly towards multi-polarity, ie in a world in which forward basing is less and less useful or possible. As for the non-nuclear concept, unless there is an existing diesel or other non-nuclear design sufficiently large to meet US requirements, it seems unlikely that the United States will purchase such craft. Design is just too complex for two attack submarine projects to run simultaneously.

In the Soviet Union, the new generation of designs (see Chapter 6) is just beginning to appear. One might speculate that, as treaty limits encroach on strategic submarine construction, reactor production resources will shift to the attack and anti-ship cruise missile classes; Soviet diesel boat production, except for export, may well decline very considerably. The great issue for the future is the extent to which the new Soviet naval emphasis on full-scale operations in the Third World will displace the submarine programme. Further, within the next two decades the Soviet Union should experience very severe economic and demographic stresses. To what extent will the Navy retain its priorities during the inter-service rivalry that must result? Surely it cannot survive on the strength of its contribution to current Soviet foreign policy, as in Afghanistan. It is not impossible to imagine a future Soviet government trying to cut costs by withdrawing from the Third World role, sharply reducing the naval building programme. Under such circumstances, the submarines might fare much better than the expensive surface ships, since they might well be perceived as defensive, ie as fulfilling very traditional Soviet roles.

The Soviet submarine industry is also significant as a builder for client states in the Third World. Soviet naval assistance policy has introduced several countries to submarine operation, the most recent being Cuba and Libya. Potential future buyers or recipients include Algeria, Syria, and Vietnam. Over the past decade, several recipients have left the Soviet sphere and have become Western customers: the submarine buyers were Egypt, India, and Indonesia. Although China has not been a Soviet client for many years, she is in much the same situation, suddenly interested in buying Western naval technology to replace Soviet-developed equipment. In fact China is probably the single largest *potential* Third World market, assuming she can solve her economic problems. One might speculate that China would be the first market Japan

WEAPONS AND TACTICS

Type 2400 (the first of an expected class of 12 was ordered from Vickers in November and it is strongly rumoured that it will be called *Upholder*, renewing the World War II 'U' class names) is the first British diesel-electric submarine to be designed since the mid-1950s *Oberon* design, itself a direct development of immediate post-1945 ideas. Both have about the same submerged displacement, 2400 tonnes (metric) for Type 2400 (hence the designation), 2450 tonnes for *Oberon*. *Oberon*, with her long narrow hull (295ft v 229ft) is marginally faster on the surface than submerged (16 knots nominal maximum speed). Type 2400 will make about 20 knots submerged but only about 10 knots on the surface.
  Like current British nuclear submarines, Type 2400 is essentially single-hulled, with external main ballast tanks at either end. Thus, virtually the same weight is devoted, 43 per cent of standard displacement, to hull structure whereas the pressure hull consumes over half (23 per cent, compared to 17 per cent in *Oberon*). This increased weight, combined with a newer hull material (HY80 equivalent with a fin/sail partly made of glass reinforced plastic), makes for a greater diving depth (over 200m/656ft v over 150m/492ft). Remarkably, the other weight divisions in the two classes also match fairly closely, although internal hull volume division does not, Type 2400 devoting over twice as much (15 per cent to 7 per cent) to its combat systems. But the new submarine actually devotes *less* space to armament proper (13 per cent v 16 per cent).
  Note that, like many modern submarines, Type 2400 has two (rather than one) primary deck levels, so *volume* division does not fully reflect deck space division. Saddle tank construction in *Oberon* is reflected in much greater reserve buoyancy (18 v 11 per cent) and in a considerably smaller standard displacement (1650 tonnes v 1870 tonnes).
  Current Royal Navy concentration on relatively short-range operations is shown in the shorter endurance (49 v 56 days) and smaller fuel load (about 215 tons v 300 tons normally); *Oberon* can carry 150 tons more in saddle tanks. The new design has a single 5300shp electric motor; its batteries are charged by 1400kW (about 1900bhp) Paxman diesels. *Oberon* has a pair of 300shp motors, her batteries are charged by 1280kW diesels. The Type 2400's submerged endurance is about 45 per cent greater.
  Each boat has six bow torpedo tubes, but *Oberon* has two more (without reloads) in her stern and carries 18 (v 12) Spearfish torpedoes, Subharpoon missiles or Stonefish mines) reloads. Advanced automation (including an autopilot for 'hands off' operation) reduces the Type 2400 crew to 46 from 71 in *Oberon*. Of all navies the Royal Navy's submarine practice is probably closest to the US Navy's. Thus the Type 2400 probably illustrates best the sacrifices (and costs) to be entailed were the US Navy to reverse its longstanding decision not to build diesel submarines.
Vickers

would approach, were she to decide to export naval goods.
  In recent years the Soviets have increasingly seen their arms trade as a hard currency source, and have sold land weapons to such non-client states as Peru. They may find it necessary to export increasingly sophisticated products to retain a competitive position, particularly if non-aligned Third World builders enter the market. The new 'Kilo' class diesel-electric submarine may represent a move in this direction.
  As for Western Europe, two of the major builders, Britain and France, no longer build export-type diesel submarines for their own fleets. There seems to be little or no prospect that they will export nuclear submarines. The new British Type 2400 is extremely sophisticated and may be attractive to such advanced navies as those of Australia and Canada, which bought British fleet submarines in the past, but is probably overdesigned for most others. It is not clear whether the new French private-venture CA 1 class can be developed without French Navy orders. Interestingly, the last French fleet diesel submarine class, the *Agosta*, began in the early 1970s as a private venture. Certainly French national defence procurement policy has sometimes been determined more by the needs of industry than by tactical or strategic requirements.
  Technologically, the next major development will presumably be a viable closed-cycle engine to provide coastal submarines with near-nuclear speed performance, albeit at the cost of very limited endurance. These would be particularly interesting to Third World buyers who cannot afford nuclear submarines, but who may also wish to mount effective coastal defence in the face of intense ASW measures. Presumably the relative success of the Argentine submarine in the Falklands (see Chapter 7) will encourage Third World navies to build up their submarine arms.
  Probably the single most important weapon development will be the widespread purchase of submerged-launch anti-ship missiles such as Exocet and Harpoon. At present their export is relatively tightly controlled. However, anti-ship cruise missiles are relatively simple, and within a decade may well be manufactured in advanced Third World countries. The underwater-launch feature is not so much more sophisticated as to preclude its manufacture, and thus its widespread export.
  Submarine development in Western Europe is bound up with the future of the Third World market. Of the three major submarine builders, only West Germany continues to build many diesel-electric craft, and indeed only she designs and builds specifically for export. The future of her own industry, then, depends first upon the extent to which the export market is or is not saturated. The other question is the extent to which new competitors may arise. First, the minor European builders, Italy, the Netherlands and Sweden, may try to export. Although not so far exporting the *Sauro* class submarine, the Italian warship industry has been relatively successful in selling surface combatants. Taiwan bought two submarines from the Netherlands, albeit under rather unusual political circumstances. Sweden has offered a design to the Royal Australian Navy, in competition with British and German designs. Although unsuccessful in exporting major weapon systems, Sweden retains an impressive defence industry and there is probably increasing internal pressure to support that industry by export. The other major current submarine builder is Japan. Although she does not currently export weapons, let alone warships, that limitation need not persist forever. Like Sweden, Japan has an impressive (and relatively independent) defence industry.
  The other source of competition is the rising industrial powers. Spain already builds submarines of French design, and she is designing her own surface combatants. Once the construction capacity has been built up, its support may become a national objective, and export sales are attractive. Although submarines have not yet been built from scratch in countries like Argentina and Brazil, both have shown interest in building up defence industries. Moreover, Third World builders

187

may find their niche in supplying countries which, like South Africa, cannot buy from the major builders of the West.

As for the market, assuming that a submarine lasts about 20 years, the German-built Type 209s should require replacement from about 1990 onwards. Yet Argentina decided to replace hers, delivered only in 1974, less than a decade later. Conversely, as this is written, several navies are still operating US-built 'Guppies', originally built during World War II and modernised in the early 1960s.

Several substantial minor navies still lack submarines – Mexico (which operates destroyers) and Uruguay in Latin America; Mexico may well be able to afford considerable naval expansion, if the price of her oil rises over the next few years. In North Africa, neither Soviet-orientated Algeria nor Western-orientated Morocco operate submarines, even though both possess substantial surface forces. It would be surprising if neither bought them over the next decade. Similarly, in West Africa, Nigeria is beginning to build a substantial fleet, but at present it is limited to surface combatants. In the Middle East, it seems likely that Saudi naval expansion will soon include submarines. The Shah of Iran had ambitious submarine-building plans, which were dropped when he fell. But, it would not be surprising if, once the war with Iraq is over and the economy stabilised, some submarine construction followed. Before the war Iraq had an ambitious naval expansion programme; at present, with her economy a shambles, no further construction is planned, but that presumably will also change in the future. Finally, in Asia, the prospects for new submarine construction must include the Philippines, Malaysia, Singapore, South Korea, and Thailand (which bought 4 coastal submarines from Japan in 1936).

So, really radical developments in nuclear submarines do not seem very likely, at least in the West. From the point of view of ASW, the Soviets threaten to continue their progress towards very high underwater speeds and very great operating depths. Their new titanium submarine is very large, which probably means that it is much quieter than the existing, relatively noisy 'Alfa'. The combination of 'Alfa' speed and depth *and* relative undetectability would be a devastating one.

Although two potential prospective technological developments in non-nuclear submarine design can be identified, the proliferation of submarines in the Third World is probably much more important, at least from the point of view of Western navies. Finally, should nuclear weapons proliferate in the Third World, the submarine may well be the ideal delivery system.

Appendix: Third World Submarine Operations

The Indo-Pakistan War of December 1971 saw the first major combat use of Third World submarines, both India and Pakistan possessing four each. The Indian surface fleet, which included the ex-British light fleet carrier *Vikrant*, was clearly superior, and the Indians feared a Pakistani surprise attack. The Pakistan Navy was credited with midget submarines and human torpedoes; the Indians feared a surprise attack on their fleet in harbour. In fact the Pakistani plan was more conventional: to keep their inferior surface fleet in harbour, deploying submarines against *Vikrant*. An Indian officer commented that they could not compromise between the two possibilities because their *Daphne* class submarines could not carry torpedoes and human torpedoes simultaneously.

A Pakistani submarine actually caught the *Vikrant* task force off East Pakistan (Bangladesh) while the carrier was attacking Chittagong, 4 December 1971. It missed with a shot on the carrier's bow, and was (apparently incorrectly) claimed sunk by her escorts, three British-built *Leopard* class anti-aircraft frigates. Meanwhile, the former US fleet submarine *Ghazi* (ex-*Diablo*) was destroyed off Vishakhapatnam harbour. The Indians suggested that she sank after triggering a mine she had just laid. Finally, a Pakistani submarine, probably the *Daphne*-class *Hangor*, torpedoed the small Indian frigate *Khukri* on 9 December in the Arabian Sea. Hit by three of nine torpedoes fired, she sank in three minutes, with the loss of 191 of her 288 crew.

The Indian submarine fleet saw no action, since the Pakistani surface fleet did not leave its bases.

Two nominally Third World navies probably envisage a rather different role for their submarines: Israel and South Africa. Although Israel faces enemies with surface fleets, she probably considers reconnaissance and agent insertion the primary role of her present three Type 206 boats. South Africa has no immediate naval neighbours, although she considers the Soviet Union an important ultimate adversary. However, given her security situation, reconnaissance and agent transportation must be vital submarine roles. Note that Argentina actually used a submarine, the ill-fated *Santa Fe*, to transport her commandos to South Georgia during the Falklands War, and that Britain reportedly used HMS *Onyx* to transport Special Air Service and Special Boat Service commandos during the same conflict. In each case, small size and handiness, for operation in very shallow water, were valuable submarine characteristics. On the other hand, the smaller the submarine, the less internal space she has for commandos. It is one thing to insert a single agent, and quite another to transport a raiding party, with its equipment.

Glossary

Only the most widely used abbreviations are listed below. They are often spelt out on first mention in the text. Miles are always nautical in this book and U-boats are always German submarines.

Asdic — Early name for sonar coined from the Allied Submarine Devices Investigation Committee that devised it from 1917. First went to sea in 1920, and by 1939 most RN ships and submarines operated one of five types.

Asroc — Anti-submarine rocket system, unguided. First deployed aboard US surface ships in 1955, 12,000 produced 1960-70. A 33in wingspan rocket delivers a parachute retarded Mk 44 or 46 homing torpedo out to about 10,000 yards, the limit of SQS-23 sonar range. The launcher has 8 barrels loaded semi-automatically, and can be fired at 2rpm. Alternative payload is a Mk 17 nuclear depth bomb.

ASW — Anti-submarine warfare.

BDI — Bearing deviation indication (sonar)

BQR — US designation for submarine sonar, B for submarine, Q for sonar, R for passive detection.

BQS — As above except S stands for search.

CG — Centre of gravity.

DASH — Drone anti-submarine helicopter (unmanned) developed for the US Navy from 1957 to take one or two homing torpedoes out to maximum sonar range, but withdrawn from service in the early 1970s after over half the 746 built were lost at sea.

DIMUS — Digital multi-beam steering, a sonar signal processing system for multi-target tracking.

ECM — Electronic countermeasures.

ELF — Extremely low frequency.

ESM — Electronic support measures.

FRAM — Fleet Rehabilitation and Modernisation (US)

FY — Fiscal Year (US), ends on 30 September (since 1976, 30 June until then), thus FY 84 began on 10 October 1983.

GHG — World War II U-boat low frequency sonar.

GIUK — Greenland-Iceland-United Kingdom gap (NATO term).

'GUPPY' — Greater Underwater Propulsive Power (US).

HDW — Howaldtswerke, U-boat and warship builders at Kiel.

HF/DF — High frequency direction-finding.

hp — horsepower.

HTP — High test peroxide.

HY — high yield (steels).

ICBM — Intercontinental ballistic missile, Polaris etc.

IFF — Identification Friend or Foe.

IKL — Ingenieurkontor Lübeck, German submarine and ship design company formed in 1946 with the staff of the old Ingenieurkontor für Schiffbau Gmbh by Prof Ulrich Gabler, former head of the U-boat development department. Submarine (and submersible) design resumed in 1955 and as of 1981 IKL had nearly 300 staff with Prof Gabler acting as consultant since 1979.

LAMPS — Light airborne multi-purpose system (US), the helicopter attack system that followed DASH (qv) and is the current US ASW equipment.

LPI — Low probability of intercept.

MAD — Magnetic anomaly detection.

ONI — Office of Naval Intelligence (US).

PUFFS — Passive Underwater Fire Control Feasibility Study (US submarine sonar system).

PWR — Pressurised water reactor.

RAPOS — 2 position sound navigation.

sail — Modern US name for conning tower which the RN calls fin.

SALT — Strategic Arms Limitation Treaty, the first was signed in 1972. The continuing talks for further agreements were redesignated START (reduction) in 1983.

shp — shaft horsepower.

snorkel — Device whereby a submerged submarine can take in and expel air.

snort — RN term for snorkel.

SOSUS — Sound Surveillance System (US), Atlantic and Pacific listening hydrophones on the seabed and linked by cable to shore stations.

SQS — US designation for surface ship sonar, S for surface ship, Q for sonar, S for search.

SSBN — Fleet ballistic missile submarine, nuclear.

SSK — Submarine, hunter killer.

SSN — Submarine, nuclear.

SSR — Submarine, radar picket.

STS — Steel tensile strength. Special treatment steel (US term).

Subroc — Submarine fired ASW nuclear rocket (US) developed from June 1958, approved for service in July 1966 and in production until 1972. Usually credited with a 35-40 mile range. Weighs 4000lb.

SURTASS — Surveillance towed array sonar system.

TMA — Target motion analysis.

UKE — British hardened steel.

VHF — Very high frequency.

VLF — Very long frequency.

WAA — Wide aperture array.

Index

All vessels are submarines unless otherwise indicated. Dates of launch or acquisition are given. Bold figures indicate drawings, those in italic indicate photographs and captions.

A-class (Jap) 40–41
A-class (RN 1941) 29, 39, 59, 66, 122
A-class (US 1910–12) *27*
A-2 (US 1902) *17*, *27*
A-4 (RN 1903) 120
A-4 (US 1910–12) *27*, 115, *155*
A-6 (US 1910–12) *27*
AL-4 (US 1915–16) *31*
AL-10 (US 1915–16) *31*
AL-11 (US 1915–16) *31*
Acoustic reconnaissance 11
Adder (US 1902) *17*
Advanced High Performance Nuclear Attack Submarine (AHPNAS) 83, 165
Aeneas, (RN 1945) 179
Agosta class (Fr 1970–) 109
Air defence *178*, 179–180
Albacore class (US 1950s) 77, 82, 108, 118, 119, 124, 126, 129, 139, 140, 178
Albacore type hull *36*, *76*, 82
'Alfa' class (Sov 1967–) 18, 82, 96, 105, 106, 134, 135, *183*, 188
Almirante Simpson (Chile 1943) *109*
Alton Closed Cycle Engine 131
Ammiraglio Cagni class (It 1939) 43
Andrew HMS (RN 1946) *168*
Anechoic coverings 14, 177, 186
Anti-aircraft missiles 179
Anti-shipping campaigns 30, 41, 42, 43–51, 93
Anti-Submarine Warfare (ASW) 9–14, 32–37, 173–176; air defence *178*, 179–180; aircraft 33, 34, 40, *44*, 49; Ballistic missile submarines 79–80; Falklands War 112–113; postwar 53, 171–173, 180; sensors 48; submarines 23, 33, 61, 63, 67–69, 68, 71, 72, 73, 74–75, 81, 105; under-ice 184; World War I 29, *31*, 32–37, 171; World War II 32, 42, 43, 47, 49, 50, 51, 52, 57, 59
Anti-Submarine Warfare Readiness Executive 172–173
Aréthuse class (Fr) 70, **70**
Argonaut, (US) 35
Arleigh Burke class (US 1977) 185
Asroc missile 81, *161*, 175, 176, 178
Automatic Target Following (ATF) 149

B-class (Jap 1918) 40–41
B-class (RN 1906) 28, 29
B-3 (RN 1916) 144
B-11 (RN 1906) 28
Balao class (US) 65, *66*
Balilla class (It) *112*
Balkon sonar 69
Ballast 17, 22–23, 24; piping 22; tanks *20*, 21, 22, 23, 42, 61, 118–120, **119**
Ballistic missiles 9, 10, 15, 75, 76, 79–80, 97, 98, *103*, 104–105, 178
Barbel class (US 1958) *76*, **83**, 118, 129
Barracuda class (US 1924) *18*
Bass (US 1924) *18*

Batfish USS (US 1945) *116*
Bathyscape 18
Bathyspheres 19
Batteries 18, 19, 20, 21–22, 23, 24–26, 27, 41, 42, 56, 59, 61, 64–65, 66, 74, 82, 101, 129, 133–134, 178–179
Battle of the Atlantic 27, 32, 42–43, 43–51, *45*, 54
Bearing Deviation Indicator (BDI) 149, 152
Blackfin (US 1946) *15*
Blast damage 180
Blockades 28, 29, 30, 31, 32
Bodies-of-Revolution 139
Bottom-bounce 67, 83, **144**, 145, 147, 151, 174–175
Brayton-cycle engine 130, 131
Bridge *12*, 21, 23–24, *28*, *29*, *31*
Britain, pre-1914 28–29; World War I 29, 30, 33, 67; between wars 37–39, 41, 44; World War II 58, 59; postwar *59*, 59–61, 61–62, *80*, *81*, 82, 83–89, **86**, *92*
British nuclear deterrent 83, 88–89 *see also* Nuclear deterrence
British Submarine Committee 29
Broeking, Fritz, U-boat designer 56
Bryant, Rear-Admiral Ben RN, 159
Buoyancy 17, 18, 24, 27, 119–120; reserve buoyancy 21–22, 23, 115–116

C-class (Jap 1938–39) 40–41
C-class (RN 1910) 22, 28, 29
C-19 (RN 1909) 24
Caiman (US 1944) 65
Capitan O'Brien class (Chile 1929) *108*
Carbon (graphite) block 130
Cargo submarine 19
Cavalla (US 1943) 70
Cavitation noise 52, 66, 67, 73, 79, 80, 81, 82
'Charlie' class (Sov 1968–) 98, 105, *167*
Charr (US 1944) 66
Chitose, midget submarine carrier, (Jap 1936–39) 41
Chiyoda, midget submarine carrier, (Jap 1963–39) 41
'Choke' points 32, 34
Closed cycle engines 130–132
Coastal defence 27–29, 42, 94, 99
Coastal submarines 27–29, 43
Codebreaking 34, 45, 47, 50, 51
Communications 10, 15, 40, 43, 47, 48, 50, 51, 57, 72, 73, 74, 75, 79–80, 94–95, 96, 99, 141–154
Compartment length 17
Conning towers *12*, 21, 23–24, **44**, **56**, 141
Conqueror (RN 1969) *81*, 86, 97
Contact-Analog (CONALOG) 126, *127*, 135
Control room 20, 24, 61, 69, *125*
Control systems 126
Convergence zone 67, 83, 144–145, 147, 174–175
Convoy strategy 30, 32, 34–36, 43, 48, 49, 50, 71; air cover 48, 49; escorts 32, 48, 49, 50, 51, 52, 57, 58, 171–172; losses 30, 48, 49
Convoy tactics 171–172, *172*
Cruise missiles 74, 75–76, *75*, *102*, 103, 104, 105, 106, 159, 165, *167*, 169, 185
Cruiser submarines 39, 40–41
Crushing 18

Cusk (US 1945) 75
D-class (Jap 1943–44) 40
D-class (RN 1906) 22, 28, 29, 120
D-class (Sov 1928–29) 99, 100
D-class (US 1909) 21
D-1 (RN 1908) 28, *28*
Daimler diesel engines 42
Daphne class (Fr 1964) **63**, 63, 108, 109, *163*, *166*, *167*
Daphne class (Pak 1968–70) 188
Darter (US 1943) 24
Davis Submarine Escape Apparatus 126
Deck area 17, 20
Decoys 14, 161, 179, 180
Deep Submergence Rescue Vehicle (DSRV) 127–128, 132
'Delta' class (Sov 1972) 9–10, 19, 97, 98, 105, 106, *182*
'Delta III' class (Sov 1975–) 106
Depth bombs, nuclear 81, *175*, 177, *177*, 178
Depth charges 9, 14, 23, 32, 35, 61, 176, 177
Depth control 54
Deutschland (Ge 1916) 13
Diesel-electric submarines 184–185
Diesel engines 23, 24, 27, 39, 41, 42, 43, *48*, 53, 54, 56, 58, 61, 68, 129–130, *131*
Digital multi-beam steering (DIMUS) 147, 149, 163
Diodon (US 1945) 67
Direct Support of Surface Forces 71, 72–74
Displacement 17, 20
Diving 120; controls *116*; depth 14, 18–19, 20, 39, 41, 42, 52, 53, 57, 61–62, 63, 64, 65, 68, 80, 82, 95, 105, 116–117, *183*; planes *19*, 20, *110*, 120, 122–126; speed 11, 12, 14, 23, 24, 41, 43, *45*, 115, 120; tanks 23
Doenitz, Grand Admiral Karl 27, 32, 34, 42, 43, 44, 47, 48, 49, 50, 51, 53, *53*, 54, 56, 57, 159, *172*
Dolfijn class (Neth, 1959–65) 64, **64**, 71
Dolphin, (US 1969) 22, *183*
Doris, (Fr 1964) *163*
Drag 20, 23, 24, 115, 139
Dreadnought, HMS (RN 1963) 72, *80*, 85, 89, 123
Drzwiecki torpedo dropping collars *13*, *163*

E-class (RN 1912–16) 29, 32, 37
E-class (US 1912) 21
E-24 (RN 1916) 32
'Echo' class (Sov 1960–) 98, 103, 104, 106
'Echo II' class (Sov 1962–) *102*
Electric Boat Company, US submarine builders 108
Electric generators 24
Electric motors 24, 54, 56, 58, 86, 101
Electronic Counter Measures (ECM) *143*, 177
Electronic Intelligence Satellites 94
Electronic Support Measures (ESM) 142
Ellis pressure-fired steam plant 131
Endurance 27, 28, 29, 37, 38, 40, 41, *42*, 43, 57, *59*, 90, 100
Engine room 20, 68, *111*
Escape 126–128
Eurydice (Fr 1960) *166*, *167*

Evasion tactics 178–179
Excalibur (RN 1947) 55, 61
Exocet missiles 113, *167*, 169, 187
Explorer (RN 1947) 55, 59, 61, *62*, **62**
Explosive Echo-Ranging (EER) 183

F-class (US 1912) 21
FY 89 (US) 136
Fairwater *see* Sail
Falklands War 36, *81*, 86, 110–113, 169, 184, 188
Fin *see* Sail
Fire control 150, 159, 160, 161–162, 185
Fisher, Admiral Sir John, First Sea Lord 28, 29
Flaming datum 9
Fleet boats 39
Fleet Rehabilitation and Modernisation (FRAM US) 171
Fleet submarine, Japan, 40–41
'Foxtrot' class (Sov 1958–) *front*, 96, 101, 106, 109, 179
Frames 19, *20*, 21, 22, *25*
France, between the wars 43; postwar 61, 63–64, 70, 71; nuclear development 89–90
Free flooding 23
Freeboard 22, 23
Fructidor (Fr 1909) *13*
Fuel cells 26, 132–133
Fuel oil 22, 23
Fuel tanks 23, 42
Furuiwa, Captain, Japanese midget submarine commander 41

G-class (RN 1915–17) 22
Gabler, Professor Ulrich, U-boat designer 23, 90, 91, 108, 123, 138
Gabler spheres 128
Gato (US 1941) 39
Gearing class, destroyers (US) 171
General Belgrano, cruiser (Arg) *81*, 86
Gentry diesel-cycle gas turbine 131
George Washington (US 1959) 76
German Naval Acoustic Torpedo (GNAT) 160
Germania Engine Works 54
Germany, pre-1914 27, 29; World War I 21 30–33, 34, 43–44, 47, 50, 51, 53; between the wars 43, 44, 50; World War II 27, 33, 42–43, 43–51, *44*, 53–58, 75; postwar *see* West Germany
Ghazi (Pak 1964) 188
Glenard P Lipscomb (US 1973) 74, 75, 137, 186
'Golf' class (Sov 1958–62) 98, 103, 105
Goodall, Sir Stanley, RCNC 58
Gorshkov, Admiral of the Soviet Union Sergei G 97, 99, 105, 106
Grayback (US 1941) 75
Greenland Iceland United Kingdom Gap (GIUK) 106
Grouper (US 1941) 69, *150*
Grumman Tracker Aircraft *178*
Guam Submarine Base 79
Gumbo closed cycle diesel engine 131
Gun mounts *16*
Gunning, M F, Dutch Naval constructor, 19, 64, **64**
Guns *15*, *168*, 169–170; deck *13*, 21, *31*, *33*, 40, 41, 43, *43*, *45*; anti-aircraft *13*, 23, *45*, 50, *50*
'Guppy' types (US) 58, 64–66, *65*, *66*, 69, 71, 80, 82, 123, 140

H-class (RN 1915–20) 23, 37, 38, *38*

H-5 (US 1919) *141, 142*
H-272 (RN) *38*
Ha 201 class (Jap) *41*, 42
Hai (Ge 1956-57) 57
Halibut class (US 1941) 74, 135
Hampshire, cruiser (RN) 32
Hangor (Pak) 188
Harpoon missiles 87, 113, 159, 164, *167*, 168, 187
Heat exchangers 18
Heat seeking missiles 179
Hecht (Ge 1956-57) 57
High frequency direction finding (HF/DF) 48, 50, 94, 104, 171, 173, 174
High speed submarine *41*, 42
High tensile steel 20
Holland, John P, American submarine designer (1841-1914) *10*, 21, 24
Holland (US 1900) *10*, *12*, 21, 120
Holy Loch Submarine Base 79
Hood, HMS (RN battlecruiser) 37
Hooded escape apparatus 126
'Hotel' class (Sov) 98, 103, *103*
Howaldtswerke, (HDW), U-boat builder, 108, *114*, 138, 186
Hull construction *20*, 21, *22-23*, 180
Hull materials and forms 20-23, 54, 61, 82-83, 86, 87, 100, 138-140
Hull openings 117
Hull volume 20
Humaita (Brazil 1927) *112*
Hunter killer submarines 67-70, 162, 171, 172
Hydrogen peroxide 14, 53-54, *53*, *62*, **133**
Hydrolysis 25
Hydrophones 13, 51, 67, 69, *141*, *142*, 143-144, 147-149, 150, 171, 176
Hydroplane console *123*

I-6, I-7, I-8, (Jap 1934-36) 40
I-16, I-18, I-20, I-22, I-24 (Jap 1938-39) 41
I-201 class (Jap 1944) 39, *41*, 42
I-202 (Jap 1944) *39*
I-351 class (Jap 1943) 42
I-361 class (Jap 1942) 42
I-400 (Jap) 19, 40
I-401 (Jap) *40*
IKL Type (Ge) 23, 25
Identification, friend or foe (IFF) 15, 36
'India', submarine transport (Sov) 126, 128
Indo-Pakistan war (1971) 188
Infra-red wakes 173
Ingenieurkontor Lübeck (IKL), U-boat design firm 90, 91, 108, 109, 123, 125, 128, 133, 138, 162
Intelligence collection 11, 24, 168, 171
Internal volume 16, 17, 20, 21, 56
Italy, between the wars 43; postwar 71

J-class (Jap) *see* A-class (Jap)
J-class (RN 1915-17) 36, 129
JT sonar 69, 70
JX sonar 70
Jack (US 1963) 137
Japan, between the wars 39-41; midget submarines 41-42, *41*; World War II 42, 57-58; postwar 71; suicide torpedoes 41
Jeune école, strategic doctrine 43, 93
Joint Tactical Information Distribution System (JTIDS) 153

'Juliett' class (Sov 1961-69) *102*, 103, 104, 106
Junon (Fr 1935) *37*

K-class (RN 1916-17) *12*, 24, 29, 36, 37, 39, 53, 120
K-class (Sov 1938-41) 100
K-class (US 1913-1914) *29*
K-class (US 1951) 74
K-1 (US 1951) 69, 70
K-3 (US 1951) *68*
K-4 (RN 1917) *12*
K-8 (US 1913-14) *29*
K-XIII (Neth 1924) *36*
K-17 (RN 1917) *12*
KD class (Jap 1921-22) *see* B class (Jap)
KD6a class (Jap 1933-35) 40
Khrushchev, Nikita S 101, 103, 104, 105
Khukri, (Indian frigate) 188
Kiev class, carrier (Sov) 106
'Kilo' class (Sov 1980) 98, *98*, 106, 109, 187
Krab (Russia 1912) 32
Kreislauf diesel 130, 131
Kurier, German 'burst' transmission 152, 154, 173

L-class (RN 1917-19) 32, 37
L-class (Sov 1931-41) 99, 100
L-class (US 1915-16) *31*
Lexington, (US carrier) 74
Life rails 21
Limbo mortar 80
Los Angeles class (US 1974-) 17, 19, 20, 23, 72, 74-75, *78*, 83, **84-85**, *122*, 126, 135, 138, 147, *148*, 152, *153*, 165, 180, 181, 182, 184, *184*, 185, 186
Lusitania 31, 34

M-class (RN 1917) *169*, 169-170
M-class (Sov 1930) 93-94, 100
M-3 (RN 1927) 32
McCann rescue chamber 127
Mackerel (US 1940) 39, *114*, 186
Magnetic anomaly detector (MAD) 15, 176, 179, 186
'Malyutka' class (Sov 1930s) 93-94
Manoeuvrability 13, 14, 23, 26, 41, 52, 65, 82, 95, 138
Maritime patrol aircraft 45, 70, 72
Marlin (US 1940) 39
Masts 20
Meteorite (RN, ex-Ge) 55
Michelsen, Vice Admiral Andreas 31, 32, 33, 34, 35, 36
Michigan (US 1979) *front*
Midget submarines 14, 40; *see also under* Japan
'Mike' class (Sov) 97, 106
'Milch cows' *see Type XIV* (Ge)
Mine chutes 32, *33*, *156*, 159
Minehunting sonar 151, 175, 180
Minelaying 29, 32, *33*, 34, 39-40, 43, 48
Minerve class (Fr 1935) 37
Mines 159, 180
Missile tubes 17, 19, 76, 104
Missiles 165-169; anti-aircraft 179; Asroc 81, *161*, 175, 176, 178; ballistic 9, 10, 15, 75, 76, 79-80, 97, 98, *103*, 104-105, 178; cruise 74, 75-76, *75*, *102*, 103, 104, 105, 106, 159, 165, *167*, 169, 185; Exocet 113, *167*, 169, 187; Harpoon 87, 113, 159, 164, *167*, 168, 187; heatseeking

179; Ikara 175; Malafari 175; Polaris 76, 86, 88-89, *92*, 165; Poseidon 79; SIAM 179; SLAM 179; SSBN *182*; Standoff *161*, 175, 180; Styx 105; Subroc 70, *161*, 162, 164, 176, 178; Trident 79, *92*, 169
Mizuho, midget submarine carrier (Jap 1936-39) 41
Mommsen lung 126
Multi-target tracing 147

Näcken class (Swe 1978) **90**, 124
Narval (Fr 1899) *129*
Narval class (Fr 1954-58) 61, 63-64, 123
Narwhal class (US 1927) 19, *35*, 74, 79, 135, 137, 186
NATO 70, 100, 101
Nautilus (US 1955) 20, 35, 40, *71*, 82, 134, 135, 139, *139*
Naval reactors group 135
Naval Underwater Sound Laboratory 83
Navigation 51, 69, 97, 154, 168
Netherlands, between the wars 56; postwar 63-64, 71, 74, *82*, *83*
Nisshin, midget submarine carrier (Jap 1936-39) 41
No 71 (Jap 1937) *41*, 42
Noisemakers 14
'November' class (Sov 1958-64) 98, 101, *106*
Nuclear accidents 98-99
Nuclear attack submarines 85, 87, 97, 98, 105
Nuclear deterrence 75-76, 79, 99, 101; *see also* British nuclear deterrent
Nuclear hull test vehicle 20
Nuclear power 23, 24, 25-26, 36, 59, 72, *73*, 74, 80-81, 103, 105, 181-182, 184-185
Nuclear reactors 79, 81-82, 83, 86, 87, 97, 98, 105, **130**, 134-136, **135**, 186
Nuclear weapons 81, 96, 101, 105, 157, 159, 162, *165*, 172, *175*, 177, *177*, 178

O-class (US 1917-18) 16
O-1 (US 1917-18) *19*
O-4 (US 1922) *16*
O-10 (US 1922) *16*
Oberon class (RN 1959) 37, **62**, 108, 126, 133, 152, 187
Observation kites 40
Odax (US 1945) 58
Odin (RN 1960) 128
Ohio class (US 1979-) *front* 19, *125*, 135, 137, 147, *164*, 181, *181*
Omaha (US 1976) *78*
Onyx (RN 1962) 188
'Oscar' class (Sov 1980-) 106, 178
Outlaw shark 154, 168-169
Overseas patrol submarine 37
'Overseas' submarines 27-29
Oxidant tanks 56

P-class (Sov 1934) 99, 100
Pacific War (1941-45) 51-52, 57-58
Passive Triangulation Ranging (TLR) 150
Passive Underwater Fire Control Feasibility Study (PUFFS) 150, 152, 157, 185
Periscopes 11, 19, 23-24, *45*, 141-142
Permit class (US 1960-66) 11, 26, 82, 135, 140, *161*, 184; *see also Thresher*

class
Pickerel (US 1944) 66
Pluvoise class (Fr 1907) *163*
Polaris missiles 76, 86, 88-89, *92*, 165
Pomodon (US 1945) 65
Porpoise class (RN 1930) 32
Porpoise class (RN 1956-59) 53, 61-62, 63, *63*
Poseidon missiles 79
Powerplants 18, 20, 24-26, 129-138; diesel or nuclear 138, 184-186; steam **132**; nuclear 134-136; closed-cycle 130-132; fuel cells 132-133; batteries 133-134
Pressure hull 17-19, 21, *21*, 22, *22*, 23, *25*, 117
Prize rules 29-31, 36
Project 611 *see* Zulu class
Project 613 *see* Whiskey class
Project 615 *see* Quebec class
Project Kayo 67
Project Migraine 71-72
Propeller shafts 19
Propulsion 129-140
Pump jets 87

'Quebec' class (Sov 1954-57) 11, 93, 100
Queenfish (US 1970) 127
Quiet speed mode 12
Quillback (US 1944) 67

R-class (Peru 1926-28) 107
R-class (RN 1919) 23, 33, 144
Radar 9, *45*, 51, *51*, 57, 66; air search 9, 34, 42, 51, 56, 57, 71; periscope detection 9; periscope ranging 59; picket submarine *143*; snorkel detection 174; submarine air warning 34, 52; surface search 142
Radar absorbent material 177
Radar pickets 36, 71-72, *72*, 95
Radio buoys 154
Radio direction-finding 45, 48, 50, 51, 74, 94, 104
Radio masts *28*
Rapid Passive Localization (RAPLOC) 157
Rasher (US 1960) *143*
Regulus cruise missiles 74, 75, 76
Repulse HMS (RN 1967) *92*, 127-128
Rescue 126-128
Resolution class (RN) 86, 89, *92*
Rickover, Admiral Hyman G 73, 74, 81, 134, 135, 138, 184
Ro 100 class (Jap 1941-43) 42
Roma, freighter (Ge) *30*
'Romeo' class (Sov 1958-61) 99, 101, 109
Rorqual, HMS (RN minelayer 1936) *34*
Rotationally directed transmission (RDT) 147

S-class (RN 1940-45) 32, 38, 39, *58*, 66
S-class (Sov 1935-47) 99-100
S-class (US 1918-22) 20-21, 23, 50
S-20 (US 1932) *131*
Shch-class (Sov 1930-41) 99, 100
Saddle tanks 21, 22, 23, *28*, *45*, *59*, 118-119
Sail 13, 20, 21, 23, 24, *59*, 69, 85, 124-126, 140, 186
Sailfish (US 1955) 72
Salmon (US 1938) 13
Salta (Argentina 1972) 110, *112*
San Francisco (US 1981) *148*

191

San Luis (Argentina 1973) 11, *112*
Santa Fe (Argentina 1960) 188
Satellite communications 154
Satellite navigation 154
Sauro class (Italy 1976–) 187
Scapa Flow 32
Scorpion (US 1968) 128
Scouting aircraft 40, 41
Scouting line 44, 45, 47, 50
Sea Cat (US 1944) 151
Sea Dog (US 1944) 67
Seahorse (RN 1932) 120
Seaplane submarines 42
Seawater inlets 19
Seawolf (US 1955) 24, 134, 135
Sennet (US 1944) 67
Sensors 14, 26, 48, 52, 141–154; acoustic 14, 26; infra-red 14, 26; magnetic 176; non-acoustic 173–175, 183; radar 14, 26
Seraph HMS (RN 1941) *58*
Shakespeare (RN 1941) 38
Ship Inertial Navigation System (SINS) 97, 105
Shock damage 180
Shore bombardment 71
'Sierra' class (Sov) 97, 106
Signal processing 149–151
Silencing 76–79, 81–82, 85, 87, 88, 95–96, 136–138, 173, 177, 183, 186
Sjöormen class (Swe 1967/68) **90, 91**
Skate class (US 1957–58) 134, 135
Skipjack class (US 1958–60) 20, 26, 61, 73, 75, 77, 81, 82, 83, 118, 135, 139, 140, 152, 186
Snorkel 11, 24, 25, 42, *44*, 49, *50*, 51, 56, 57, 58, 59, *59*, 63, 66, 67, 101, 129, 133, 174
Sonar 9, 20, 36, 43, 50, 51, 52, 58, 61, 66, 67, 68, 69–70, 73, 79, 87, 142–154; active 12, 13–14, 15, 25, 26, 57, 79, 81, 83, 143–144, 147, 149, 156, 172, 173, 176, 177, 183; anti-sonar measures 14; 'Balkan' 69; bottom bounce 67, 83, **144**, 145, 147, 151, 174–175; convergence zone 67, 83, 144–145, 147, 174–175; countering 175–176; fixed array 147, 149; hydrophones 13, 51, 67, 69, *141*, *142*, 143–144, 147–149, 150, 171, 176; JT sonar 69, 70; JX sonar 70; low frequency 146, 174–175; minehunting 151, 175, 180; multi-target tracking 147; multiple transmission **144**, passive 9, 11, 13, 15, 26, 34, 57, 67, 69, 74, 79, 83, 90, 94–95, *141*, 143–144, 147, 149, 151, 155–156, 159, 173, 176, 177, 183; Rotationally directed transmission (RDT) 147; scanning 9, 147; searchlight 13; signal processing 149–151; supersonic 146–147, 159; towed arrays 147–149; transducers 146–147, 149, 151; variable depth 144–145, 175–176
Sonobuoys 175–176, 179, 183
Sound detectors 142–144
Sound Surveillance System (SOSUS) 157, 171–172, 173, 176, 183
Sound Under Sea 144–145
Soviet Union, between the wars 93, 96, 99–100; World War II 93; postwar 53, 67, 72, 75, 82, 93–106
Spartan HMS (RN 1978) 184
Speed 18, 20–21, 23, 24, 25, 27, 36,
37, 72, 79, 95, 105, 129, 130, 138–139, 182, 183; battery power 182; nuclear submarines 182, 186; surface 39, 41, 53, *53*, 54, 57, 58, 65, 68; underwater *41*, 42, 53, *53*, 54, 56, 57, 58, 59, 61, 65, 66, 68, 80–81, 82
Spinax (US 1945) *72*
Spruance, (US destroyer) 17
Squalus, (US 1939) 127
Stability 22, 24, 82, 118–120, 139
Stealth 9, 11, *13*, 14, *14*, 15
Steam and steam turbine engines 24–25, 36, 53–54, 55, 64, 72
Steel 20, 61, 62, 82–83, 90, 91
Steering console *123*
Stern design 124
Stern plane *36*
Stern plane jam 18, 124
Stirling piston engine 131
Streamlining 140
Sturgeon class (US 1969) 11, 24, **84–85**, 95, 135, **153**, 184, *184*, 186
Styx anti-ship missiles 105
Submarine-borne aircraft 40
Submarine hunter-killer operations 67–70, 162, 171, 172
Submarine Integrated Control (SUBIC) *115*
Submersibles 18, 21, 22, 26, 27
Submersible aircraft carrier 16
Subroc missiles 70, *161*, 162, 164, 176, 178
Superstructures 20; freeflooding 21
Surcouf (Fr 1929) 40, 43, *43*
Surface Towed Array Sonar System (SURTASS) 183
Surfacing 120–122, **121**
Sweden 71, 89, **90, 91**
Swiftsure class (RN 1971–79) 86, 87, **86–87, 89**, 136, **136**, *183*
Swordfish class (RN 1931) 38

T-class (RN 1937–45) 32, 37, 39, *59*, 66
T-class (US 1918–19) 18, 65
Tactics 42, 94–95, 154–157; convoy 171–172, *172*; World War II torpedo 159–160; evasion 178–179
Tang class (US 1951–62) 24, 53, 60, *60*, **61**, 65, 71, 80, 82, *132*, 140, 151, 152, 161, 162
'Tango' class (Sov 1972–) 97, 98, 106, 179
Tanks 21, *21*, 22, 23, **118**; ballast *20*, 21, 22, 23, 42, 61, 118–120, **119**; diving 23; fuel 23, 42; oxidant 56; Q-tanks 120; saddle 21, 22, 23, *28*, *45*, *59*, 118–119; torpedo 119, 163; trim 118
Target A class (Jap) 41
Target B class (Jap) 41
Target, range 156; bearings 159, 162; speed 159
Target Motion Analysis (TMA) 151, 156, 162
Tautog (US 1940) **153**
Tench class (US 1944) *65*
Thames class (RN 1932) 37
Thermidor (Fr 1907) *13*
Third World 107, 114, 186–188; export to 107–109
Thorough (RN 1943) *59*
Thresher (US 1960) 20, 61, 62, 73, 74, 81, 82, 83, 120, 121, 124, 127, 135, 137, 145, 147, 152, *161*, 163
Thyssen, Emden, U-boat builder
108, 109
Thyssen TR 1700 U-boat 130
Tiburon (Peru 1954) *114*
Ticonderoga (US cruiser) 17
Titanium 18, 83, 97, 105
Torpedo boats 43
Torpedo Data Computer 159
Torpedo Inspectorate (Germany 1912) 29
Torpedo-mines 32
Torpedo rooms 20, *47*, *155*, *164*
Torpedo stowage 164–165
Torpedo tanks 119, 163
Torpedo tubes *13*, 19, *19*, *33*, *37*, 43, 46, 52, 57, *59*, 61, 106, 159, 162–164, 185–186; swim out 162; reloading 163
Torpedoes 9, *15*, 23, 24, 42, 43, 52, 57, 68, 70, 80, 96, **157**, 157–165, *168*, **173**, *174*; acoustic 50, 51, 52, 67, 160–161; Advanced Lightweight Torpedo 130–131, 158; air 157; anti-escort 179; ASW 162, 179–180; fire control 160, 161–162; guided 13, 51, 57, 59, 86, 160; helicopter-borne 175; homing 13, 52, 59, 70, 81, 160, **160**, 161, 176, 177–178, 180; internal combustion 158; Japanese suicide 41; nuclear 96, 101, 105, 157, 159, 162, *165*,178; range 159, 162; salvoes 159; speed 178; stand off **160**; Tigerfish 86, 87; wakeless electric 9, 51, 157, 158, *158*, 162; World War II tactics 159–160
Trafalgar class (RN 1981–) 87, **89**, *183*
Transducers 146–147, 149, 151
Transport submarines 71, 74
Trident missiles, *front*, 79, *92*, 169
Trieste bathyscape 18, 19
Trigger (US) *60*
Trim control 20, 24, 118, 119
Triton (US 1956) 36, 72, 135
Truant (RN 1939) 59
Truculent (RN 1950) 127
Tullibee (US 1960) 68, 73, 74, 81, 135, 137, 138, 145
Type IA (Ge) 23
Type IIB (Ge) *44*
Type VII (Ge) 23, 42–43, 56
Type VIIC (Ge) 27, 42, *45*, **45**, 53, 54, 57, 58, 140
Type VIID (Ge) 32
Type IX (Ge) 43, *44*, *47*, *48*, *49*
Type IXC (Ge) 50, 151
Type IXD (Ge) 139
Type IXD2 (Ge) *46*
Type XB (Ge) 32
Type XIV (Ge) 43, 140
Type XVIIB (Ge 1945) *54*, **55**
Type XVIII (Ge) 54–55, 130
Type XXI (Ge 1944) 19, 42, 49, 53, 55, **55**, 56–58, *57*, 58, 66–67, 68, 100–101, 138, 139, 140, 151, 163
Type XXIII (Ge 1945) 21, 49, **56**, 57, 57, 90, 140
Type XXVI (Ge) 55, 58–59, 140
Type 201 (W Ge) 90, **91**
Type 202 (W Ge) 90
Type 205 (W Ge) 90, 91
Type 206 (W Ge) 91
Type 207 (W Ge) 91
Type 208 (W Ge) 91
Type 209 (W Ge) **112**, *113*
Type 2000 (W Ge) *185*
Type 2400 (RN 1983) 183, *187*
Typhoon class (Sov 1980–) 19, 93, 97, 98, 106, 117, 126, 178, *182*

U-class (RN 1940–43) 32, 38, *39*
U-cruisers 31, 32
U-1 (Ge) 29
U-2 (Aus) *117*
U-17 (Ge) 29
U-35 (Ge 1912) *30*
U-47 (Ge 1939) 32
U-111 (Ge 1917) 27, *33*
U-142 (Ge) 40
U-151 (Ge 1920) *13*
U-251 (Ge) *45*
U-505 (Ge) *47*
U-873 (Ge) *46*
U-889 (Ge) *50, 51*
U-3008 (Ge) *55*
UB types (Ge) 23
UB-I (Ge 1915) *30*
UB-III (Ge) 23
UC class (Ge) 23, 32
UC III class (Ge 1914–1918) *156*
UC-31 minlayer (Ge 1916–1917) *33*
UC-58 minelayer (Ge) *33*
UE-class (Ge) 23, 32, 39
UF-class (Ge 1917) 23
UG-class (Ge) 23
Under-ice operation 69, 184, 186
Underwater control 117–118
'Uniform' class (Sov) 106
United HMS (RN 1944) *39*
United States, pre-1914 27–28, *29*; between the wars 39–41, 50; World War II 34, 35, 51–52; postwar 58, 61, 64–83, 83–85
Upholder (RN 1983) 187

V-4 (US 1927) 24
V-80 (Ge) 53, 54, **54**
Valiant, HMS (RN 1962) *25*, **89**
Valiant class (RN 1963–70) 85, **89**, **136**
Vastergötland class (Swe 1981–) **91**
Ventilators *28*
Ventose (Fr 1907) *163*
'Victor' class (Sov 1967–75) 75, 105, 106, 149, 185
Vikrant, (Indian carrier) 188

Walrus (US 1946) *21*
Walrus class (Neth) **82**, 124
Walter, Helmuth, U-boat designer 25, 53–56, *53*, 58, 59, 101, *138*, 140
Walter steam gas turbine 130, 131, 132, **133**
Water density 120
Waterplane area 22, 24
Watertightness 19
Weapons 154–170
Weight 17
Weight critical 17, 18
Welding 20
West Germany 71, 89, 90–91, 130
Whale (US) *184*
'Whiskey' class (Sov) 93, *93*, 95, *99*, **99**, 100, 101, 103, 105, 106
Wide Aperture Array (WAA) 150, 185
Wilhelm Bauer (W Ge) *55*
Wolf packs 10, 15, 34, 35, 43–48, 49, 50, 51, 53, 56, 57, 59, *172*

X-1 (RN) 40, 43
X-1 (US) *14*

'Yankee' class (Sov) 19, 97, 98, 105–106, *182*
Yuro Maru, (Jap tanker) *168*

'Zulu' class (Sov) 93, 100, 101, 103
Zwaardvis (Neth 1970) 83, 108